Markets
and Macroeconomics

Markets
and Macroeconomics

*Macroeconomic Implications
of Rational Individual Behaviour*

SCOTT J. MOSS

Basil Blackwell

First published in 1984 by
Basil Blackwell Publishers Ltd,
108 Cowley Road, Oxford OX4 1JF.

Basil Blackwell Inc,
432 Park Avenue South, Suite 1505,
New York, NY 10016, USA.

British Library Cataloguing in Publication Data

Moss, Scott, J.
   Markets and macroeconomics.
   1. Macroeconomics
   I. Title
   339   HB172.5

ISBN 0-85520-756-6

Typeset by Unicus Graphics Ltd., Horsham
Printed and bound in Great Britain by
T.J. Press Ltd., Padstow

To
Adolph Lowe
whose work inspired crucial aspects of my
macroeconomic analysis and who has long
been my model of scholarly integrity and
personal courage; and
to
Alfred Chandler
whose work has been a source of inspiration in
developing my microeconomic analysis and
whose encouragement greatly eased the
burden of working alone for long periods
of time.

I am grateful to them both.

Contents

viii

List of Figures

Preface

My purpose in writing this book has been to establish a new theoretical foundation for microeconomic analysis and to draw the macroeconomic implications of the resulting microeconomic theory.

I was moved to write it because the failure to resolve controversies in macroeconomics appeared to be the result of different schools' assumptions about how markets work. That is, both the monetarist and the temporary equilibrium schools presumed that all markets work in the same way: one school assumes that prices are flexible, the other that quantities are flexible. If markets differ, it is only in their speeds of adjustment. Keynesians assume that different markets work in different ways. Prices in the product markets are determined in relation to costs of production; prices in the financial markets are determined by speculative or psychological factors; prices in the labour market are determined by social considerations.

Conferences bringing together some of the best minds in the discipline yield confusion and an inability to determine the points of difference – much less to resolve them (cf. Harcourt, 1977). Sometimes the differences seem to depend on what is thought to be rational behaviour; sometimes they turn on how markets work. That is why I decided to concentrate on the implications of rational individual behaviour in determining how markets work.

This approach led me to the two crucial differences between my theory and previous theories. First, I deduce that long-run equilibrium is a concept that causes far more analytical and logical difficulty than it solves. This difficulty does not depend on convexity assumptions, though convexity makes long-run equilibrium even less compatible with the assumption that individuals behave rationally.

Second, if non-convexities are recognized to prevail in the technologies required to undertake exchange activities, the assumption of rational individual behaviour enables us to deduce how markets work. This makes it possible to drop the assumption that markets are maintained by auctioneers and the like. Moreover, the abandonment of long-run equilibrium makes it possible to rely on these non-convexitities to deduce the properties of *allocatively efficient* markets. I hope that readers will stop at this point to consider who else among modern economists has considered allocative efficiency *inside* markets. Even Okun (1981), whose analysis of exchange was published simultaneously with my own theory of markets (in Moss, 1981), considered efficiency only on each side of the market. Indeed, not even Okun defined the market. I believe mine to be the first economic definition in modern times.

I have been exceptionally fortunate while writing this book to have had encouragement and constructive criticism from eminent economists of widely differing views. Early drafts of the first five chapters were read and commented upon by Mark Casson, George Yarrow, Jan Kregel and Denis O'Brien. All of them were most encouraging. Later drafts were read in whole or part by Meghnad Desai, Michael Artis and Ian Steedman. Professor Desai read the whole manuscript in detail. He forced me to consider how best to make the reasons for my approach clear to mainstream economists by explaining what they would find difficult to accept by virtue of their training and commitment to received ideas and analytical techniques. His criticism led me to specify my rational markets hypothesis and my generalized Lucas critique. Michael Artis provided the same kind of criticism, in particular with respect to the policy analysis in chapter 9. Ian Steedman read an earlier draft of chapter 6 and pointed out a fundamental error in my analysis of joint production.

I am also grateful to Professors Artis and Steedman for having me appointed a Research Fellow in Economics in the University of Manchester during the final stages of work on this book. The University's Department of Economics is a marvellously stimulating environment in which to work.

Yvonne Thomas and Philippa Abbott word-processed several drafts of the manuscript. They were efficient and good-humoured throughout, thereby easing my task.

The errors and omissions are, of course, my responsibility.

University of Manchester and Manchester Polytechnic
December 1983

1

The Issues

1.0 INTRODUCTION

The assumption that individuals behave rationally is common to all schools of economists. Indeed, without the rationality assumption it is hard to see how general theoretical statements could be made about any social processes. For this reason, the assumption of rationality as the guiding force of individual behaviour should be given pride of place among all of the assumptions on which economists rely. Whenever other assumptions conflict with the assumption that individuals are rational, logical consistency dictates that those other assumptions be abandoned – no matter how much they simplify analysis or appeal to intuitive or other preconceptions.

It will be shown in this book that all of the mainstream schools of economists – particularly macroeconomists – rely on assumptions that are logically consistent with the fundamental rationality assumption only in special and empirically implausible conditions. Taken by itself, of course, this result can be dismissed as unimportant by appeal to the aphorism that theories are tested by their predictive power and not by the 'realism' of the assumptions. Although such aphoristic methodology is philosophically and economically dubious, I will not take issue with it here. Instead, I will demonstrate that strict adherence to the fundamental rationality assumption leads to the adoption of auxiliary assumptions which are consistent with and possibly are implied by rational individual behaviour, and which, in addition, are more general and descriptively accurate than the auxiliary assumptions of the various mainstream theories. Moreover, the resulting collection of realistic and general assumptions yields a more general, simple and powerful theoretical structure. In particular, this structure resolves the controversies over the microeconomic foundations of macroeconomics and provides a theoretical basis for policy prescriptions that are richer than any provided by previous theories.

Unless assumptions that are special and empirically implausible are for some reason to be preferred to assumptions that are general and descriptively accurate, the theory reported here is an unambiguous advance over previous theories of microeconomic and macroeconomic processes.

The importance of the rationality assumption makes it imperative that it be stated clearly at the outset. Our formulation of the assumption must be sufficiently strict that it actually guides our analysis, while, at the same time, it must be wide enough to avoid closing off possible avenues of enquiry. I shall therefore adopt a definition which, by virtue of its generality, includes as special cases all of the particular behavioural assumptions made by economists. We shall say that an individual is rational if he formulates well defined objectives and refrains from acts that he believes will frustrate the attainment of those objectives.

I recognize fully that, as it stands, this definition is too wide to provide much guidance for our subsequent analysis. More particular assumptions about the rationality of entrepreneurs will be developed in chapter 2 and, though the theory reported here does not depend on it, I shall not reject the standard choice theoretic assumption that households maximize utility. If individual entrepreneurs are not rational in the meaning of this general definition, they cannot rationally maximize profits or growth or anything else. This is all that we shall require here.

The purpose of this chapter is to resolve an expositional difficulty. The difficulty stems directly from my strict reliance on the fundamental rationality assumption. We shall find that certain key presumptions and concepts which are crucial to all of the various mainstream economic theories turn out to be so special as not to be worth serious consideration because, in the world as we know it to be, they either imply or depend upon irrational behaviour. But giving up these concepts and presumptions necessarily changes the meanings of important words; for the analytical attitudes and concepts that underlie the exposition of my argument are, in important cases, simply different from the attitudes and concepts underlying previous theories.

In an attempt to avoid the problems associated with the holding of different analytical frameworks, I shall describe two main results derived formally in the substantive sections of this book and prove a special case of a third result. To do so will have the added advantage of sign-posting the general direction of the arguments pursued in subsequent chapters. The density of those arguments and the complex relationships among them makes an outline of the main points and the relationships among them especially desirable.

The three results stand out in importance.

1   Long-run equilibrium cannot in general prevail in economic systems comprising rational households and rational entrepreneurs (or, equivalently, rationally managed firms). However, special conditions can be adduced that make long-run equilibrium compatible with individual rationality.

2   Even if the conditions for the existence of long-run equilibrium are satisfied, the set of markets that can exist in economies composed of rational individuals will not be complete because they cannot be both profitable and allocatively efficient. As a result, market signals to direct individual economic agents collectively to full employment of labour or full utilization of capital equipment will not be generated. There can be Keynesian and structural unemployment even if all markets that do exist are cleared continuously by flexible prices.

3   Keynesian economic policy prescriptions are neither necessary nor sufficient to achieve or maintain either full employment or full capacity utilization in the short run or the long run. If demand management is to be a tool of public policy, it must be supplemented by industrial and other policies that have well specified effects on the supply side of a decentralized market economy. The general characteristics of efficient and effective industrial and other policies are implied by the theory reported here.

The validity of each of the first two results is independent of the validity of the other. Together they lead to the third result and to a conceptual foundation for the analysis of long-run economic processes in conditions of uncertainty.

1.1   INDIVIDUAL RATIONALITY AND THE NECESSARY CONDITIONS FOR LONG-RUN EQUILIBRIUM

Long-run equilibrium in Walrasian and most Keynesian theories is defined by the simultaneous maximization by all agents in the economy of long-run variables subject to long-run constraints. The long-run maximand of each firm could be growth, but, more generally, it is assumed to be profits or the discounted value of a long – possibly infinite – stream of profits arising either in successive short-run equilibria or in a single equilibrium covering a long sequence of trading dates. Households maximize intertemporal utility subject to income and wealth constraints.

The crux of the *logical* objection to this conception of long-run equilibrium is that, for strictly mathematical reasons, some or all of the long-run constraints must be exogenous, but the very exogeneity of long-run constraints is generally incompatible with the assumption that individuals are rational maximizers.

Rational maximizers will always seek to shift binding constraints in order to increase the attainable values of their maximands. Indeed, such constraint-shifting is always the purpose of investment by firms and the education and training demanded by households. It is, of course, common ground in economics that firms will seek to shift constraints on the scale and scope of their activities whenever the benefits from such shifts exceed the costs of the requisite investments. It is also well known that replication of existing capacities by the firm would, on technological grounds alone, enable outputs to be increased without limit at constant average cost. In competitive conditions, therefore, there would be nothing to limit the size of the firm.

The usual way round this obvious problem is to assert that there are diminishing returns to the scale of the organization. However, there is no dearth of evidence to show that, when organizational forms are devised to shift that constraint, the particular forms devised depend upon the particular problems faced by each firm. That is, when the binding constraint on the firm's maximizing propensities is its organization, a new organizational form is devised and implemented to shift the organizational constraint so that it is no longer binding. In practice, the same phenomenon occurs when there are supply or demand constraints faced by the firm. Technical changes are developed so that innovative investments shift the binding constraints. These organizational and technological innovations are often developed either by the firms whose maximizing propensities are constrained or at their behest. The objective of these innovations is to change the benefits of constraint-shifting relative to the costs. It follows that the process of constraint-shifting is endogenous in the long run.

Although the evidence supports this contention, the argument is not empirical. It is logical. If the objective of firms' managers is to maximize some long-run variable, then to accept any constraint on the maximand without seeking to shift or eliminate that constraint is to fail to pursue the avowed objective. To treat organizational or technological or any other relationships as being somehow sacrosanct is irrational behaviour. Either agents seek rationally to maximize, or they do not. If they do, then by any definition of the word 'rational' they will not treat binding constraints as being exogenous – a logical implication which extends equally to constraints on their abilities to shift constraints.

It must be recognized immediately that, if there really are no exogenous constraints, then the realized values of rational maximizers' objective functions will become infinite within an infinitesimal interval of time. And this is the crux of the usual objections to this line of argument. Something must limit either the size or the rate of growth of the firm. If it is not technology, it must be organization. If it is not organization, then what is it?

Once stated, the answer to this question is blindingly obvious to anyone who either teaches or develops new ideas or new applications of old ideas. It is an inherent characteristic of mortal man that the rate at which he learns is limited. Some learn more quickly and some learn more slowly. But no one can learn everything all at once. To assume that learning rates are limited is wholly compatible with the assumption that individuals are rational, and it explains why binding constraints cannot be shifted the moment they are encountered. If this assumption were not adopted, then we should require to assume that some other law of nature makes the shifting of some constraints physically impossible or, alternatively, that all agents always believe that the costs of shifting constraints – or finding out how to shift them – will always exceed the benefits. While both of these alternatives are patently unrealistic, they are not *logically* inconsistent with the assumption that individuals behave rationally. And if the concepts associated with long-run equilibrium are to be maintained, then so-far-unspecified natural laws, or the assumption that individuals hold peculiar (because empirically false) expectations about the costs and benefits of investments, must be retained in preference to the more natural (because obviously true) assumption that individuals learn at limited rates. The more natural assumption cannot be adopted in long-run equilibrium theory because it violates a necessary condition for the existence of general equilibrium where trading is an on-going activity.

This condition was first demonstrated by Radner (1966). He showed that, if agents learn at limited rates, then in the fullness of time the information acquired simply by engaging continuously in market exchange will exhaust these limits. Once that happens, agents will be unable to calculate their optimal responses to additional flows of information even up to a subjective probability distribution. In consequence, no equilibrium predicated upon successful maximization by individual economic agents can exist. But the alternative, we have just seen, is to assume unlimited learning rates which themselves preclude the existence of long-run equilibrium of the individual unless supplemented by special, implausible assumptions.

This conclusion applies not only to Walrasian general equilibrium models but to all models incorporating the rational expectations hypothesis. For that hypothesis is predicated only partly on the assumption of individual rationality. It also requires the assumption that learning rates are effectively unlimited.

The specific way in which rationality is incorporated into the rational expectations hypothesis is by assuming that individuals will not formulate persistently and systematically falsified expectations. Although the formal specification of rationality in expectations – that errors be serially uncorrelated with zero means – turns out to be stronger than is required here, the essential insight that rational individuals will not willingly repeat the same errors time after time is both plausible and, we shall see, fruitful.

If information is scarce, then rational individuals would clearly seek to use that information so that none is wasted. Models incorporating the rational expectations hypothesis thus require some way of limiting the information that becomes available to individuals. Lucas and Prescott (1974/1981), for example, followed Phelps (1969) in assuming that individuals trade on islands at each date and the information available on each island is limited to that arising from markets located there. They do not have information about current events on other islands. Now, if scarcity has any meaning at all here, it must be that if more information were freely available it could and would be used in the formulation of expectations. But to say that more information could always be used is precisely to say that the capacity of individuals to use information always exceeds the information that is available. In particular, the rate at which individuals can learn from the past and the present about the future must never be a constraint.

Thus, it is not only Walrasian models but also Keynesian models incorporating the rational expectations hypothesis (e.g. Buiter, 1980) that cannot be predicated upon the assumption that individuals are constrained by the rates at which they learn. This result will be demonstrated mathematically in chapter 2 in the framework of a dynamic optimal control model. In the meantime, I simply note that nothing in this argument implies any difficulties at all for either short-run equilibrium concepts or for the proposition that individuals will not willingly formulate expectations that are systematically and persistently proved false. By maintaining these two sets of concepts, both of which are logically compatible with rationality and limitations on individuals' learning rates, we are led naturally to a theoretical framework for the analysis of decision-taking and long-run macroeconomic processes in conditions of uncertainty, hence in conditions where long-run equilibria cannot exist.

1.2 RATIONALITY IN EXCHANGE: THE RATIONAL MARKETS HYPOTHESIS

Macroeconomic controversy has been less about individual behaviour than about the ways in which markets work. The particular focus of much of the controversy has been the flexibility of prices. The monetarists and new classical macroeconomists assume that all markets work in the same way and are cleared by continuously flexible prices. Price inflexibility, they aver, would be irrational. Keynesians of various schools argue that inflexible prices prevail in some or all markets.

All of these arguments over price flexibility and the effects thereof turn on the efficient markets hypothesis, although this is something of a misnomer. That hypothesis is not about markets in any institutional sense. It is about prices.

The efficient markets hypothesis has it that all prices fully reflect available information so that there are no persistent, systematic opportunities for arbitrage. Provided that expectations are rational, so that deviations of expected from actual prices are serially uncorrelated with zero means, then any divergences of prices from their market-clearing values will be random and transitory. In addition, there must be market prices for all assets as well as all newly produced goods and services. In particular, it must be possible to buy and sell second-hand equipment (as distinct from firms) as easily as new goods and services. It makes no difference to the efficient markets hypothesis whether there are auctioneers or multilateral recontracting arrangements or trading posts or islands or any of the other institutional arrangements or procedures for transactions that economists have from time to time assumed. All that is required is that prices fully and continuously reflect available information and that agents are rational.

The main problem with the efficient markets hypothesis is that it takes no account of efficiency in the use of resources required to effect transactions. This is a most curious lapse since, in economics, rationality implies allocative efficiency. Yet, there is an implicit, universal presumption among economists that market efficiency in the restricted sense of the efficient markets hypothesis is always and everywhere compatible with individual rationality; hence, for the sake of logical consistency, the efficient use of resources in exchange. This presumption is false.

In order to see just what is involved here, it will be convenient to distinguish between price-efficient markets and allocatively efficient markets. Price efficiency is what is described by the efficient markets hypothesis. The criteria for allocative efficiency in exchange are the same as the criteria for allocative efficiency in production. It is quite possible that allocatively efficient markets will also be price-efficient, but this is a special case. Analysis of the requirements for allocative efficiency in markets leads naturally to what I shall call the rational markets hypothesis which, in special cases, entails the efficient markets hypothesis. Before specifying this hypothesis, let us be clear why it is important to distinguish between price efficiency and allocative efficiency in exchange.

The efficient markets hypothesis and current macro economic controversy

Price-efficient markets clear continuously apart from random and transitory (i.e. serially uncorrelated with zero mean) excess supplies and demands. This follows from the efficient markets hypothesis. It also follows from this hypothesis that persistent and systematic deviations from the simultaneous clearing of all markets is a consequence of either price inefficiency or individual irrationality. The argument of the temporary equilibrium theorists is that markets are price-inefficient, while income–expenditure theorists (using one or another variant of the *IS–LM* model) have it that households are selectively irrational.

From Clower (1965, 1967/1969) and Leijonhufvud (1968) onwards, temporary equilibrium theorists have argued that, in practice, prices do not reflect all available information. If, in the face of excess supplies for their factor services, households allow factor prices to fall, firms will not thereby be induced to hire those factors because they do not know that to do so would increase the demands for their outputs as households' incomes are increased. The only effective signal in this circumstance would be for households to increase their purchases of firm's outputs before actual demands for factor services are increased. In consequence, prices do not convey information about conditions of excess demands and supplies because markets are not organized in a way that makes that possible. Quantity signals dominate price signals. Markets are therefore price-inefficient.

Income–expenditure models presume no such market inefficiency. Excess supplies in the labour market persist because wages are sticky downwards but not upwards. This asymmetrical wage rigidity is the basis of the reverse L-shape of the aggregate supply curve. Since excess supplies in the labour market would be eliminated by falling real wages, households' refusals to lower their reservation wages are irrational. But this irrationality is decidedly selective, since the same households are assumed to buy and sell bonds in a wholly rational manner. They accept and respond to price rises (interest rate reductions) and price reductions (interest rate rises) in a way that clears the bond markets, and, moreover, they do so without a murmur of protest. Of course, it might be argued that households do not realize the consequence of downward wage rigidity. If so, prices in the labour market do not reflect the available information and the labour market is, by definition, price-inefficient.

Evidently, the main opponents of the monetarist/new classical school of macroeconomists base their opposition on some rejection of the efficient markets hypothesis. Either they believe that prices do not in practice reflect all available information about supplies and demands, or they believe that households are selectively irrational. In either of these cases, excess supplies or demands can be persistent (i.e. serially correlated) and systematic (i.e. having non-zero means). The monetarists/new classicals reject temporary equilibrium and income–expenditure theories outright on the grounds that any rejection of any aspect of the efficient markets hypothesis is *ad hoc*.

There is a third aspect of the efficient markets hypothesis which, if rejected, makes the question of price flexibility one of secondary importance. That is, price flexibility is neither necessary nor sufficient to prevent persistent and systematic deviations from market-clearing if markets are not complete and continuous. In such cases there are no continuously determined market prices for some assets or commodities and, therefore, no prices to reflect available information about the supplies of and demands for those assets and commodities. As will be shown in section 1.3, the absence of markets for second-hand plant and equipment, or the services thereof, makes possible an

indefinitely sustained period of Keynesian and/or structural unemployment, even though all markets that do exist are continuously
cleared by flexible prices. Of course, in relation to the efficient
markets hypothesis, this result is as *ad hoc* as those of the temporary
equilibrium and income–expenditure theories. One of the implications of the rational markets hypothesis, however, is that to assume
the validity of the efficient markets hypothesis itself is *ad hoc*
because the technological conditions in which it is applicable – if
agents are rational – do not characterize actual economic systems.

The rational markets hypothesis

Unlike the efficient markets hypothesis, the rational markets hypothesis is concerned with markets. A market is defined here as a set of
mutually independent agents who produce and use a commodity
together with all other mutually independent agents whose activities
are required to get the commodity from its producers to its users.

The rational markets hypothesis is that, given the prevailing technology of exchange, markets will be so organized that private profits
(gross of depreciation but net of transactions costs) are maximized
and, in consequence, social transactions costs are minimized. Whenever it is the case that, for any commodity or asset, private gross
profits after the deduction of transactions costs have a negative maximum, then no markets for that commodity or asset will exist.

Note carefully here that the rational markets hypothesis stands or
falls with the assumption that individuals are rational in precisely the
sense in which all economists assume agents to be rational. Indeed,
the rational markets hypothesis has a more thoroughgoing reliance
on rational behaviour by individuals than does Walrasian theory with
its assumption of an auctioneer who does not rationally maximize
profits or anything else. Since the efficient markets hypothesis has
no standing independently of Walrasian theory, the rational markets
hypothesis evidently entails individual rationality at least as consistently as the efficient markets hypothesis – and in a less *ad hoc* way.

We shall find in chapters 3, 4 and 5 that there are circumstances in
which, if the rational markets hypothesis is correct, individual
markets will be cleared by flexible prices. However, flexible, continuously market-clearing prices would require irrational behaviour in
other – perhaps most – markets. In addition, we shall see in chapter 4
that there are clear conditions in which, *if agents are rational*, continuous markets for some real assets will *not* exist. Among these
assets are items of capital equipment already in use.

The conditions in which continuous markets for second-hand capital equipment can be maintained by rational individuals and cleared by flexible prices are determined by the physical characteristics of these assets in relation to the technology of exchange. The more compact, durable and well standardized is any item of capital equipment, the lower will be the transactions costs incurred in its exchange. If all items of capital equipment are so well standardized that they are effectively homogeneous, and so compact and durable that they are in effect costlessly malleable, then markets for capital equipment will meet the conditions of the rational markets hypothesis for continuity of existence and clearing by means of flexible prices.

This is an important result. It amounts to the proposition that, if capital equipment is to all intents and purposes homogeneous and costlessly malleable, then the economy can function as if its market structure were Walrasian in character and, equivalently, as if it were chracterized by the circular flow of income assumed by mainstream Keynesians. For the capital equipment could change hands as often as anyone wanted at virtually no transactions cost. If firms are owned by households, then the economy will work as if households were to sell factor services to firms at each date and buy final commodities – including capital equipment. Conversely, if a substantial element of the capital equipment in the economy is not effectively homogeneous and costlessly malleable, then macroeconomic processes cannot work as if the economic structure were Walrasian or mainstream Keynesian. The transactions costs will simply be too high to enable anyone to make a profit.

1.3   MACROECONOMIC IMPLICATIONS

Keynesian economics has always been marked by the presumption that sufficient real expenditure can always generate full employment and full utilization of existing capacities in the short run. Moreover, if full employment and capacity utilization can be maintained in the short run, then the long run will look after itself.

No one has expressed this presumption better than Keynes (1936, pp. 378-9):

[I]f our central controls succeed in establishing an aggregate volume of output corresponding to full employment as nearly as is practicable, the classical theory comes into its own again from this point onwards.... To put the point concretely, I see no reason to suppose that the existing system [of decentralized, private investment] seriously misemploys the factors of production which are in use.... It is in determining the volume, not the direction, of actual employment that the existing system has broken down.

This, surely, is the justification for operating macroeconomic policies that rely on demand management to generate employment and growth to the virtual exclusion of policies intended to increase employment and growth by acting directly on the supply side of the economy. Supply-side policies in Britain have been either abortive (e.g. the Labour Government's National Economic Plan in the 1960s) or adopted only to correct regional disparities in unemployment rates. The position in America is even more stark. And yet, there is no theoretical reason to believe *both* that Keynesian unemployment is possible *and* that the direction of investment will always be appropriate to the achievement and maintenance of full employment provided only that the real value of investment is sufficient.

To be sure, multiplier–accelerator models from Harrod (1939) onwards have shown that supply-side reactions to even accelerating growth of consumption, government and export demands could cause deviations from full employment. But these models ignore issues connected with the direction of investment, by one of two devices. One is to assume that a single commodity serves as both consumption and investment commodity in the economy. Investment can then proceed in only one direction by assumption. The other device is less obvious. It is to assume that every commodity that is not a consumption commodity enters directly or indirectly as inputs to the production of all commodities including itself. The mathematical representation of this assumption is to specify indecomposable input–output matrices, a point that will be taken up in detail in chapter 6. I shall indicate here only how the microeconomic results discussed in the two preceding sections imply that the direction of investment in the economy is important and can frustrate attempts to achieve and sustain full employment by means of demand management alone.

If individuals learn at limited rates (so that long-run equilibrium cannot exist), and if capital equipment is not effectively homogeneous and costlessly malleable (so that continuous markets in second-hand capital equipment, if any exist, are not ubiquitous), then there will be no market signals to induce entrepreneurs either collectively or individually to respond to increases in demands by investing in directions that either lead to full employment or sustain full employment once it is achieved. Consider separately the effects of the non-existence of long-run equilibrium for the whole economy and the effects of the non-existence of continuous markets for second-hand capital equipment.

If long-run equilibrium cannot exist or, in practice, does not exist, investments cannot be determined even contingently on a complete set of forward markets. If it were possible for rational entrepreneurs profitably to provide the services required for the maintenance of such markets, then long-run equilibrium would exist whenever these markets were simultaneously cleared. Without such a complete set of cleared markets, long-run equilibrium does not exist and entrepreneurs cannot insure their investments against failure. In consequence, entrepreneurs will require to formulate expectations about future demands entirely on the basis of such information about past events and current circumstances as they have the learning capacity to acquire and use.

If markets for second-hand capital equipment are not complete and continuous, then firms that invest in capacity expansion will be unable to dispose of that capacity without incurring substantial transactions costs – if they can dispose of the equipment at all without simply scrapping it. A mistaken investment decision in the short run cannot be rectified subsequently by transferring equipment to other uses that turn out to be more profitable.

Taking these two points together, it follows that increases in current demands do not signal to an entrepreneur whether those increases will or will not last long enough to warrant investment in capacity expansion. The only market signal is that it will be profitable to increase the rates at which existing capacities are utilized. These are the market signals that Keynes identified and on which his analysis was predicated. That is, he had every theoretical justification to conclude that public works or any other expansionary demand management measures would increase utilization rates of under-utilized capacities and, therefore, demands for labour. There is nothing in my theory to cast doubt on the validity of that conclusion. Indeed, it is an important element of the theory reported in this book. But the effect of increased capacity utilization and corresponding increases in employment can be weak, strong or even perverse depending upon whether there are consequent investments in capacity expansion as well as capacity utilization. If, moreover, there is any population growth at all, some investment in capacity expansion will be required simply to maintain a constant unemployment rate. It turns out, moreover, that the direction of investments in capacity expansion are of crucial importance in determining the effectiveness of demand management.

This result turns on the identification of two distinct categories of commodities. The commodities in one category enter directly or indirectly as inputs to the production and exchange of all commodities produced, traded and used in the economy. The commodities in the other category, though they might enter as inputs to the production and exchange of some commodities, do not enter even indirectly as inputs to processes for the production and exchange of other commodities. Obviously, the second category of commodities are not used even indirectly in the production and exchange of commodities in the first category. Commodities in the first category are basic commodities in the sense of Sraffa (1960) as developed by Manara (1980) and Steedman (1980). Commodities in the second category, including some capital commodities and all consumption commodities, are non-basic. The distinction, although it was developed in order to solve problems in value and capital theory, turns out to be a powerful concept in the analysis of real and important macroeconomic processes. Provided that we can distinguish between basic and non-basic commodities and processes, then a two-sector model can be used to demonstrate the key properties of complex economic systems.

The theory of markets derived from the rational markets hypothesis implies that it is possible to make this distinction provided that we take the technology of exchange fully into account. There are some processes for the exchange of consumption commodities alone and some for the exchange of capital commodities alone. Even where there are establishments that sell to both firms and households, it is possible and, indeed, natural to describe the corresponding technology mathematically as two distinct processes. The outputs from one of these processes are sales to firms; the outputs from the other are sales to households. In this way, we can identify some processes for the production and exchange of basic commodities and other processes for the production and exchange of non-basic commodities. Consequently, although the theory of markets makes it both possible and necessary to take into account the richness of the institutional diversity of markets in actual economies, that theory also suggests the means of simplifying the analysis very considerably and of proving that that diversity is a phenomenon of secondary importance in macroeconomic processes.

1.4 THE BASIC MACROECONOMIC MODEL

We have three propositions that are derived from microeconomic analysis predicated on the assumption of rational individual behaviour. These are (1) that, learning rates being limited, there is no long-run macroeconomic equilibrium; (2) that, if capital equipment is not very like homogeneous and malleable capital, then investments in capacity expansion entail long-run commitments by the investing firms; and (3) that basic and non-basic commodities and corresponding processes will characterize the macroeconomic technology.

With these three propositions, it is a straightforward matter to demonstrate that and *why* market signals cannot be relied upon to convert increases in demands into increases in capacity and employment growth sufficient to achieve and maintain full employment. There is no better theoretical reason to expect expansionary demand management to increase capacity and employment growth rates than to diminish them except for minor expansionary deviations from trend. This result is easily demonstrated in a two-sector model incorporating the three microeconomic propositions discussed above. Although it requires some highly artificial specifications, the advantage of the two-sector model is that it shows the essential simplicity of the structure of the argument as it affects real (as distinct from financial) macroeconomic relationships. Moreover, when the model is generalized in chapter 6 the artificialities vanish, while no fundamental changes are required in the conclusions reached by means of the two-sector model.

The structure of the model is by no means novel. Like the notation, much of it is taken from Hicks (1965). What is novel is the way in which the distribution of the basic commodity is determined over time and its implication that market signals in general – whether price signals or quantity signals – are *not* sufficient to bring about full employment of labour or full utilization of capital equipment. In particular, this result is not affected by the fullest degree of market-clearing price flexibility.

There is a consumption commodity, called corn, which is assumed not to enter as an input to any production process – not even its own. Corn is therefore a non-basic commodity. The basic commodity is a machine. Machines and homogeneous labour are required to produce machines, and, in different input proportions, machines and labour are required to produce corn. Labour is non-basic because it is a primary input the production of which is not described by input coefficients.

We begin by considering the supply of and demand for corn. The determination of corn supplies and demands in this model is part and parcel of the determination of the employment multiplier.

The employment multiplier

If the production of consumption goods is profitable, the wage bill in each firm producing consumption goods must, by definition, be less than the market value of the firm's consumption good output. Thus, even if consumption-good sector workers were to spend their entire wage incomes on consumption goods, there would be some surplus output left over for consumption by other workers, by those receiving property income or other transfer payments and by those spending their wealth on current consumption. In the model of this section, corn production will be profitable only if the output of corn per worker is greater than the corn-wage per worker. The employment multiplier is a consequence of this relationship. A diagram invented by Joan Robinson (1960, pp. 79–80) will make clear just what is involved here.

The vertical axis of figure 1.1 measures quantities of corn per worker. The horizontal axis measures employment of labour. $O\bar{C}$ on

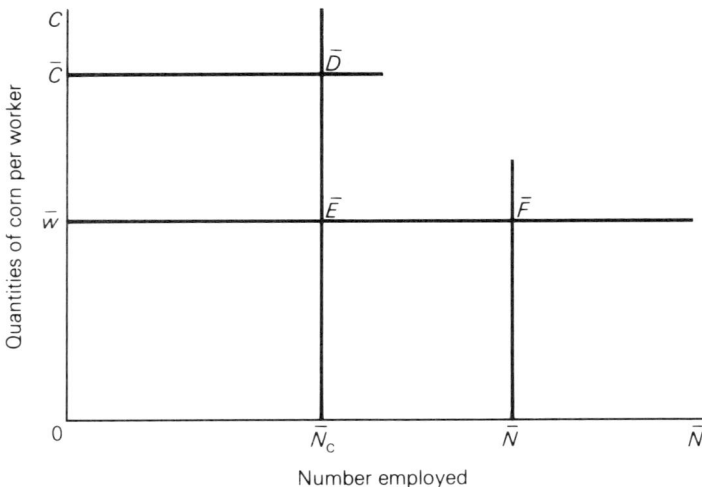

Figure 1.1   Corn-market clearing

the vertical axis is the average product of labour in the corn sector and $O\bar{w}$ is the wage per worker denominated in units of corn, i.e. $O\bar{w}$ is the corn-wage. $O\bar{N}_c$ is the employment of labour in the corn sector so that $O\bar{w}\bar{E}\bar{N}_c$ is the corn-wage bill in the corn sector and $O\bar{C}\bar{D}\bar{N}_c$ is the total corn output. Gross profits in the corn sector (revenue less wages) is evidently the area $\bar{w}\bar{C}\bar{D}\bar{E}$.

It will be convenient in the following discussion to refer to the amount of corn produced but not consumed by corn-sector workers as the net supply of corn. It is the amount of corn available for consumption out of profits and wealth or transfer payments of any kind or out of machine-sector wages. If the corn market is cleared, the demand for corn from these sources – the net demand – will equal the net supply. Most importantly, any increase in these net demands will generate additional corn-sector employment until the net supply has again become equal to the net demand. To take the simplest possible example, suppose that all wages are consumed and the wage rate is the same in both the machine and the corn sectors. If there is no consumption out of profits, transfer payments or wealth, the corn market will clear if the net supply of corn is equal to the machine-sector wage bill. That is, the area of rectangle $\bar{w}\bar{C}\bar{D}\bar{E}$ in figure 1.1 will equal the area of rectangle $\bar{N}_c\bar{E}\bar{F}\bar{N}$ where $\bar{N}_c\bar{N}$ is machine-sector employment. An increase of ΔN_I in the machine-sector labour force ($=\bar{N}\bar{\bar{N}}$ in figure 1.2) will require an increase in the net corn supply equal to the area of rectangle $\bar{N}\bar{F}\bar{\bar{F}}\bar{\bar{N}}$. If this incremental net corn supply is equal to the area of $\bar{E}\bar{D}\bar{\bar{D}}\bar{\bar{E}}$, then the value of employment multiplier is $(\bar{N}_c\bar{\bar{N}}_c + \bar{N}\bar{\bar{N}})/\bar{N}\bar{\bar{N}}$ or $[1 + (\Delta N_c/\Delta N_I)]$.

If there is consumption out of profits, the value of the employment multiplier will be larger as a result of the increased corn- and machine-sector profits. If there is any saving out of wages, the value of the employment multiplier will be smaller because the net corn supply per corn-sector worker will be larger and the net demand from each machine-sector worker will be smaller. The essential point here, often ignored in macroeconomic models, is that the employment multiplier, *and therefore the standard investment multiplier,* depends on the clearing of the corn market in this model and the clearing of the markets for consumption commodities in more general models.

Accelerator processes

The accelerator in macroeconomics is typically specified as a relationship between aggregate investment and aggregate demand and output.

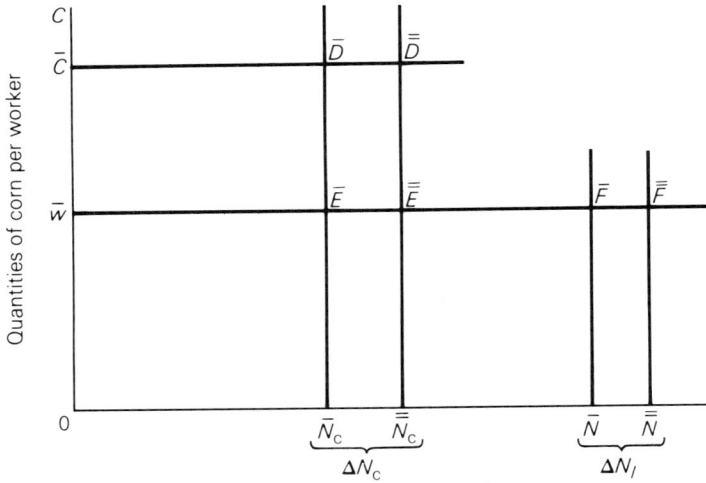

Figure 1.2   The employment multiplier

Each firm is assumed to have some desired capital–output ratio and some function describing its reaction to changes in demand. Thus, a change in demand and output induces each firm to change its level of net investment in order to re-establish its desired capital–output ratio. The macroeconomic accelerator relationship is simply the sum of all firms' changes in investments divided by the sum of all firms' changes in output. Some specifications of the accelerator relationship entail a fixed accelerator coefficient; others entail variable accelerator coefficients represented by functions of a variety of independent variables. As far as I know, however, no specification of the accelerator relationship has proved to be empirically satisfactory. This is just what the theory reported here would lead us to expect.

The reason is apparent even in our simple two-sector model in which, we shall see, the aggregate response of investment to changed demands depends on the extent to which the investment expands machine-sector production capacity relative to corn-sector production capacity. That is, the direction of investment is a crucial determinant of the time-path of the value of investment over time, and so of the measured relationship between investment and demand changes.

In addition, limited learning rates and the heterogeneity and/or non-malleability of capital equipment make an entrepreneurial decision *not* to invest in capacity expansion no less rational than a decision to invest in capacity expansion when current demands are increasing. Thus, even if the direction of investment were not an important determinant of the measured accelerator relationship, there would still be no microeconomic foundation for the belief that there is any *stable* fixed or variable accelerator coefficient.

The key issue, as manifested in our two-sector model, is the sectoral distribution of machines. At any time t, the distribution of machine stocks is given by Φ_t^*, which is the fraction of all machines held by firms in the machine sector of the economy. $(1 - \Phi_t^*)$ is then the fraction of machines held in the corn sector of the economy. We shall denote by Φ_t the proportion of machines actually employed in machine production at time t. Φ_t is the basic stock ratio and Φ_t^* is the maximum basic stock ratio. The rate of capacity utilization in the machine sector (the proportion of that sector's machines actually in use) at time t is Φ_t/Φ_t^*. The rate at which the distribution of machines changes over time is determined by the sectoral distribution of new machine outputs and the quantity of machines produced. The distribution of new machine outputs is given by ϕ_t, which is the proportion of current machine outputs held for use in the machine sector. ϕ_t is the basic flow ratio.

These basic ratios determine the rates at which the capacities and outputs of each sector can grow. Since machine-sector firms determine both their own rates of capacity utilization and the customers to whom they will sell current outputs, production and investment decisions in the machine sector have a crucial role which is not shared with firms in the corn sector. This, we shall see in chapter 6, is a perfectly general result. Taking all basic commodity producers together, their production and marketing decisions are uniquely important in the determination of macroeconomic growth.

A simple, if somewhat lengthy, algebraic and diagrammatic exposition will help us to see what is involved here.

Let a be the input of machines required to produce one machine and let α be the number of machines required to produce a unit of corn. Then

$$X_t \equiv ax_t + \alpha c_t + \tilde{X}_t \tag{1.1}$$

where X_t is the existing stock of machines in the economy at the beginning of period t, x_t is the output of new machines during period t, c_t is the output of corn during period t and $\tilde{X}_t$ is the stock of machines kept idle during the same period. It is in keeping with the desire for analytical simplicity here that the gestation periods of machines and corn are assumed to coincide with the length of the unit time-period.

The number of machines used to produce machines during period t is evidently $\Phi_t X_t$. That is,

$$\Phi_t X_t \equiv a x_t \tag{1.2}$$

and

$$x_t \equiv \frac{\Phi_t}{a} X_t. \tag{1.3}$$

Evidently, (Φ_t/a) is the rate of growth of the whole economy's stock of machines if machines do not depreciate. This assumption will be dropped in the more general analysis of chapter 6, but for the present it simplifies the exposition of the points at issue. It follows from this assumption that (Φ_t^*/a) is the maximum feasible rate of growth of the machine stock during time-period t. In consequence, the determination of any changes in the maximum basic stock ratio is a key element in any analysis of expansionary accelerator processes. For that ratio – hence, the distribution of machine stocks among the sectors – together with the technical conditions of machine production as described by the input coefficient a, determine the maximum feasible real investment in capacity expansion in the short run. We require to determine how this maximum changes over time. Since the technology of machine production is a datum in the short run, changes in the maximum rate of growth of the machine stock require changes in the maximum basic ratio. It is clear from identity (1.3) that, the higher the proportion of machines held in the machine sector, the higher is the maximum rate of growth of the economy-wide machine stock. That is, the maximum rate of growth of the economy-wide machine stock can be increased only by increasing the maximum basic ratio and is diminished whenever the maximum basic ratio falls.

It is in the determination of changes in the maximum basic stock ratio and the maximum rate of growth of machine stocks that we require the basic flow ratio. The stock of machines in the machine sector during period $t + 1$ is

$$\Phi_{t+1}^* X_{t+1} \equiv \Phi_t^* X_t + \phi_t x_t. \tag{1.4}$$

Subtracting $\Phi_t^* X_{t+1}$ from both sides of this expression, noting that

$X_{t+1} = X_t + x_t$ and substituting from equation (1.3), we have

$$\Delta\Phi_t^* \equiv (\phi_t - \Phi_t^*) \frac{\Phi_t}{\Phi_t + a}. \tag{1.5}$$

Evidently, the maximum basic stock ratio and therefore the maximum rate of growth of the economy's machine stock is increased in any period in which the proportion of current output held in the machine sector – the basic flow ratio – exceeds the proportion of machines already held in the machine sector. And if the basic flow ratio is below the maximum basic stock ratio, then the maximum rate of growth of the machine stock will be falling over time. Of course, the rate at which the maximum basic stock ratio rises or falls depends upon the actual basic stock ratio (or, equivalently, the rate of capacity utilization) as well as the basic flow ratio. The larger is the basic stock ratio, the larger will be the change in the proportion of machines held in the machine sector. The direction of that change depends entirely on whether the basic flow ratio is above or below the maximum basic stock ratio.

If there is full capacity utilization in the machine sector, then we can substitute $\Phi_t \equiv \Phi_t^*$ into identity (1.5) so that

$$\Phi_t^* \equiv (\phi_t - \Phi_t^*) \frac{\Phi_t^*}{\Phi_t^* + a}. \tag{1.6}$$

This expression can also be written as

$$g_t^* \equiv (g_{mt} - g_t^*) \frac{g_t^*}{1 + g_t^*} \tag{1.7}$$

where $g_t^* = (\Phi_t^*/a)$, the maximum possible rate of growth of the economy-wide machine stock at t, and

$$g_{mt} \equiv \frac{\phi_t x_t}{\Phi_t^* X_t} \equiv \frac{\phi_t}{\Phi_t^*} g_t^* \equiv \frac{\phi_t}{a}. \tag{1.8}$$

It is clear from identities (1.6) and (1.7) that the rate of growth of the economy-wide machine stock converges towards the rate of capacity growth in the machine sector because the maximum basic stock ratio converges towards the basic flow ratio in conditions of full capacity utilization. The phase diagram for identity (1.7) or equivalently identity (1.6) is particularly simple. Above the steady-state locus ($g = g_m$) in figure 1.3(a), the rate of growth of the economy-wide machine stock (g) is falling, and below the locus it is

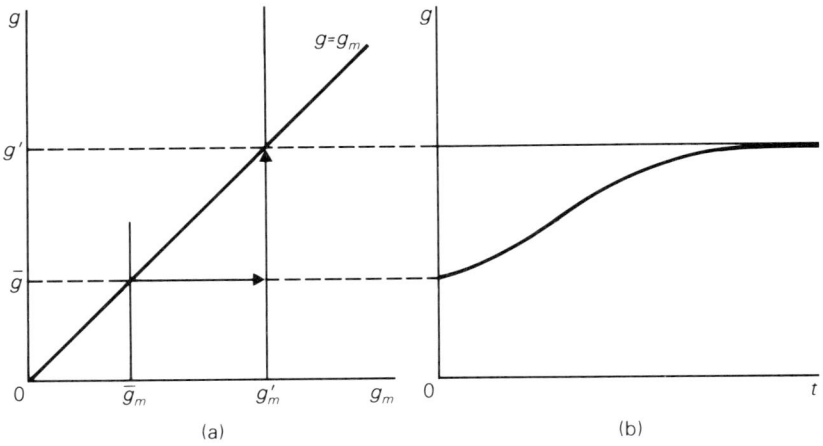

Figure 1.3   The effect of increased machine-sector growth on the growth of the economy-wide machine stock

rising. The steady-state solution is the intersection of the $(g = g_m)$ locus and the vertical from $\bar{g}_m$ on the horizontal axis. $\bar{g}_m$ is the value of the given rate of capacity growth in the machine sector. An increase in g_m to g'_m in figure 1.3(a) has no immediate effect on the economy-wide growth rate g. But as the maximum basic stock ratio catches up to the basic flow ratio, the economy-wide rate of machine stock growth converges towards the rate of capacity growth in the machine sector. The time-path of this convergence is represented in figure 1.3(b). The two diagrams in figure 1.4 depict the same phenomena after the rate of capacity growth in the machine sector has fallen from $\bar{\bar{g}}_m$ to g''_m.

That there is a short-run trade-off between machine and corn production in conditions of full capacity utilization in both sectors is obvious from identity (1.1). In addition, the short-run trade-off is related to the distribution of machines between the two sectors. The time-path of that trade-off once the rate of machine-sector capacity growth has changed is of crucial importance in accelerator analysis.

The rate of corn-sector capacity growth (i.e. the rate of growth of that sector's machine stock) at time t is

$$g^*_{ct} \equiv \frac{\Delta\left[(1 - \Phi^*_t)\,X_t\right]}{(1 - \Phi^*_t)\,X_t} \equiv \frac{1 - \phi_t\,\Phi^*_t}{1 - \Phi^*_t\,a} \tag{1.9}$$

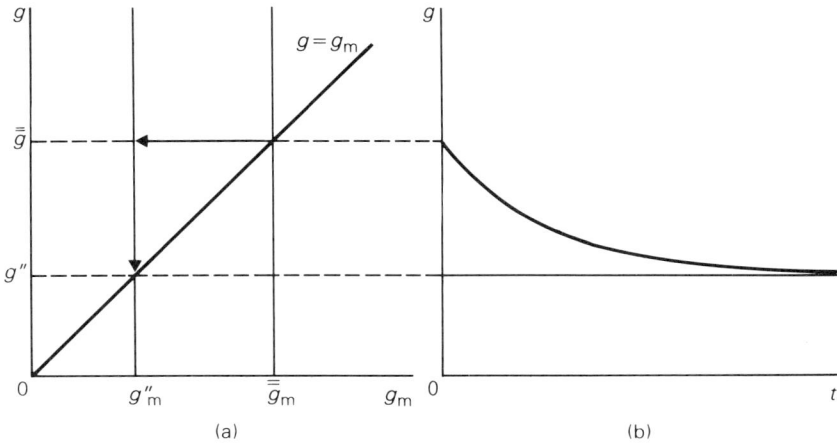

Figure 1.4 *The effect of diminished machine-sector growth on the growth of the economy-wide machine stock*

or

$$g_{ct}^* \equiv \frac{1 - \phi_t}{1 - \Phi_t^*} \, g_t^*. \qquad (1.10)$$

We have already found that the maximum basic stock ratio Φ_t^* converges towards the basic flow ratio and, in conditions of full capacity utilization, the rate of growth of the economy-wide machine stock converges to the rate of machine-sector capacity growth. It follows that the ratio on the right side of identity (1.10) converges towards unity while the value of g_t^* converges to g_{mt}. The steady-state solution of expressions (1.9) and (1.10) is therefore $g_{ct}^* = g_{mt}$. If g_{mt} should be increased, g_{ct}^* will rise towards that increased value in the long run. Similarly, g_{ct}^* will fall in the long run towards any reduced values of g_{mt}.

In the short run, there must be a trade-off between the two sectoral rates of capacity growth. Eliminating ϕ_t in expressions (1.8) and (1.9), we find that

$$g_{ct}^* \equiv \frac{\Phi_t^*}{1 - \Phi_t^*} \left(\frac{1}{a} - g_{mt} \right) . \qquad (1.11)$$

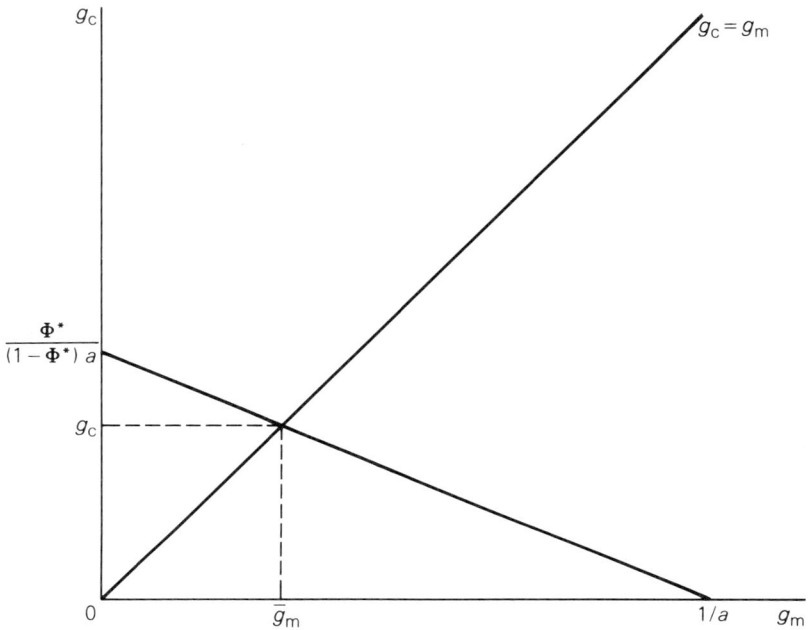

Figure 1.5   Short-run trade-off between corn-sector and machine-sector growth: the steady-state solution

This trade-off is shown in figure 1.5. The horizontal intercept $(1/a)$ is a technological datum. It is the average product of machines in machine production, and so the maximum rate of growth of the machine stock. The vertical intercept is the rate of growth of corn-sector capacity corresponding to a given maximum basic stock ratio – hence the distribution of machine stocks between the sectors – with the whole of full capacity output from the machine sector being sold to corn-sector firms. The vertical intercept obviously increases as the maximum basic stock ratio increases and declines as the maximum basic stock ratio falls.

The steady-state solution in figure 1.5 is the intersection of the short-run trade-off of sectoral growth rates and the $(g_c = g_m)$ locus.

The effect of an increase in the rate of machine-sector capacity growth is demonstrated in figure 1.6. That growth rate is assumed to be increased from $\bar{g}_m$ to g'_m in figure 1.6(a). The initial effect of that

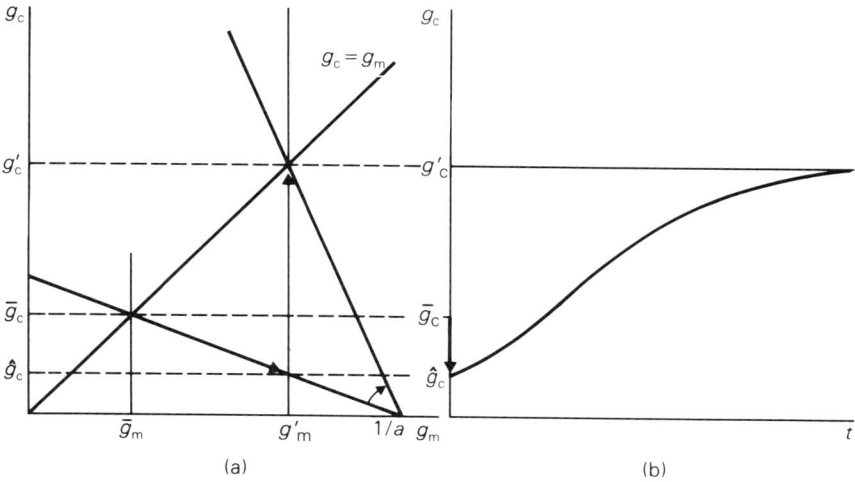

Figure 1.6   *Corn-sector growth path after an increase in the machine-sector growth rate*

increase is a reduction in the rate of corn-sector capacity growth along the short-run trade-off from $\bar{g}_c$ to $\hat{g}_c$. In the long run, however, the vertical intercept of the short-run trade-off rises with the maximum basic stock ratio. Since the horizontal intercept is fixed, there will be a sequence of short-run trade-offs rotating clockwise about the g_m intercept. The rate of corn-sector capacity growth will be determined by the intersection of the short-run trade-off with the vertical from g'_m. In consequence, the rate of corn-sector capacity growth will rise each period until the new steady-state solution is reached at $g_c = g'_m$. In other words, the corn-sector capacity growth rate converges to g'_c. The shape of the time-path of the corn-sector capacity growth rate is depicted in figure 1.6(b).

The consequences of a reduction in the rate of machine-sector capacity growth are wholly analogous. They are shown in figure 1.7. The short-run effect of the reduced machine-sector growth rate is shown in figure 1.7(a), where g_m is assumed to fall from $\bar{g}_m$ to g''_m and the rate of corn-sector capacity growth therefore rises from $\bar{g}_c$ to $\tilde{g}_c$. The reduced machine-sector growth rate causes the maximum basic stock ratio to fall until its steady-state value – equal to the now lower basic flow ratio – is reached. As a result, the vertical intercept

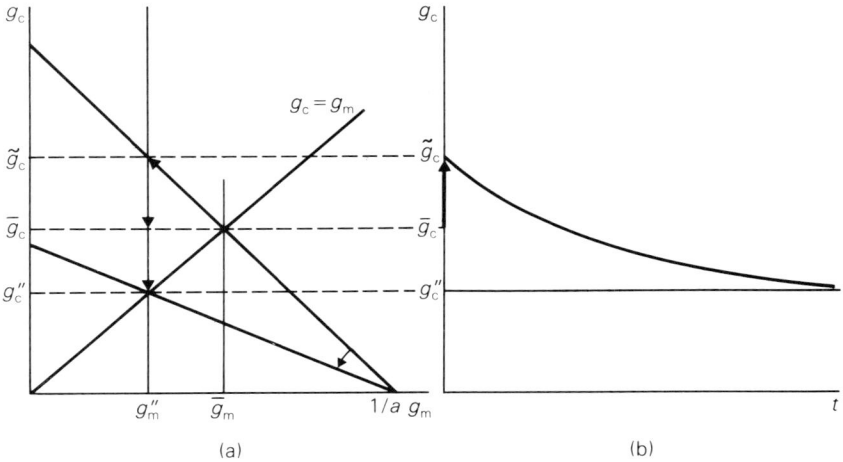

*Figure 1.7   Time-path of the corn-sector growth rate after a reduction in
the machine-sector growth rate*

of the short-run trade-off falls and the trade-off itself rotates counter-
clockwise. Since the value of g_c is determined by the intersection of
the vertical from g_m'' and the growth trade-off, the corn-sector capacity
growth rate evidently declines until the trade-off intersects the
$(g_c = g_m)$ locus at $g_c'' = g_m''$. The time-path of the rate of corn-sector
capacity growth is depicted in figure 1.7(b).

   These results define two types of accelerator process corresponding to full capacity utilization in both sectors. A third type is possible
in which there is under-utilization of capacity. All three of these
accelerator types are identified on the basis of strictly microeconomic
assumptions. Nothing has been assumed about macroeconomic
processes or relationships.

Three types of accelerator processes

Accelerator processes in general being investment responses to
changes in demands, we require, when using a multisectoral model,
to specify the nature of the demands that are changing. The particular demand change that I assume here has been chosen to make
two points. One is that Keynesian demand management is not
sufficient to bring about and sustain full employment because the

appropriate market signals will not be generated. The other is that our results are independent of the role of money as means of payment. Thus, Clower (1967/1969) was wrong when he contended that the use of money makes quantity signals dominate price signals and that this is responsible for Keynesian unemployment. Even without money and with fully flexible prices, both Keynesian and structural unemployment can persist indefinitely in economies composed of rational agents.

It will suffice to make both of these points if we assume a barter economy in which the government borrows corn for the payment of real wages to workers hired for a programme of public works. That is, the government demands corn from corn-sector firms which it promises to repay – perhaps from future corn taxes – at some subsequent date. In consequence, firms in the corn sector increase their outputs until their capacities are fully utilized. Entrepreneurs in the corn sector have two choices here: they can make no changes in their previously formulated investment plans while fully utilizing their existing capacities, or, alternatively, they can take full capacity utilization as a reason for increasing their investments in capacity expansion. If they learn at limited rates, then, even if there were a complete set of forward markets in corn and machines, they would be unable even to formulate a complete, subjective probability distribution of the outcomes of current investments. It is possible and by no means irrational that they will decide not to invest in capacity expansion because they cannot be certain of recovering their investment costs – in this case the purchase costs of machines. Since the machines are not sufficiently compact to be traded in continous markets, failure to recover the purchase costs would amount to a loss. The profit-maximizing strategy would turn out to have been not to invest.

In general, I define a *Type I* accelerator process to entail investments in working capital but not in capital equipment. Since there is no working capital in this model, the Type I accelerator entails no investment response to the increased demand for corn. There will therefore be no change in the derived demand for machines, and so no reason for entrepreneurs in the machine sector to increase their investments – if any – in capacity expansion.

There is a *Type II* accelerator response when entrepreneurs in the corn sector increase their demands for machines as a result of the increased demands for corn and entrepreneurs in the machine sector meet those demands without changing their own investment plans. If the corn-sector entrepreneurs respond to the government demand for corn by increasing their investments in capacity expansion, but not by so much that machine sector capacity is fully utilized, the Type II accelerator response clearly entails rational behaviour by machine-sector entrepreneurs. Even if the increases in corn-sector demands for machines result in fully utilized machine-sector capacity, a Type II accelerator process could still ensue without any violation of the rationality assumption; for the increased demands for machines could be either a once-over increase or the start of a period of increased growth of demands for machines. Current market signals cannot distinguish between the two possibilities. If the costs of purchasing machines cannot be recovered by selling them at will, then machine-sector entrepreneurs will not invest in capacity expansion unless they believe that the resulting capacities will be so fully utilized that, at prices that they deem likely to prevail in the future, the cost of those machines can be recouped. If they do not hold those expectations, then they will rationally refrain from increasing their own rates of capacity growth.

We have seen that increases in the rate of corn-sector capacity growth require reductions in the rate of machine-sector capacity growth in the short run. In order then to avoid long-run reductions in the rate of corn-sector capacity growth, the capacity growth rate in the machine sector will have to decline continuously. This result is readily demonstrated in relation to figure 1.7(a). As the short-run growth trade-off rotates counter-clockwise, the value of g_c can be maintained only by shifting the vertical corresponding to the current value of g_m continuously to the left. In this way, the long-run tendency for the corn-sector capacity growth rate to converge on the machine-sector capacity growth rate is offset by short-run trade-offs from machine-sector growth in favour of corn-sector growth.

In short, the Type II accelerator process involves a period of increased or possibly rising rates of corn-sector capacity growth with declining rates of machine-sector capacity growth. Clearly, this process is of limited duration since, eventually, the machine-sector growth rate will fall to zero and no capacity growth will be possible anywhere in the economy.

The *Type III* accelerator process is essential for a sustained increase in employment, capacity and output growth. It arises when increased derived demands for machines induce entrepreneurs in the machine sector to increase their own rates of capacity growth. This will happen when they believe an increase in current demand growth to presage a sustained increase in the rate of growth of demand for machines. As we have already seen, increases in the rate of machine-sector capacity growth entail short-run reductions in corn-sector capacity growth followed by a long-run convergence to the higher rate of growth of machine-sector capacity. As long as the machine-sector growth rate continues to rise, the corn-sector growth rate must lag behind. In principle, the machine-sector growth rate could reach its technological maximum, after which there could be no corn-sector growth at all because the basic flow ratio would be unity.

Such extreme results of Type II and III accelerator processes are precluded by the effects of interaction with the multiplier process.

Multiplier–accelerator interaction

It remains now to describe the multiplier–accelerator interaction corresponding to each type of accelerator process. In order to be as clear as possible that price flexiblity is not an important macro-economic issue, I will assume here that the three markets (for corn, machines and labour) are characterized by flexible relative prices. I cannot assume that all markets clear continuously without assuming that neither Keynesian nor structural unemployment is possible. I will therefore suppose that the two commodity markets clear continuously and that the wage rate relative to the two commodity prices can fall when there is Keynesian unemployment and rise when there is full employment with, perhaps, excess labour demands.

There are two price mechanisms that are common to all three types of multiplier–accelerator interaction in conditions of flexible prices. The first concerns the multiplier and the other concerns the accelerator.

1   Whenever the rate of capacity growth is higher in the machine sector than in the corn sector, the rate of employment growth will also be higher in the machine sector. Unless the real wage rate – the wage rate relative to the price of corn – falls in these circumstances, the net demand for corn must be growing faster than the net supply. A falling real wage rate diminishes the net corn demand by reducing the demand from each worker in the machine sector. In addition, the falling real wage rate reduces corn consumption per worker in the corn sector, thus increasing the net supply per corn-sector worker. The faster the decline in the real wage rate, the slower will be the rate of growth of net corn demand relative to the rate of machine-sector capacity and employment growth and the faster will be the rate of growth of the net corn supply relative to the rate of capacity and employment growth in the corn sector. It follows that, whenever the rate of machine-sector capacity and employment growth is rising,

falling real wage rates will be required to clear the corn market. As long as the marginal propensity to consume out of wages is not less than the non-negative propensity to consume out of profits, this result is not affected by the parameters of the aggregate consumption function.

2   If there is an increased demand for new machines, the machine market will be cleared if the machine price rises fast enough relative to the corn price. As the relative machine price rises, the quantity of new machines that corn-sector firms can buy out of any given revenue or even with external finance (if that were included in this model) would decline. If the machine price is also rising relative to the wage rate, then the profits of machine-sector firms will be growing faster than the machine-sector wage bill. That is, the share of profits in machine-sector income will be rising while capacity and output growth are increasing. It follows that the financial constraint on the machine-sector firms' abilities to invest in capacity expansion will be weaker than the financial constraint on corn-sector firms. Thus, the rising relative machine price will tend to clear the new-machine market by reducing demands by corn-sector firms.

We now investigate the three types of multiplier–accelerator interactions corresponding to the three types of accelerator processes identified above. In each case, we shall begin from a depressed state of the economy with a bout of expansionary demand management. As before, we shall assume deficit spending on corn by the government in a barter economy.

Demand management can always bring about a Type I multiplier–accelerator interaction – that is, an interaction between the multiplier process and the Type I accelerator process. If the government hires the unemployed for a programme of unproductive public works, each worker so employed will increase the net demand for corn and therefore corn-sector output and employment. In the nature of a Type I accelerator process, once corn-sector capacity is fully utilized, the rate of growth of corn output cannot exceed the previous rate of capacity growth in the corn sector. If the government persists in expanding employment in its public works programmes, the resulting excess demand for corn will drive up the corn price relative to the wage rate. Thus, the real wage rate falls and will continue to fall so that the utility-maximizing consumption out of wages is restrained to the full capacity level of output in excess of any consumption out of profits at each date.

Unless corn-sector entrepreneurs believe that the government will and can maintain a higher rate of demand for corn in the long run, they will not rationally increase their rate of capacity growth. They will however find profits growing as the corn price rises relative to the price of the only direct input: labour. At the same time, as long as there is only a Type I multiplier–accelerator interaction, the corn price will be rising relative to the machine price since there will be nothing to generate excess demands for machines. As the profit on each unit of corn sold rises relative to the price of machines, the corn-sector firms will find that the duration of sustained demands required to cover the costs of the new capacity is declining. Eventually, the cost of a machine will be recovered immediately it is installed. In such a circumstance, entrepreneurs in the corn sector will rationally increase their demands for machines since the resulting profit will be virtually certain. That is, the Type I accelerator process will give way to a Type II accelerator process with the corresponding Type II multiplier–accelerator interaction or, possibly, to a Type III accelerator process.

In the Type II multiplier–accelerator interaction, the increased growth of demands for machines from corn-sector firms is met first by increased utilization of existing machine-sector capacities and then by reducing the rate of capacity growth in the machine sector. As the rate of capacity utilization in the machine sector rises in response to growing corn-sector demands, employment in the machine sector also grows, so that there is an additional contribution to the growth of net corn demands by workers. If corn prices have been rising relative to wages as a result of employment in public works programmes, the relative price of corn will rise yet faster as the wage bill in the machine sector grows. So long as there are excess capacities in the machine sector, however, the machine price relative to the corn price cannot, under present flexible-price assumptions, be rising and will, if anything, be falling. These are the same as the price movements we found to characterize the Type I multiplier–accelerator interaction. If they persist long enough, the growing demands for machines will eventually exhaust machine-sector capacity and give rise to excess demands which can be eliminated only by a rising machine price relative to the corn price. The rising relative machine price might, *but need not*, induce a Type III accelerator process and multiplier–accelerator interaction. Let us see why it need not.

The initial increase in the utilization of machine-sector capacity yields an expansionary multiplier effect. But once there is full capacity utilization and the basic flow ratio either falls or simply remains below the maximum basic stock ratio, the rising rate of capacity growth in the corn sector can be maintained only at the expense of a declining rate of capacity growth in the machine sector.

If machine-sector employment growth is determined by its capacity growth, then the growth of net corn demands from the machine sector will be declining. At the same time, employment and output growth in the corn sector will be increasing. In consequence, at any given real wage rate there will be growing excess supplies of corn unless these are taken up by the government.

If the government does maintain corn demands by borrowing corn in order to feed workers on public works programmes or to pay real unemployment benefits, the government's share of aggregate demand will continually increase while the machine sector's share will decline until it simply vanishes. If the government does not act to maintain corn demands, the elimination of growing excess corn supplies during a Type II multiplier–accelerator interaction will require a falling corn price relative to the wage rate. In addition, as long as machine-sector capacities are fully utilized (albeit they are growing at an ever-diminishing rate), there will be no such downward pressure on the machine price. As a result, the corn price will be falling relative to the machine price. These relative price movements are precisely the opposite of those that led from the Type I to the Type II multiplier–accelerator interaction. Diminishing growth of corn sector profits relative to the machine price will increase the possible losses from machine purchases which turn out to be unwarranted. And the period of time required to recoup the cost of a machine out of the revenue generated from its corn outputs will be increasing.

Eventually, corn-sector entrepreneurs will cease to buy additional machines if only because the average and marginal value product of labour falls below the wage rate: they would make losses by hiring additional workers to operate new machines. Once the demand for machines by corn-sector entrepreneurs declines and possibly vanishes, there will again be unutilized machine-sector capacity and falling employment. In short, the expansionary phase of the Type II multiplier–accelerator interaction will give way to a contradictory phase. As a result of the expansionary phase, the distribution of machines in the economy will have shifted in favour of the corn sector, so that the maximum feasible rate of growth of the aggregate machine stock will be lower after the upturn in corn output and employment growth than during the previous slump.

It is by no means inevitable that the expansionary phase of the Type II multiplier–accelerator interaction should give way to a contraction. Indeed, it will do so only if entrepreneurs in the machine sector believe the expansion will be too short to warrant investments in their own productive capacities. If they are more optimistic, the rising demand for machines by corn-sector entrepreneurs could lead them to investment in new machine-sector capacity. If that happens, the Type II multiplier–accelerator interaction will give way to a Type III process which is self-sustaining.

In the Type III multiplier-accelerator interaction, the growth of corn-sector demands for machines induces machine-sector entrepreneurs to increase their own desired growth of investment in capacity expansion. Since, in this model, such investment growth requires only that machine-sector entrepreneurs retain a rising proportion of their current outputs for their own use, realized machine-sector growth rates are determined entirely by entrepreneurial expectations in the machine sector. The mechanism is different in the more general analysis although the effect is the same. Once the rate of capacity growth in the machine sector begins to rise, the rate of capacity growth in the corn sector must initially decline and then lag behind the rising machine-sector growth rate. This is the nature of the Type III accelerator process. Since employment is then growing faster in the machine sector than in the corn sector, unless the corn price rises relative to the wage rate there will be growing excess net demands for corn. The rising price of corn relative to the wage rate, together with full capacity utilization in the corn sector, will naturally induce corn-sector entrepreneurs to demand more machines. The resulting excess demand for machines can be eliminated only by a rising machine price relative to the corn price. That is, during a Type III multiplier–accelerator interaction with flexible prices, the machine price rises relative to the corn price, which in turn rises relative to the wage rate. The corn-sector demand for machines is held in check by the rising price of machines relative to corn-sector profits. The machine-sector demand for machines is encouraged by rising profits on each machine sold to the corn sector and therefore by the increasing internal corn-finance available to pay wages (this being a barter economy). At the same time, profits on each unit of corn produced are rising because the real wage rate is falling. Thus, corn-sector entrepreneurs' demands for machines will remain strong, and, should the relative machine price fall, they will naturally invest in capacity expansion. So although the short-run growth trade-off at each date is restraining the supply of machines to the corn sector, there is likely to be some increase in the rate of corn-sector capacity growth as the trade-off itself begins rising in the manner seen in figure 1.6.

We shall find in the general case that any of three phenomena can bring about a downturn from an expansionary Type III multiplier–

accelerator process. Two of them depend on financial relationships, and so are not conveniently introduced in this chapter. The third is manifest here as the falling real wage rate. Ignoring non-price phenomena such as strikes, the labour supply will grow at an ever slower rate, either because there will be a Malthusian decline in the rate of population growth or because the utility-maximizing supply of labour by each household declines with the real wage rate. In the end, full employment will be reached for one or the other of these reasons – or workers will simply strike for higher real wage rates. Whichever might be the case, the labour constraint will eventually bring the expansionary Type III multiplier–accelerator process to an end if financial forces do not do so first.

Major and minor macroeconomic cycles

We have found that expansionary demand management can always bring about a Type I multiplier–accelerator process and, provided that the government is sufficiently persistent and bold in its demand management, a Type II expansion as well. Even the Type II expansion is weaker and shorter than the expansion generated by a Type III multiplier–accelerator process. The difference between Type II and Type III expansions is the response of entrepreneurs in the machine sector to increased growth in the demand for their outputs. In a general equilibrium model, the response of entrepreneurs in the machine sector would depend on the time-preferences of households as manifest in the markets for the services of machines. These markets do not exist in the present model because the machines are assumed to be sufficiently different from malleable, homogeneous capital that profit-maximizing firms could not rationally provide the services required for exchange in second-hand machines. Moreover, the response of machine-sector entrepreneurs depends on their expectations formulated only on the basis of current demand growth, which itself provides no unambiguous signals regarding future demand growth. The lack of such signals, together with the unrecoverable capital costs of machine acquisition, make a contractionary response no less rational than an expansionary response. In consequence, rational microeconomic behaviour could give rise to either a Type II or a Type III accelerator process, and therefore to either a short weak upswing in macroeconomic activity followed by a downswing or a long, robust upswing which sustains itself until full employment is reached or financial forces impose a downturn.

We shall see in chapter 8 that there are endogenous forces which induce expansionary Type III multiplier–accelerator processes followed by analogous contractionary forces. That is, there is a relatively strong, long-lasting macroeconomic cycle implied by rational microeconomic behaviour. This cycle could be the Kondratieff cycle – the long wave of economic activity – but that cannot be concluded on the basis of the present theory. To avoid confusion with the literature on the long wave, I shall refer to the cyclical form characterized by Type III accelerator processes as the *major macroeconomic cycle*. The short, weak cycle characterized by Type I and II accelerator processes will, correspondingly, be called the *minor macroeconomic cycle*.

If spontaneous or endogenous forces or expansionary demand management measures bring about a minor cycle, it will be led by consumption or exports or government spending. The upswing of the cycle will peter out with no increases in the growth of investment in capacity expansion or, possibly with capacity expansions that are confined to the industries producing consumption, export and government (e.g. public works) commodities. The major cycle will be investment-led with a growing proportion of investment taking placed in industries producing such basic commodities as machine tools, electronics, steel and other base metals. (The general identification of basic commodities will be discussed in detail in chapter 6.) These phenomena are well known. The minor cycle is often characterized as a weak, consumption-led recovery from a deep recession or depression.

In order to analyse and prescribe policies to control these macroeconomic cycles, it is necessary to abandon the efficient markets hypothesis. While it is well known that Keynesian unemployment can be justified if markets are not price-efficient, we have seen in this chapter that, at least for one simple case, the abandonment of the efficient markets hypothesis is implied by the assumption of individual rationality in both production and (what is novel here) exchange. Together with the rationality assumption, we need assume only that individuals learn at limited rates and that capital equipment is not, to all intents and purposes, homogeneous and costlessly malleable in order to arrive at a fully general analysis of the major and minor macroeconomic cycles. This analysis leads naturally to a set of general criteria for policy measures that will maintain full employment growth in either an open or a closed, decentralized, market economy with fully developed financial markets, monetary arrangements and labour markets.

2

Equilibrium and Imbalance Theories: The Necessary Conditions

2.0 INTRODUCTION

The critique of long-run equilibrium suggested in section 1.1 is important not only for its demonstration of the implausibility of important concepts and analytical devices in mainstream economics, but also because it suggests a theoretical development that is both plausible and more powerful as a replacement for the notion of long-run equilibrium. This development is the imbalance theory of the firm, which shows how rational responses to short-run constraints on maximizing behaviour within firms determine the directions of firms' investments.

In this chapter, I develop the formal argument underlying the remarks of section 1.1 by showing, in the framework of optimal control theory, that long-run equilibrium of the firm either requires implausible and special assumptions to make the existence of that equilibrium compatible with rational, short-run constrained maximization or, alternatively, leads to an infinite regress. We shall see that the standard convexity assumptions substantially reinforce this argument.

The infinite regress follows from the proposition that rational maximizers will rationally seek to eliminate any constraint that frustrates their maximizing propensities. Each constraint with a corresponding positive Lagrangean multiplier falls into this category, since the multiplier measures the increase in the value of the maximand that would follow from a marginal relaxation of the constraint. Thus, it is not rational maximizing behaviour to accept the exogeneity of any effective constraint unless the expected cost of shifting effective constraints exceeds the expected benefit. However, the costs of shifting constraints will, in any equilibrium model, follow from the prices of inputs to constraint-shifting and the technology or organization of constraint-shifting. The rational maximizer will then seek some means of changing that technology or organization or will search for lower input prices. If the costs of constraint-shifting exceed the expected benefit, the maximizer will seek to shift the constraints resulting in that cost–benefit relationship. If those constraints are too expensive to shift, he will seek to reduce that cost by shifting the underlying constraints, and so on. Apart from assuming that there are immutable constraints – which is simply to ignore the requirements of logical coherence – the only way of avoiding the infinite regress is to prove that rational maximizers will maximize their objective functions by accepting some set of constraints. If the problem of the infinite regress is not solved, then agents are effectively unconstrained in their rational maximizing behaviour, and so there can be no finite solutions to their respective maximizing problems.

The imbalance theory of the firm arises naturally from the analysis of the infinite-regress problem and its solution. As suggested in chapter 1, that solution rests on the assumption that individuals learn at limited rates. We shall see that it is rational behaviour for firms' managers to maximize gross trading profits in the short run and, in so doing, to determine the optimal directions in which to invest in the shifting or elimination of short-run constraints. The rates at which the personnel of the firm can identify and then devise the means of shifting constraints is limited by their learning rates. Limited learning rates thus limit the rates of growth of the firm by either expansion or diversification or integration. This limit is obviously microeconomic in character. Macroeconomic limitations on firms' investments are no less important, although we will not be in a position to consider these until chapter 6.

In sections 2.1 and 2.2 I demonstrate the assumptions that are necessary for the existence of long-run equilibrium when firms are rationally managed. The imbalance theoretic approach is then described in sections 2.2–2.4, where it is also shown to be more general and no less simple than equilibrium theory.

In section 2.5 we shall see that imbalance theory specifies the institutional structure within which the determinants of the directions and magnitudes of investment, technical changes and other dynamic phenomena can be analysed.

2.1 A TAXONOMY AND ANALYSIS OF THE LONG-RUN EQUILIBRIUM OF THE FIRM

In this section we shall consider in some detail a largely diagrammatic analysis of firm equilibrium. The reason for analysing the equilibrium of the firm rather than the equilibrium of the household is primarily that the logical coherence of firm equilibrium has been the subject of analysis ever since the equilibrium theory of the firm took shape. The issues are therefore clear, and it is possible to build upon much previous work. A second reason for considering only firm equilibrium is that household equilibrium alone has no theoretical standing. If the concept of firm equilibrium is abandoned, the analyst is left with neither product-market supply curves nor factor-market demand curves. Since the remaining product-market demand and factor-market supply curves alone determine nothing, the equilibrium of the household is rendered otiose by the abandonment of the equilibrium of the firm.

My purpose in this section is not to analyse or model firm behaviour, but rather to analyse the whole class of long-run equilibrium models of the firm by, in effect, modelling models. I have therefore devised a model of the firm that incorporates the relevant features of a wide class of models in the literature on the firm. Those features that are relevant concern the limits to the magnitude or growth of the firm. Their relevance here stems from the nature of the problem of the infinite regress. That problem relates entirely to the limits on firm activity in the long run since, in the absence of exogenous constraints, the rational maximizer will find no finite value for his maximand.

It is well recognized that there is no technological impediment to the firm in attaining any size whatever. If diminishing returns are encountered with one plant or set of plants, they can be replicated.

The two classes of impediment that have been identified are competitive or market impediments and managerial impediments. In this section, we shall consider only the managerial impediments because the market impediments raise a different set of problems which will occupy the three chapters following.

There are, as far as I am aware, two lines of long-run equilibrium analysis of the managerial limits to the firm. One of these lines began with Kaldor's (1934) article, 'The Equilibrium of the Firm' and was developed mainly by Penrose (1959) in her *Theory of the Growth of the Firm*. The second line of analysis had its inception in Coase's (1937) 'The Nature of the Firm' and has been developed in classic works by Alchian and Demsetz (1972) and Williamson (1975).

The Kaldor–Penrose approach takes as given a limit to the amount of coordination of a firm's activities that can be undertaken by any one entrepreneur or, in Penrose's terms, any member of the management team. The main difference between Kaldor and Penrose is that, where Kaldor assumes that expanding the management team will not increase the team's coordinating capacity, Penrose assumes that it will.

The line of analysis stemming from Coase concentrates on the reasons for diminishing managerial effectiveness as the firm becomes larger. Coase himself ascribed increasing costs of managerial coordination to the costs of agreeing and supervising contracts. Alchian and Demsetz developed this approach by asserting that, for technological reasons, increased size gives increased opportunities to the employees of firms to shirk, i.e. to become wilfully inefficient in order to minimize the disutility of work. Williamson argues that there are market sources of diminishing managerial efficiency arising from the costs of enforcing contracts when one party has more information than the other or perhaps some other monopolistic advantage in exchange.

Even though these two approaches have different starting points and focus upon different concerns, all of the particular theories and models within each tradition essentially explain the limit to the size or growth of the firm by assuming that there are diminishing marginal returns to managerial coordination. I have sought to capture this feature in a model that is as conventional as I could devise and at the same time is as amenable as possible to diagrammatic analysis. The model is particularly useful in that it yields a variety of possible equilibria ranging from the standard, textbook, stationary equilibrium of the firm to a neoclassical version of the Penrose growth theory with a receding managerial limit. It is important to show that wholly standard equilibria arise from this model in order to be clear that I have not simply devised a straw man. It is then possible to consider the conditions in which constraint-shifting could be an uneconomic activity within the established analytical framework. In all other conditions, of course, the problem of the infinite regress predominates.

The model

In order to capture the various standard equilibria of the firm, it is necessary to employ dynamic, optimal control techniques. The model used here assumes discrete time-periods and constraints which can be represented diagrammatically in order to make the discussion accessible to those who are not mathematically oriented.

The firm is therefore assumed to produce one commodity by means of labour and real capital. The latter input is assumed to be homogeneous, costlessly malleable and indestructible. As a result, there are no costs of capital to the firm once the capital has been acquired. This assumption will be relaxed in chapter 3 and thereafter with the consequences indicated in chapter 1.

The technical possibilities open to the firm are fully described by a neoclassical production function. Apart from convexity, no particular assumptions about the form of the production function are required in algebraic analysis. For diagrammatic simplicity, the production function is assumed to be linear homogeneous. The argument in no way depends on this specification.

In addition to the standard technological production function, I have taken up a recent suggestion by Caves (1980) that an 'organizational production function' be specified. This will be seen to be a neoclassical specification of Penrose's managerial limit. The particular form of the managerial limit adopted here entails inputs of management to the acquisition of additional managers and to the coordination of investment. In order to facilitate diagrammatic exposition, the managerial-limit function is assumed to be additively separable.

The real capital available to the firm at any time t is

$$K_t = K_0 + \sum_{\tau=t_0}^{t-1} I_\tau \tag{2.1}$$

where K_0 is the firm's initial stock of real capital at t_0 and I_τ is real investment at time r.

The number of managers available to the firm at t (measured in some arbitrary efficiency unit of management) is

$$M_t = M_0 + \sum_{\tau=t_0}^{t-1} \Delta M_\tau \tag{2.2}$$

where ΔM_τ is the acquisition of efficiency units of management at time τ.

If we assume that the firm is a perfect competitor in all markets, the problem of the firm is:

$$\max_{\{I_t, \Delta M_t\}} \sum_{t=t_0}^{t_1} \langle \{F(K_t, N_t) - wN_t - [r + sm_k(I_t)] I_t \\ - sm_\mathrm{m}(\Delta M_t) \Delta M_t\} (1+i)^{-(t-t_0)} \rangle \tag{2.3}$$

subject to

$$K_t \leqslant K_0 + \sum_{\tau=t_0}^{t-1} I_\tau \tag{2.4}$$

$$m_k(I_t) I_t + m_m(\Delta M_t) \Delta M_t \leqslant M_0 + \sum_{\tau = t_0}^{t-1} \Delta M_\tau \qquad (2.5)$$

$$I_t \geqslant 0; \quad \Delta M_t \geqslant 0. \qquad (2.6)$$

There are three prices denominated in units of the firm's output: the wage rate w, the salary of an efficiency unit of management s and the price of a unit of real capital r. The discount rate i we take to be the long-term interest rate. The 'organizational production function' is described by the variable input coefficients $m_k(I_t)$ and $m_m(\Delta M_t)$. $m_k(I_t)$ is the input of managerial capacity required to coordinate the acquisition of a unit of real capital. It is assumed that the first and second derivatives of $m_k(I_t)$ are both positive, in keeping with the standard assumption of diminishing marginal returns to managerial coordination. For the same reason, the first two derivatives of $m_m(\Delta M_t)$ are also assumed positive.

The assumed objective of the firm's management team is to maximize the discounted value of profits from now to kingdom-come. Under the present assumptions, this is equivalent to maximizing the net present value of the firm.

We shall see that there are four possible equilibrium phases in the life of the firm. Three of these phases can be of infinite duration: (1) the standard stationary equilibrium of the textbooks, (2) a constant-investment equilibrium in which the managerial constraint (2.5) is not binding and (3) a constant-investment equilibrium in which the managerial constraint is binding. In addition, there is (4) a managerially constrained exponential growth phase with declining growth rates. This phase degenerates over time into the third type of equilibrium. Since our purpose here is to consider the role of constraints in the rational maximizing process, it will be convenient to group the analyses of these equilibria under the headings of their most binding constraints. We shall therefore take first the two equilibria, which are only capital-constrained, and then those that are also managerially constrained.

Capital-constrained equilibria

The capital constraint (2.4), but not the managerial capacity constraint (2.5), will be binding whenever the managerial capacity inherited from previous time-periods is more than sufficient to coordinate the long-run profit-maximizing rate of investment. In general, if there is an equilibrium it will entail a constant rate of investment and, therefore, a constant input of managerial capacity.

In the special case of the stationary equilibrium, no increase in the firm's stock of real capital will increase long-run profits, so the equilibrium rate of investment will be nil. In other words, the firm will be in stationary equilibrium whenever the discounted value of the profits resulting from a marginal increase in the stock of real capital is less than the cost of the investment.

The conditions for a stationary equilibrium are clear from figure 2.1. Part (a) of the figure is a standard isoquant map. Let us suppose

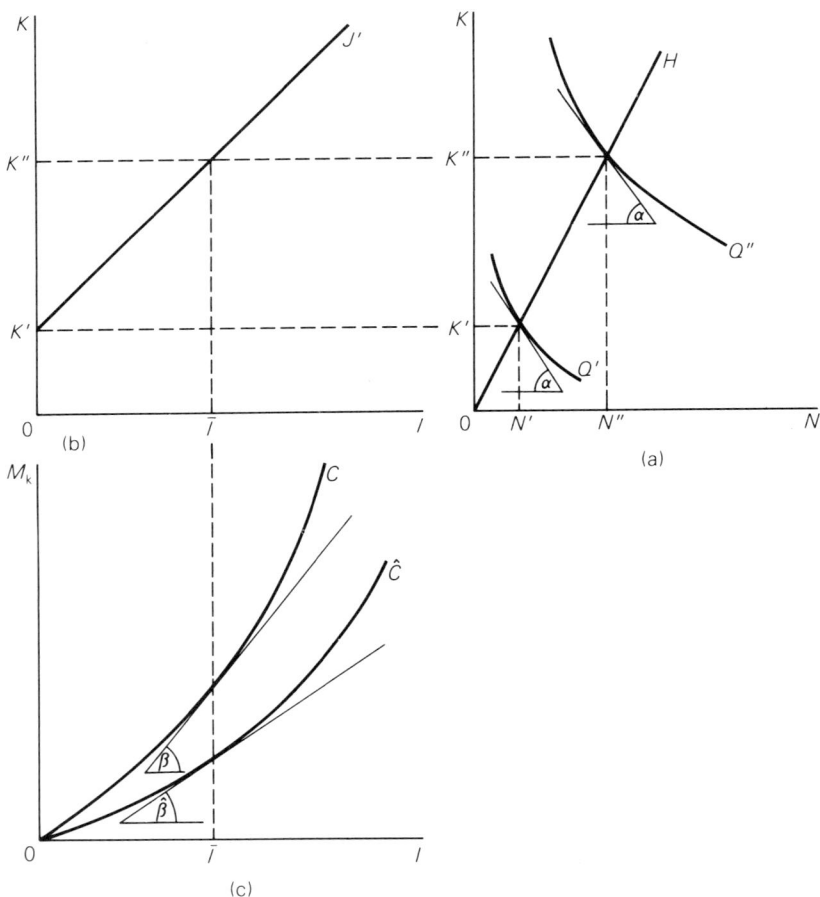

Figure 2.1   Stationary equilibrium of the firm

that the firm is considering an increase in output from Q' to Q'' requiring an increase in the stock of real capital from K' to K'' and an increase of employment from N' to N''. The resulting increase in the firm's profits at each date would be the increase in output $(Q'' - Q')$ less the increase in the wage bill $w(N'' - N')$. The present value of the additional profits will be insufficient to induce the firm to invest if, for all positive values of I,

$$\frac{1}{i} \left(\frac{\Delta Q}{\Delta K} - w \frac{\Delta N}{\Delta K} \right) < r + s \frac{\Delta M_k}{\Delta I} \tag{2.7}$$

where $M_k = m_k(I) \cdot I$. Evidently, the right side of the inequality is the marginal cost of investment. From Euler's Theorem, it is easy to show that the left side of the inequality is the marginal product of capital in a linear homogeneous production function for a given wage rate (so that both outputs are produced along the ray OH).

The $45°$ line $K'J'$ in figure 2.1(b) simply maps the real capital stock at the two dates on the vertical axis into the horizontal investment axis. This enables us to plot the required managerial input M_k against the rate of investment in figure 2.1(c). The relationship between them is OC, which for convenience we shall call the investment-coordination function. We thus see that the increase in output from Q' to Q'' requires a once-over investment $\bar{I}$. The marginal input of management at that rate of investment is evidently $\tan \beta$, the slope of OC at that point. Thus, condition (2.7) for a stationary equilibrium of the firm amounts in figure 2.1 to

$$\frac{1}{i} \left(\frac{\Delta Q}{\Delta K} - w \frac{\Delta N}{\Delta K} \right) < r + s \tan \beta. \tag{2.8}$$

Clearly, there will be a positive equilibrium rate of investment if, for some $I > 0$, condition (2.7) is replaced by the equation

$$\frac{1}{i} \left(\frac{\Delta Q}{\Delta K} - w \frac{\Delta N}{\Delta K} \right) = r + s \frac{\Delta M_k}{\Delta I} \tag{2.9}$$

with the corresponding change in condition (2.8).

In both of these and the subsequent equilibrium, the slope of the equilibrium point on the isoquants is

$$\tan \alpha = w \left/ \frac{1}{1+i} \lambda_k \right.$$

where λ_k is the shadow price (Lagrangean multiplier) of real capital and is therefore equal to the marginal contribution of real capital to the value of long-run discounted profits. That is,

$$\lambda_k = \frac{1+i}{i}\left(\frac{\Delta Q - \Delta N}{\Delta K}\right) = \frac{1+i}{i}\left(1 - w\frac{\Delta N}{\Delta Q}\right)\frac{\Delta Q}{\Delta K} \tag{2.10}$$

where $Q = F(K, N)$. Thus, $\tan \alpha$ is determined entirely by the interest rate i, the wage rate w and the production function $F(\cdot)$. It is not determined by the price of real capital r, since that price is a once-over cost of investment and not a cost of capital utilization.

Given $F(\cdot)$, i and w, the equilibrium ray OH determines the marginal product of capital and, therefore, the value of the left side of equilibrium conditions (2.7) and (2.8).

Any change in the parameters of the model that generates a larger or, indeed, a rising stream of future profits with a present value in excess of the cost of generating them will be found desirable by any management team seeking rationally to maximize the objective functional (2.3). Those changes that raise the left side of inequality (2.7) and those that lower the right side of that inequality are conveniently considered separately. Both are important because, if they are of sufficient magnitude, then the stationary equilibrium condition (2.7) gives way to the constant-investment equilibrium condition (2.9). This latter equilibrium is preferable because it entails a rising long-run profit stream acquired at a current cost each period that is less than the present value of those profits. Since constant output is always one option that is open to the firm, the constant-investment (hence increasing-output) equilibrium must dominate the stationary equilibrium with output Q'. Let us now see how such a change in equilibrium conditions can be brought about.

The left side of inequality (2.7) is increased either by reductions in the rate of interest or by technical changes that increase the marginal product, hence profit contribution, of capital. In general, however, reductions in the rate of interest will be of diminishing effectiveness in improving the long-run profits of the firm in this model while technical changes need not be. The reason for this difference is that, in perfect competition, a technical change that increases the firm's marginal product of capital will have no effect on the rate of interest while a fall in the rate of interest will reduce the firm's marginal product of capital. The latter effect follows from the increase in the value of $\tan \alpha$ that is implied by any reduction in the rate of interest. The resulting increase in the capital–labour ratio entails a lower marginal product of capital at each level of output. Thus, the increase in the left side of the stationary equilibrium condition (2.7) resulting from a reduction in the rate of interest will be offset by a reduction in the marginal product of capital. Depending on the elasticity of substitution, the effect of a reduction in the rate of interest could even be perverse, with the proportional reduction in the marginal product of capital exceeding the proportional increase in the value of $(1/i)$.

As the rate of interest continues to fall, the cumulative effect on the marginal product of capital will be ever more pronounced, and any benefits of technical change will, for that reason, rise continuously relative to the benefits of further reductions in the interest rate.

We get much the same sort of result when considering the right sides of equilibrium conditions (2.7) and (2.8). The value of those expressions clearly will be reduced by any reductions in either the price of real capital r or the managerial salary s. For sufficiently small values of these prices, there will be some value of $\tan \beta$ corresponding to a positive rate of investment that yields equality between the marginal acquisition and coordination costs of investment and the discounted marginal product of capital. Moreover, the smaller the values of r and s, the greater will be the equilibrium value of $\tan \beta$ and so the greater will be the constant, equilibrium rate of investment.

The alternative to reductions in the real capital price and the managerial salary is an organizational change that reduces the required input of managerial coordination for any given rate of investment. Evidently, if the organizational change is effective for all feasible rates of investment, then the investment coordination function is in effect shifted as from OC to $O\hat{C}$ in figure 2.1(c). Provided that $m_k''(I_t)$ is everywhere positive both before and after the organizational change, then the slope of the investment-coordination function will be smaller at all rates of investment for which it is defined. Let us compare a price change that transforms a stationary equilibrium into a constant-investment equilibrium at $\bar{I}$ in figure 2.1(c) with an organizational change having the same effect by reducing the slope of the investment-coordination function. Depending on the required price and organizational changes, the total investment costs will be reduced more by the price change in some cases and by the organizational change in others – provided that we are concerned only with moderate increases in the equilibrium rate of investment.

However, with a strictly convex investment-coordination function, any increase in the equilibrium rate of investment will be offset by increasing values of dM_k/dI (i.e. $\tan \beta$). The steeper the investment-coordination function becomes, the greater will be this offset until, as is evident from the function *OC* in figure 2.1(c), significant increases in the rate of investment are rendered impossible by the organizational limitations on the firm. In such cases, the benefits (ignoring costs) of organizational changes, which in perfect competition have no effect on input prices, will clearly rise relative to the benefits of price changes – even if the latter could be secured.

Evidently, in both types of equilibria considered so far, the benefit of constraint-shifting continues without any obvious source of decline unless costs are assumed to increase as one technical or organizational change succeeds the last. However, the benefit to the firm from any favourable price change must diminish ever more sharply as one price improvement follows on the last. This result is quite general since it follows from the second-order conditions for a constrained-maximization equilibrium. It does not appear to depend on the particular assumptions of the present model.

Although the point has been demonstrated here only in the context of a deterministic (i.e. non-stochastic) model, it patently applies equally to stochastic models. This is a point that will be taken up below in some detail. It will suffice for the present to point out that, with the technology and organization assumed here, the mathematical expectation of the benefit from a marginal extension of search activity will diminish with the scale of the search. This could be because, for any given probability distribution, the expectation of a further price improvement declines as ever more favourable prices are turned up by the search or because the benefit from a non-declining expected price improvement is itself declining. As suggested in chapter 1, the assumption of immutable constraints upon the firm in a stochastic model requires special implicit assumptions about the subjective probability distributions that attach to the search process.

We have now taken the first step in our infinite regress. That is, if a rationally profit-maximizing firm is in stationary equilibrium, either it will seek favourable price changes – which are excluded by assumption in a deterministic, but not in a stochastic, perfectly competitive equilibrium – or, as that search becomes increasingly uneconomic, it will seek to shift the binding constraints that determine that stationary equilibrium. The preservation of the concept of long-run equilibrium requires the assumption that there is some constraint on the ability of the firm to shift those constraints. Although there are many possible assumptions about the constraints on constraint-shifting, the particular assumption considered here is that the next level of constraint is managerial. This has the virtue, already noted, of complying with the essential features of the established long-run equilibrium theories of the firm.

Managerially constrained equilibria

The firm that succeeds in making the organizational and technical changes necessary to rise above stationary equilibrium and then continually to increase its constant equilibrium rate of investment might, but need not, require ever more managerial capacity. The firm that increases its equilibrium rate of investment by securing favourable price changes will inevitably run up against a managerial constraint as it moves up its investment-coordination function. Given the investment-coordination function and the managerial-augmentation function relating inputs of management to acquisition of additional managers, there will be some price configurations at which the firm does not seek to increase its managerial capacity and others at which the managerial capacity of the rationally profit-maximizing firm will grow at an exponential rate. However, this exponential rate of managerial growth will decline over time, and so, although it characterizes an equilibrium time-path, this is not an equilibrium state in the same sense as the other three equilibria.

In order to see what is involved here, we begin with the managerially constrained constant investment equilibrium. This equilibrium is depicted in figure 2.2. The diagrams there have the same axes as in figure 2.1. The production function yielding the isoquants of figure 2.2(a) and the investment-coordination function OC of 2.2(c) are the same as in the corresponding diagrams of figure 2.1. The economic meanings of $\tan \alpha$ and $\tan \beta$ are also identical. The main difference between the two figures is that in figure 2.2 it is assumed that there is a limited managerial capacity $\bar{M}$ available to the firm.

Given the set of relative prices and the interest rate, the equilibrium value of the slope of the investment-coordination function OC (i.e. $\tan \beta$) yields a managerially unconstrained equilibrium rate of investment I^* in figure 2.2(c). Taking just two consecutive time-periods ($t = 0$ and $t = 1$), then starting with real capital stock K_0 at $t = 0$, hence output Q_0, the managerially unconstrained equilibrium will result in a capital stock K_1^* and output Q_1^* at $t = 1$. However, given the managerial constraint $\bar{M}$, the maximum feasible rate of investment is only $\bar{I}$ ($<I^*$), resulting in a capital stock of only $\bar{K}_1$ and output $\bar{Q}_1$ at $t = 1$. Clearly, the question now to be considered is whether and under what conditions the rationally maximizing firm will devote existing managerial capacity to its self-expansion. The answer to this question is demonstrated in relation to figure 2.3.

Parts (a), (b) and (c) of this figure have the same axes and curves as the previous diagrams. The managerial-augmentation function is

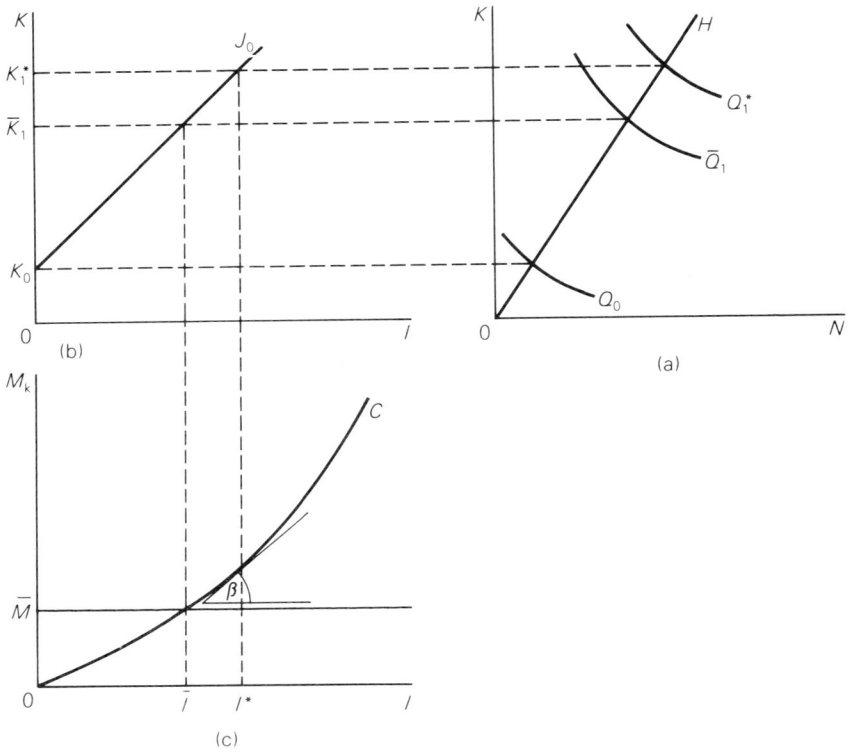

*Figure 2.2   Managerially constrained, constant-investment equilibrium of
the firm*

now introduced as curve OD in part (e) – its shape determined by the
assumption that the first and second derivatives of the variable input
coefficient $m_m(\Delta M)$ are strictly positive. At any point on the locus
$\bar{M}'\bar{M}''$ in part (f), the entire managerial capacity (i.e. $\bar{M}$) of the firm
is fully utilized in either self-expansion or investment coordination.
The slope of $\bar{M}'\bar{M}''$ will obviously be -1. The curve $\bar{L}'\bar{L}''$ in part (d)
is the mapping of points on $\bar{M}'\bar{M}''$ into points in the $(\Delta M, I)$ space.
The mapping from $\bar{A}$ in part (f) into point $\bar{B}$ in part (d) is shown
explicitly. Curve $\bar{L}'\bar{L}''$ in part (d) is clearly the managerial limit to
investment and managerial self-expansion.

One standard property of the managerial limit that will be of considerable importance in the present discussion is that the slope of the

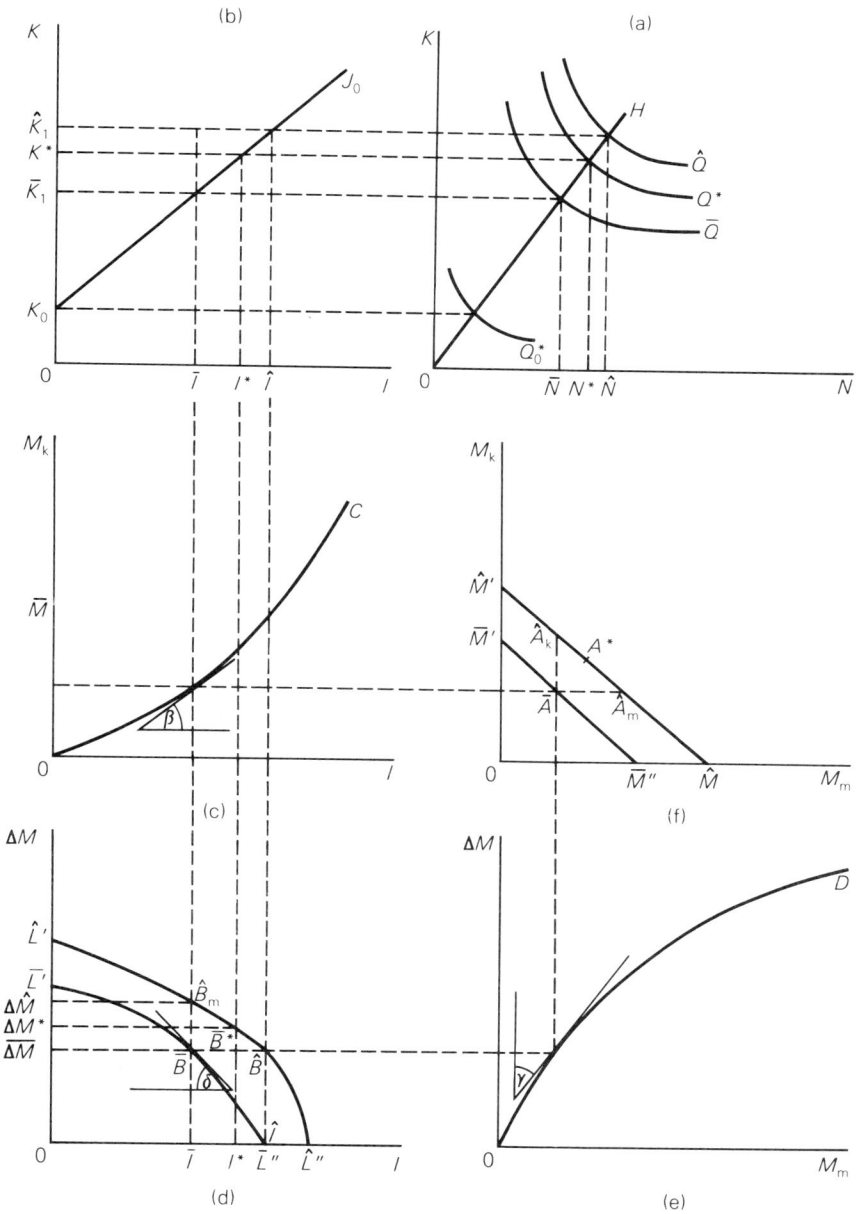

Figure 2.3   The managerial limit

managerial limit is the ratio of the slope of the investment-coordination function to that of the managerial-augmentation function; for along $\bar{M}'\bar{M}''$ we have

$$\bar{M} = M_k + M_m$$

and

$$\Delta\bar{M} = 0 = \frac{\Delta M_k}{\Delta I}\Delta I + \frac{\Delta M_m}{\Delta(\Delta M)}\Delta(\Delta M)$$

so that

$$-\frac{\Delta(\Delta M)}{\Delta I} = \frac{\Delta M_k/\Delta I}{\Delta M_m/\Delta(\Delta M)}. \tag{2.11}$$

In terms of figure 2.3, this property amounts at point $\bar{B}$ on the managerial limit to

$$\tan\delta = \frac{\tan\beta}{\tan\gamma}. \tag{2.12}$$

One thing is immediately clear: the managerially constrained, constant-investment equilibrium will prevail whenever the profit-maximizing point on the firm's managerial limit is its horizontal intercept. In that case, $\Delta M = 0$ whatever the managerial limit and, for managerial limit $\bar{L}'\bar{L}''$, investment will be represented by $O\bar{L}''$. Since this is clearly a special case, it is best to begin by demonstrating the general properties of a profit-maximizing equilibrium path.

The problem of the firm here is to find the profit-maximizing allocation of managerial capacity as between investment coordination and managerial augmentation. In equilibrium, the standard result applies: the marginal profit of managerial capacity allocated to the coordination of investment will equal the marginal profit of managerial capacity allocated to the augmentation of that capacity. For reasons shortly to become apparent, it will be useful to know not only when this marginality condition is satisfied but also the marginal profit to be had from a marginal notional increase in the current managerial capacity (i.e. the shadow price of managerial capacity). It will therefore be convenient to develop the appropriate marginal conditions as a comparison of the optimal allocations with two, slightly different, managerial capacities $\bar{M}$ and $\hat{M}$. It will also be convenient to define two additional variables: μ_k, the marginal present value of future profits arising from a marginal increase in

M_k, and μ_m, the marginal present value of future profits arising from a marginal increase in M_m. We begin by determining μ_k.

Suppose that the entire notional increment to managerial capacity is allocated to investment coordination. That is, the firm's managers choose point $\hat{A}_k$ on $\hat{M}'\hat{M}''$ in figure 2.3(f). The resulting increase in investment increases the firm's stock of real capacity by $\bar{K}_1\hat{K}_1$ in every period starting one period hence. Given the linear homogeneity of the production function, there will be a corresponding increase in output from $\bar{Q}$ to $\hat{Q}$, starting one period hence, together with an increase in employment of $\bar{N}\hat{N}$. Thus, in every period starting one period hence, the firm will generate an additional gross trading profit of $\Delta Q - w\Delta N$. The present value of this stream is, of course, $(1/i)(\Delta Q - w\Delta N)$. The cost of acquiring this additional stream of profits is this period's additional investment cost $r\Delta I + s\Delta M_k$. Letting V be the present-value operator; we have

$$V(\Delta P) = \frac{1}{i}(\Delta Q - w\Delta N) - (r\Delta I + s\Delta M_k) \qquad (2.13)$$

$$\mu_k = \frac{V(\Delta P)}{\Delta M_k} = \frac{1}{i}\left(1 - w\frac{\Delta N}{\Delta Q}\right)\frac{\Delta Q}{\Delta I} - \left(r + s\frac{\Delta M_k}{\Delta I}\right)\frac{\Delta I}{\Delta M_k}.$$

Bearing in mind that in this is a comparison in which $\Delta I \equiv \Delta K$, this expression can be rearranged to yield

$$\mu_k = \frac{(1/i)\,[1 - w(\Delta N/\Delta Q)]\,(\Delta Q/\Delta K) - r}{\Delta M_k/\Delta I} - s. \qquad (2.14)$$

In turning to the derivation of μ_m, we note immediately that the notional increment to managerial capacity cannot be allocated entirely to managerial self-expansion if it is to be profit-maximizing. To see this, suppose that such an allocation, $\hat{A}_m$, is chosen. This will entail a current cost to the firm of $s\Delta M_m$ with no corresponding increase in investment, or therefore in future real capital stocks or outputs. In that case, the present value of the additional profits accruing to the firm as a result of the notional increase in managerial capacity is simply $-s\Delta M_m$, which is, of course, negative. Let us therefore suppose that the allocation of the notionally increased managerial capacity chosen by the firm's managers is A^*. It is then evident from figure 2.3 that there will be an increase in investment of $\Delta I = \bar{II}^*$, an increase in the capital stock $\Delta K = \bar{K}K^*$, increased output and employment being, respectively, $\Delta Q = Q^* - \bar{Q}$ and $N = \bar{N}N^*$. The increase in M_m yields a higher rate of investment at every period starting one period hence. The present value of the profits from each of those increases in investment *at the time they take place* will be equal to the right side of expression (2.13). Thus, an increase in the allocation of existing managerial capacity to its own replication will generate a stream of present values which themselves have a present value. The discounted stream of additional profits from an increase in the rate of managerial expansion will be the present value of a stream of present values less the cost $s\Delta M_m$ of acquiring that stream. Formally, this will be

$$V(\Delta P) = \frac{1}{i}\left[\frac{1}{i}(\Delta Q - w\Delta N) - (r\Delta I + s\Delta M_k)\right] - s\Delta M_m, \quad (2.15)$$

from which, noting again that in this context $\Delta I \equiv \Delta K$,

$$\mu_m = \frac{V(\Delta P)}{\Delta M_m} = \frac{\Delta(\Delta M)}{\Delta M_m}\frac{\Delta I}{\Delta(\Delta M)}\frac{1}{i}\left[\frac{1}{i}\left(1 - w\frac{\Delta N}{\Delta Q}\right)\frac{\Delta Q}{\Delta K}\right.$$
$$\left. - \left(r + s\frac{\Delta M_k}{\Delta I}\right)\right] - s$$

or

$$\mu_m = \frac{\dfrac{\Delta I}{\Delta(\Delta M)}\dfrac{1}{i}\left[\dfrac{1}{i}\left(1 - w\dfrac{\Delta N}{\Delta Q}\right)\dfrac{\Delta Q}{\Delta K} - \left(r + s\dfrac{\Delta M_k}{\Delta I}\right)\right]}{\Delta M_m / \Delta(\Delta M)} - s. \quad (2.16)$$

If there is an equilibrium with a positive value of ΔM, then the marginal contributions to the present value of long-run profits from the allocation of managerial capacity to its own expansion and to investment coordination will be equal (i.e. $\mu_k = \mu_m$). Equating the right sides of expressions (2.14) and (2.16), we find that

$$\frac{\dfrac{1}{i}\left[\left(1 - w\dfrac{\Delta N}{\Delta Q}\right)\dfrac{\Delta Q}{\Delta K}\right] - r}{\dfrac{\Delta I}{\Delta(\Delta M)}\dfrac{1}{i}\left[\dfrac{1}{i}\left(1 - w\dfrac{\Delta N}{\Delta Q}\right)\dfrac{\Delta Q}{\Delta K} - \left(r + s\dfrac{\Delta M_k}{\Delta I}\right)\right]} = \frac{\Delta M_k / \Delta I}{\Delta M_m / \Delta(\Delta M)}.$$
$$(2.17)$$

The value of the right side of this equilibrium condition is, from expressions (2.11) and (2.12), the slope of the managerial limit in figure 2.3(d). The value of the left side is directly related to the prices r, s, w and i. In consequence, any favourable price change found or faced by the firm will reduce the equilibrium slope of the profit-maximizing point on the managerial limit. Looked at the other way round, it is always possible to find prices that are high enough to ensure that a corner solution prevails at $\Delta M = 0$. There always exists a range of prices that are sufficiently low that all managerial capacity is utilized in investment coordination, but it is none the less unprofitable to use any managerial capacity for the expansion of the managerial limit. This equilibrium is what is shown in figure 2.2.

It follows that, in such a managerially constrained, constant-investment equilibrium, there will always exist favourable price changes of sufficient magnitude that they will raise the firm to a growth equilibrium with a receding managerial limit. The characteristics of this equilibrium will be considered presently.

An alternative way of transforming a managerially constrained constant-investment equilibrium into an exponential growth equilibrium is by means of an organizational change, which reduces the managerial capacity required to expand the managerial limit. Such an organizational change is depicted in figure 2.4 as a shift in the managerial-augmentation function $O\bar{D}$ to $O\hat{D}$. This organizational change has no effect on the horizontal intercept of the managerial limit, but it does raise the vertical intercept and all other points corresponding to a feasible allocation of managerial capacity (e.g. point A in figure 2.4(f)). It is clear from figure 2.4 that the effect of this organizational change is to render the slope of the managerial limit steeper over the entire range of feasible rates of investment. Since this change does not affect the left side of equilibrium condition (2.17), it is clear that, for upward shifts of sufficient magnitude in the managerial-augmentation function, the slope of the managerial limit can be made sufficiently steep that the equilibrium value of that slope will be found for some positive value of ΔM.

Technical changes, which increase the profitability of capital (i.e. $(1 - \Delta N/\Delta Q)(\Delta Q/\Delta K)$), reduce the value of the left side of equilibrium condition (2.17) and so move the equilibrium point on the managerial limit upward to the left. The profit-maximizing value of ΔM is thereby increased, possibly from zero, while the current optimal rate of investment is reduced. Such technical changes are therefore capable of transforming a managerially constrained constant-investment equilibrium into an exponential growth equilibrium.

The effect of an organizational change that improves managerial efficiency in the coordination of investment is ambiguous. A reduction in $(\Delta M_k/\Delta I)$ will certainly reduce the slope of the managerial limit, shifting the I-intercept outward but not affecting the ΔM-intercept. However, it will also reduce the slope of the equilibrium point on the managerial limit (i.e. the left side of condition (2.17)).

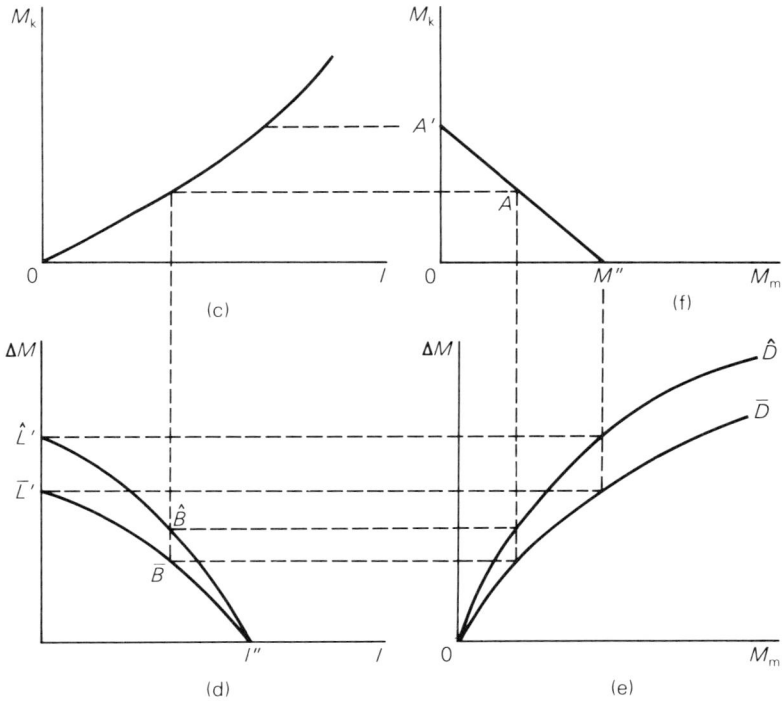

Figure 2.4   The effect of organizational change on the dynamic equilibrium of the firm

Whether it reduces the equilibrium slope faster than it reduces the actual slope everywhere on the managerial limit depends on the firm's production function and the market prices faced by it. None the less, such an organizational change does unambiguously increase the rate of investment that can be undertaken with a given managerial capacity.

Let us now put together these points on price changes, technical changes and organizational changes. It is not, of course, surprising to find that organizational changes are preferable to price changes since it will always be the case that the costless relaxation of a binding constraint increases the value of a constrained maximum. It is surprising, however, that in a managerially constrained equilibrium the effect of a technical change is equivalent to a favourable price change, even though the firm is on its production function and is utilizing all of the real capital it has inherited from the past. Why should this be so?

The reason is that managerial capacity in the present model is basic in the same sense as the machine is basic in the two-sector model in chapter 1. In any economic system, including such open systems as the firm, basic commodities have a crucial function in limiting the growth of the system which non-basic commodities do not. This function makes the relaxation of constraints on the availability or growth of availability of basics more effective than similar relaxations of constraints on non-basics. The reason for this difference is apparent when we consider a (declining) growth equilibrium in the present model.

The relevant diagrammatic apparatus is presented in figure 2.5. This apparatus differs from that of figure 2.4 in the addition of two diagrams. Part (h) maps the acquisition of managerial capacity at any time t into the total managerial capacity at $t+1$ by means of the $45°$ lines M_0F_0, M_1F_1, etc. Part (g) simply transfers the value of M at any time from the horizontal to the vertical axis in order to fix the vertical intercept of the locus of feasible allocations of managerial capacity after that capacity has been augmented. All of the other diagrams are the same as in the previous figures.

It has already been shown that the growth path of the firm is determined by the shape of the managerial limit and the slope of the equilibrium point on the managerial limit given by the left side of equilibrium condition (2.17). In figure 2.5, we follow the growth path of the firm over three time periods ($t = 0, 1, 2$). The initial conditions are given by the initial stocks of real capital K_0 and managerial capacity M_0. Assume that the value of the left side of condition (2.17) is $\tan \delta_0$. In that case, the equilibrium point on the managerial limit is B_0, corresponding to the allocation A_0 of managerial capacity in part (f). The profit-maximizing equilibrium augmentation of the management team at $t = 0$ is ΔM_0, which yields a managerial capacity M_1 the following period (as shown in part (h)). The feasible allocations of managerial capacity at $t = 1$ are then given by the locus $M_1'M_1''$ in part (f). In the now usual way, this allocation maps into the managerial limit $L_1'L_1''$ in part (d). The equilibrium point on this managerial limit will have a steeper slope than the equilibrium point on the previous period's managerial limit – say, $\tan \delta_1$ ($\delta_1 > \delta_0$). This increase results from the assumed diminishing efficiency of the managerial coordination of investment, since the equilibrium rate of investment is increasing and, in consequence, $\Delta M_k/\Delta I$ is larger at $t = 1$ than at $t = 0$. It is evident by inspection that this increases the value of the left side of equilibrium condition (2.17).

Repeating this procedure, we find the managerial limit at $t = 2$ is $L_2'L_2''$ and again the equilibrium point on that managerial limit will

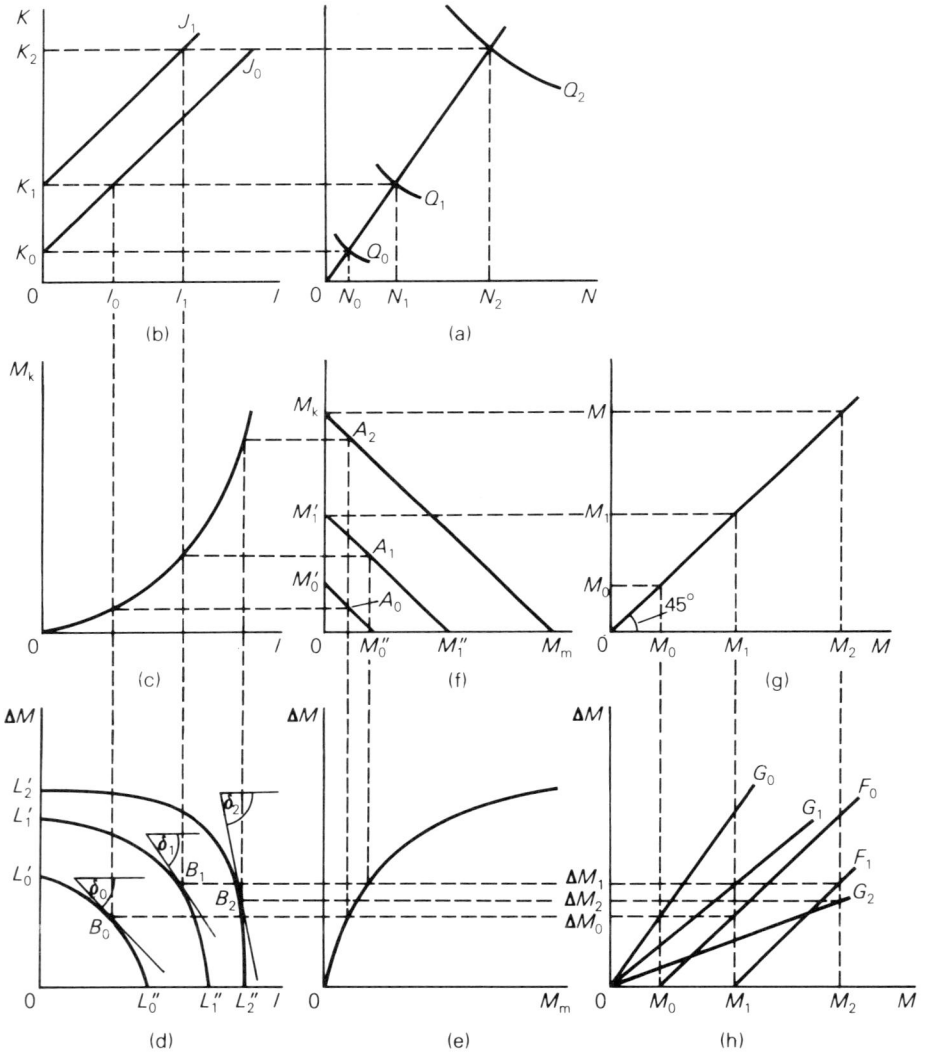

Figure 2.5   The receding managerial limit

have a steeper slope than was the case at $t = 1$. In addition, this managerial limit has a more pronounced bulge than its predecessor, which itself had a more pronounced bulge than $L_0' L_0''$. This, too, is a result of diminishing returns to managerial coordination. The value of the slope of the investment coordination function at points close to that corresponding to the horizontal intercept of the managerial limit tends towards infinity as the maximum feasible rate of investment increases with the expansion of the managerial limit. As a result, the slope of the managerial limit itself tends towards infinity. Similarly, the inverse of the slope of the managerial augmentation function OD (i.e. $\Delta M_m / \Delta(\Delta M)$) tends towards infinity as the maximum feasible acquisition of managerial capacity increases over time. Thus, the slope of the managerial limit close to its vertical intercept tends increasingly towards zero as the managerial limit recedes. This increasingly pronounced bulge, together with the increasing slope of the managerial limit at its equilibrium point, puts downward pressure on managerial self-expansion and results in a falling proportion of managerial capacity being allocated to managerial self-expansion.

The rate of growth of managerial capacity, and therefore the rate at which the managerial limit recedes, can now be seen to fall over time. In part (h), the ray from the origin OG_0 passes through the point $(M_0, \Delta M_0)$, OG_1 passes through point $(M_1, \Delta M_1)$, and so on. The slope of these rays are therefore equal to $\Delta M_t / M_t$ ($t = 0, 1, 2$). Since each of these rays is less steep than that of the preceding period, it is clear that the rate of growth of managerial capacity is declining over time. Eventually, the growth equilibrium declines into a managerially constrained, constant-investment equilibrium that can, in principle, last for ever.

In this case, favourable price changes reduce the slope of the equilibrium point on the managerial limit at every date, thus reducing the rate of deceleration of the managerial growth rate. They also increase the present value of long-run profits. The same effect is achieved, as we have seen, by technical changes that improve the profitability of capital. And, as before, organizational improvements must become increasingly desirable relative to either of those alternatives. In addition, we now find that organizational changes, but neither price nor technical changes, can prevent the rate of managerial growth from declining in the long run.

To see why price and technical changes cannot forestall declining growth for ever, consider what happens when all prices have fallen to zero. It is easily seen that the left side of equilibrium condition (2.17) will then be zero, implying that the equilibrium point on the managerial limit is its vertical intercept. All managerial capacity will then be devoted to its replication, but, because of diminishing returns, the exponential rate of expansion must be falling (i.e. the vertical intercept rises at a diminishing exponential rate).

This is a property of all systems with diminishing returns to basic commodity production or basic resource acquisition. The proof could hardly be more elementary.

The allocation of managers to the acquisition of additional managers (M_m) at any time t is

$$m_m(\Delta M_t) \cdot \Delta M_t = a_t M_t \qquad (2.18)$$

where a_t is simply the proportion of existing managerial capacity allocated to its own replication. In figure 2.5, this proportion at each date is $M'_t A_t / M'_t M''_t$ ($t = 0, 1, 2$), which is readily seen to decline over the equilibrium time-path there represented. Cross-multiplying in equation (2.18), we have

$$\frac{\Delta M_t}{M_t} = \frac{a_t}{m_m(\Delta M_t)}. \qquad (2.19)$$

At best, prices could fall so low that $a_t = 1$. In, for example, a steady-growth equilibrium, not only is the total managerial capacity growing at the constant, equilibrium rate, but so too is the rate of acquisition of managerial capacity ΔM_t. With positive first and second derivatives of $m_m(\cdot)$, the denominator on the right side of expression (2.19) must be increasing over time, implying a fall in the rate of managerial growth on the left side.

Clearly, in this case, as in those previously considered, the second-order conditions for a constrained-maximization equilibrium leads to the conclusion that, ignoring costs, constraint-shifting must eventually offer a greater expectation of benefits than is offered by the search for favourable price changes. In addition, shifting constraints on the availability of basic resources is preferable to shifting the constraints on non-basic services. What about the costs? It is always possible to assume that the costs of constraint-shifting are such that the expected *net* benefit of search for improved prices in a stochastic world would exceed the expected net benefit of any search for less binding constraints.

Clearly, this assumption would be another step in the infinite regress. Therefore, in avoiding the temptation to follow an infinite regress to its end, I shall indicate how the analysis would proceed without reporting it formally.

The only limit to the assumptions that could be made about the possibilities of and benefits from constraint-shifting is that they must be amenable to representation by a convex set defined at least up to a probability distribution. Within this limit it is possible to assume organizational changes handed down from heaven that, for example, reduce the variable input coefficients $m_m(\cdot)$ and $m_k(\cdot)$ by the same proportion for every value of their respective arguments. If this rate of organizational change were such as to keep $\Delta M_k / \Delta I$ and therefore the left side of condition (2.17) constant, then the firm would be in a long-run, steady-growth equilibrium, since $M_t' A_t / M_t' M_t''$ will be constant. Indeed, the committed model-fetishist could introduce assumptions of organizational innovation possibilities frontiers or organizational progress functions relating rates of organizational change to relative prices, acquisitions of vintage managers or what-have-you.

Suppose that all of this is done and several alternative assumptions are found that yield steady-growth equilibria of the firm. This surely could not be the end of the matter. Why should not the managerial maximizers of long-run profits prefer an accelerating growth of profits or, if that is achieved, profits growing at an accelerating rate that is itself accelerating? In a deterministic model, it must simply be assumed that we reach some (probably early) point in the infinite regress at which one or more constraint functions are for some unexplained reason immutable and exogenously determined. The point at which immutability is assumed will no doubt depend on the nature of the problem. In models concerned only with predictions of prices and quantities in markets, the immutability assumption is made at the first point: the production function. There has arisen in the past few years a minor industry (so-called transactions-cost economics) concerned virtually entirely with the elaboration of the sources of diminishing efficiency of managerial coordination as the size of the firm increases. Economists working in this field (cf. Williamson, 1981) in effect analyse the parameters of the managerial limit but do not, as far as I am aware, analyse how those parametric relationships came to exist in the first place or how they might or should change endogenously. Evidently, the point at which immutability is assumed depends on the problem being considered. Whatever the problem, however, the approach amounts to assuming that the problem of the infinite regress does not exist.

In stochastic models – including those comprising the 'new classical macroeconomics' – it is not necessary to assume that any constraint is itself immutable if it is assumed instead that there are exogenous and immutable subjective probability distributions that ascribe sufficiently low probabilities to the prospect of successful outcomes of searches for constraint shifts. A probability will be sufficiently low if it renders the mathematical expectation of the net benefit of the search for less binding constraints lower than the mathematical expectation of the net benefit from (say) a search for a marginal price improvement. What is involved here is a corner solution to the stochastic problem of the optimal search.

There are two difficulties with this 'solution' to the problem of the infinite regress. One is that it depends upon special specifications of agents' subjective probability distributions. The other is that there are no criteria implied by the assumption of individual rationality to indicate at what point in the infinite regress the corner solution will be found.

If this line of argument is right, then evidently stochastic models can simply be given a more sophisticated version of the immutability assumption than is available for deterministic models. But the effect is precisely the same in that the problem of the infinite regress is simply assumed away.

2.2. LIMITED RATES VERSUS LIMITED DIRECTIONS OF LEARNING

The alternative to assuming that firms face exogenous sets of technological and organizational possibilities is to assume that the rate at which such possibilities can be discovered is inherently limited.

We know that general equilibrium of a sequence economy cannot be proved to exist if the rate at which agents learn as a result of market activity is a binding constraint on them. This is the Radner (1968) problem. It arises from a proposition of network information theory that the amount of information made available to each trader from his trading activities alone increases exponentially from each date to the next. This information enables traders to formulate probabilistic specifications of the market constraints upon their respective activities. These constraints result from the strategies adopted by other traders, that is, from the correspondence between the economic environment (or state of nature) that might occur at any future date and other traders' supplies of and demands for commodities.

If the ability of each trader to process and then act upon the exponentially growing body of information available to him is limited, then each such trader will know that there is relevant information but he will be unable to use that information to calculate his own optimal acts. In the case of the firm in a stochastic world, the entrepreneur or management team will be unable to calculate which strategies will maximize the mathematical expectation of long-run profits because the managers will not know the market constraints within which they must operate (including the supply and demand functions they face), *even up to a subjective probability distribution.* In particular, the firm's managers will be unable to calculate the optimal search strategy to maximize expected long-run profits (or anything else).

The implications of Radner's result for the present analysis are clear.

We have already found that the problem of the infinite regress can be avoided in stochastic models only by assuming that the optimal search entails a corner solution at which the optimal allocation of resources devoted to the search for new technological and organizational information – either within or outside the firm – is precisely nil. We have now seen that, in addition, the capacity of the firm to collect, process and act upon market information must be effectively unlimited. In order to be effectively unlimited, however, the computational capacity of the firm must either be infinite or must grow at least as fast as the available information is growing.

But how is this computational capacity to grow? In practice, advances in information technology, administrative organization, operational research and accounting methods are all means of improving the abilities of firms to collect and use information. The implication of Radner's analysis, then, is that such changes must be available to be called forth as required to keep the growth of each firm's computational capacity ahead of the growth of the stock of information.

This brings the issue to a head. Either the expected net benefit of the search for technical and organizational change is sufficiently high that the search is undertaken, and, once undertaken, is sufficiently successful that the computational capacity of the firm keeps ahead of the growth of information, or market constraints upon the firm cannot be sufficiently well defined for long-run, constrained-optimization equilibrium to exist. This is just a jargon-ridden way of saying that the rate at which firms learn about technical and organizational changes that increase their computational capacity must be unlimited, so that whenever computational capacity becomes a binding constraint that constraint is profitably shifted. This, in turn, implies that the problem of the infinite regress can be avoided only on the assumption that technical and organizational changes are always found profitable if they shift constraints on computational capacity, but not if they shift constraints on productive or managerial capacity.

If the foregoing argument is correct, all those analyses that are predicated upon the existence of long-run equilibrium of the firm, and, by analogy, the household, require the implicit assumption that rates of learning about external market phenomena are unlimited (such assumptions often being expressed as statements about the behaviour of an auctioneer or similar *deus ex machina*), while rates of learning about any internal aspects of the firm's activities must be specifically and exogenously limited. We can allow for the possibility of functional relationships among the various rates of learning in the different areas of the firm's internal activities, thus enabling models of technical and organizational change to be formulated. None the less, the structure of the system of constraint functions in any mathematical programming problem must be exogenous to that problem. In a constrained-maximization model of firm behaviour, the constraint functions typically include the production function of the firm, possibly some organizational production function as in the model of section 2.1 and, conceivably, some relationship between inputs of, say, management and outputs of constraint shifts. No matter how complicated such assumed relationships might become, it remains necessary for the structure of constraints (including any relationship between managerial or other inputs to constraint-shifting) to be specified exogenously rather than determined endogenously to the model.

Since the exogeneity of the structure of the constraints upon a rational maximizer amounts equivalently to an exogenous restriction on rates of learning or possible directions of learning, a necessary condition for the existence of equilibrium in the long run is that firms must learn about their environments but cannot profitably learn about themselves. If they learn about their environments and their environments include the distribution of prices in the various markets, then as we saw in section 2.1 the net benefit from price search must decline as ever more favourable prices are found. It is, therefore, at least possible that some rational maximizers will conclude that the investment of resources in learning about the internal activities of the firm, including the making of technical and organizational inventions, has a larger expected net benefit than learning more about the environment. In such cases, unless their learning behaviour can somehow be exogenously limited, long-run equilibrium cannot exist. It follows that, whenever agents believe (i.e. have subjective probability distributions that indicate) that the mathematical expectation of the net discounted benefit of searching for endogenously defined technical and organizational changes – or, indeed, any other endogenously determined constraint shift – is greater than searching and learning in any other direction, then rational maximization will not imply the existence of long-run equilibrium.

Although the assumption of individual rationality is not generally compatible with the existence of long-run equilibrium, there is no reason to suppose that it is ever incompatible with the existence of short-run equilibrium. And in short-run equilibrium, many standard economic propositions remain valid; most importantly, the efficacy of the most powerful techniques of economic analysis remains undiminished.

In adopting an analysis of short-run equilibrium with no corresponding conception of long-run equilibrium, we appear to be standing on its head several centuries of economic theorizing. Certainly from Adam Smith onward – with the major exceptions of Keynes and Kalecki – it has been assumed that long-run analysis yields predictions and propositions about 'natural' outcomes to which short-run outcomes conform. The more obvious examples of these 'natural' outcomes are natural prices, natural rates of interest and, more recently, natural rates of unemployment. Without some conception of long-run equilibrium, the whole idea of this sort of 'natural' outcome is vacuous.

I am evidently here proposing to abandon the notion of long-run equilibrium and the assumption that there are long-run variables to be maximized. This clearly amounts to the rejection of classical and Marxian economic analysis as well as the modern monetarist theories. Moreover, without the possibility of maximizing long-run variables, the textbook conception of the marginal efficiency of investment ceases to have any clear analytical foundation. I am therefore rejecting textbook Keynesianism as well.

In abandoning these pillars of established theory, we lose the key element in the conventional, theoretical derivations of decision rules for firms because short-run processes have conventionally been analysed in relation to their long-run equilibrium consequences. We therefore require to replace long-run equilibrium with an alternative concept which enables us to formulate decision rules for individuals. The alternative concept on which I shall rely is that of short-run imbalance. This approach has the very considerable advantage of preserving the utility of the standard tools of analysis employed by economists because it rests on constrained maximization, albeit only in the short run.

As we shall see presently, the imbalance theory of firm behaviour entails propositions about the endogenous determination of the direction of learning (hence organizational and technical change) and investment. It is not open to us, therefore, to assume that limitations on the direction of learning prevent the firm from achieving infinite values of its maximand, since the rationally maximizing firm will eliminate first any constraints upon its rate of growth and then the rate of acceleration of that growth rate and then the rate at which that rate of acceleration itself accelerates, and so on. In light of the previous analysis, the alternative is to assume that the rate rather than the direction of learning is exogenously limited. Because this assumption has been derived inductively as well as for reasons of logical coherence, it has the advantage of being descriptively accurate.

In keeping with this inductive spirit, I shall not assume that a constant, exogenous rate of learning can be defined but rather that the rate of learning depends upon the problem for which the solution requires new information or knowledge. In some cases, the solution to a problem requires no more than routine applications of well understood principles to well defined objectives. Indeed, this sort of technical and organizational change almost certainly predominates. However, it is by no means the only sort of technical and organizational change that takes place. In the course of inventing new techniques and organizations that require the establishment of new principles of science, technology or organization, the requisite knowledge cannot be called forth at will. Indeed, examples of inventions that had long been desired but had to await the development of such principles abound in the literature. (See, e.g., Rosenberg, 1976; Langrish et al., 1972.) Most particularly, Chandler (1962) has shown that the lags in the process of inventing and applying new organizational principles are generally quite lengthy – especially if one takes into account the need to modify them in light of experience in order to render them efficient. Even in semi-conductor-based technology, three decades elapsed between the invention of the first germanium transistor by Shockley and his colleagues and the beginnings of the widespread diffusion of silicon-chip-based computers and microcomputers. Since these represent a major advance in information technology, it appears that on historical grounds there is no warrant for assuming that computational capacity or the scale and scope of technological capacity can be increased at will. Indeed, history supports the opposite assumption: rates of learning are always limited although their limits are different in different areas of endeavour.

Thus, in choosing to assume that the rate rather than the direction of learning is subject to exogenous limitations, we are on the side of history as well as logic.

2.3   SOME ELEMENTS OF IMBALANCE THEORY

The aim of the foregoing argument was to show not that the assumptions of equilibrium theory are unrealistic – which they are – but rather that the cost of the analytical convenience they afford is, in terms of generality and logical coherence, enormous. An advantage of the logical dissection of the established theory is that it shows not only where there are inconsistencies within the theory but also which of the various parts of the theory are plausible and useful.

None of the criticism developed above affects short-run analysis, which, in the altogether standard definition, entails the exogeneity of constraints associated with the given resources and organization inherited from the past. Provided that we define the firm in the short run as a collection of given resources that embody the technology and organization of the firm, there is no logical difficulty in assuming there to be exogenous short-run constraints.

This short-run definition of the firm does, however, raise a problem about what we mean by the firm in the long run. Since in practice the resources and organizations of firms change over time, our short-run definition of the firm would lead us to distinguish as different firms what anyone would call a single firm at different times. For this reason – and because it conforms to the long-run analysis of business history and the theory of business strategy (cf. Chandler, 1962, 1977; Penrose, 1959; Rosenberg, 1976; Moss, 1981) – the firm will be defined here as a collection of physical and human productive resources and organizational structures that evolve *endogenously* over time. This is not to imply that there are no exogenous forces acting upon the direction of firm growth and investment, but if there are such forces their effects are mediated by forces that are internal to the firm.

Our objective here is to develop a concept that replaces that of long-run equilibrium in the specification of individual's decision rules. It is not possible, however, to analyse the determinants of decision rules without first specifying the motivations that underlie decisions. We therefore require an alternative to the assumptions that underlie previous theories of long-run economic processes that individuals act only with reference to long-run maximands.

The most plausible and fruitful assumption is that the prime motivation of managers is to ensure, in so far as they can, that their firms will survive in the long run. The assumption is plausible because managers' incomes, career prospects and (often) their wealth are bound up with the survival of the firms they manage. Presuming that income and wealth are preferred to poverty and penury, the assumption of the survival motive warrants consideration on utility-theoretic grounds alone. Even so, it is the analytical fruitfulness of this assumption that is the compelling reason for its adoption.

In the first place, the survival motive implies that, in the short run, firms' managers will want to maximize gross trading profits which are quickly realizable as cash flows. The cash-flow proviso is included because the *sine qua non* of firm survival is that the firm pay its bills more or less as they fall due – a condition that implies that on average the firm must generate a positive cash flow from trading over any substantial period of time. It follows that, if firms maximize the cash receipts in excess of cash payments that arise from their trading activities (i.e. not including use of funds for long-run investments), then any negative cash flows that might be incurred in an uncertain future will be more likely to result in reduced financial reserves or increased use of borrowing capacity than in late payment or non-payment of bills or (in the extreme) in liquidation of the business. Thus, one analytical advantage of the assumption of the managerial survival motive is that it preserves the fundamental analysis of firm behaviour in the short run. Since technological, organizational and capacity constraints are all immutable in the short run, the survival motivation implies the short-run constrained maximization of profits that do not take the form of unrecoverable trade credit.

A second advantage, which will become apparent presently, is that the assumption of the survival motive leads naturally to our theory of the direction of investment and the direction of technical and organizational change by the firm. This development is of obvious importance in light of the conclusion described in chapter 1 that the macroeconomic direction of investment is a crucial determinant of the strength and duration of improvements in macro-economic activity.

In addition, the survival motive underlies the theory of markets implied by the rational markets hypothesis, the theory of speculation reported in chapter 5, the theory of macroeconomic cycles reported in chapters 6 and 8 as well as a related theory of money and interest reported in chapter 7. These developments are novel not least because they rely on the future being uncertain as a result of limited rates of learning by individuals, and they yield well defined, falsifiable predictions and policy prescriptions. Even if the survival motive were not plausible and compatible with standard choice theory, the power of the analyses to which it gives rise would warrant its adoption.

Given the foregoing definition of the firm and the assumed short-run maximand of managers, the central proposition of imbalance theory is that decision-makers turn their attention first to those problems most urgently requiring solution. This proposition is developed as far as possible here using the model of section 2.1.

The two equilibrium conditions on which this development is based are reproduced here for convenience:

$$\mu_k = \frac{(1/i)\,[1-w(\Delta N/\Delta Q)]\,(\Delta Q/\Delta K) - r}{\Delta M_k/\Delta I} - s \tag{2.14}$$

and

$$\mu_m = \frac{\dfrac{\Delta I}{\Delta(\Delta M)}\dfrac{1}{i}\left[\dfrac{1}{i}\left(1-w\dfrac{\Delta N}{\Delta Q}\right)\dfrac{\Delta Q}{\Delta K}-\left(r+s\dfrac{\Delta M_k}{\Delta I}\right)\right]}{\Delta M_m/\Delta(\Delta M)} - s. \tag{2.16}$$

Consider the declining exponential growth phase of the equilibrium time-path of the firm in that model. We know that I and ΔM will take values that ensure that the marginal contribution to profits of the managers employed in coordinating investment and managerial self-expansion will be equal ($\mu_m = \mu_k$). Since this is the marginal contribution of management to the value of the objective functional, it is the value of the Lagrangean multiplier (i.e. the shadow price and costate variable) attaching to managerial capacity. The reason that the growth rate of managerial capacity, and therefore the scale of all of the activities of the firm, declined over time was that, as the scale of managerial acquisitions (ΔM) and investment (I) increased, the values of $\Delta M_m/\Delta(\Delta M)$ and $\Delta M_k/\Delta I$ also increased. These latter increases can be seen by inspection of conditions (2.14) and (2.16) to reduce the values of both μ_m and μ_k, and therefore to reduce the shadow price of managerial capacity. It is easily seen that the shadow price of management falls throughout the declining growth equilibrium.

From condition (2.14),

$$(\mu_k + s)\frac{\Delta M_k}{\Delta I} = \frac{1}{i}\left(1-w\frac{\Delta N}{\Delta Q}\right)\frac{\Delta Q}{\Delta K} - r. \tag{2.20}$$

Substituting this result into condition (2.16),

$$\mu_m = \frac{1}{i}\,\mu_k\,\frac{\Delta M_k}{\Delta I}\,\frac{\Delta(\Delta M)}{\Delta M_m} - s. \tag{2.21}$$

Setting $\mu_m = \mu_k = \lambda_m$ and noting that $(\Delta M_k / \Delta M_m) = -1$,

$$\lambda_m = -\frac{i \cdot s}{i + \Delta(\Delta M)/\Delta I}. \qquad (2.22)$$

We know from the argument of section 2.1 that in equilibrium $\Delta(\Delta M)/\Delta I$ is negative and declining over time. Given the rate of interest and managerial salary, therefore, the value of λ_m is positive but declining over time until the constant-investment equilibrium is reached or investment itself declines.

That the rational management team would in this circumstance seek some organizational change that would relieve the effect of diminishing returns to managerial capacity is wholly consistent with the standard investment choice criteria. For as the shadow price of managerial capacity continues to fall, the opportunity cost to the firm in using such capacity in some different way is falling. Indeed, these are just two ways of saying precisely the same thing. In particular, employing incumbent managers to devise a less constraining organizational form will become increasingly cheap as the shadow price of management comes to be ever lower. In the absence of such a diversion of managerial capacity, managers are increasingly employed in the acquisition of capital (i.e. in coordinating investment) because the shadow price of capital, being constant in terms of the firm's output, is rising relative to the shadow price of managerial capacity. In other words, given the return that can be expected from any investment project, or, in an uncertain world, given that the total gross return is not affected by the provenance of the resources employed, the opportunity cost of the project is lower, as there are more existing resources with low or falling shadow prices which the firm can use in bringing it to fruition.

The extreme example of this proposition is where the firm has resources with excess capacities. In that case the shadow price is of course nil, implying that the firm will incur no opportunity cost whatever in so far as the excess capacity of such a resource can be employed in some alternative activity or in so far as the utilization of that resource can be increased by replicating other complementary resources that are inputs to existing activities.

In addition, one would normally expect the personnel of the firm to have knowledge and experience derived in part from working with the resources of which the firm is composed. They will be particularly well placed to find or invent technologies or organizational forms that are uniquely suited to the capacities and the imbalances characterizing that firm. In effect, the rates of learning by such personnel as they seek to overcome the most pressing imbalances (identified with the lowest or most rapidly falling shadow prices) within the firm are likely to be higher than the learning rates of outsiders in the same situation – even though the outsiders might be equally well qualified on other grounds. And once a new investment project were completed, so that the new coordinating practices or production processes were implemented, the theory of learning-by-doing suggests that the running-in costs would be lower than if none of the firm's existing resources had been employed; that is, the workers and managers of the firm would start further along the learning curves associated with the techniques and organization associated with such an investment project.

Evidently, reducing the opportunity costs of an investment project by employing existing, low-shadow-price resources of the firm and, at the same time, increasing the early net revenues by reducing the costs of learning-by-doing will increase the value of any of the standard measures of goodness of investments, whether internal rate of return, net present value, pay-back period or any of the others. It follows that investment projects that are defined in order to raise the lowest shadow prices of the firm's complement of resources or to offset falling shadow prices will also be the investment projects most likely to satisfy the standard investment choice criteria.

It remains to consider the forces that result in low and falling shadow prices more generally than we have done so far. In the model of section 2.1 and the discussion of that model in this section, the only force we have considered that has such consequences is diminishing returns to a resource that is basic to the firm. There are, however, a large number of forces internal to the firm that have the same effect. Many of these I have previously discussed both extensively and in detail in *An Economic Theory of Business Strategy* (Moss, 1981). I shall not repeat that discussion here. It should none the less be clear from the foregoing discussion that, even in an uncertain world, the existence of imbalances and, most particularly, increasing imbalances among the profitabilities of the various resources comprising the firm will lead managers rationally to focus their attention on ways of redressing those imbalances. The process that leads to this focusing of attention, and particularly the search for ways of using the existing physical and human resources of the firm to solve the problems created by the imbalances, is called the *focusing effect*.

In addition, however, there are clearly external forces that create imbalances within the firm. Once again, the exposition of these forces is facilitated by referring to the model of section 2.1.

It can be seen directly from expressions (2.14), (2.16) and (2.22) that both μ_m and μ_k, and hence λ_m, the shadow price of managerial capacity, are related inversely to the market price of real capital r, the wage rate w, the managerial salary s and the interest rate i. Thus, rises in the prices (relative to the output price) of the firm's physical and human inputs and the cost of external finance cause shadow prices to fall. The foregoing argument suggests that such price movements will create or exacerbate imbalances among the shadow prices of the firm and so focus the attention of managers upon what are rationally seen as the most urgent problems facing the firm. Although in a perfectly competitive firm such as that modelled here it is only adverse price movements that can be considered, in a more general analysis supply and demand shortages are readily seen to have the same effect on some shadow prices. Clearly, if some essential direct input is in such short supply that available fixed resources cannot be fully utilized, then the shadow prices of those resources will be nil. The same will be true if demands do not warrant the full utilization of some capacities.

Some shortages will result from the competitive strategies of other firms or from technical changes that alter the inputs required by customers or the outputs produced by suppliers. Output prices might fall relative to input prices because of a price war. All these possibilities are commonly treated under the heading of 'microeconomics'. All of them can induce firms to take some action because of the imbalances they create within the firms. Clearly, the optimal action will be channelled by the same considerations that were considered in the discussion of focusing effects. In order to distinguish these external influences from those that arise internally and require the consideration of a different set of phenomena, I have called them *inducement effects*.

It will also be convenient to distinguish between those inducement effects that arise in the ordinary course of commercial and competitive activity, that is from microeconomic processes, and those that arise from wider macroeconomic processes and relationships. It is natural to call the one 'microeconomic inducement effects' and the other 'macroeconomic inducement effects'.

Although each of these three effects has a different origin, all of them work by creating imbalances within the firm that rational managers will seek to redress. Since these imbalances result from the particular complements of resources comprised by the individual firms in the short run, it is clear that long-run processes will be the outcomes entirely of decisions taken in the context of the short run.

Since the nature of short-run processes need not be supposed to conform to long-run outcomes, there is no need to consider what a long-run equilibrium might be.

2.4   IMBALANCE THEORY AND RATIONAL EXPECTATIONS

The imbalance-theoretic framework described in the preceding section has implicit within it a description of the formation of expectations by individuals. This description does not suffer from the defects of Muth's (1961) rational expectations hypothesis, while it does retain Muth's insight that individuals will rationally make use of information about their environments in formulating expectations of future events.

The crux of the Muth hypothesis is that information is scarce and will be used efficiently by rationally maximizing agents. The imbalance-theoretic resolution of the paradox of long-run equilibrium, however, implies that it is not information, but each agent's capacity to make use of it, that is scarce. Thus, where Muth asserts that agents act as if they have an econometric model of the economic system that is relevant to them – whether a single market or a whole macroeconomic system – an imbalance-theoretic argument could allow, at most, that agents act as if they have an incomplete econometric model, which is known to be incomplete even if the nature of the incompleteness is not well understood. The limit to the complexity – and therefore the completeness – of such models is the computational capacities of individuals.

When we say that agents act as if they had such models, we mean nothing more than that it might be possible to formulate a model that will predict agents' decision rules in a specified range of circumstances. Let us therefore consider the extent to which formal modelling techniques can be used to predict decision rules. In so doing, we shall have to go behind the 'as if' assumption to elucidate as far as we can the processes that lead individuals to act according to one set of rules or another. It is only in this way that we can determine the limits of 'as if' modelling, and also the ways in which the 'as if' models evolve over time.

The starting point for this consideration is Penrose's distinction between objective knowledge (which can be taught) and subjective knowledge (which cannot be taught). Objective knowledge is often the more general of the two. An engineer, for example, will learn the broad principles of engineering (mechanics, materials science, etc.) at university and will, in employment, learn more deeply about the specific principles that he uses most often. Thus, some of his knowledge will be quite general and some will be more specifically related to particular applications. In addition, most individuals, in the course of performing tasks that are related in one way or another, become adept at choosing efficient means of performing them and, equivalently, at rejecting irrelevant, erroneous or inefficient means of approaching and performing such tasks. To the extent that this adeptness is acquired by experience, and cannot be (or simply is not) taught to one individual by another, it constitutes subjective knowledge.

An essential proposition of imbalance theory is that the knowledge held by personnel of the firm will be a key determinant of the characteristics of the potential investment projects that will be defined within the firm. Undoubtedly, some of this knowledge will be objective, but, equally, some will derive from the experience that individuals have had in working with the existing resources comprising the firm. The latter category of knowledge is clearly subjective in the sense of Penrose. This subjective knowledge is an important element of the firm's comparative advantage in the implementation of those projects that its focusing effects lead it to define. These two categories of knowledge are also important elements in determining how expectations are best formed by rational individuals.

One limitation of the rational expectations hypothesis is its failure to explain how individuals come to know the 'correct' model of the economy in the limited sense that it yields unbiased predictions. If rational maximizers act as if they have incorrect models, which yield biased predictions about the variables that enter their decision rules as inputs, they will consistently and systematically fail to optimize. In the usual 'new classical macroeconomic' example, decision-makers who interpret general price changes as changes in some relative prices – usually the prices they notice first – will plan consumption and production on the basis of relative prices which will not be realized. On average, therefore, these decision-makers will not be at the tangencies of their budget lines and indifference curves or their isocosts and isoquants. With unbiased predictions, the average outcomes of their decisions will be optimal even if on any one occasion they are not. If there are some agents with models yielding biased predictions of relevant variables and other agents with models yielding unbiased predictions, then the latter agents will be able to sell their predictions to the former to the profit of both. As a result, all agents will be using models yielding unbiased estimators of prices or any other relevant variables.

In a world characterized by long-run equilibrium, in which the structure of the economy and therefore the correct model of the economy does not change, the issue of how agents determine the correct model is of scant importance. If, however, the economy is characterized by ongoing technical and organizational changes by firms or changes in households' tastes, then it is important to know that agents are able to modify their decision rules accordingly. Indeed, it is inherent in the new classical macroeconomic view of rational expectations that any change in the environment that introduces biases into the estimates of relevant variables will soon be taken into account as those biases come to be manifest as systematically falsified expectations (see Lucas, 1977/1981).

Since the relevant equilibrium for Muth's rational expectations hypothesis, and particularly for the new classical macroeconomic models using that hypothesis, is long-run equilibrium, the main current protagonists of monetarism are undoubtedly right in placing detailed analysis of the process of model change well down the agenda of their research programme. If, however, my critique of long-run equilibrium is sound, then there can be no general analysis of either comparative equilibria or the stability of equilibria. The only analysis to be undertaken in this regard is that of the process by which decision rules change and expectations are formulated. In this analysis, the distinction between objective and subjective knowledge comes into its own.

In the present analysis, two elements of the new classical analysis have been retained and, indeed, given pride of place. One is that the assumption that agents are rational is a fruitful assumption which prevents the analyst from employing *ad hoc* behavioural postulates chosen for either convenience or ideological appeal. As we have seen, strict adherence to the rationality assumption leads straight to the rejection of the single most important concept on which the new classicals have relied for their specification of the 'correct theory' of the economic system. The second element of new classical analysis retained here is the wholly plausible view that changes in the information (including the knowledge) available to individuals will affect their decision rules and expectations. But where the new classicals assume that it is only market information and, possibly, announcements of policy changes by the government that enter into the information set of agents, it has been argued in this chapter that the set of information and knowledge that is relevant to *rational* agents is far wider than this. In particular, it is recognized here that information arises within the firm, and often does so in a way that focuses attention on specific problems and opportunities. This process is essential to the focusing effect. Other information is generated externally, but such information is not restricted to prices and government announcements. It can include failures of demands for a firm's outputs or supplies of its inputs. We shall see below that similar information is made available to (or imposed upon) households. Such information gives rise to both microeconomic and macroeconomic inducement effects. Now, in so far as focusing and inducement effects together determine the direction and magnitude of investment by firms, the information giving rise to these effects implicitly generates expectations about the profitabilities of various courses of action over periods of time sufficiently long for the firm to recoup its investment costs. Thus, the analysis of focusing and inducement effects, and therefore the whole imbalance theory of the firm, can be seen as an analysis of rational expectations formation by agents with limited rates of learning and limited computational capacities. If it is convenient to analyse the corresponding decision-making processes by devising formal models which mimic the outcomes of these processes, then the complexity of those models and the generality of their application will be limited not only by learning rates and computational capacities, but also by the endogenously determined direction of learning by the personnel of the firm. In other words, focusing and inducement effects provide the basis of a theory of the kind of information that agents will acquire as a result of undertaking economic activities.

The possibility of such modelling is limited by the extent and importance of the objective knowledge that is employed in the making of decisions. The observer can undoubtedly take objective knowledge into account in formulating models intended to throw up the same decision rules as those that implicitly guide decision-makers. It is hard to see how the observer can take subjective knowledge – the fruits of experience – into account unless he is also a participant. Thus, although the importance of subjective knowledge has been and will continue to be recognized in the development of the theory of this book, explicit account can be taken only of those determinants of individuals' decision rules that constitute objective knowledge. I can see no other way of developing the broad framework within which to develop a logically coherent macroeconomic theory with clear policy implications for an economy in which decision-makers are rational maximizers in the short run and devise survival protecting business strategies for the long run.

2.5 IMBALANCE THEORY AND THE ANALYSIS OF THE LONG RUN

One of the undoubted advantages of equilibrium theory has been the order it has provided for the analysis of such long-run phenomena as economic growth and development, technical change, the functional and personal distributions of income and so on. The complexity of the phenomena that economists have been able to study has surely been far greater than would have been possible with a theory less bold in its simplifications. None the less, the complexity of the phenomena studied by equilibrium theorists has not been matched by the range of their concerns. Virtually the only issue that has been analysed by general equilibrium theorists has been the sufficiency of various conditions for general equilibrium to exist. A rather broader range of issues has been considered by temporary equilibrium theorists, although their analyses have presumed very particular structures of the economy. In partial equilibrium theory, a limited range of competitive states is analysed with a limited range of assumed characteristics of firms and market processes. The precise limitations to these various equilibrium theories will be considered in some detail in the two chapters following. For the present, it will be useful to demonstrate that, in principle, imbalance theory can be used to evaluate long-run trends. That is, imbalance theory does not predict that the long run is characterized by economic chaos or that every short period entails a revolution in either the resources comprising individual firms or the institutional structure in which they operate.

I have previously considered how the institutional compositions of markets evolve as a result of investments by firms (Moss, 1981). It would be easy, but wrong, to infer from this concentration on evolution that markets are continuously in a state of flux. Such an inference would be wrong on both logical as well as empirical grounds.

While there is no long-run equilibrium of the institutional market structure of the economy, there does appear to be a punctuated stability. Historically, market institutions usually evolve only gradually – if at all – although there are occasional periods of relatively rapid change. These periods of rapid change follow either from changes in the technology of production or the technology of exchange or both. Some technical changes generate inducement effects that lead some firms to integrate vertically either in production, in order to eliminate some markets altogether, or in exchange, in order to take on some of the transactions services that previously had been provided by independent firms. Other technical changes give rise to inducement effects that create new markets, either in new geographical locations or for new commodities; or they lead to the creation of new, independent market institutions. Any analysis of the long-run development of an economy must take these inducement effects explicitly into account if that analysis is to be complete.

Although the market structure of any growing, technologically progressive economy does change over time, it is unlikely to change so rapidly that the structure cannot normally be presumed effectively constant. There are two reasons for this presumption to be normally valid.

In the first place, limits on the magnitude of investment and the rate of learning restrict the number of problems to which managers can devote their attention and as a result of which they define investment projects. This realization has led to the proposition that firms' managers will concentrate their attention on the most pressing problems faced by their firms. Since it is unlikely that the nature and functioning of market institutions will always generate the most pressing problems for firms, it is also unlikely that firms will continuously be seeking to modify those institutions in any substantial way.

In the second place, it does not seem to be the case that firms continually lurch from one crisis to the next. Certainly, there is nothing in imbalance theory to suggest that they do. When there is no particular crisis in their affairs, firms are guided only by focusing effects to the definition of investment projects. Thus, firms that are dominated by their production interests are more likely to define investment projects that utilize the knowledge and skills that their personnel have developed by using the production (rather than exchange) resources and technologies of the firm. If they are able to acquire the supplies they need, and if fluctuations in demands for their outputs are well explained by seasonal and cyclical factors, government policies and the like, then it is hard to see why focusing effects would often indicate investments in vertical integration to supplant the market. Of course, those firms that provide the services that are essential to exchange will be likely to seek improvements in the process of exchange – and hence in the ways in which their markets work – by virtue of focusing and, possibly, normal inducement effects. None the less, such improvements will not change the institutions that comprise markets unless those institutions cease to provide the essential services of exchange.

It follows that, while imbalance theory is well suited to the analysis of firm behaviour that is changed by, or itself changes, the way in which markets function and the institutional structure of the economy, there will normally be no serious loss if we simply show that rational maximization by individuals implies that different markets work in particular and different ways. In those apparently exceptional cases in which market structures do change materially over relatively short periods of time, the particular changes must be explained and included in the analysis of macroeconomic growth and development. Since I have already reported the theory of the evolution of market structures and institutions, I shall restrict the analysis of markets in this book to the determinants of those structures in order to explain why and how different markets function differently in the determination of prices and outputs. This will be the subject of chapter 3. We shall then be able to analyse, in chapters 4 and 5, both the optimal institutional arrangements and the optimal processes of exchange in economies comprising rational maximizing agents.

The issues involved here are of considerable importance in current macroeconomic debate, since the new classical macroeconomists argue that the Keynesians have only *ad hoc* theories, by which they mean theories without a thoroughgoing foundation in rational behaviour by individuals. The Keynesians argue, to the contrary, that the assumed structure of the economy in new classical macroeconomic theory is not the 'correct' structure, while the new classical policy conclusions are sensitive to the assumed structure. What we shall find is that, in the main, Keynes's (if not all 'Keynesian') assumptions about the market structure of the economy conform to what would be expected in an economy composed of rational individuals, but the Walrasian structure assumed by the new classicals does not.

3

The Theory of Markets

3.0 INTRODUCTION

The economic analysis of exchange is an exercise in metaphysics. In that analysis, the process of exchange yields outputs – reciprocal transfers of commodities and assets – but has no apparent inputs. Clearly, no such processes are found in the physical world. It is this metaphysical aspect of the economic analysis of exchange that distinguishes it from the economic analysis of production; for all analyses of production in economic theory or in empirical work require or determine some specification of technological relationships between inputs and outputs. Yet a moment's consideration will show this dichotomy to be insupportable.

Exchange is a process not only of transfer, but of reciprocal transfer. In bilateral exchange, the transfer of goods, service-rendering resources or information requires the transfer of some other good, resource or information in the opposite direction. In multilateral exchange there will evidently be a network of such transfers. In order to effect these transfers, each of the parties to an exchange must know what will be received and how much is to be sent. That is only to say that the various dimensions of the commodity and of the price paid and received must be known. And since, in the physical world, transfers cannot usually be made instantaneously, there will be some need to store the subjects of an exchange at least over the interval between their dispatch and their receipt. Moreover, the laws of physics preclude the parties to exchange from occupying the same space so that some transportation will be required in order to effect the exchange.

Simply to recognize that exchange entails storage, transportation and communication immediately removes the study of exchange from the realm of the metaphysical. For each of these activities requires physically specified inputs to yield a physically specified output. That is, each of these activities has a technology, and these technologies together comprise the technology of exchange.

Like the technology of production, the technology of exchange is embodied in the capital equipment operated within firms. There is no reason to apply different criteria of rationality to firms producing the services of exchange from the criteria that are applied to firms producing other commodities. It is therefore assumed here that the managers of firms producing services employed in exchange seek to maximize their firms' gross short-run profits realizable as cash flows in furtherance of the survival motive. In generating maximum short-run gross profits and cash flows, each firm will be constrained by its previously established complement of productive resources (including capital equipment) and organization. It follows that firms producing exchange services will do so by allocatively efficient means in the short run, whether their long-run behaviour is described by means of imbalance or equilibrium theory.

The proposition that exchange will be allocatively efficient is, in effect, the rational markets hypothesis specified in section 1.2. Since it rests only on the assumption that firms maximize short-run profits, the rational markets hypothesis is evidently as compatible with partial and general equilibrium theories as with the imbalance theory of the firm. Its effect on established equilibrium theories will be to eliminate the fundamental conceptual distinction between the theory of production and distribution and the theory of exchange. In particular, even an equilibrium theory of markets must make nonsense of models of pure exchange.

In the theory of markets reported here, I will take it for granted that short-run constraints on exchange processes are altered in the long run in accordance with the focusing and inducement effects implied by the imbalance theory of the firm. The reason for taking this approach is that the imbalance theory leads to specifications of market functions in whole economic systems that are simpler, more precise and more robust than any specifications that might be implied by a theory of markets predicated on the existence of long-run equilibrium. This property of imbalance theory is obviously important in the context of current macroeconomic controversies.

No doubt it is because propositions derived from the mainstream macroeconomic theories are so sensitive to assumptions about market characteristics that much current controversy in the field turns on specifications of the way in which markets communicate information about supplies and demands. In general, monetarists assume that prices are the main vehicle of communication within markets while Keynesians and post-Keynesians assume that quantities demanded or supplied (depending on which is the short side of the market) are the main vehicles of communication. Because of its reliance on clear specifications of the technology of exchange, the theory of markets predicts that there are some well defined conditions in which the one assumption will be correct and other well defined conditions in which the other will be correct. Among other things, the truth of the matter will depend on who it is that communicates prices, effective supplies and effective demands within any market because different agents in markets have different limitations on their abilities to perceive and communicate information. They will also have different decision rules concerning exchange which, as we shall see presently, depend upon the technologies of production as well as exchange and upon the physical characteristics of the commodities being traded.

The theory of markets is concerned with what goes on within markets – in what might be called the interior of the market – while the established theories of exchange are concerned only with two sides of the market – the supply side and the demand side. To open the interior of the market to analytical inspection is arguably an important advance. By identifying the actual institutions that comprise the interior of the market, i.e. those that undertake the activities of communicating effective prices and quantities, and transporting and storing the commodities traded, it is possible to analyse the economic forces predisposing these institutions to act in one way or another. In this way, the argument over the extent of systematic discrepancies between effective and notional prices and quantities in the long run and the relative flexibilities of prices and quantities in the short run – and, indeed, any other presumed characteristics of market processes – can be subjected to prior analysis and therefore direct empirical investigation. The alternative is to continue to assume the market to be a *deus ex machina* such as the Walrasian auctioneer or Clower's 'central "market authority"' (1969, p. 289). To adopt such an alternative is merely to beg the most important and controversial questions of macroeconomics.

In this chapter I set out a brief, slightly modified, statement of the theory of markets that I have previously reported (in Moss, 1981, chapters 4–8). This theory is developed further in the three succeeding chapters, both to determine the conditions in which the assumptions relied on by the various schools of macroeconomic thought are appropriate and, more importantly, to determine how allocatively efficient markets for various commodities and assets function to set prices and determine physical volumes of transactions.

3.1 THE DETERMINANTS OF MARKET INSTITUTIONS

For all that is written about the market and market forces, it is remarkably difficult to find a definition of 'the market' in the textbooks or other economic literature. Perhaps this is another aspect of the metaphysical nature of the established economic theory of exchange. The rational markets hypothesis leads naturally to a definition of the market in which the interior is composed of firms. Specifically, the market is here defined as the set of producers actually comprising an industry together with the set of users of the closely substitutable commodities produced by the industry and all economic agents who, directly or indirectly, buy these commodities from the producers only in order to sell them to users, or who arrange the direct sale of commodities to the users by the producers.

With this definition, the analysis of focusing and inducement effects described in chapter 2 can be applied to the institutions and processes of exchange as well as to the institutions and processes of production. Investments in exchange are those that enable traders to communicate more cheaply and effectively with one another and to increase or improve the requisite storage and transportation capacities. Moreover, this definition preserves what is usually meant by the supply (i.e. producing) side of the market and the demand (i.e. consuming) side of the market.

In order to determine how markets as defined here can be expected to function in determining prices and quantities, it is essential to identify the economic forces that induce firms comprising market interiors to act in one way or another. In order to identify these inducement effects, we must know something about the resources and market connections of these firms. So much follows from the analysis of short-run imbalances in section 2.3.

There are three categories of economic agent that might undertake the activities of communication, storage and transportation. These are the producers, the users and the agents, whose business involves neither the production nor the use of the commodities but who undertake the activities required for exchange between mutually independent producers and users. The agent, who is neither producer nor user, is the intermediary. A key conclusion of the theory of markets is that the economic agents who provide the services of exchange in their respective markets are those who can achieve economies in exchange that are not available to other agents.

Consider first the conditions in which intermediaries can provide a market interior. Being firms, intermediaries will require to generate a positive cash flow on average over time simply in order to remain in business. In addition, firms on each side of the market will have an incentive to trade through intermediaries only if intermediated exchange yields to them a larger cash flow on average over time than does direct exchange between producers and users. This situation is possible only if the total transactions costs incurred by all parties to intermediated exchange are less than the total transactions costs that would be incurred by producers and users alone in direct exchange.

If there are such savings to be had, then the intermediaries in a market will be able to realize as revenue only a part of the savings, the rest accruing to the firms on either side of the market. The only revenue that intermediaries can realize derives from selling commodities at prices that are higher than the prices at which the same commodities are purchased. The difference is the jobber's turn or the broker's commission. Of course, these price differences must be greater than the unit transactions costs actually incurred by the intermediaries if they are to realize a positive net cash flow from their trading activities. None the less, the price difference cannot exhaust the total unit savings since some of these savings must be passed on to the producers and users. It follows that the transactions costs incurred by the intermediaries alone must be less than the *savings* in total transactions costs afforded by intermediated over direct exchange.

The sources of the savings in transactions costs incurred by intermediaries but not available to agents on either side of the market in direct exchange are undoubtedly economies of scale in the three exchange activities: communication, storage and transportation. These savings, however, are by no means ubiquitous since storability and portability both require that the commodity be durable and compact. Moreover, some degree of standardization is necessary if the price, quality and quantity of the commodity is to be communicated to users and if demands are to be communicated to producers on a large scale.

These physical characteristics of commodities cannot be assigned any absolute meaning. Durability is clearly determined by storage technology – a clear example here being the increased durability of meat and ice as a result of inventions and innovations in refrigeration technology. Similarly, compactness is relative to the technology of transportation since, for example, the development of waterways, railways, roads and large lorries have rendered economic the transportation over long distances of commodities that previously were too bulky to be moved very far from the point of production (e.g. coal in the eighteenth century). Even standardization is relative to the technologies of production and use. An example is the finer tolerances required in the thickness of steel sheet by, among others, airframe and motor car manufacturers and the consequent developments in steel-rolling technology that have made it possible to meet these tolerances (see Langrish et al., 1972, pp. 197–218).

These technology-related physical characteristics of commodities not only render it technologically feasible to engage in transactions on a large scale, but they also afford substantial economies of large-scale exchange. The arguments and evidence in favour of economies of scale in transportation, communication and storage are sufficiently elementary and well known that they will be taken for granted here. The essential point is that these economies can be achieved only in respect of transactions in commodities that are durable, compact and standardized. Given that these conditions are met, we require to determine the circumstances in which intermediaries, but not producers or users, will be able to realize these scale economies. In addition, we require to demonstrate that in those circumstances producers and users will be able to reduce their transactions costs in intermediated exchange below the level of transactions costs incurred in direct exchange.

The first of these issues is the more straightforward.

If there are many producers and many users of a commodity, it is possible that the physical volume of transactions in which any one of the firms on either side of the market engages is a small proportion of the total transactions volume. Certainly, this must be the case for at least some firms on each side of such a market. There can then be a relatively small number of intermediaries, each of which buys the outputs of several (and perhaps many) producers and sells them to several (or many) users. In so doing, the intermediaries will be able to reap the benefits of economies of specialization in exchange which are entirely analogous to the Smithian division of labour in production.

A second source of economies of scale in exchange is the fuller use of indivisible resources, which are available to intermediaries but not to individual producers and users. This will be the case when there is substantial product differentiation in a market or where the technological requirements of storage, transportation and communication are similar for a range of commodities purchased by each of a large number of individual users. In such markets, each intermediary can stock the outputs from many producers of competing commodities or of commodities produced in technologically distinct processes. Wholesalers and retailers are clear examples of such intermediaries. Shops can be fully stocked with a wide assortment of goods produced by many, often competing, producers for sale to many users, and large lorries can be filled with many producers' outputs for delivery to the intermediary's customers. Without intermediation in such markets, each producer would have to sell his outputs to each of many users and there would be many more transactions – each on a much smaller scale than in intermediated exchange. These two sources of intermediaries' economies of scale in exchange themselves give rise to savings in producers' and users' transactions costs.

A producer will realize economies of bulk transactions by selling all of his output to one or a few intermediaries rather than to many users. These economies are available only if the producer's rate of output is large in relation to the demands of any individual user. Similarly, a user will realize economies of bulk transactions by purchasing all of his requirements for a particular commodity from a single intermediary rather than from a large number of users. This latter condition is unlikely to be realized, however, since it requires users to have utilization rates considerably in excess of the output rates of any of the individual producers with whom they might trade in direct exchange.

Economies of joint exchange are more likely to be available to producers and users alike in intermediated but not direct exchange. That is, producers will be able to sell an entire product range to intermediaries although users will typically require only a fraction of the number of products from that range. In addition, users will be able to satisfy their demands for a range of commodities by trading with an intermediary, although no one producer can supply as extensive a range, either because of product differentiation by competing producers or because different technologies are employed in the production of the various commodities conveniently sold by a single intermediary (hence the same exchange technology).

Both economies of bulk transactions and economies of joint exchange reduce the number of transactions in which each producer and user must engage. Since, however, economies of scale in exchange are related to the number of transactions as well as the size of each transaction, it is likely that the cost per transaction will be higher in intermediated than in direct exchange and it cannot be ruled out entirely that the costs per transaction will be higher by a greater proportion than the number of transactions will be lower. Consequently, it is possible that total transactions costs will be higher in intermediated than in direct exchange. As we shall now see, economies rather than diseconomies are more likely as the commodities involved are more compact, durable and highly standardized.

It is an elementary proposition of optimal inventory theory that the optimal number of transactions for a cash-flow-maximizing firm is inversely related to the cost of executing each transaction and directly related to the carrying costs associated with holding the commodity over a given period of time. In general, therefore, bulk transactions and joint exchange are more likely to maximize short-run cash flows, thus favouring intermediated over direct exchange, as the cost of a transaction is higher and the time-rate of carrying costs is lower. There can be no doubt that carrying costs will be lower, as the commodity is more compact (requiring less storage space) and more durable (entailing less deterioration). The net effect of standardization is less clear, since that characteristic reduces the information cost of effecting a transaction and makes bulk transactions possible to begin with. In consequence, standardization appears to favour direct exchange by virtue of its effects on the cost per transaction, while at the same time being necessary if traders on each side of the market are to benefit at all from intermediated exchange. Compactness and durability unambiguously increase the benefits of intermediated over direct exchange.

The final condition for intermediation turns on market concentration. Just as there is a minimum efficient scale in production above which further unit cost reductions are insignificant, so there are certain to be minimum efficient scales in exchange. Indeed, the reasons for these are well known as regards storage, transportation and communication. Given that there are minimum efficient scales in exchange, the intermediaries in any market will be able to secure unit transactions costs below those of producers and users only if they approach such scales more closely than the agents on either side of the market. It is therefore not only the physical characteristics of commodities but also the degree of buyer and seller concentration that determine whether intermediated or direct exchange will be the more economic in any market. If there are no intermediaries, then the market comprises only producers and users who themselves provide the necessary communication, transportation and storage of commodities.

To identify the determinants of the institutions that constitute markets, as we have done here, is in itself an advance over previous analyses of exchange. Its importance in the present context is that it provides the basis of an analysis of the locus of price and quantity determination in markets and processes whereby prices and quantities change over time. As a result, the theory of markets will enable us to argue from first economic principles in specifying the conditions in which each of the various assumptions about market processes made by the different schools of macroeconomic analysis are economically intelligible.

3.2   MARKET POWER

One undoubted effect of the metaphysical approach to the analysis of exchange is that it has enabled economists to build upon the empirical observation that markets, by and large, are orderly without requiring them to explain that orderliness. However, once it is recognized that exchange entails technological relationships that do not differ in importance from the technological relationships of production, it is no longer difficult to explain the general absence of market anarchy. Instead of assuming that the power necessary to maintain order in markets is vested in a *deux ex machina*, we can seek to determine which earthly institutions can claim and maintain that power.

There can be no question that what is involved here is an issue of power. Economic agents who can determine market prices or output directly, or who can dominate the interior of a market in order to coordinate a more diffuse process of competitive or collusive activity (e.g. enforce goodwill competition to the exclusion of price competition, maintain cartels, etc.) must be able to ensure that their views and decisions are accepted by other agents trading in the same markets. That is, they must have market power. By market power I mean the ability to inflict unacceptable consequences upon competitors, suppliers and customers without provoking unacceptable consequences for oneself.

Clearly, the consequences of any act that different management teams find unacceptable will differ according to the long-run strategies they have adopted and the strength of their commitments to those strategies. None the less, if the weak assumption of managerial motivation is right, all management teams will find effective threats to the survival of their firms to be unacceptable. Since the *sine qua non* of firm survival is a positive average cash flow over any substantial interval of time, any consequences will be unacceptable to a management team if they entail the systematic erosion or elimination of cash flows.

This observation leads to the identification of three sources of market power in the short run and one that takes effect only in the long run.

The first source of market power is the susceptibility of competitors, suppliers and/or customers of a firm to shortage costs. These are the costs to a firm resulting from shortages in either supplies of required inputs or demands for outputs completed for sale. The sensitivity of a firm to shortage costs is directly related to its operating leverage – the elasticity of the firm's cash flow with respect to physical sales volume. The higher is the break-even output of a firm relative to capacity output from any of its production activities, the greater must be the operating leverage of that activity. Moreover, break-even outputs – and hence operating leverages – are increased and cash flows reduced by any price reduction in greater proportion as the operating leverage before the price rise is greater. It follows that a firm will enjoy greater market power as its own operating leverage is smaller and the operating leverages of other firms that are active in the market are larger.

The second source of market power is financial strength, in the sense of large liquid and other financial reserves in relation to normal outputs together with low financial leverage and, hence, large untapped borrowing capacity. The firm that is financially strong in this sense will be able to suffer a reduction in cash flows over a longer interval of time than will financially weaker firms.

The third source of market power is one that has been accepted by all of the various schools of economic thought: buyer or seller concentration. The loss of supplies from a firm producing a very small proportion of total output of a commodity can easily be made good by that firm's competitors so that no significant shortage costs are imposed on that firm's customers. If, however, a firm producing a large proportion of the total output of any commodity were to withhold supplies, then the resulting shortage could not so readily be made good by that firm's competitors. In that case, the users of the commodity will face shortage costs of a magnitude that will depend on their operating leverages unless they have effectively inexhaustible stocks of the commodity in question. The effect of buyer concentration is entirely symmetrical with that of seller concentration.

The extent to which a firm will be willing to expose itself to shortage costs by holding small stocks of inputs will evidently depend on the carrying costs of those stocks and therefore the compactness, durability and degree of standardization of the inputs. Similarly, the extent to which a seller will react to demand shortages by reducing rates of production will depend upon the costs of holding stocks of outputs completed for sale – costs that again depend on the physical characteristics of the commodities in question. Thus, it is not only the operating leverages of individual firms that determine distribution of market power. The same characteristics of commodities and exchange technologies that determine the institutions comprised by markets also determine the intensity of the effects of operating leverages and, therefore, the intensity of market power.

A firm with superior technical (or cost) efficiency will be able to achieve a concentration of market power in the long run either because of superior price competitiveness or because of the financial strength that would accrue to it over time. This source of market power, however, is less relevant here since it makes possible the analysis of changes in the identity of an industry leader without indicating more generally whether market power will lie on the demand side, the supply side or among intermediaries in any market.

The concept of market power developed here implicitly underlies the analysis of intermediated and direct exchange in section 3.1. The essential point there is that intermediaries will be able to function in markets not only if they can generate a positive cash flow from exchange activities but also, more to the present point, if they can enhance the cash flows of their own customers and suppliers. The other side of this coin is that established intermediaries can refuse to buy from or sell to individual producers or users, respectively, and thereby can systematically reduce the cash flows of such agents.

The firms with which intermediaries refused to trade would evidently incur higher transactions costs than those with which the intermediaries continued to trade. A producer denied access to intermediated exchange either would require to set higher output prices than his competitors to cover his higher transactions costs or would generate a smaller cash flow. At higher output prices than those set by competitors engaged in intermediated exchange, a producer could hardly expect to maintain the same volume of sales that could be expected at the lower prices made profitable by intermediation. The magnitude of the reduction in cash flows will of course depend on the operating leverage in the activities directly or indirectly related to production for and sales in the markets in which the producer was denied intermediaries' services.

Similarly, if a commodity user in a market in which intermediaries are active were denied access to their services, then such a user would necessarily incur higher transactions costs than other buyers in the same market. In so far as those other buyers were competitors in other product markets, the higher transactions costs would place the user in the position of having either to accept a lower profit margin or to set higher prices than other firms producing competing products. Alternatively, the user that has to engage in direct exchange in a market where indirect exchange is the rule will need to offer producers lower prices for their outputs than the intermediaries offer. In consequence, such a user would be at the end of any queues for the commodity and would thereby suffer shortage costs on that account both earlier and to a greater extent than other firms, including its competitors, using the same commodity. In any of these cases, the user will clearly suffer a systematic erosion of cash flows, the magnitude of which will depend upon the firm's operating leverage and financial strength and the degree of buyer concentration in the market.

In the light of the arguments of section 3.1, these conclusions depend absolutely upon the realization of economies of scale which are not available to traders on either side of the market. Thus, a necessary condition for intermediaries to have market power is that there must be sufficiently few of them to enable each to approach minimum efficient scale in exchange; alternatively, a few of the intermediaries must be sufficiently large that they are able to set prices for smaller intermediaries as well as the two sides of the market. This is not a sufficient condition even in intermediated markets, since producers and users can in principle achieve production and utilization rates that bring them as close to minimum efficient scale in exchange as any intermediary can achieve. Intermediaries will be unable to reduce the cash flows of such buyers and sellers by refusing to trade with them since, in the long run, these buyers and sellers can bypass the intermediaries, who have their own operating leverages. This threat denies market power to the intermediaries in such markets.

I indicated at the end of section 3.1 that the theory of markets enables us to determine the conditions in which the various assumptions of market characteristics used by different schools of economists are economically intelligible. It is now possible to show more precisely how these various conditions are determined.

If we identify the intermediary with the market, the foregoing discussion of market power gives the neoclassical, partial equilibrium accounts a superficial plausibility if they are restricted to markets for compact, durable, standardized and undifferentiated commodities; for when there are many buyers and many sellers in such a market, none of which approach minimum efficient scale in exchange, then market power will reside with the intermediaries who will thus be able to set prices to both sides of the market. If, however, there are any sellers who can achieve minimum efficient scale in exchange in a market of this type, those sellers will themselves have at least as much market power as the intermediaries *vis à vis* buyers. These concentrated oligopolists will be able to set the market prices of their own outputs and will not have to take prices from any intermediary. There might still be a role for the intermediary, but he will be a taker of prices from his suppliers. Similarly, any buyers who can achieve minimum efficient scale in exchange will, like the concentrated oligopsonists of partial equilibrium theory, have sufficient market power *via à vis* sellers in the market to set rather than take prices. Thus, provided that the interior of the market is treated as a 'black box', both sides of the market are price-takers in the absence of either buyer or seller concentration; the sellers are price-makers and the buyers are price-takers in conditions of concentrated oligopoly; and the buyers are price-makers and the sellers price-takers in conditions of concentrated oligopsony. An important difference between partial equilibrium theory and the theory of markets, of course, is that the theory of markets gives an explanation of this result based on clear technological criteria while partial equilibrium theory can explain it only in terms of demand elasticities in conditions of long-run equilibrium.

The foregoing defines the conditions in which intermediaries act as the embodiment of the invisible hand in any one market. However, intermediaries do not function in all markets, and in any one market there is typically more than one intermediary. Moreover, the neo-classical parable has been shown here to have a certain plausibility only with respect to partial equilibrium analysis. When we turn to consider macroeconomic systems, and especially general equilibrium analysis, account must be taken of interactions among markets. Even if all such markets were characterized by intermediated exchange, there is no reason in theory or practice to expect a single intermediary to set prices and agree quantities traded in every one of them. Clearly, this is an issue of crucial importance to macroeconomic analysis because of the importance of assumptions of market interactions in the various theories of inflation, employment and aggregate output. We shall return repeatedly to this issue in the chapters that follow.

The other issue at the centre of macroeconomic controversy concerns the relative flexibilities of prices and quantities. In considering this issue, the focus of our attention shifts from market characteristics to individuals' decision rules. Since market characteristics are seen in the present analysis to result from allocative efficiency in exchange, which itself is a consequence of rational individual behaviour, it follows that decision rules determine market characteristics no less than market characteristics determine decision rules. In previous theories, only the latter direction of causation has been taken into account.

3.3 THE MICROECONOMICS OF PRICE FLEXIBILITY AND FIXITY

There is a presumption in macroeconomic analysis that either prices or outputs must change in response to macroeconomic deviations from equilibrium. While this view is not, as we shall see in section 3.4, strictly true, it does dominate the argument between the monetarists and Keynesians. In this section we consider the determinants of price flexibility separately – in so far as we can – from the determinants of quantity flexibility.

As far as I am aware, no one argues that prices are inflexible in the long run. The main area of contention is whether prices are flexible enough in the short run to respond to excess supplies and demands in a way that provides agents with useful market signals. To put the same issue in a slightly more general way, the differences between the various schools of thought concerning the role of prices in clearing markets turn on whether prices are established in markets with respect to short-run criteria (e.g. continuous market-clearing) or long-run criteria. Since we have abandoned the auctioneer and all other metaphysical price-setting agents, the only question that is meaningful in the present analysis is whether firms with the market power to do so set their prices in light of short-run or long-run considerations. Evidently, in those markets where firms engage in long-run pricing (i.e. with respect to long-run considerations), short-run excess supplies and demands cannot be eliminated by rapid movements in market prices. The only markets in which excess supplies and demands can be eliminated in this way are those in which price-setting firms engage in short-run pricing (i.e. with respect to short-run considerations). I shall argue presently that these two classes of markets generally co-exist and there is no clear division between them.

The differences between markets characterized by long-run pricing and by short-run pricing stem from the dual role of the commodity price from the point of view of the selling firm. That is, the price that any firm will seek for its outputs is necessarily an element in both the competitive and the investment strategies of the firm. The role of the pricing decision in the competitive strategy of the firm is that which virtually all economists have always claimed for it. Firms can attempt to set prices below those of their competitors in order to increase market share, although such a strategy is fraught with the uncertainty that arises from the likelihood that competitors will react to one's own price cut, thus setting in motion cumulative reductions in all competitors' prices. For this reason, uncertainty-averse management teams will prefer goodwill competition which generates only a limited degree of uncertainty. The success of competitors' attempts to avoid price competition, however, will depend upon the concentration of power in the market. Where power is concentrated, the power-holders will be better able to control market prices, and thereby to avoid price competition, than in markets with no significant concentration of market power.

Pricing and financial policies

The role of prices in the investment strategy of the firm is financial. The mark-up on costs and the volume of sales together determine the availability of internally generated funds. Some of these funds cannot be allocated at the discretion of the management team. There are prior statutory and contractual claims by government and creditors. In addition, quoted firms seek to maintain credibility on the stock exchange by avoiding in so far as possible any reductions in dividends during periods of adverse trading conditions and by increasing dividends roughly in line with profits in more favourable conditions. It is, of course, the excess of gross trading profits over such non-discretionary expenditure which is available as internal finance for investment.

These observations led Eichner (1973, 1976) and Wood (1975) to argue that specific investment plans of oligopolostic firms – represented by their marginal efficiency of investment schedules – determine their mark-ups over direct costs of production. The essence of their argument is that the uncertainty-averse management team will prefer to finance the planned investment of its firm internally rather than externally provided that the opportunity cost of the finance is not increased thereby. The basis of this proposition is that internal finance results in smaller claims upon the firm's financial reserves by external agents, and so leaves the firm financially stronger in the event of unforeseen reverses, than does external finance. Thus, any increases in planned rates of firm investment will typically be financed partly from the proceeds of increased mark-ups. Of course, such proceeds can be anticipated only if demands faced by such firms are inelastic in the short run. The costs of such finance are long-run reductions in sales revenues which follow from price rises as cutomers change their tastes or technologies and substitute other commodities with now-lower relative prices, the increased likelihood of entry by firms not already in the same industry and, possibly, increased likelihood of government intervention on anti-trust grounds.

Neither Eichner nor Wood suggests that all investment will be financed internally. Increasing the mark-up on costs increases the long-run costs of the finance at an increasing rate in this theory so that there will be a critical price and mark-up increase beyond which the costs of external finance are less than the costs of internal finance. Obviously, this critical increase will depend on the level of the rate of interest on external debt.

The main difference between the Eichner–Wood view of oligopoly pricing and the neoclassical-cum-game-theoretic view is that in the Eichner–Wood analysis the time-patterns of quantities and investment are determined simultaneously with prices, while in neoclassical oligopoly theories prices and quantities are determined separately from (or prior to) investment. In so far as investment is a consideration in, or joint outcome of, the pricing process, the determination of prices clearly has a substantial long-run element. If investment plans are given pride of place in the determination of prices, then anticipated long-run conditions of demand and competition completely dominate short-run conditions of supply and demand. Certainly, Eichner takes the view that oligopolistic industries face inelastic short-run demands, so that prices can always be raised by the price leaders in these industries (but only in these industries) to generate internal finance for long-run investment plans.

Such direct evidence as there is indicates that firms set prices by establishing a normal mark-up on costs. The reasons for so doing were well established by Andrews (1949, 1964). They also fit well within the imbalance theory of the firm, which implies that uncertainty-averse entrepreneurs will rationally prefer goodwill competition to price competition. It will hardly increase a firm's goodwill with its customers if, every time sales are sufficiently buoyant to induce the firm to increase its production capacity, it jacks up its prices. It makes no difference to a firm's customers whether price increases are intended to generate internal finance for investment, to increase dividends or, indeed, to increase managers' salaries and perquisites.

Price rises in conditions of excess demand, if repeated, will soon lead customers to formulate an implicit model of the firm that predicts this pricing pattern. In such a circumstance the customers will rationally seek alternative sources of supply. In particular, they will seek out firms that hold their prices in conditions of excess demand. Customers will rationally buy from such firms in periods of excess supply. For the benefits of goodwill accrue to both customers and suppliers: the suppliers minimize shortage costs during the slump by having priority from a hard core of customers for their demands in a buyers' market, while customers minimize shortage costs during the boom by having priority over whatever supplies are available in a sellers' market. Thus, it will always be a sound competitive strategy for producers not to raise mark-ups during precisely those periods when strong demand would provide an incentive and opportunity to do so – whether to finance investment internally or to increase reserves against the next slump. Similarly, it will be a sound competitive strategy for buyers to avoid attempts to force prices down during periods of weak demand.

The foregoing conclusion also applies to industries with strong price leadership. the industry that is characterized by price increases during periods of strong demand will be ripe for entry by potential competitors with the appropriate resources. The scale on which entrants operate is not typically marginal – particularly in industries with sufficient seller concentration to have a substantial concentration of market power. Either firms within such an industry will have operating leverages high enough to make the market power of the largest firms effective, and therefore the minimum scale of operations by an entrant will be significant, or operating leverages will be small and the minimum efficient scale will also be small enough to make entry relatively easy. In the first case, attracting one or two entrants will have a significant effect on the market shares of the industry's incumbents, and the implicit cost of internal finance generated by increased mark-ups will turn out to be substantial. There will be no question of comparing the marginal cost of internal finance with the marginal cost of external finance. In the second case, the number of entrants might well be large relative to the number of incumbents, and entry – requiring resources on a smaller scale than in the first case – could then make the period of inelastic demand very short and the elasticity of demand in the long run very high indeed. In this case the marginal cost of internal finance generated by mark-up increases will be large.

Evidently, in industries based on technologies with high operating leverages, the cost of Eichner–Wood pricing could well be so large that, even allowing for short-run demand inelasticities, the expected discounted cost of the marginal internal finance will very quickly exceed the cost of external finance. In industries based on technologies with low operating leverages, the ease of entry could result in high demand elasticities becoming dominant, because of the entry factor, so quickly that only a very limited amount of internal finance would in fact be generated while the loss of internal finance would come early and last long. Once again, it seems likely and is certainly conceivable that only a very small – if any – element of internal fiance could be raised before it came to exceed the cost of external finance.

This argument suggests that, at the extremes of possible operating leverages, a constant mark-up is likely to be adopted by the rationally maximizing, survival-motivated management team. It is conceivable that there is a broad watershed between these extremes where the Eichner–Wood theory is apposite. This is strictly an empirical matter. I know of no direct evidence that firms act in this way, and the indirect statistical evidence indicates no more than that prices in manufactures and the non-financial service industries are far more sensitive to costs than to demands. This evidence is compatible with a constant mark-up on costs.

The question thus remains. What determines the mark-up? Since the mark-up is an important determinant of available internal finance, it is altogether plausible that it will be set to provide the finance necessary to carry out firms' long-run investment plans. Mark-ups will be changed, if at all, to generate a flow of internal finance over the whole of the seasonal and the trade cycle appropriate to a changed rate of expansion or diversification by the firm. Increased sales volumes during regular periods of strong demands will evidently provide cash flow surpluses which will be offset by cash flow deficits during the regular periods of slack demands. Given the financial leverage available to any firm and its commitments to service its debts and pay out dividends, a mark-up that is too low will constrain investment to the point where the firm will need continually to contract its rate of investment or use up its reserves. A mark-up that is higher than its financial commitments and investment plans require will lead to ever-increasing liquid reserves, which will make the firm attractive to take-over raiders. Thus, although the Eichner–Wood price mechanism is, in general, compatible in some circumstances with the managerial survival motive in conditions of uncertainty, the mark-up will not be determined or altered rationally in the light of the firm's investment plans for a single 'planning period'. Because the issues involved here will turn out to be of crucial macroeconomic importance, let us consider afresh the relative costs of finance from alternative sources.

Suppose that the management team(s) of some industry leader(s) come to anticipate that a higher trend rate of growth of production capacity will be required. The circumstances in which such anticipations are likely to arise will be considered in chapter 8. For the present we simply assume this change in expectations. If the industry's capital–output ratio is roughly constant, the increased rate of capacity growth will require an increased ratio of investment to trading income.* Thus, firms in the industry will need to increase the sum of the flows of internal and external finance relative to total sales revenue. This increase can come from increased financial leverage, from increased retention ratios, from periodic issues of new equity shares, from increased output prices in conditions of inelastic demand or from some combination of these. If technical changes are involved that reduce the capital–output ratio or reduce direct unit costs so that mark-ups but not prices can be increased, then these changes will reduce the requirement to increase leverage, equity and/or retention ratios. For the present technical change is ignored here, although it, too, will be considered in chapters 6 and 8.

All of these methods of generating the necessary long-run finance entail notional and real long-run costs. Increased financial leverage increases the contractual debt repayment and servicing commitments relative to current income, thereby reducing the ability of the firm to set aside reserves against the possibility of unexpectedly deep or prolonged slumps in demands. In any case, for wholly rational reasons to be considered in chapter 5, lending institutions typically limit their borrowers' financial leverages, and, after a point, any further increases entail rapidly increasing rates of interest unless the additional borrowing is proscribed altogether by previous loan contracts.

Unless *rentiers* share the optimistic expectations of the management teams of firms seeking to finance more rapid growth, increases in retention ratios and new share issues will also entail substantial and increasing long-run costs. Without such shared optimism, *rentiers* will perceive a rise in retention ratios only as a reduction in the divided income derived from their share holdings. They will also perceive new share issues as increased supplies of the firm's shares with no apparent prospect of increased demands to prevent share

---

* If Y is the real value of the firm's output, I the rate of investment, K some measure of the fixed capital stock and constant $v = K/Y$, then $g = I/K = (1/v)\,(I/Y)$ and sgn Δg = sgn $\Delta\,(I/Y)$.

prices from falling. But if the firm can convince the life assurance and pension fund managers and other actual and potential shareholders that current reductions in its retention ratio or new share issues will enable the firm to increase future dividends at a faster rate, or that an increased rate of growth will result with associated capital gains on shareholdings, then the desired internal finance can more safely (albeit within limits) be raised by these means. In both cases, of course, the consequent increased value of net assets will enable the firm to increase its external finance and the growth thereof without increasing its financial leverage.

For the sake of logical completeness, we must consider the long-run cost of a once-over increase in the mark-up to accommodate a higher rate of growth of investment. I have argued that increased mark-ups associated with each wave of investment are generally too costly to contemplate. However, it is conceivable that some buyers in a market will have a substantial interest in the growth of their suppliers. This might be the case if the buyer used the commodity in some process that was itself to be expanded at a more rapid rate than previously and the buyer's rate of use was such that it exhausted the capacities of one or more producers. In this circumstance, however, it is likely that the buyer would rationally integrate backwards either by establishing new production facilities or by taking over existing independent producers. If these options were not thought likely to be profitable, almost certainly such a user would prefer to finance his supplier's increased investment growth by share purchase or loans rather than by paying a higher price for the commodity. For having paid the higher price, the user has no claim on the producer for a future return or the recovery of any part of the higher cost; while, by lending or taking an equity share in the firm (a sort of partial acquisition), there can be some prospect of repayment or a return that does not depend on the future course of an informal goodwill relationship between supplier and customer.

On balance, then, we conclude that mark-up increases are likely to entail a high marginal cost of finance and so will be limited in extent and in application. That is, the mark-up would rationally be increased only when equity finance and profit retention increases are expensive because the optimism of managers is not shared by *rentiers*, and when the firm cannot easily increase its financial leverage. In any case, while the mark-up might (if anything) be increased in response to entrepreneurial optimism about long-run demand, it is unlikely to be related to any particular investment project or investment plans for a single planning period.

Prices and market-clearing

It would be quite wrong to infer from the foregoing discussion that mark-ups are held constant in all markets all of the time. The maintenance of constant mark-ups requires both sufficient concentration of power in the market to preclude price-cutting by survival-motivated competitors and the perception of a stable or at least predictable contribution to internal finance for investment from the trading activities of the firm. There are some markets, however, in which neither of these requirements can be met; and, as we shall see in section 3.4, rational price-setters will then raise and lower prices to eliminate excess supplies and demands.

That prices can be determined for a market only by agents with sufficient market power to threaten the survival of pricing deviants was demonstrated in section 3.2. We also saw in that section that sufficient concentrations of power to keep prices or mark-ups constant are unlikely to be found in markets for commodities that are produced and used in processes entailing small operating leverages, and where there is no substantial buyer or seller concentration and no concentration of financial strength. In such markets, price and mark-up stability depend on the mutual confidence of all sellers that none will seek to undercut the others' prices. This is the situation that is commonly considered in oligopoly theory. Although there is no definitive model of oligopolistic behaviour, the usual conclusion that collusive agreements will rationally be broken by individual sellers lest others secretly break the agreement first is entirely plausible. Even in markets with no power concentrations, however, the value of strong goodwill relationships between buyers and sellers and the need to generate non-negative contributions to internal finance on average over time will tend to limit the fluctuations in prices and margins. In general, the less the concentration of market power, the larger will such fluctuations be, although the analysis of goodwill competition leads to the conjecture that price competition and fluctuations in prices will not respond entirely to excess supplies and demands on account of the absence of market power alone.

If, in addition to an absence of power concentrations, the relationship between supplies and demands is volatile and unpredictable, the financial benefits of stable mark-ups are likely to be very small indeed. This is not because it would be impossible to set a mark-up that, on average over sufficiently long periods of time, would provide a positive cash flow; it is because the variance of the cash flow would be much greater than the financial requirements of investment strategies. For any investment decision typically commits the firm to a definite and inflexible time pattern of expenditures. A firm could enter such commitments while relying on managers' expectations of future cash flows only if the managers were quite certain that the flows would not be of large negative magnitude over a period of time that was so long as itself to require substantial additional external finance for the firm to survive. In other words, the variance of cash flows from trading activities might simply be too large for such cash flows to be relied upon in the finance package associated with any substantial investment commitments. In those circumstances, firms would rationally seek some other means of limiting the threat to their survival from occasionally large, negative cash flows.

In chapter 5 we shall see why institutions have evolved to limit the threats to firm survival in markets without concentrations of power where commodities subject to volatile fluctuations in excess demands and supplies are traded.

Between the extremes

Markets that are characterized either by constant prices or mark-ups or by short-run market-clearing prices represent extreme cases. Even in markets with some concentration of power, management teams will sensibly allow only for seasonal and cyclical fluctuations of magnitudes and durations previously experienced. Thus, a slump that is of a severity and length regularly experienced in the past is not especially likely to lead management teams substantially to revise previous investment, financing and pricing decisions. But if a slump should prove to be unusually severe and/or prolonged, so that demands and internally generated finance are smaller than managers had anticipated on their most pessimistic assumptions, then some action will be required in order to protect the cash flows, and hence the viability, of the firm. Investment plans may be curtailed, or profit margins changed and external finance increased, or possibly new markets will be sought or some combination of these. Clearly, the response will be conditioned by the actual effect of the slump on cash flows – the magnitude of which will depend upon the operating leverage of the firm as well as on certain other sources of shortage costs to the firm. These other sources will be considered in the section following.

(It should be noted that the direction of change in the profit margin cannot be specified on the basis of the analysis undertaken so far. If demands are thought to be inelastic with respect to price in the short run, profit margins could well be increased. In the opposite case they could be reduced. The effect of the slump on costs will also be important here. All of these issues will be considered below.)

It will soon become apparent that the determinants of the direction and magnitude of price changes in markets characterized by short-run pricing are not wholly dissimilar to the determinants of price changes in markets characterized by long-run pricing. They are, none the less, sufficiently different that it will be convenient to consider these two types of market separately.

Markets with short-run pricing

In the previous section, we found that short-run pricing will predominate in markets in which the physical volume of transactions is inherently volatile and uncertain. In such markets, either supplies or demands (or both) are volatile and cannot be expected generally to move in the same direction or by the same magnitude. The gross profits of firms are rendered uncertain by the unpredictability of supplies and/or demands. Consumers, too, will be subject to unpredictability of exchange costs or, perhaps, simply to the inconvenience of having to forgo the consumption of desired commodities.

In light of the assumption that firms' managers are motivated primarily to ensure the survival of their firms, and consequently seek to maximize short-run cash flows from existing activities, we must be concerned here to identify the pricing policies that can be expected to maximize these cash flows over future periods of time and are sufficiently near that managers can actually form clear expectations concerning them. What we cannot do, however, is to assume there to be some functional relationship either between prices and supplies or between prices and demands, since the aim of this discussion is to identify the nature and sources of these relationships.

This issue is best approached by comparing potential shortage costs with carrying costs. Consider, for example, the position of a producer faced with market conditions of excess supply. If the shortage costs of responding to expected demand deficiencies by curtailing outputs exceed his best estimate of the highest unrecoverable carrying costs the producer might incur, then production levels will rationally be maintained with the difference between outputs and sales being held as stocks. Clearly, there will be some limit to the volume of stocks that a producer can carry, since in the short run storage capacity will be limited. Even before such limits are reached, however, it is possible that marginal carrying costs will exceed the marginal shortage costs that might be expected to arise from curtailed production rates. In such cases the producer will rationally reduce his rates of output. The only alternative is to induce customers to incur the carrying costs of the producer. To do so, the producer can reduce his supply price to the level at which his customers expect the difference between present and future prices to be greater than the unit-carrying costs of stocks over the same interval of time. In addition, a commodity user might wish to hold stocks against the time when conditions of excess demand arise – a possibility that is important in the sort of market being discussed here. Thus, as users' carrying costs are lower and their own potential shortage costs are higher, they will be increasingly willing to purchase more of a commodity as a result of lower prices. Of course, they, too, will be able to do so only as long as they have unutilized storage capacity.

In conditions of excess demand, it is commodity users who face the prospect of incurring shortage costs. Users with the highest operating leverages face the greatest shortage costs in relation to normal sales revenue. Evidently, users facing shortage costs will rationally offer a premium for commodities in short supply, and this premium will be larger as the potential shortage costs are greater. The maximum price offered by users will be limited by the magnitude of the shortage costs they face and the proportion of total costs accounted for by the inputs in short supply.

In addition, the standard analysis of the relationship between derived demand elasticities and the elasticity of output–demand applies here. If the demand for the *users'* outputs is relatively inelastic in the short run, firms will be able to pass on to their own customers the bulk of any increases in input costs. If, however, the demand for the user's outputs is relatively elastic, then the users will be able to pass on a smaller proportion of the increased costs.

There is an asymmetry between conditions of excess demand and excess supply. Conditions of excess supply involve at least the possibility of a glut on the market. In consequence, the costs of carrying stocks of commodities for which there is deficient demand become relevant. In conditions of excess demand, however, the problem is that stocks of the commodity are smaller than users would like. The carrying costs associated with a commodity might enter into the determination of optimal stocks in the short run, but there seems no reason for them to have any effect on price movements resulting from deficient supplies.

The arguments upon which these propositions are based are inherently dynamic. For example, producers' shortage costs do not determine *whether* there will be a large or a small fall in supply price but only *when* the supply price will fall. High carrying costs will tend to increase the speed of supply price adjustment, although, in addition, higher carrying costs are likely to lead to larger supply price reductions before production is stopped. Moreover, smaller carrying costs in relation to future price rises expected by buyers will induce the buyers to increase their rates of purchase of a commodity, but increased acquisition in relation to subsequent sale or use will eventually exhaust buyers' storage capacities. Thereafter, no further reductions in price can induce buyers to maintain, much less augment, the higher rates of purchase.

Finally, there is the problem of changing expectations. If producers expect demand deficiencies to be short-lived, they will be reluctant to reduce prices in order to reduce stocks that they believe will be required in the near future. If, however, demand continues at a low level or continues to fall, producers are likely to revise their expectations and seek desperately to reduce stocks by reducing both prices and output rates – the latter perhaps to zero. Similarly, once supply prices begin to fall, buyers will have to form expectations about the likely magnitude and speed of the fall – expectations that will be revised in light of further experience. A more complete account of expectations formation along lines first suggested by Hahn (1973) will be given in chapter 5 and developed more fully in chapter 8.

Even without a full analysis of expectations, however, the foregoing argument is sufficient to indicate the economic reasons, based in technology, for prices to fall in the face of excess supplies and to rise in the face of excess demands. It should be remembered, however, that this argument applies only to that limited class of markets in which traded commodities are standardized, supplies and demands move unpredictably in relation to one another and there is no significant concentration of power on either side of the market.

We turn now to consider markets in which long-run pricing is economic.

Markets with long-run pricing

The standard textbook expositions of the income–expenditure approach to macroeconomic income and employment determination rest on two assumptions that are of importance in the present context. One is that commodity prices and wages are sticky at less-than-full employment; the other is that firms (or their managers) seek to maintain some optimal level of stocks of commodities completed for sale. I have already suggested that the first assumption is not necessarily accurate on theoretical grounds alone. There is, in addition, the obvious fact that prices on some markets are volatile. That is, in some markets short-run pricing predominates. But even if we restrict our attention to markets characterized by long-run pricing, there are theoretical as well as empirical reasons to accept that in some of these markets goods are not produced for stock at all. In such markets, firms obviously do not maintain positive optimal inventories.

It hardly needs pointing out that the reasons firms hold stocks of any goods – finished or unfinished – is to enable production rates to differ from rates of sale and for both of these to differ from rates of use of the same goods. For some commodities, however, it is not economic to hold stocks, and in such cases commodities can be produced only to order.

What is involved in the choice of production to order or for stock is a comparison of the transactions and carrying costs associated with each. Producing commodities to order entails higher transactions costs and lower carrying costs than producing the same commodities for stock. The reasons for this are perfectly obvious. If commodities are produced only to order, the terms of each order must be agreed but the producing firm will need to hold virtually no stocks of commodities that have been completed for sale. If commodities are produced for stock, then the producing firm will incur the carrying costs of those stocks but can sell from stock to customers as they come along without having first to agree the details of what and how much is to be produced.

Production for stock is evidently more likely in the case of commodities that entail low carrying costs (commodities that are compact and durable) and are highly standardized and in general demand so that the needs of each individual customer need not be determined in advance of production. Producers of such commodities can then establish production capacities to meet the average flow of demand for their outputs and to allow the volume of stocks to vary seasonally or even cyclically as the level of demand varies.

If the requirements of the producer's customers are highly specialized so that the firm cannot sell standard commodities all of which are in general demand, then the firm's rate of stock-turn must be relatively low. In such cases, either the specialized outputs of the firm must be produced to order, or stocks of each of a large variety of specialized commodities must be maintained. If there are any significant carrying costs associated with the holding of these specialized commodities, the producer is likely to find that the savings on carrying costs that result from production to order will exceed any increased transaction costs. If this line of argument is right, then compactness, durability and standardization – the commodity characteristics that also favour market intermediation – favour production for stock rather than production to order.

In order to avoid the shortage costs resulting from fixed and other indirect costs of production during periods when demands fall short of full-capacity output rates, firms queue their customers so that variations of demand in either direction are taken up by variations in the sizes of firms' order books. Of course, such a procedure is economically feasible only if the users of such commodities are actually prepared to join the queues. Whether they will or not depends upon the technological characteristics of the user's production processes.

The technologies of production by commodity users will determine the lapse of time between the manifestation of a need for an input and the requirement to meet that need. If the commodity is some direct material input to the production of some output for which the demand has increased, then the user will need to increase his inputs of that commodity very quickly in order to satisfy his own customers. How quickly the user will have to increase throughput rates will depend on his own stocks of both inputs and outputs completed for sale. But once these stocks have been depleted, the user will begin to incur shortage costs, the size of which will depend upon his operating leverage. If the operating leverage and therefore shortage costs are high, the firm could profitably offer a premium to producers in order to jump the queues for their outputs. It is possible that in such cases the offers of premiums replace goodwill relationships.

In other circumstances, the need for a commodity will be less urgent once it is manifest. This will be the case with some inputs to capital investment projects. Those inputs that are required early in the production of new plant and equipment, for example, will be the subject of more urgent demands than will the later inputs. Thus, builders might need to purchase bricks and cement from suppliers' stocks in order to construct a factory building, while the machinery, which cannot be put in place until the building is completed, could more readily be ordered with no loss to the purchaser from taking his place at the end of the queue. More generally, queueing theory is well able to take into account differing urgencies in customers' need to reach the front of the queue as well as the different lengths of time required to fill different customers' orders.

3.5 THE CONVERGENCE OF EXCHANGE TECHNOLOGIES

This chapter has been concerned with the relationships between, on the one hand, allocatively efficient technologies of exchange and, on the other, given physical characteristics of commodities and technologies of commodity production and use. That allocatively efficient technologies of exchange will in fact be chosen is a proposition about the long run that is justified by the basic premises of imbalance theory. Moreover, imbalance theory implies the likelihood of convergence in the technologies of exchange of commodities with diverse physical characteristics, production processes and uses. That is. to say, there is not a wholly different exchange technology for every commodity but, rather, there are technological genotypes of exchange.

In general, new activities or new ways of undertaking existing activities arise first within firms where focusing effects concentrate the attention of managers or other personnel upon particular problems. Once these new activities or products are developed as the results of such focusing effects, there will be an inducement effect upon other firms either to adopt or to adapt for their own use the innovation arising from the original focusing effect. When problem-solvers have defined a problem with precision, and perhaps have developed a partial solution which is incomplete in some highly specific way, they frequently discover knowledge developed by others, in the context of rather different problems, that with adaptation completes the solution to their own problem or sets them off on a new line of enquiry resulting in a complete solution (see, e.g. Langrish et al., 1972, Watson, 1970). This process undoubtedly lies behind the process of technological convergence identified by Rosenberg (1976, pp. 9–31). There is no reason to suppose that the same phenomenon does not affect technical and organizational change in exchange.

When new or modified techniques of exchange are developed they can hardly be kept secret, since, unlike production, the process of exchange involves several independent firms and, possibly, households. Thus, if a technical change reduces the total of transactions, storage and transport costs, it will quickly become widely known, and there will therefore be a clear inducement effect upon the innovator's competitors to employ or adapt the same technique of exchange. In addition, other firms producing or using different commodities might find that an innovation in a market in which they do not trade will reduce their own transactions costs or the transactions costs of their own customers or suppliers. It seems likely that a firm is more likely to imitate exchange innovations in other markets if exchange has been the subject of a focusing effect within the imitating firm. And once one firm in a market adopts an innovation that renders exchange more efficient, its competitors will face an inducement effect to adopt the same innovation. This reasoning, of course, is but an application of a general theoretical underpinning of the phenomenon of technological convergence.

If we accept the convergence of exchange technologies – whether on theoretical or empirical grounds – it renders far more tractable the task of theorizing about macroeconomic systems. It becomes possible to specify genotypes of production and exchange technologies. The theory of markets then relates these genotypes to one another without requiring us to specify the actual technologies employed by firms trading in every market in the economy.

We shall see in the following three chapters that the identification of these genotypes leads to a macroeconomic analysis of capacity, output and employment growth which, though simple, robust and powerful, takes explicit account of the fullest possible complexity of price regimes in different markets as well as the interactions among those markets. The simplicity, robustness and power of that macroeconomic analysis is a consequence of the implication of the theory of markets, discussed in this chapter, and the imbalance theory of the firm that there is a macroeconomic technology which has the same structure as that assumed in the basic model of chapter 1. That is, the imbalance theory of the firm and the theory of markets predicated upon the rational markets hypothesis implies the existence of two mutually exclusive and exhaustive sets of processes and commodities: a set of basic processes and commodities and a set of non-basic processes and commodities. In consequence, the three types of multiplier–accelerator interactions identified in the basic model are found equally in the most general macroeconomic analyses.

4

Firms, Markets and Auctioneers in Macroeconomic Theory

4.0 INTRODUCTION

Macroeconomics is the study of interactions between various parts of integrated economic systems. The parts of such systems that are actually studied are not those that exist in reality but rather economists' conceptions of how reality is best simplified. Such is the nature of scientific enquiry. The scientist establishes categories of phenomena and entities with broad strokes of his intellectual brush – he is an impressionist.

In economics there has long been tacit agreement about the entities that are to be studied, although there is considerable disagreement about the phenomena to which the behaviour of those entities gives rise. Basically, there are households, which sell factor services and buy outputs produced by firms; there are firms, which buy factor services and sell output to households; and there are markets, in which these transactions take place. It is, of course, common in macroeconomic models to add to this basic list a government, which buys output and factor services and sells financial assets, and a 'rest of the world', which buys and sells produced commodities and financial assets.

One of the main differences between the theory reported in this book and previous macroeconomic analysis is that the list of basic entities is different. The firm of established theory is a production function, or marginal efficiency of investment function, and an objective function. The market in established theory is an independent – indeed, a metaphysical – entity. In the preceding two chapters, however, I have argued that the established definitions of the firm and the market lead to logical difficulties. These are resolved by defining the firm as a collection of resources and independent organizational structures and by defining the market as a collection of rational maximizing agents – both firms and, in final markets for consumption goods, households. In consequence, it is market institutions and characteristics that are determined by the rational behaviour of firms and households and not, as is customary to assume, the rational maximizing behaviour of firms and households that is determined by market characteristics.

This new approach solves problems of logic and removes the economic analysis of exchange from the realm of the metaphysical. In so doing, it enables us analytically to evaluate both the new classicals' contention that Keynesian theory is *ad hoc* and the Keynesian contention that the general equilibrium model underlying new classical analysis is not the correct model of the economy. These views are considered in detail in this chapter and the next. We will find that there is some justice in both.

We shall begin by examining the Walrasian specification of the economy to determine the conditions in which macroeconomic processes can be represented either as the monetarist/new classicals assume or as the neo-Walrasian temporary equilibrium and dis-equilibrium theorists assume.

The auctioneer

In both general and temporary equilibrium theory, the role of the auctioneer is essential. Without the auctioneer, there could not be an equilibrium of the whole economic system in either the short run or the long run. The problem that this raises is not simply methodo-logical. The question is not whether such an institution actually exists but, instead, whether such an institution is logically compatible with the assumption that individuals are rational. If there can be rational agents in the economy who carry out the functions ascribed to the auctioneer, and if it can be shown that agents on both sides of markets benefit from such agents' activities, then the case for the assumption that the economy functions as if there were an auctioneer is analytically strengthened. If we should find, however, that the functions ascribed to the auctioneer are in logical conflict with the fundamental rationality assumption, then there is no analytical foundation for the assumption that the economy functions as if it had a Walrasian structure. In that case, it is hard to justify using Walrasian models to devise and support any policy prescriptions at all, whether they are monetarist and derived from general equilibrium theorizing or 'Keynesian' and derived from temporary equilibrium theorizing.

Of course it would not be convincing to dismiss the auctioneer-based theories simply by relying on assumptions that conflict with those underlying general and temporary equilibrium analysis. It must also be shown that some of the assumptions of these equilibrium analyses are mutually incompatible. This caveat is particularly important here because the imbalance-theoretic definition of the firm makes sense only if firms hold productive resources in the long run. In equilibrium theories, to the contrary, firms are assumed only to hire productive resources from households in the short run. Our first objective in the analysis of the market structure of the economy will therefore be to determine the conditions in which either of these characterizations of the firm is compatible with the assumption, common to both, that firms and households are rational. This determination is the subject of section 4.1.

4.1 THE FIRM IN WALRASIAN AND NEO-WALRASIAN THEORY

All topological proofs of sufficient conditions for the existence of general or temporary equilibrium require that, among other things, there be continuous excess demand functions for each and every market. In particular, specifications of the firm and firm behaviour must preclude discontinuous jumps in product supplies and factor demands as prices notionally vary. This is the reason for two widespread assumptions in both Walrasian and neo-Walrasian models.

The first assumption is that all indivisible commodities yielding factor services are owned by households and are not themselves traded. Thus, firms hire producers' durables (or buy their services) only for the interval of time between transactions, which are assumed to take place at every 'date' – even if all transactions are agreed at one date. The second assumption is that no firm can become bankrupt.

If firms were to own or to hire, over extended periods of time, the indivisible resources that yield productive services, then the firms would incur fixed costs in the short run. As is well known from partial equilibrium analysis, the presence of these fixed costs for any one firm would imply that there is a positive price, equal to minimum average cost at the prevailing price vector, at which the supply of outputs and the demand for inputs would fall discontinuously to zero. That is, the assumption of profit maximization, together with ownership of resources by firms, introduces discontinuities in their supplies, hence in product-market excess demand functions, and in their demands, hence in factor-market excess demand functions.

The same problems, for analogous reasons, would occur if firms could become bankrupt – and therefore cease to buy or sell in any market – in the long run.

It is not impossible to relax these assumptions, but the ways that have been found to relax them (e.g. in Arrow and Hahn, 1971) are limited and highly restrictive.

I have nothing to add to the existing literature on bankruptcy in general equilibrium. The artificiality of the no-bankruptcy assumption is perfectly well recognized. A clear and concise summary of the present position taken by Walrasians and neo-Walrasians is Weintraub's (1979, p. 105):

The major difficulty with these models has been a lack of agreement about the manner in which *firms* should be introduced to create production economies. ... In the temporary equilibrium model with production, the time profile of production is of some importance, and, further, the firm must usually choose specific plans both for financing production and paying out dividends over time. ... [I]f firms supply bonds ... to finance current production, there must be some 'natural' way to bound the supply of bonds. Yet the expectations of bankruptcy which in fact restrain real firms, are immensely difficult to model since such fundamental discontinuities in behaviour 'mess up' existence proofs.

It is clear that the theory of the firm and market described in chapters 2 and 3 is basically incompatible with any theory that cannot allow for the bankruptcy of the firm, since the threat of bankruptcy is essential to the plausibility of the assumption that managers seek to maximize short-run cash flows from existing activities. That assumption follows from the prior assumption that the primary objective of firms' managers is the survival of their respective firms. If firms cannot become bankrupt, their survival is thereby assured – whatever their cash flows might be in the long or the short run.

While imbalance theory is incompatible with the no-bankruptcy assumption of neo-Walrasian theory, it can accommodate the assumption that firms hire resources for short periods of time but enter into no long-run resource commitments. This accommodation has some limited interest *per se* and, more importantly, it exhibits the role for imbalance theory in any further development of neo-Walrasian theory.

The two assumptions, (1) that firms own no assets (including fixed capital equipment) and (2) that all productive services are sold by households to firms, amount to assuming that households intermediate in exchange between the producers and the users of fixed, though not necessarily circulating, capital goods. Sales of durable capital equipment directly to users by the producers would violate assumption (1). At the same time, households must buy items of durable capital equipment and then rent them out to firms in conformity with assumption (2).

We already know from the theory of markets that certain physical characteristics of commodities favour intermediation and their absence favours direct exchange. These characteristics are standardization, compactness and durability. We shall now see that these same characteristics, and the relevant technical conditions of production and exchange, also favour the particular form of intermediation required to satisfy assumptions (1) and (2).

It is important to note here that the rental activity specified in Walrasian and neo-Walrasian theory is short-term rental only. The rental contract is always for a single date although, to be sure, a number of such contracts for consecutive dates is always possible. None the less, such a sequence of dated contracts cannot be necessary. If there were long-term rental contracts spanning several dates, then the firms using rented capital goods would incur positive rental and, possibly, maintenance costs even if no outputs were produced at one or more of those dates. The rental costs would then amount to precisely the sort of fixed costs that we have seen to engender inadmissible discontinuities in the market excess demand functions. In consequence, long-term rental contracts must be excluded from the analysis by assumption. (In any case, the practice of long-term rental amounts only to a means of financing the purchase of capital goods – a practice that corporate taxation provisions sometimes render financially attractive.)

To the user of capital goods, the advantage of hiring rather than buying them is that, by so doing, there is a reduction in the potential shortage costs faced by the firm. If all resources can be hired only for the length of time they are actually required for use in production, then hiring will reduce operating leverages to unity if direct unit costs are constant or to below unity if direct unit costs are positively related to the volume of throughputs. Since we have seen that shortage costs are closely and positively related to operating leverage, it is clear that the hiring of capital goods reduces these costs.

The reduction of potential shortage costs made possible by hiring rather than buying capital goods has an analogous role in the present analysis to the role of savings in transactions costs in the analysis of intermediation. The magnitude of the savings in shortage costs imposes a maximum to the rental charges that the users of hired resources can economically incur. And just as the intermediation considered in chapter 3 results in a transfer of transactions costs to the intermediary, so hiring transfers shortage costs from the user to the rental agent – in Walrasian and neo-Walrasian theory to households. Clearly, if the rental agent is to gain from engaging in the rental activity, such an agent (whether firm or household) will have to incur shortage costs that are less than those that owner-users of the same capital goods would incur.

The saving of shortage costs made possible by hiring results from the ability of the rental agent to hire out the same capital goods to different users who require them at different times. Indeed, this is just how actual rental agents generate custom and revenue. Car-hire agencies rent their cars to drivers whose need for a car in a particular place is infrequent, and the rental firms count on the probability that there will always be enough such drivers – although the individuals in the population will vary considerably from day to day – to utilize the pool of cars owned by the agencies. The drivers thus avoid the costs of maintaining idle cars in places where they need them only infrequently (although the cost of such rentals would, if incurred every day over the lifetime of a car, far exceed the cost of buying and maintaining such a car themselves). In effect, rental agents make it possible for many individual users of capital goods to share each unit of that good without having to enter into complex multilateral arrangements. There is therefore a very considerable saving in the transactions costs of the sharing arrangements which itself reduces shortage costs.

In general, then, the shortage costs incurred by a rental agent will be smaller the larger the number of users to whom such an agent can hire out the capital goods he owns. This implies that these shortage costs will be smaller as the capital good is better standardized, and so is known to be utilizable by many users in perhaps many different employments. In addition, the more compact and durable is the capital good, the greater is the possible dispersion over time and space of the points of use; for compactness and durability reduce the costs of transporting and storing any commodity, including capital goods. In consequence, both the user's and the rental agent's costs of completing a transaction – which may involve transportation and certainly involves storage of the capital good – will be lower as the good is more durable and compact.

In summary, standardization, durability and compactness of the capital good increase the number of likely users who will share in its utilization and therefore reduce the shortage costs incurred by the rental agent who owns it. Moreover, compactness and durability reduce the transactions, storage and maintenance costs that are incurred either by the rental agent, and covered by the rental price, or by the user, and therefore added in his calculations to the cost of the rental. Of course, the latter costs will be important only to the extent that they exceed the transportation, storage and maintenance costs that would be incurred even if the user owned the capital good. None the less, it appears from this argument that standardization, compactness and durability are necessary to some degree both to establish a savings in social shortage costs out of which the extra costs associated with rental must be met and to reduce those extra costs so that the rental agent can generate a positive cash flow from engaging in the rental activity.

I might be objected here that, unlike Walrasian and neo-Walrasian theorists, I am supposing the rental agent to be a firm. I believe that this objection would be false, since households acting as rental agents are providing productive services to firms. The difference is that rental agents in the present analysis provide a complex of productive services of which the service of the capital good itself is but one. A related objection is that it now becomes more difficult to distinguish clearly between firms and households, since households, too, have a production set in the present analysis, whereas in Walrasian and neo-Walrasian theory they are identified only by initial endowments and preference sets. This, too, seems to be a false objection, since in the more traditional analyses of this type there is a relationship between endowments of capital goods and the possible supply of the productive services of those capital goods. In my argument, it is simply that the relationship between endowments of capital goods and the supply of their productive services is more complex and more explicit than is usual in these analyses. In principle, there is nothing to preclude these relationships entering neo-Walrasian analysis through the specification of household feasible consumption sets.

The only valid objection that I have found is that I have introduced indivisibilities, and therefore discontinuities, into excess demand functions via the households rather than the firms. This is undoubtedly correct, and it implies that to be compatible with the implications of imbalance theory neo-Walrasian theorists will require to come to terms with indivisibilities and other non-convexities.

But this desideratum is one that the best neo-Walrasians themselves have recognized and attempted to achieve. Once this has been achieved, however, the implications of increasing returns to scale and indivisibilities, which are essential to imbalance theory, can be introduced directly through specifications of the firm as a collection of productive resources.

In the meantime, the foregoing arguments suggest that rational behaviour by individuals implies the economic structure assumed in Walrasian and neo-Walrasian theory only if all commodities are standardized, durable and compact. This is a point to which I shall return repeatedly in the remainder of this and the following chapter.

Although the foregoing arguments have been concerned exclusively with those aspects of firm behaviour that are relevant to the hiring-versus-purchasing decision, I have shown, for that case at least, that the rational markets hypothesis prescribes reasonable economic behaviour independently of any assumption about the prevalence of equilibrium. It is apposite to argue here that, as a result, this hypothesis is also of potential importance to current neo-Walrasian developments.

There is a developing neo-Walrasian literature on disequilibrium processes and approaches to equilibrium. This literature, although highly mathematical, is well and comprehensibly surveyed and evaluated by Hahn (1977), Fisher (1976) and Weintraub (1979). These writers agree that neo-Walrasian disequilibrium analysis has been unsatisfactory because of the difficulty of specifying reasonable disequilibrium behaviour. The central problem is that disequilibrium behaviour requires firms and households to change their offer prices in the markets in which they sell and to change their bid prices in the markets in which they buy in order to strike bargains over quantities to be traded. At the same time, however, continuity of excess demand functions generally requires the assumption of perfect competition, so that the quantities bought or sold by any single agent has no effect on any prices. Clearly, agents cannot be both price-setters or negotiators and perfect competitors. The bargaining process is a characteristic of disequilibrium, while the state of perfect competition is characteristic of equilibrium.

Neo-Walrasians have sought a way round this incompatibility by introducing continuity-preserving price expectations. None the less, these assumed expectations are highly restrictive and artificial, and do not in fact lend the sort of realism to neo-Walrasian analysis that its practitioners are seeking.

Arguably, a consistent standard of what constitutes reasonable and rational disequilibrium behaviour is required. Equilibrium analysis has clearly failed to offer any useful pointers in this direction – perhaps because of the logical incompatibility of long-run equilibrium and the short-run rational maximization assumption of the disequilibrium models. Whatever the ultimate source of the difficulty, however, it is clear that those neo-Walrasians who have abandoned both general and temporary equilibrium have found no satisfactory replacement to enable them to deduce plausible decision rules for agents. This is a direct result of either the rational-maximization assumptions employed or the assumptions about expectations required to deduce decision rules. Since the method adopted in this book is to follow the implications of the assumption that individuals are rational even when it conflicts with other assumptions, we shall consider here the utility of the assumptions about expectations.

Where, in imbalance theory, various technological determinants of decision rules are specified, the neo-Walrasian disequilibrium theorists have specified particular price expectations. Indeed, in so far as they have relied on pure-exchange models, they have had little choice, since, in such models, whatever constraint is assumed to limit the maximizing proclivities of individuals must be subjective. It is not altogether surprising that the subjective approach has led to an analytical morass: one analyst's introspectively plausible assumption can easily strike another analyst as merely *ad hoc*. To rely instead on specifications of technological conditions at least has the advantage of yielding assumptions that can be tested for descriptive accuracy. Either technologies have the assumed characteristics or they do not. When they do, either the predicted outcomes are systematically found false or they are not. Indeed, this is one of the strengths claimed for imbalance theory, since in that theory decision rules as well as market characteristics are deduced both from the assumption of rational short-run maximization by individuals and from testable assumptions about the technological conditions in which decisions are taken.

There remains, of course, the difficulty that imbalance theory presupposes indivisibilities of productive resources, which generate discontinuities in excess demand functions. That, however, is a problem for Walrasians and neo-Walrasians only because of their mathematical techniques. If the mathematics are found wanting, then it is surely better to find techniques of analysis that are appropriate to the subject rather than to tailor the subject to inappropriate techniques.

4.2   MARKETS IN WALRASIAN, NEO-WALRASIAN AND NEO-KEYNESIAN THEORY

In section 4.1 I outlined the conditions in which it would be economically rational for there to exist a set of agents who conform to the Walrasian and neo-Walrasian parables in which firms hire only capital goods that involve fixed costs of production. In this section, that discussion is extended to the market. The conditions to be specified are those in which there could economically exist an agent who neither produces nor uses commodities and whose sole role is to communicate information between producers and users of commodities (including such productive services as labour).

Just such an agent was identified in chapter 3. It is the intermediary who actually generates a cash flow by providing the service of communication that, in one way or another, is provided by Walras's auctioneer or the alternative sorts of *deus ex machina* assumed by the neo-Walrasians. That is, if all commodities are compact, durable and standardized, and if there are many buyers and many sellers relative to the number of intermediaries in each market, then there can exist intermediaries with sufficient market power to determine market prices and to communicate the existence of demands to commodity producers and the existence of supplies to commodity users. In order to establish whether intermediaries can fulfil the role of the auctioneer, central market authority (Clower, 1965/1969), price-setting agent (Barro and Grossman, 1976, p. 30), trading post (Muellbauer and Portes, 1978, p. 790) or whatever, we must be clear as to the analytical role of such a *deux ex machina*. Moreover, in the neo-Keynesian analyses typified by the income–expenditure model, one finds no mention of such a *deux ex machina*. It will be convenient in this section to determine whether this is an oversight or if those analyses simply do not require an auctioneer.

We begin with the auctioneer in Walrasian and neo-Walrasian economics.

It is an elementary tenet of general equilibrium theory from Walras onwards that there is no false trading. The auctioneer starts the processes by which transactions are agreed by calling a set of prices – one for each output and asset – *au hazard*, and then prices are changed in response to the resulting excess supplies and demands. Only when the market supply and demand curves for each asset, good and service intersect simultaneously in every market is trading allowed at the corresponding price vector. In the elementary economics textbooks, it is said that the Walrasian stability conditions result from the responsiveness of prices to excess demands rather than from the responsiveness of supplies and demands to prices. Thus, if we were to suppose that there exists an actual agent who fulfils the role of the Walrasian auctioneer, that agent would act upon information about both existing prices and notional excess demands. Notional excess demands, of course, are the differences between the amounts that one side of the market would purchase and the amounts that the other side of the market would sell if they could each buy or sell all that they wanted in every other market at the prevailing price vector.

Neo-Walrasians from Clower onwards have allowed false trading, which they have introduced by limiting the information upon which the auctioneer acts or that he provides to buyers and sellers in the various markets. In neo-Walrasian theory, the auctioneer or his equivalent knows and communicates only prices and the lesser of effective supplies or demands in each market. Notional excess demands are neither communicated nor acted upon. The reason for this rejection of the basic Walrasian assumption is its lack of realism as perceived by the neo-Walrasians. That is, there appears to be no way in practice for workers to let an entrepreneur know that if they were in employment they would purchase their own outputs or create the demands for other entrepreneurs' goods which would lead indirectly to the creation of demands for their own outputs. Neo-Walrasians assert that there are no actual agents in markets to pass on that kind of information. The sort of agent that could do so would need to have information not only about prices but also about excess notional demands in every market, as well as information about the actual demands backed by existing purchasing power and the actual supplies rendered possible by the availability of inputs to sellers' production processes.

Granted that the Walrasian parable of the auctioneer is highly unrealistic, are the neo-Walrasian parables of central market authorities, trading posts, suitably programmed computers, etc., any more realistic? Neo-Walrasians would presumably argue that realism is enhanced by doing away with the assumption that there is no false trading. Perhaps so, but if realism is the objective, then why keep the analytical equivalent of the auctioneer whose existence is no more realistic than the assumption of general market-clearing? The answer, I suppose, is that it somehow makes more palatable the assumption that there are no effective limitations on computational capacity anywhere in the neo-Walrasian economy. We have already seen in chapter 2 that such limitations cannot be accommodated in long-run equilibrium theories – including those derived from Walras.

In order to demonstrate this point, let us suppose that all commodities produced or traded in a neo-Walrasian economy are compact, durable and highly standardized. We know from the theory of markets that, if such an economy is also competitive in the sense that there are many buyers and sellers of each commodity, every market can have an intermediary who determines prevailing prices and who receives all intimations of a desire to trade from both sides of the market. We also know from section 4.1 that all firms can economically hire rather than buy capital goods which would otherwise engender fixed costs of production by the firm. These are the circumstances that embody those technological conditions of production and exchange that are most favourable to the economically (if not mathematically) simple Walrasian and neo-Walrasian parables.

There is a difficulty here in that these are also the conditions that favour the holding of inventories rather than the queueing of customers for producers' outputs. The issue then is one of comparison between inventory-holding as a means of taking up discrepancies between effective supplies and demands and the existence of inter-mediaries who ensure that in every market supplies (including new outputs from production processes) either maximize profits or utilities at the existing price-vector, or they are just equal to demands that are constrained by outcomes in other markets. Evidently there are two aspects to this issue. One is that intermediaries ensure that transactions in every market are agreed simultaneously on the basis of knowledge of the simultaneous outcomes of the trading processes in every other market. The second aspect is that only one side of the market is rationed, so that actual transactions are determined by either the profit-maximization behaviour of firms or the utility-maximizing behaviour of households.

Consider the first aspect of this issue.

In neo-Walrasian theory the assumption that trades in different markets must be agreed simultaneously involves the assumption that expenditure in the current period must be met in full or in part from this period's income. Otherwise, shortness of demand in the labour market would have no effect on the demand for consumption goods and, therefore, would not imply shortness of demands in the goods market. However, if we are to insist that incomes in this trading period finance expenditures in this period, we shall require intermediaries to acquire, process and disseminate a very considerable quantity of information. Having acquired the information about the notional supplies and demands of every household and firm, the intermediary will have to inform each of them of their incomes – which must of course be calculated from the raw information about notional quantities. This latter calculation itself requires the prior determination of the magnitudes of the shortnesses of supplies and demands in the markets for all commodities. Even if we ignore the Radner problem, a tremendous amount of computational capacity is required by the intermediaries. If we maintain our assumption that intermediaries are rational, allocatively efficient firms, it is surely reasonable to consider means of reducing the requirement for computational capacity. For it must be remembered that inter-mediaries can function in a market only if their collective transactions costs are less than the savings on both sides of the market that are made possible by intermediated exchange. For this reason, reductions in information and computing costs render the position of the intermediaries more secure and also increase their profits.

It is not necessary to invent new institutions to reduce these costs. All that is required is to assume that the finance for expenditure during the current period was arranged during preceding periods. For there is no obvious mathematical or other analytical reason to preclude the assumption that consumption this week or month is paid for out of liquid resources inherited from the preceding week or month. In the case of households, such liquid resources would include, in addition to previous savings held as cash, bank deposits, last period's wage or salary, any profit, interest or other transfer receipts *plus* any net borrowings arranged before the purchases are made. In the case of firms, expenditures are financed from previously accumulated liquid reserves and from previously arranged borrowings. The survival-motivated management team will hardly commit its firm to expenditures without first assuring itself that the finance necessary for the expenditures will be available. Any expenditure must be met either by prior incomes or by borrowing unless purchasers are to pass fraudulent cheques and default on their debts.

This is hardly to suggest that firms and households fail to take into account their expectations of current incomes when deciding upon current expenditure. It is entirely plausible that expectations of earnings in the current period will be held with complete confidence. None the less, there is no obvious difference of kind between the expectations of income in the current period and expectations of incomes in future periods. Even the concept of time preference only indicates that earlier incomes are valued more highly than later incomes. Both present and future incomes are still valued according to the same principles, while past incomes either have become wealth or no longer exist.

What the proposed procedure does is to require both notional supply and notional demand decisions to be made in advance of trading in every market. We still have to have some way of reconciling the inevitable differences between notional supply and notional demand decisions by individual firms and households.

Two such means were identified in chapter 3. These are fluctuations in inventory levels and fluctuations in order-books. Since we already know inventory fluctuations to be the more compatible with a world in which all commodities are compact, durable and highly standardized, and such commodities are required if the Walrasian and neo-Walrasian parables are to make economic sense, I shall first consider inventory fluctuations as a means of reconciling actual supplies with actual demands when the notional magnitudes differ.

Inventory fluctuation

No new theoretical propositions are required to show that inventories render the auctioneer redundant in the reconciliation of supplies and demands. The elementary textbook versions of Keynesian theory will suffice.

The role of inventories in Keynesian theory is to render firms' output decisions subsequent in time to the relevant demand decisions manifested in the markets in which firms sell. The elementary textbooks maintain that an unanticipated increase in demand is communicated to sellers by an unanticipated reduction in inventories, while an unanticipated fall in demand is made manifest by an unanticipated increase in inventories. This is the essence of the mainstream Keynesian account of the income multiplier. That is, the unintended reduction (say) in inventories leads to an increase in firms' outputs and a simultaneous increase in demands for direct inputs, including labour. The increased incomes of workers and other sellers in the factor markets lead to further increases in demands and reductions in inventories until rising incomes raise savings to equality with investment and net autonomous expenditures.

This entirely standard account of the multiplier process evidently requires that information about changing supplies and demands be conveyed by the passage of time rather than by the Walrasian or neo-Walrasian auctioneer. Any increase in demands in this period reduces inventories in this period, leading to increases in both outputs and incomes next period. The increased incomes lead income recipients to increase demands in the following period so that the cycle repeats itself on an ever smaller scale – provided, of course, that savings and other leakages from the rounds of expenditure continue to be significant.

The virtue of this procedure is that it represents a tremendous saving in information costs over the Walrasian and neo-Walrasian parables. At any one time, each firm and household has to take limited decisions on the basis of limited previous experience. Production decisions are taken in response to previous manifestations of demands, and consumption decisions are taken in response to previous changes in incomes. No one is required to consider the manifestations of conditions of demand or supply in more than one market at any one time. The passage of time replaces the auctioneer in communicating supply and demand constraints to agents.

One aspect of the auctioneer's role in Walrasian and neo-Walrasian theory that is not explicitly represented in neo-Keynesian theory is that of ensuring that the magnitude of desired transactions on the short side of each market is determined by either the profit-maximizing behaviour of firms or the utility-maximizing behaviour of households. Without the auctioneer or some similar arrangement to provide information to both sides of every market, it is possible that actual trades will not satisfy even the short side of any market. That is, even in markets where there are excess demands (the supply side is the short side of the market), would-be purchasers will not actually buy up the entire supply because of ignorance about the identities or locations of the effective suppliers. In markets where there are excess supplies (the demand side is the short side of the market), ignorance can prevent the satisfaction of even that constrained demand.

While ignorance of the sort just described renders it difficult, if not impossible, to tell the detailed stories about temporary equilibrium and disequilibrium processes that are attempted by neo-Walrasians, it is not clear that it has any such crucial effect on the simple Keynesian parables. Undoubtedly, such ignorance in Keynesian models will affect the quantitative results, but it will not affect predictions of the directions of changes.

To see this, let us suppose that, after an increase in some autonomous expenditure, some effective demands are unsatisfied as a result of a lack of buyers' information about the identities or locations of commodity producers. This ignorance will reduce the magnitude of the decrement to producers' inventories, thereby reducing the strength of the expansionary market signals. But all that is involved here is a reduction in the aggregate marginal propensity to consume out of additional income and wealth. The effect of that reduction in the realized propensity to consume out of increments to income is, of course, a lower value of the expansionary multiplier. Unless ignorance is absolute, however, some multiplier effects will still be realized. That is, income will rise by more than the initial increase in autonomous expenditures, and employment will increase by more than is required to satisfy the demands that gave rise to that increment of autonomous expenditure in the first place.

These comments are less likely to apply to downward multiplier effects since it is not necessary to know who supplies particular commodities in order to refrain from buying them. If there is any significant reduction in the downward magnitude of multiplier processes it is more likely to be an inheritance from a previous expansion. That is, ignorance during an expansionary phase of the trade cycle does not necessarily imply that effective demands are never satisfied. It might be that it takes more time for would-be purchasers and sellers to identify and locate one another. In consequence, the earlier rounds of the multiplier process will entail smaller magnitudes but the later rounds will entail larger magnitudes. To the extent that ignorance delays rather than eliminates actual transactions, it lengthens the interval of time required for the multiplier process to work itself out and does not actually reduce the eventual magnitude of the multiplier. In consequence, as the economy moves from a phase of expansion into a phase of contraction, the effects of the downward multiplier are more likely to be mitigated over a longer period of time by the inheritance of the multiplier process from the expansionary period. There is nothing surprising in this, however, since it is just another twist to the Goodwin–Hicks theory of the trade cycle (cf. Goodwin, 1951; Hicks, 1950).

It is important to be clear that ignorance does more than simply affect the time-pattern of the multiplier processes. If the interval of time between an increase in incomes, which creates a specific demand, and the discovery of a supplier is sufficiently long, it is altogether possible that a reversal of fortunes will extinguish that demand before it is satisfied. One role of the auctioneer is in effect to preclude this possibility. Since, as far as I am aware, no Keynesian has suggested an alternative means of limiting this ignorance, we must consider whether it indicates a crucial oversight. If it does, then

Keynesians, like Walrasians and neo-Walrasians, must rely on the auctioneer or its analytical equivalent.

In considering this issue, I shall continue to adopt the approach that has informed the previous developments in the theory of markets. That is, I shall determine whether there is a rational agent who will find it worthwhile to limit the extent of ignorance in the market.

Ignorance of the sort that was considered above generates what in chapter 3 were called 'shortage costs'. I argue that the existence of shortage costs is essential if there is to be a concentration of power in any market. Although that analysis is not predicated on any assumption that the magnitude of threatened shortage costs would always be known, the prospective source generally will be clear. Once we turn to consider shortage costs that are macroeconomic in origin, the specific sources cannot be anticipated any more than can their magnitudes.

Without an auctioneer, sellers' shortage costs can arise from either effective demand failures or ignorance of the identities and locations of would-be buyers. Although the sellers in such cases will know only too well the magnitude of their own excess supply, there is no market signal to distinguish between a failure of demand and ignorance. On the other side of the market, if buyers are suffering shortage costs because they are unable to obtain needed supplies, they will have no means of distinguishing between their own ignorance about an existing and willing seller on the one hand and, on the other hand, the absence of any seller willing to part with the commodity at the current price. One thing is clear, however. If either buyers or sellers believe that they might face significant shortage costs owing to ignorance, they will rationally undertake the expenditure of any amount that is less than the expected, consequent reduction in shortage costs. In a sense, they will try to engage in an optimal search, but the search will be concerned with the shifting of constraints rather than just the sampling of market information.

The ignorance-reducing activities that are in fact given considerable attention by businessmen are those required to establish strong goodwill relationships with their customers and suppliers. It is these relationships that are intended to minimize ignorance and uncertainty over supplies of inputs and demands for outputs. Indeed, this concern to minimize uncertainty as well as ignorance leads to goodwill competition among rival firms.

The essence of the goodwill relationship is reliability. Not least, the users of a commodity are anxious to ensure that they will be able to acquire inputs to their production processes – or, in the case of households, consumption goods – as and when they require them. If such commodities are in short supply from time to time, users will want to be given some priority in the allocation of whatever commodities are available in order to minimize the consequential shortage costs. Similarly, the producers of any commodity will want to minimize the fluctuations in demands for their outputs – even in the event of failures of effective demand in the markets in which they sell – by getting priority in the orders placed by their customers. These goodwill relationships reduce uncertainties on both sides. Even if future demands or supplies are uncertain in the aggregate, goodwill relationships can at least avoid the vagaries associated with uncertain sources of what custom or supplies are available. In other words, strong goodwill relationships reduce uncertainty by reducing precisely the sort of ignorance that the auctioneer is assumed by neo-Walrasians to prevent.

In general, then, goodwill renders superfluous the position of the auctioneer in so far as his role is to eliminate ignorance about effective supplies and demands in the market.

What we have now found is that three of the roles of the auctioneer in Walrasian and neo-Walrasian theories are economically filled in markets for compact, durable and standardized commodities by rationally maximizing agents. It is even possible that in some markets all of these roles will be economically filled by a single class of agent: the intermediaries who occupy the interiors of the markets. They will set prices to both sides of the markets if they have a predominance of power resulting from insufficient producer and user concentration to allow any agent on either side of the market to approach minimum efficient scale in exchange. In addition, inter- mediaries who hold inventories of the commodities in which they trade can respond to fluctuations in those inventories by reducing or increasing their purchases from producers, who can change their own production rates accordingly. If, at the prevailing set of market prices, producers are unwilling to meet existing demands, then intermediaries can ration users. Both economy in the transmission of information about excess supplies and demands and orderly rationing are provided by the goodwill relationships that agents on both sides and in the interior of each market will rationally maintain. Thus, the third of the economic functions of the auctioneer is fulfilled.

The only remaining function of the auctioneer is the holding up of transactions until all agents on both sides of every market have settled upon their optimal (but possibly rationed) supplies and demands. However, this function is nothing but a logical artefact to render equilibrium analysis possible. Because it does not describe any activity that is actually undertaken in real markets, it is unlikely to be a profitable activity, and so it will not be undertaken by rational agents. It thus has no place in the present analysis. If, moreover, the present line of argument is right, equilibrium analysis requires this function to be undertaken by some *deus ex machina*. In consequence, as long as – but only as long as – economists theorize within the framework of the equilibrium of general economic systems, it seems likely that they will be unable to do away with the auctioneer.

Queue fluctuations

Markets in which commodities are produced only to order, and in which customers queue for outputs, will be characterized by brokers if there are any intermediaries at all. For, as we saw in chapter 3, the commodities traded on such markets are likely to be bulky, perishable and/or specialized in use. These characteristics severely limit economies of scale in storage, transportation and communication. We have also seen that the scale economies in storage and transportation are important to intermediaries who buy commodities and hold them in stock for resale – that is, for jobbers. Brokers, however, depend less on economies of large scale in transactions than on frequency of transactions in the market. Buyers or sellers who come to the market only infrequently are unlikely to find it worthwhile to maintain a wide range of goodwill relationships in that market, and they will not in general have a great deal of experience, expertise and current knowledge of market procedures, prices and trends in supplies and demands. The broker who continually arranges transactions for the occasional traders will have such experience, expertise and knowledge. His commission is in effect the price he charges for it. The savings to buyers and sellers is a savings of exactly those information costs that are specified in search theories.

In order to have a role in the market, the broker's costs in arranging transactions, like those of the jobber, must be less than the savings on these information costs that brokerage affords to producers and users. It is often the case, however, that brokers do not restrict their activities to intermediation, but provide that service as part of a package. It is possible that such brokerage services are provided as a loss-leader to make the whole package more attractive. In that case, the broker's transactions costs might be no less than producers' and users' savings. In general, however, there must be some producers' and/or users' savings, and it is these that will provide the basis of any market power that brokers might have.

We have seen, in regard to markets in which commodities are suitable for intermediation by jobbers, that both sides of the market will be price-takers only when there is a sufficient concentration of market power among the intermediaries. This concentration requires that intermediaries be able to reduce the cash flows of producers and users without facing any serious threat of a loss of cash flow from retaliatory action. This position is possible if the jobbers can realize economies of scale that the traders on either side of the market cannot.

The position is similar in markets with brokers. Provided that neither producers nor users come to the market sufficiently frequently to acquire as much experience, expertise and current knowledge as the brokers, the brokers will be able to reduce cash flows to firms on both sides of the market by increasing their information costs. If they do this selectively, they will impair either the profits or the competitive position of the firms with which they refuse to trade. However, it is unlikely that brokers will be in such a position of power with respect to both sides of the market.

The producers of commodities are not in practice infrequent traders in their product markets. Users, on the other hand, often are. Archetypical products that are produced to order for queueing customers are buildings and ships. Even large shipping lines do not purchase a passenger liner or a freighter more than once a year and sometimes not more than once in four or five years. Office buildings and factories are long-lived. Firms purchase factory buildings only as part of major investment projects. Net additions to firm's office buildings are acquired only when the firm has enjoyed a period of substantial growth, requiring increased numbers of administrative personnel. In consequence, producers will rely on brokers not for general information about the state of demand or prevailing prices, but only for the identities of potential customers. If, in these circumstances, brokers attempt to use their market power to reduce output prices, the large operating leverages and therefore potential shortage costs of the producers will rationally induce them to integrate forward and thereby to eliminate the independent broker altogether. It follows that the broker in such markets will have market power *vis à vis* users that is greater than his market power *vis à vis* producers. This will enable the broker to exact his commission but not otherwise to determine the general level of prices.

For these reasons, it does not seem at all likely that the broker in markets where queue fluctuations take up discrepancies between supplies and demands will be able to fulfil the price-setting role of the Walrasian and neo-Walrasian auctioneer. It is equally clear that the broker can fulfil the auctioneer's role in limiting users' ignorance of current supplies in the market and producers' ignorance of current demands.

Finally in this regard, we consider the effect of queue fluctuations on simple Keynesian models.

One effect of having queue fluctuations accommodate excess supplies and demands is clearly to reduce the magnitude of any multiplier processes in the short run. To the extent that any increases in demand are reflected only in thicker order-books, there is no corresponding increase in expenditure to give rise to further consequential rounds of spending by households. Thus, in the short run the effect of queueing for outputs is the same as the effect of ignorance, since both reduce the reliance that can be placed on multiplier effects.

There is, however, an important long-run difference in the effects of ignorance and queueing. Demand deficiencies resulting from ignorance carry with them no market or other signals that such deficiencies will be made good in the future. Increases in demands that result in thicker order-books, to the contrary, do carry with them a clear signal that increases in output are warranted. Firms with growing order-books thus have an incentive to increase the rate at which orders for their outputs can be filled. There is an inducement effect to invest in increased production capacity. It follows that, even though demands are unlikely to result directly in upward multiplier effects, they are likely to generate upward accelerator effects provided that the trend is maintained over substantial periods of time. The usual multiplier–accelerator interactions can then proceed. This is a point of more than passing theoretical interest. Its policy implications are important and will be developed in some detail in chapters 6–9.

5

Expectation, Survival and Economic Structure

5.0 INTRODUCTION

Two lines of analysis have been developed in the two preceding chapters. One is concerned with the institutional composition of different markets; the other is concerned with the ways in which prices and quantities are determined in different markets. Although the exposition of each of these issues has been distinct from the other, the analyses are integral parts of the theory of markets. In this chapter, both lines of analysis are seen to be essential to the development of our macroeconomic theory. We shall see that the theory of markets generates a specification of the institutional structure and dynamic processes that characterized macroeconomic systems comprising rational firms and households.

Once we specify the structure and dynamics of the sort of economic systems with which we are concerned in this book, we meet head-on the most controversial issue of contemporary economic debate: the issue of pricing. If prices are sufficiently flexible, then it is claimed that all is for the best in the best of all possible worlds. If the assumption of price flexibility is thought to be unrealistic, then quantities are assumed to be flexible and incomes change to eliminate excess supplies and demands. The argument of the two preceding chapters indicates that the degree of price flexibility will be different in different markets, and, moreover, that if we adhere strictly to the assumption that firms rationally maximize short-run gross profits then the price and quantity responses to excess supplies and demands can be determined analytically rather than by controversial assumption.

We shall find in this chapter that the macroeconomic structure deduced within the framework of imbalance theory is much more like that assumed by Keynes than that assumed in Walrasian and neo-Walrasian theory. The fundamental reason for the similarity between imbalance-theoretic propositions and Keynes's assumptions appears to be the crucial importance accorded in both theories to the passage of time in the processes of production and exchange. As was pointed out in section 4.2, the only element in the logical role of the Walrasian auctioneer that cannot be undertaken by rationally maximizing agents is to render exchange instantaneous. It will be seen in section 5.2 that Walrasian and neo-Walrasian theories require that production be effectively instantaneous as well.

In taking the time-consuming nature of production and exchange into account, the theorist has no choice but to include expectations and, possibly but not necessarily, uncertainty in his analysis. In Walrasian and neo-Walrasian analyses, however, it is possible but not necessary to take expectations into account and, because of the Radner problem, wholly impossible to analyse uncertainty. Uncertainty is at the heart of imbalance theory because that theory is predicated upon limited rates of learning. This limitation prevents agents from perceiving any well defined constraints upon long-run maximizing activities. The same limitation renders the rational expectations hypothesis logically incompatible with imbalance theory. The fundamental assumption of the rational expectations hypothesis – that information is scarce relative to the capacity to use it – is a necessary condition for the existence of long-run equilibrium, and at the same time it is wholly incompatible with the logical foundation of imbalance theory. This hypothesis is, in consequence, a natural extension of any long-run equilibrium theory and in particular of Walrasian and neo-Walrasian theories.

We have seen in section 2.3 that the assumption that rates of learning are limited implies that the rationally managed firm will have a comparative advantage in the undertaking of investment projects that raise the shadow prices of its resources, especially if the project also entails increases in the scales of those of the firm's resources having the highest shadow prices. As a result, the short-run composition of the firm's resources, by determining the relative shadow prices of those resources, effectively determines the most profitable directions in which the firm should shift its resource constraints in the long run. The implication of this result can be stated in two equivalent ways: first, the constraints on the rational-maximizing propensities of the firm's managers are endogenous in the long run, and, second, the optimal directions of learning and investment by firms are determined endogenously. Using the first form of words, it is clear that the necessary conditions for the application of mathematical programming algorithms are not met in the long run.

Using the second form of words, it is clear that imbalance theory overcomes an incompleteness of the rational expectations hypothesis. Let us consider this second point in some detail.

The endogeneity of directions of learning and investment in imbalance theory leads to the specification of focusing and inducement effects. In particular, firms will seek technical and organizational changes that utilize existing, preferably under-utilized, physical and human resources. Some of these resources will undoubtedly be specialized in exchange. The human resources (i.e. the personnel) of the firm that are specialized in exchange activities will be able to render services to the firm as a result of knowledge acquired in the course of engaging in those activities. Indeed, the development of such knowledge is a key element in the imbalance theory of firm behaviour. In effect, this developing knowledge can be treated as the evolution, by the personnel of the firm, of models of the markets in which the firm trades – models that yield the decision rules they employ.

It is a necessary condition for the existence of long-run equilibrium that directions of learning are specified exogenously and in advance of the undertaking of any economic activities at all – whether in production or in exchange. To assume that this condition is satisfied is tantamount to assuming that there is no endogenous evolution of decision rules, or therefore of the models that might describe those rules. Since the rational expectations hypothesis can be used only in tandem with equilibrium theories, it does not seem possible to generalize that hypothesis to explain the choice or development of the models that agents in effect use to formulate unbiased expectations and associated decision rules. Because the models that yield unbiased estimators (or expectations) must be determined before the rational expectations hypothesis can be used, the hypothesis itself cannot be used to show any particular equilibrium model less 'correct' than any other. It is therefore equally permissible for the new classicals to add the rational expectations hypothesis to a Walrasian model of a sequence economy to demonstrate that no government policies have real effects, and for Keynesians of various schools to add rational expectations to an income–expenditure model (e.g. Tobin, 1980; Buiter, 1980) or to a neo-Walrasian model (cf. Hahn, 1977, 1980) to demonstrate that government policies do have real effects.

It would, however, be quite wrong to reject, with the rational expectations hypothesis, Muth's (1961) essential insight that rational agents will seek efficiently to use the information available to them and that they will try to avoid forming systematically false expectations. In this chapter, therefore, we shall *deduce* a macroeconomic structure and set of dynamic decision rules within the various markets on the assumption that buyers and sellers can recognize systematic errors in their expectations. To do so, we shall need to determine the limits to possible dynamic outcomes in the various classes of product and financial (or asset) markets. Provided that all propositions are deduced within the framework of imbalance theory, then limited rates of learning, endogeneity of the directions of learning and the evolution of agents' 'models' giving rise to unbiased expectations will be implicit in our results. We shall see in section 5.4, however, that the role of expectations in the determination of money wages and employment – that is, in the labour market – is more muted than in the other markets, although the survival assumption remains of central importance.

5.1 THE PRODUCT MARKETS

The proposition that the only essential role of the Walrasian auctioneer is to eliminate the passage of time as an aspect of production and exchange does not appear to have been recognized by economists working to eliminate that logical artefact. Economists developing models of both general disequilibrium and temporary equilibrium have been trying mainly to resolve the issue first raised by Arrow (1959). He had pointed out that there is no one in competitive models to set prices, since every trader in every market must be assumed to be a price-taker. To assume a rationally maximizing price-setter is to assume that competition is not perfect, and this, generally, entails the introduction of discontinuities in the excess demand functions. We have already seen in section 4.1 that the avoidance of these discontinuities in a disequilibrium framework requires special assumptions about expectations and firm survival. With regard to temporary equilibrium models, Hahn (1977) has scotched the notion that Clower or Leijonhufvud or Malinvaud or anyone else contributing to this literature has manage to do away with the auctioneer. In Hahn's words (1977, pp. 35-6),

It has become commonplace to say that Keynesian economics is economics without the Walrasian auctioneer. . . . In the 1960s a number of non-tâtonnement models of adjustment were studied. Trade took place at 'false' prices and the value at going prices of what was actually bought was always equal to the value of what was actually sold. These models, however, still need the auctioneer.

Moreover, during the adjustment process agents were quantity constrained just as they are in the papers which are so popular now. In the later versions even Clower's axiom that only money buys goods was included, and still the auctioneer appeared. He did so because no one had the faintest idea how prices were actually changed and it seemed reasonable to suppose that, when more was known, it would be found correct that prices rose when there were unsatisfied buyers and fell when there were unsatisfied sellers. . . . Now this last supposition may turn out to be far from correct.

What then about the neo-Keynesian income–expenditure model developed by Hicks, Hansen, Klein, Tobin et al.? The usual assumption in these models is that prices are constant or perhaps rise 'slowly' over the range of unemployment equilibria, and that they rise quickly and apparently without limit whenever any attempt is made to expand the economy beyond the full-employment equilibrium level of output. The process by which prices and wages are established or raised was, until very recently, left to intuition rather than analysis. The need for a theory to explain how and why different markets work differently was recognized by Okun (1981), who distinguished between 'auction' markets and 'customer' markets corresponding roughly to markets with short-run pricing and long-run pricing, respectively. Unfortunately, Okun's analysis is incomplete, since he did not explain who will be the auctioneer in the auction markets or how price-setters will achieve that position in either class of market. However, in so far as he considers the technology of exchange at all, his analysis and my theory of markets (Moss, 1981) described in chapter 3 are compatible.

Although neo-Keynesians have had remarkably little to say about the nature of the exchange process, Keynes, the post-Keynesian school and the neo-Walrasian school have all been concerned with this issue. There are, or so I shall argue, substantial insights to be derived from Keynes, and from some of the post-Keynesians and neo-Walrasians. However, in some cases the two schools use the same words for different concepts and assume that their own definitions of those words are Keynes's. This is particularly the case with 'effective demand'. As will be seen in section 5.2, the different definitions attached to the same words entail fundamental differences in analysis. It will be helpful, in the presentation of the present theory, to sort out the analytical relationships between Keynes, the post-Keynesians and neo-Walrasians in order to be clear which of their analytical categories are useful and where imbalance theory stands in relation to these established schools of economic thought.

We begin with Keynes.

In the *General Theory*, Keynes (1936) assumed that output decisions are reached by entrepreneurs on the basis of both the costs that they expect will be required to produce outputs started now, and the prices that they expect to prevail for different volumes of current production starts when the resulting outputs are completed for sale or use. Thus, the supply curve that is relevant to the current production decisions of the firm is that which relates costs incurred over the period of production to outputs one period of production hence – the period of production being the interval of time between the decision within a firm to change its rate of throughput and the consequent change in the rate of output completed for sale or use. The demand function that is relevant to the production decisions of a firm relates the various rates of output one period of production hence to the prices at which it is expected that those volumes will be able to be sold (Keynes, 1936, pp. 24, 46–7, 55). The key passages in the *General Theory* are these:

Time usually elapses . . . between the incurring of costs by the producer (with the consumer in view) and the purchaser of the output by the ultimate consumer. Meanwhile, the entrepreneur has to form the best expectations he can as to what consumers will be prepared to pay (directly or indirectly) after the elapse of what may be a lengthy period; and *he has no choice but to be guided by these expectations if he is to produce at all by processes which occupy time.* (p. 46; emphasis added)

Keynes identified two classes of expectation, short-term expectation and long-term expectation:

[Short-term expectation] is concerned with the price which a manufacturer can expect to get for his 'finished' output at the time when he commits himself to starting the process which will produce it; output being finished (from the point of view of the manufacturer) when it is ready to be used or to be sold to a second party. Long-term expectation relates to prospective returns on investments in capital equipment. (pp. 46–7)

Evidently, Keynes presumed that both outputs and price expectations (not prices) are determined within individual firms at the time when production is started or the level of throughput is changed. The actual volume of throughput is determined in the light of the decision-makers' state of short-term expectation, i.e. their expectation of the price that that volume of output will fetch when completed one period of production hence. The volume of production starts chosen now is that volume which is expected to maximize the gross profit of the firm when the resulting output is completed for sale. This amounts to the assumption that all product-market pricing is short-run pricing.

The problem with Keynes's presumption here is the finding in sections 3.3 and 3.4 above that the conditions in which short-run pricing will characterize any particular market are not at all general. Moreover, to the extent that it is economically feasible for firms to determine their output prices on the basis of long-run investment considerations, they will rationally do so – even though there will inevitably be some short-run, competitive factors taken into consideration. Indeed, in those markets where outputs are produced only to order, the state of short-term expectation must always entail virtually complete confidence, since both outputs and prices one period of production hence are already contractually determined. Only long-term expectations have any role in such markets. Since queueing by customers is common in these markets because suppliers are subject to substantial shortage costs arising from high fixed costs of production, it is likely that any decision in light of long-term expectations to increase production capacities will entail substantial and time-consuming investment projects. Clearly, the cash flows from trading – and therefore the mark-ups and sales volumes – of such firms will have to be such as to support these investment projects in capacity expansion. Thus, it will be costs and long-term expectations, but not short-term expectations, that will determine the pricing and output strategies of firms in such markets.

At the other extreme are markets in which only short-term expectations enter into the pricing decision. These are markets for commodities for which carrying costs might be substantial (because they are either bulky or perishable) and which certainly are highly standardized so that they can be produced in the speculative hope that they will be sold even though supplies and demands are volatile in relation to each other. In such markets, it is clear that only short-term expectations will affect price and current output decisions although investment by the producers of those commodities will require them to formulate favourable long-term expectations. Both classes of expectation are important, but each affects a different set of decisions.

Between these two extremes are markets for commodities that are sufficiently well standardized to be produced for stock and are sufficiently durable and compact that their carrying costs are not prohibitive and for which supplies relative to demands are not highly volatile. The markets for these commodities will be characterized predominantly by long-run pricing. None the less, if demand conditions should deteriorate with unusual severity and/or persistence, then, as I argued in section 3.4, these prices are altogether likely to decline.

If the foregoing remarks are correct, the roles of the states of long- and short-term expectations are evidently different in the markets for different commodities.

In those markets where customers queue and production is undertaken only to order, we have seen that there is no role whatever for short-term expectations. In these markets, realized changes in queue lengths (hence the state of short-term demand) are very likely to affect long-term expectations and therefore desired magnitudes of investment in capacity expansion. One would obviously expect increasing queue lengths to focus the attention of managers of firms producing for these markets on the potential for profitable expansion of their existing capacities. If the focusing effects were sufficiently strong, they might be led to increase mark-ups in order to provide the necessary internal finance for a permanently increased rate of capacity growth.

But what if the state of short-term demand in markets with strict long-pricing processes were declining? The manifestation of such a decline will be shortening queue lengths, which give rise to inducement effects. That is, if a firm with a high operating leverage in conditions of declining demand is to survive, it will have to diversify into expanding markets, to reorganize, to merge with another firm in the same industry or to seek some vertical integration to improve the efficiency (from its own point of view) of the market. What seems wholly unlikely is that such a firm could reduce its prices significantly and remain in business. The reason such firms adopt their marketing methods is because short-falls of demand or price reductions relative to costs quickly become ruinous. In these circumstances, the firm can survive only as long as its cumulative losses do not exhaust its liquid reserves and its borrowing capacity. In practice, borrowing capacity is likely to shrink in the face of sustained losses by a firm, and a high operating leverage implies that liquid reserves will be used up at a rapid rate. Of course, those firms that are bankrupted first will enable the survivors to increase their market shares. But this implies a reduction in employed production capacity rather than any significant reduction in prices relative to costs. On balance, one would expect the losses to firms producing for these markets to result almost entirely from volume rather than mark-up reductions.

In markets characterized by short-run pricing alone, the states of long- and short-term expectation are likely to have limited, if any, interaction. Short-term expectation in these markets determines current production intentions (hence the planned flow of outputs one period of production hence), while long-term expectations determine the magnitude of investments. The uncertainties of future demands relative to supplies militate against wholesale revisions of long-term expectations on the basis of failures to realize previously held short-term expectations. At the least, we would expect short-term expectations to be falsified in the same direction continuously over a long period of time before there were any substantial effect on long-term expectations.

The dynamics of pricing in such markets were analysed in section 3.4. We saw there that excess demands will lead price-setters rationally to raise prices as the prospect of users' shortage costs rises relative to the carrying costs of the commodity. Excess supplies lead price-setters rationally to reduce prices in order to induce users to hold larger stocks, provided that producers expect that their shortage costs would otherwise exceed any lost profits on the volume sold at the lower prices. What was not considered in section 3.4 was who the price-setters would be in such markets. This issue will be taken up in section 5.3 since, although of relevance to the product markets, it is most germane to the organized financial and commodity exchanges. Indeed, a complete analysis of short-run pricing is not possible without an integral analysis of the organized exchanges.

The remaining category of markets is for commodities that are produced for stock and in which, because supplies and demands are not volatile, long-run pricing is the norm although short-run considerations lead exceptionally to revisions of long-term expectation. In such markets, the under-fulfilment of short-term expectation creates inducement effects that necessarily limit long-run investment plans. However, the over-fulfilment of short-run expectations will, at most, generate only a focusing effect. That is, excess finance could lead sufficiently ambitious management teams to seek avenues for increased rates of investment. According to the theory of prices reported in chapter 3, these upward-focusing effects might entail some increases in profit margins to provide internal finance that is additional to the unexpected reserves. The extent to which it does so will depend on the extent to which increased growth rates are expected to be permanent. The investment-constraining inducement effect results from unexpectedly low or negative additions to financial reserves. The firm that was counting on cash flows from trading to finance the investments to which it is already committed will either have to find additional external finance or have to curtail or delay

work on current investment projects. The first of these options –
increasing the external finance of the firm – is not always feasible or
economic when the need for the finance is a result of sustained
adverse trading results. At the very least, one would expect lenders to
exact a higher rate of interest for such finance than the firm is accus-
tomed to pay in less difficult times. This will in itself reduce future
cash flows, and therefore internal finance and borrowing capacity.
The second option – curtailment and delay of current projects – is
also unlikely to be attractive and will certainly reduce the future
investment capacity of the firm. As a matter of definition, the firm's
rate of return on capital will be reduced by such a course of action,
since it will have additional assets equal to the costs of the curtailed
or delayed project but no corresponding increases in income. Since
the problem will have arisen from reduced current net earnings, the
future ability of the firm to generate increased external or equity
finance cannot be enhanced by curtailment. Whichever way the firm
turns, its financial ability to undertake long-term investment will be
constrained by the under-fulfilment of its short-term expectation –
a consequence that is independent of the state of long-term expectation within the firm.

Even in adverse trading conditions, there are forces that would
make firms' managers reluctant to reduce their mark-ups. If demand
conditions are inelastic in the short run, the difficulty and increased
cost of acquiring external finance would if anything lead firms to
raise profit margins in order to generate additional internal finance
with which to meet their current obligations. The extent to which a
firm would react in this way will clearly depend on its ability to draw
down existing liquid reserves which had been built up to meet
precisely this circumstance. If demands are elastic but the conditions
of demand faced by a firm are deteriorating, prices can decline as
long as the resulting revenues are sufficient to meet the firm's financial commitments. We shall see presently, however, that these
financial commitments typically impose strict limits on short-run
price flexibility – even in elastic demand conditions.

Macroeconomic price flexibility: preliminary conclusions

Although the issue of price flexibility has typically been considered
in macroeconomic (including general equilibrium) terms, the dynamics
of price adjustment are microeconomic in nature. Once one attempts
to analyse the microeconomic dynamics of macroeconomic price
flexibility, it becomes clear just how much the assumption of price

flexibility depends on the auctioneer and how much conclusions that price flexibility is or could be optimal depend upon the assumption that firms do not hold productive resources in the long run.

There can be no doubt that rationally managed firms will seek to hold in the long run those productive resources that are specialized and bulky. The holding and acquisition of these resources by individual firms renders long-run pricing preferable to short-run pricing. That is, to the extent that the costs of acquiring such resources are greater than the available revenue over any short period of time, firms will set prices to generate the necessary flow of internal finance and the repayments and servicing of debts incurred to purchase the resources. When the fixed and other indirect costs of production of firms in these circumstances are large in relation to normal income, and therefore to available reserves and borrowing capacities, firms producing non-standard commodities will seek to isolate themselves from the consequences of short-run demand variations. This explains the practice in some industries of queueing customers.

In general, then, long-run pricing will characterize such markets with the relationship between prices and costs (the profit margin or the mark-up) being determined by the state of long-term expectation of those with, collectively, sufficient market power to determine prices. If prices are to respond to excess supplies and demands, it must be because either mark-ups or costs or both respond to changing conditions of demand in relation to production capacities. Let us consider these in turn.

Declining sales volumes have been seen above to imply increased mark-ups, if anything, unless managers believe that declining demands are elastic. Even if such a belief is held, however, mark-ups must be set in the short run to provide the cash flow from trading that is required to meet long-run commitments. Since the major source of such commitments is investment, mark-ups can fall more readily as current investment projects are completed or abandoned – thereby requiring no further internal finance – and as previously incurred debts are repaid. This is simply the converse of the relationship between capacity growth, current revenue and required finance noted above. As the rate of capacity growth falls, investment costs fall relative to current revenues, and so the proportion of current revenues committed to long-run expenditure must decline. In order to generate this decline in the mark-up, however, the state of long-term expectation must be rendered sufficiently pessimistic that planned growth rates are reduced. Even then, the reduction will not be realized until current projects are completed and past debts repaid, or until expectations are so depressed that current projects are actually abandoned before completion. We must therefore anticipate that mark-up reductions will not follow from moderate declines in demand over time-intervals regularly experienced in the past. What is required significantly to reduce mark-ups is an unusually deep depression.

If a firm's costs are to be reduced as a result of excess demands in the markets for its outputs, it can only be as a result of price reductions by its suppliers. It can hardly be a general phenomenon that one firm will reduce its prices to a customer in trading difficulties for very long, if at all; it is far more likely that a supplier will face some downward pressure on prices when his own demands are in general decline. Even then, they will fall only if his costs fall. In the end, we are left to conclude that prices will fall first in markets characterized by short-run pricing and in other markets to the extent that their inputs to production processes are themselves purchased at short-run prices markets. Since primary products are in practice traded in markets characterized by short-run pricing, then virtually all commodities' production costs directly or indirectly reflect the state of demand in the primary commodity markets. It follows that those markets must be taken explicitly into account before we can have a complete theory of macroeconomic price flexibility.

First, however, we investigate why it is that macroeconomic pricing processes can be discussed without assuming the existence of the auctioneer in the present analysis but not in more conventional analyses.

5.2 KEYNESIAN AND NEO-WALRASIAN DEFINITIONS OF EFFECTIVE DEMAND: IMPLICATIONS FOR THE ANALYSIS OF MACROECONOMIC EXPECTATIONAL STATES

A theme of the previous chapter was that those theories that have their origins in the writings of Keynes do not require assumptions of auctioneers because they rely instead on the passage of historical time to convey information about quantities supplied and demand. The difference between this approach and that adopted in neo-Walrasian 'Keynesian' theories of Clower, Leijonhufvud et al. is bound up with the difference between these economists' definition of effective demand and that of Keynes. We begin with Keynes's (1936) definition:

Let Z be the aggregate supply price of the output from employing N men, the relationship between Z and N being written $Z = \phi(N)$, which can be called the *Aggregate Supply Function*. Similarly, let D be the proceeds which entrepreneurs expect to receive from the employment of N men, the relationship between D and N being written $D = f(N)$, which can be called the *Aggregate Demand Function*.... The value of D at the point of the aggregate supply function, will be called the effective demand. (p. 25)

The aggregate demand function relates various hypothetical quantities of employment to the proceeds which their outputs are expected to yield; and the effective demand is the point on the aggregate demand function which becomes effective because, taken in conjunction with the conditions of supply, it corresponds to the level of employment which maximises the entrepreneur's [*sic*] expectation of profit. (p. 55)

It is clear from these passages that Keynes defined effective demand as that quantity of commodities that entrepreneurs anticipated that their customers would want to purchase and would be able to purchase one production period hence. Of course, the intervals of time that constitute the periods of production of different commodities by different firms will themselves differ widely. The purpose of formulating the concept of effective demand was to determine not the volumes of various outputs one production period hence, but the volume of employment now. That effective demands of different entrepreneurs relate to conditions of demand that are expected to prevail after the passage of different intervals of time is of no consequence in Keynes's theory of employment. After all, if production takes time, a theory of employment is not the same thing as a theory of current output; for current output is always the consequence of decisions, including employment decisions, taken by entrepreneurs at a number of widely differing points of time in the past. Conversely, current employment decisions are taken in order to produce outputs that will be ready for sale at different future times.

This concept of effective demand cannot be adopted by neo-Walrasians because they assume that supply and demand decisions in all markets are taken simultaneously in the sense that nothing happens during the interval of time between the taking of all notional demand and supply decisions in the various markets and the revision of those decisions in light of the supplies and demands made known by the auctioneer. In other words, the quantity constraints on individual supply and demand decisions are perceived at the same time as the constrained supply and demand decisions are assumed actually to be taken. This is the essence of Clower's dual decision hypothesis as generalized by, e.g., Barro and Grossman (1976) and Malinvaud (1977, 1980). By eschewing any role for the passage of historical time in the process of communication, the neo-Walrasians can, and indeed must, eschew Keynes's definition of effective demand.

I am not arguing here that the neo-Walrasians should not have developed their concept of effective demand because it is different from that of Keynes. I am pointing out that it is wrong to suggest, as for example Hahn (1977, p. 31) does, that 'it is of course true that Keynes thought of effective demand as demand backed by purchasing power'. What is far more important, however, is that Keynes's conception of effective demand is the more fruitful of the two because it gives a clear role to the passage of the historical time and therefore takes fully into account the importance of those factors that affect the formation of short-term and long-term expectations by rational individuals.

We should be clear, however, that the acceptance of the Keynes approach to effective demand and the importance of historical time does not entail the wholesale acceptance of the Keynes theory. Kregel (1976) has pointed out that Keynes's analysis and the analyses of the post-Keynesians rest on various, particular assumptions about expectations and about relationships between the states of long- and short-term expectation in all markets. As we have seen in section 5.1, there is a variety of relationships between these two states of expectation and their effects on prices, outputs and investment in different product markets. Keynes did not capture them all.

None the less, of all Keynes's contributions, the one that is most important to the present theory is that he distinguished between the two expectational states in such a way that short-run processes were not dominated by long-run processes as in the pre-Keynesian orthodoxy and in Walrasian theory. If I am right, he went too far in this direction by supposing that long-run expectations would be accommodated to persistent changes in short-run expectations. This is what Kregel (1976) called Keynes's 'shifting-expectations model'. We saw in the framework of the two-sector model developed in chapter 1, however, that Keynes's supposition here is in some circumstances false. An unchanging state of long-term expectation in that model's machine sector was found to overwhelm and reverse an improvement in the state of short-term expectation.

If the direction of investment were unimportant – as in a one-sector or one-commodity model it must be – then Keynes's analysis of the short-run determinants of output and employment would have been complete. The analysis in chapter 1 showed that the direction of investment can be important; in the chapters following we shall see that, in general, the direction of investment will be of the utmost importance.

5.3 THE ORGANIZED EXCHANGES

The organized exchanges for transactions in financial assets and contracts to buy or sell commodities have long been taken for archetypical Walrasian markets. Unfortunately, this view is wrong on both historical and logical grounds.

The logical grounds are already familiar from the arguments of chapters 2 and 3. In essence, buyers and sellers do not always find it economically optimal to trade in organized exchanges or in any other market with short-run pricing. Short-run pricing is optimal only in circumstances that are dominated by uncertainty with regard to the conditions of supply and demand. These, of course, are also the conditions in which long-run equilibrium – including general equilibrium – cannot exist. Moreover, the history of the development of the organized exchanges confirms that they have a role only in conditions where uncertainty is economically important.

The historical fact is that the organized exchanges were created precisely in order to reduce the depressing effects of uncertainty upon the production of commodities. In general, their purpose is to enable producers, users and intermediaries to purchase relief from uncertainty by, in effect, paying others to assume some part of that burden in their stead. In order to achieve this purpose, organized exchanges have evolved in directions that make trading attractive to a wide range of wealth-holders who, individually, will accept a limited burden of uncertainty. Indeed, major changes in the organization of the exchanges have resulted from manifestations of unanticipated sources of uncertainty.

Illustrative historical episodes in the evolution of the organized exchanges

After the enactment of the Joint Stock Companies Act of 1856 in Great Britain, a large number of companies registered the limited liability of their respective 'bodies corporate'. Within six years of enactment, 2479 companies had registered under the 1856 Act. That economic forces led to the overwhelming of deep-seated opposition to the Act is amply documented by Shannon (1931). For business-men were being frustrated in their efforts to increase their scales of operation while *rentiers* were finding it difficult to acquire small investments that did not entail the prospect of ruination instead of the anticipated profit. The inducement effect here arose from the prudential separation of enterprise and capital – entailing a refuge from uncertainty. Even so, once limited liability by registration was made general, experience showed that the early legislation created or allowed anomalies which were gradually removed either by legislative enactment or by the adoption of less anomolous practices by firms and *rentiers* in order to serve their own interests. An example here will be instructive.

In the early years of limited liability by registration, it was thought prudent to issue shares that were not fully paid up. If the face value of a share were (say) £100, it might be sold by the issuer for (say) £5. The remaining £95 could be called, but the typical understanding was that further calls would not be made. Usually it was the creditors of limited companies who required this 'cushion'. The problem to which it gave rise became apparent with the first financial crisis after the coming of general limited liability. In the crisis of 1866, the negative cash flows of many companies led them to call up the unpaid portions of their outstanding shares. But the owners of those shares were not sufficiently liquid to meet the calls – their wealth being very largely in shares. During the crisis these shares – even when there were no calls for further payments – could not be sold and banks refused to lend against them. Far from increasing financial stability and providing creditors with a cushion against adverse cash flows, the practice of issuing high-denomination shares that were not fully paid up actually increased the uncertainties faced by firms, creditors and share-holders. Thereafter, it gradually became the practice to issue small-denomination, fully paid-up shares – a practice that had the added advantage of attracting the small middle-class *rentier*, thereby widening and deepening the market for shares (cf. Jefferys, 1946).

The role of uncertainty in the development of the commodity exchanges is similar to the role of uncertainty in the development of the stock exchange. The first organized commodity exchanges arose in the nineteenth century as economic growth, technical change in communication and transport and population growth combined to generate a large increase in international trade in raw materials. In order to avoid the prospect of serious shortage costs on account of failures of supplies, merchants and manufacturers held ever-larger stocks of raw materials. To a considerable extent, however, these stock-holdings, which were financed by borrowings, replaced the fear of shortage costs with a fear of capital losses on the stock-holdings. Adverse movements in prices would simply wipe out the values of intermediaries' stocks, thereby leaving them with no means of repaying the debts incurred to acquire those stocks. It was in order to limit this capital uncertainty that the forerunners of the commodity exchanges evolved in City coffee shops, where merchants, shippers and processors met to do their business. They began trading in forward contracts by which one individual would contract to supply another with a specified amount of a specified commodity at a specified price on a specified date. If the price should rise during the interval of time between the signing of the contract and the date of delivery, the seller would have forgone a capital gain but the buyer would have avoided a possibly ruinous capital loss. Should the price fall during that time, the buyer would have forgone a windfall gain and the seller would have avoided the capital loss. Evidently, the motivational basis of these contracts was that traders feared for their survival in business more than they desired a possible windfall gain.

The problem with forward contracts, however, was that, in the event of a harvest failure or some political or climatic event that reduced available supplies of agricultural or mineral raw materials, traders who had agreed to supply commodities could find that the goods that they had anticipated selling simply failed to materialize. In such cases, they had to go to the market in order to purchase, at whatever price was prevailing, the commodities they had contracted to deliver. As a result, the avoidance of capital uncertainty that was to be provided by the forward contract was not in the event provided. Futures contracts were devised precisely to get round this source of commercial uncertainty. Futures contracts are between 'the market' (a group of cooperating jobbers) and a trader who agrees either to buy or sell a commodity that is specified only by its characteristics in relation to an arbitrary standard (or contract) grade for delivery during a specified month at one of a number of specified locations. Since the holder of a futures contract to sell (say) hard March wheat can always cancel that commitment before March by taking a contract to buy the same amount of hard March wheat, he need never actually supply or take delivery of the commodity itself. Indeed, in most organized commodity markets, less than 2 per cent of all futures contracts result in spot deliveries being made or taken, and in no market is the figure as much as 5 per cent (Goss and Yamey, 1978). It is this feature of futures markets that makes possible the avoidance of the capital uncertainty that is associated with forward contracts.

The 'auctioneer' in the organized exchange

The 'auctioneer' in the organized exchanges is just what would be expected from the theory of markets. It is a group of jobbers: intermediaries who buy assets in order only to sell them. That the organized exchanges satisfy the necessary conditions for a market to be characterized by intermediated exchange is not mere chance. A good deal of effort goes into ensuring that assets or commodities traded on any organized exchange are completely standardized, compact and durable and that the volume of transactions, on average, supports intermediaries operating at minimum efficient scale in exchange.

Standardization is achieved by the exchanges' own systems of inspection of assets or commodities offered for sale on the exchange or, particularly in the United States, by governmental authorities. In the commodity exchanges, commodities are deemed suitable for spot delivery only if they are certified to be either of contract grade or some standard alternative. In addition, the futures contract on any exchange is designed by the exchange's governing authority and its terms are completely standardized. On the exchanges for financial assets – the stock exchanges – it is clear that the securities issued by one firm are not like those issued by any other firm. None the less, it is not permissible for the issuer of any asset to discriminate among different holders of the same class of security, and this renders each bond, debenture or share certificate identical to any other bond, debenture or share certificate, respectively, issued by the same firm.

Financial assets traded on the stock exchanges are durable by nature. It would be possible to insist that share certificates be inscribed in stone, thereby to render them bulky, but printing them on paper affords economies of both issuance and storage that are advantageous to all traders. The quality of certificates must be such as to ensure that in normal circumstances they will not physically perish before their maturity dates, and that when there is no specified maturity date the certificates can be replaced if they should perish. The same is true of the futures and other contracts traded on the commodity exchanges. More to the point, no commodities that are traded on these exchanges are so perishable and bulky that they cannot economically be transported from their point of production to an authorized place of delivery or held in stock at least as long as the longest permissible future contract. In fact, the durability and compactness of the commodity must be such that it can economically be held for substantial periods of time both before delivery to authorized warehouses and after delivery is taken by the ultimate users. If that were not the case, then producers, merchants and users would find the commodity exchanges to be of such limited usefulness that the exchanges could not have arisen in the first place. Moreover, the longest maturities of futures contracts must be such that producers and users can hedge their commitments to engage in real transactions at a time that is sufficiently far into the future that no very firm expectations can be formulated about the conditions of supply and demand that will prevail when the commitments must be met.

Of course, it is also necessary, for the dominance of price-setting intermediaries in a market, that the commodities traded there be standardized, compact and durable. The scale of transactions must be large enough that the intermediaries can achieve minimum efficient scale in exchange, or at least come closer to that scale than traders on either side of the market. It is, moreover, well recognized in the literature on futures trading that the volume of transactions on any organized exchange must be large in relation to the size of the average transaction; otherwise, a spate of hedging on either the short or the long side or a substantial security issue on the stock exchange would significantly affect prices. If the taking of a short hedge (sale of futures) were to depress the futures price, then the subsequent closing of the hedge (offsetting purchase of futures) would entail a larger net loss or smaller net gain on the hedge than if the price had not been depressed by the initial hedging transaction. If a new issue of securities depresses securities prices significantly, then the finance raised by the issue will be smaller although the absolute cost of the finance will not. Thus, the effective rate of interest will be higher. To reduce the costs of hedging and finance by firms, therefore, the markets for futures and/or securities are made as wide and as deep as possible. In order to achieve the requisite large transactions volume on the exchanges, the governing authorities of the exchanges seek to make them as attractive as they can for wealth-holders in general and speculators in particular. To this end, standards of trading behaviour are set and maintained to ensure that the nature of the risks and uncertainties that traders face are in some ways limited and in all ways known. This is why futures contracts are designed to make it virtually impossible for any trader or consortium of traders to establish a corner in the market. There are, in addition, back-up powers to suspend trading in any commodity where it appears that transactions are in any way irregular. The same powers exist and are often used in the stock exchanges. And no effort is spared in eliminating the uncertainties arising from moral hazard.

Income and capital uncertainty

The circumstances of some *rentiers* (wealth-holders and speculators) make them averse to uncertainty regarding the incomes yielded by their wealth. Other *rentiers'* circumstances make them averse to uncertainty regarding the capital value of their wealth.

The income-uncertainty-averse are typified by the proverbial widow and orphan who rely upon their wealth to yield an income because their time-horizon is sufficiently long that they wish to maintain, in so far as is possible, the stream of purchasing power that their wealth provides. In addition, the 'widow-and-orphan' class of *rentier* faces no claims upon the capital values of their wealth. For such wealth-holders, bonds are the appropriate form in which to hold their wealth because the interest income is contractually fixed. They will not wish to sell their bonds in order to realize their capital value because to do so would result in a long-term reduction in income. Even in inflationary times, such *rentiers* will want to hold bonds yielding incomes in money unless some other asset will promise similar certainty of income in a form that is confidently expected to hold its exchange value better than money.

The capital-uncertainty-averse are concerned more with maintaining the values of their assets because of the structure and nature of their liabilities. The financial institutions in particular – including banks, insurance and pension funds and finance houses – generate their incomes by borrowing at one interest rate or prospective cost and lending at a higher rate. Since their borrowings are typically in a form that entails capital repayments – e.g. from insurance claims or withdrawals of time deposits – any excess of claims over income and new borrowings will require such firms to realize some part of the capital values of their assets. Any diminution of these values as a result of falling securities prices or speculative losses on the commodity exchanges increases the proportion of the holdings – and therefore the proportion of their long-run incomes – that must be liquidated to meet any net claims in excess of current incomes. That is, the institutions' incomes are broadly proportional to the values of their assets, so that any reductions in their asset bases reduce their incomes, thereby causing larger losses in future incomes as a result of future net claims on their assets. It follows that significant capital losses at a time when the institutions' creditors are seeking to become more liquid could well set up a survival-threatening, vicious circle of increased claims which must be met from diminishing incomes and asset values.

Although income- and capital-uncertainty aversion will be seen to be important in several contexts, they have been introduced at the present stage of the argument in order to show that continuity of supplies and demands is essential to the existence of the organized exchanges and therefore to the survival of the jobbers who occupy the interiors of those markets.

Clearly, the income-uncertainty-averse will not trade in the commodity exchanges for the simple reason that there is no income to be had from so doing. All returns are in the form of capital gains from successful speculation. In so far as speculators buy and sell futures to make a capital gain, they will obviously need to be able at any time to close positions in which they anticipate capital losses. If they cannot do so, the uncontrollable losses that they face are necessarily greater than if they can buy and sell futures at will to offset previous sales and purchases, respectively. The same point applies to the stock exchanges, although there its importance depends on the relative magnitudes of assets held by the income- and the capital-uncertainty-averse. Provided that their income is secure, the coupon-clipping widows and orphans might like to be able to sell their holdings when they expect interest rates imminently to rise, thereby enabling them to purchase larger income streams as bond prices fall. But such an option is not essential, particularly since they do not actually suffer reductions in incomes as a result of falling interest rates (and rising bond prices). In general, then, market continuity is likely to increase the number of *rentiers* active in the markets by attracting more of the capital-uncertainty-averse than would be attracted to discontinuous asset markets. Conversely, market continuity is more easily maintained as the number of traders is larger. In practice, the archetypal capital-uncertainty-averse *rentiers* – the financial institutions – have very sizeable holdings of assets traded on the stock exchanges, and so enable those markets to function efficiently for the issuers of new securities and profitably for the jobbers and brokers.

In order to maintain continuous markets, the jobbers must maintain minimum stocks of the assets in which they trade so that their customers' demands can always be met. Being survival-motivated firms themselves, however, the jobbers will seek to limit their own exposures to uncertainty and financial charges by keeping their stocks from greatly exceeding their likely requirements. Thus, if there are excess supplies of securities or commodity futures, the jobbers will reduce their bid and offer prices until enough speculators believe that those prices are likely to rise in the near future, or at least that prices are unlikely to fall further and faster than any interest yield will offset. This result lulls *rentiers'* feelings of capital uncertainty, thereby inducing them to stop selling and start buying. Similarly, if there are excess demands jobbers will rationally raise their prices until enough speculators believe that prices must fall and so will stop buying and perhaps start selling their securities or futures. In the language of the exchanges, the aim of the jobbers in conditions of excess supply will be to convince enough bearish speculators that a bull market is at hand, and in conditions of excess demand will be to convince enough bullish speculators that a bear market is in the offing (cf. Keynes, 1930/1971, I, pp. 222–6).

This account of the source of price flexibility in the organized exchanges evidently depends on the presumption that speculators always believe that current price rises and reductions can be large enough that they must soon be reversed. There is, of course, no warrant for relying on this presumption unless it can be shown to be implied by rational individual behaviour.

The issues involved here are hardly novel. That individual behaviour in conditions of uncertainty (as distinct from risk) cannot be modelled by means of equilibrium analysis is well known. The Radner problem, which itself is crucial to our rejection of long-run equilibrium, is a manifestation of the general incompatibility between uncertainty and the existence of long-run equilibrium. The consequence of rejection of long-run equilibrium concepts is that, for reasons developed in section 8.1, we cannot generate either deterministic or stochastic models of behaviour with long-run implications. In general, we shall find that the limits to rational behaviour in the short run are imposed by the constraints of existing resource capacities and the technological characteristics of those resources. The assumption that managers of firms are motivated to secure their respective firms' survival implies that financial limits on rational behaviour are important in both the long run and the short run.

In the remainder of this section, this approach to the analysis of rational behaviour in conditions of uncertainty will be applied to the analysis of speculative activity in the organized exchanges. In addition to providing a clear introduction to this method, the argument is interesting *per se* because it advances the theory of speculative activity.

The limits to speculative activity: real and subjective

The proposition that prices in the organized commodity exchanges tend to fall as stocks of the actual commodities rise relative to rates of use, and that prices rise as stocks fall relative to rates of use, amounts to no more than conventional wisdom. The problem here is to bring this conventional wisdom into our analysis. The way that is not open to us is that which now dominates economic analyses of price variance in the organized exchanges and markets for primary commodities: rational expectations modelling (cf. Newbery and Stiglitz, 1979, 1981, 1982; Wright and Williams, 1982). The reason this approach is not open to us is discussed in detail in section 2.4. The approach that is taken here is to identify the real limits to speculation and the way in which they will vary in the organized exchanges for different commodities, and then to consider how these real limits affect the expectations of rational individuals with limited computational capacities and rates of learning.

It is an elementary tenet of the economics of the organized exchanges that the upper limit to any futures price is the current spot price plus the unit carrying costs of the actual commodity from now to the maturity of the futures contract. This limit is maintained by arbitrageurs who, if it were exceeded, would buy spot and sell futures, thereby to obtain a riskless profit equal to the difference between the contango (excess of the futures price over the spot price) and the carrying cost (including any interest charges or interest forgone). It follows that speculatively sustained upward movements in futures prices require, after a time, upward movements in spot prices arising from speculative demands alone; for, if spot prices were not rising and contango were at its maximum, futures prices could not rise. We therefore need consider only how speculators can keep spot prices rising.

We know that jobbers in the exchanges will continue rationally to raise prices only in conditions of continuing excess demands. A continuing bull market arising from speculative activity alone thus requires that speculators' net demands exceed the positive difference between new production and users' purchases, that is, any 'real' excess supplies. Our first question then is, What are the limits to these speculative excess demands for spot commodities?

Like intermediaries, speculators buy only in order to sell. Unlike intermediaries, they do not themselves provide any service of exchange. None the less, they engage only in exchange (even if, in a different aspect of their activities, they produce or use the commodities). It follows that any real limitations on their activities must arise from the technology of, or resources available for, exchange. Of the three services of exchange, two – communication and transportation – can be eliminated from the discussion straightaway. For the whole object of maintaining organized exchanges is to ensure that communications resources are sufficient to cope with the requirements of any except the most unexpectedly large transactions volumes. Since transportation can only limit the rate at which commodities can be delivered to authorized warehouses, any constraints resulting therefrom have the same effect on the present discussion as constraints on production. That is, we can legitimately identify real supplies with delivered supplies of newly produced output. If there is a real limit to net speculative demands, it can only be a limit to storage capacities.

The point here is perfectly simple. If speculators are to keep spot prices rising – this being a necessary condition for cumulatively rising futures prices – then they must collectively enter the spot market on the demand side. In consequence, they must be continuously accumulating stocks of actual commodities. If there is any storage limit at all, eventually it will cease to be possible for them to take delivery of the commodity. Possibly they will have to use increasingly unsuitable storage facilities which will entail larger carrying costs, perhaps through increased deterioration. Whatever the particular case might be, in conditions of limited storage capacity storage costs must eventually approach infinity, if only in the sense that there is no finite price at which additional storage capacity can be had. Since a net speculative profit can be realized only if the rate of capital gain exceeds the marginal time-rate of carrying costs, positive speculative gains will be impossible to generate in these circumstances. Speculators must either cease buying spot as a rational-maximizing decision, or they must use all of their liquid reserves and borrowing capacity, and so become bankrupt. Once the storage limit is reached, excess speculative demands cannot remain positive and the rate of capital gains from speculative sources falls to zero.

In this circumstance, spot prices could continue to rise only if there were net excess real demands. However, there is no reason to suppose that production has fallen off with such high spot prices, while, if anything, these prices will cause users to economize as much as possible on their own stock-holdings. Thus, demands will not exceed, and are quite likely to fall short of, time-rates of use as user's stocks are drawn down in anticipation (or hope) of spot price reductions. On balance, therefore, one would expect excess real supplies, no further excess speculative demands and, in consequence, declining spot prices. Given the maximum contango, futures prices cannot be expected to have an upward trend either. Indeed, as stocks are drawn down and marginal storage costs therefore fall, the maximum contango itself will decline, thereby reinforcing a declining ceiling on futures prices.

As for speculatively sustained price reductions (or bear markets), there is no positive lower limit to either futures prices or spot prices. If there are no spot buyers, there will be no spot prices. If the spot price is positive, there is no limit to the positive difference between spot and futures prices as long as both are positive. That is, the maximum backwardation is the magnitude of the spot price.

There is, however, a limit to the ability of speculators to force spot prices down. There can be net speculative supplies only as long as speculators hold stocks of spot (actual) commodities of contract grade. Thus, the cumulative excess speculative stock-supply is always limited – in the extreme by available storage capacity. It only remains to consider the limits to speculatively sustained bearish movements in futures prices.

The object of a bear position in futures is to sell futures now at a price that is below the spot price that will prevail during the contracted delivery period. If the present futures price is below the future spot price, the difference will be the speculator's profit. Evidently, if speculative excess supplies in the futures markets are to continue to force futures prices down, bearish speculators must be able to remain active in the market. If they are to remain active in the market, they must generate a profit, since sustained losses will eventually bankrupt them. Thus, spot prices must always be below previous levels of futures prices on currently maturing contracts for spot deliveries; otherwise, speculators will be making losses that, if they continue long enough, must eventually bankrupt them.

It is now clear that, if storage capacity is a real constraint on the magnitude of speculatively held stocks of any commodity, then speculative transactions can dominate real transactions only over limited periods of time. No matter how bullish speculators might be feeling, once the granaries, warehouses or vaults are full, prices can continue to rise only as a result of excess real demands of a sort that are hard to explain when stocks are abnormally large. When speculators' holdings of spot commodities are low, then bearish sentiment cannot put downward pressure on prices. If prices are to fall it will be because of excess real (rather than speculative) supplies.

The latitude for speculative activity in any organized exchange is evidently limited in extreme cases by the magnitude of the storage capacity available for speculative stocks. But for speculation to dominate real trading, the volume of speculative transactions must be greater than the volume of real transactions within the limits imposed by storage. This pattern of relative transactions volumes itself requires that stocks available for speculative sale or purchase be large relative to rates of new production and use in further production or in consumption. We know from chapter 3 that, in general, stocks of any commodity held for use will be larger as the commodity is more compact and durable (standardization already being required for there to be an organized exchange in the first place) and as producers' and users' operating leverages are greater. These factors indicate no more than that stocks held for real purposes will be large in relation to use. Unless available storage capacities are sufficient to accommodate this magnitude of stocks, taking seasonal and cyclical fluctuations into account, there will be an inducement effect to expand storage capacity. And if there is normally a large demand for speculative stocks, we would expect inducement effects to ensure in the long run that the capacity is available for these stocks as well. How much capacity? This will depend on the compactness of the commodity in relation to its market price (or the compactness of a pound's or dollar's worth) and the value of speculative commitments in the particular exchange.

Unlike producers and users, speculators are not directly concerned with the physical characteristics of the commodities in which they trade. Their speculations are in market values alone: so many pounds' or dollars' worth of the various commodities or assets. If the bulk of a pound's worth of commodity is relatively large, the requisite cost and space for storage will also be relatively large. If a commodity is compact in relation to both the technology of exchange and its market price, then the value of stocks that can be accommodated by existing storage capacity will be greater and speculators' willingness to hold stocks of actual (spot) commodities will also be greater. Thus, rational speculators will be able to force prices up further and either faster or over a longer period of time, and will have the stocks to force prices down further and either faster or over a longer period of time, as commodities are compact in relation to price. In general, compactness and durability of commodities traded on the organized exchanges imply that stocks will be large in relation to rates of production and use and that speculators will be more willing to trade in spot commodities. It follows that speculators will be better able to maintain excess demands for stocks over a longer period, and therefore to maintain excess supplies for a longer period as commodities are more compact and durable.

This, no doubt, is a major part of the reason why speculative trading has a far more dramatic effect on (say) gold prices than on (say) cereals or frozen pork-bellies. It is, however, only a part of the explanation. The other part turns on the financial exposure of the speculators.

In a bull market that is speculatively fuelled, spot prices are rising because speculators collectively enter the market on the demand side. In consequence, bullish speculators are committing ever more of their financial resources to the holding of actual commodities and commodity futures. The holding of actual commodities, of course, requires an additional commitment of finance to meet the carrying costs. It follows that a severe downturn in prices will impose a larger cost on bullish speculators as the period of time over which the speculatively fuelled bull market has prevailed is longer. If there should be a reversal in the price trend, then those speculators who sell off their holdings will obviously realize the largest possible capital gain. Those who sell off later will realize smaller capital gains than the earlier sellers and, if they are very late in selling, will realize capital losses. If, however, speculators had collectively continued to be net purchasers of spot commodities and futures, then all would have continued to enjoy notional capital gains, which some speculators could have realized from time to time in order to finance consumption, or perhaps production requiring their speculative holdings as inputs or to finance different speculations.

Even if there were no physical limits to the duration of the bull price trend, the potential loss faced by active speculators increases with no obvious reason to suppose that the likelihood (or subjective probability) of incurring a loss is diminishing. Thus, rational speculators will eventually conclude that they should dispose of their speculative holdings unless there is some prospect that realizable capital gains will grow at an increasing rate in the future. It is this latter prospect that is limited by the bulk and perishability of the commodities in relation to their prices. In part, the carrying costs per unit of time are higher as the commodities are less compact and durable, and, in part, the storage limitation is more evident. Speculators who are experienced as well as rational will recognize that rising stocks relative to rates of use of commodities necessarily presage a downturn from a rising price trend. Since they will want to be among the first to dispose of speculative holdings, they will not wait for storage capacities to be fully utilized. They will rationally begin selling. If speculators generally recognize the nature of this situation they will rationally be looking for signs that their fellow speculators have begun selling. Since rising stocks in relation to rates of use indicate that such selling is likely, we would expect that, after a long bull trend in an organized exchange for bulky and possibly perishable commodities, once selling starts the desire to sell will become widespread. In these circumstances, jobbers will rationally begin to lower their bid and offer prices. The bull market will give way to a bear market. The ratio of stocks to flow-demands will be a consideration of less importance in markets for the more compact and durable commodities.

The same considerations will apply to the stock exchanges with little modification. Rates of use in the commodity exchanges correspond to the redemption of financial assets (including the maturity of bills and bonds) in the stock exchanges; rates of commodity production correspond to rates of issue of new securities. Existing stocks of securities are very large in relation to new issues and redemptions – as we would expect, since financial assets are designed to be as compact and durable as any asset can be. Thus, financial assets are also compact in relation to their market prices. These are the circumstances in which we have found speculative latitude to be at its widest and, therefore, least affected by 'real' factors. Thus, the range of prices over which speculative transactions can be dominant will be greater in the stock exchange than is economically possible in the exchanges for the bulkier and less durable commodities.

These are all matters that will be taken up again in chapters 7 and 8, where analysis of the limits to speculation is completed and shown to be an essential component of our theory of major macroeconomic cycles.

5.4 THE LABOUR MARKETS

Either labour markets function in much the same way as any other market or they are in some essential way different. The first view underlies both partial and general (including temporary) equilibrium theories. The second view is that taken by the classical economists, Keynes and those (apart from the temporary equilibrium theorists) who claim to be their intellectual descendants. More particularly, while the orthodoxy has it that both wage rates and employment are economically determined, the classical and Keynesian assumption is that wage rates are socially rather than economically determined.

Excepting the post-Keynesian school (e.g. Davidson, Kregel, Eichner, S. Weintraub and Minsky), who, it must be said, have not had a substantial impact on mainstream macroeconomic policy analysis, economists in general have maintained the presumption that supply and demand functions play the same role in the labour markets as in any other markets. If there are any differences between the functioning of the labour and other markets, these are assumed to turn on lag structures. Thus, Friedman (1969 and elsewhere) has argued that, while the labour market will clear in the long run just like any other market, households' price expectations adapt more slowly than firms' price expectations so that any short-run excess demands or supplies will result in price movements in the product markets first and then in the labour and other factor markets. The new classical macroeconomists follow Friedman in assuming a Walrasian economic structure but alter the lag structure by assuming statistically unbiased (rational) rather than adaptive expectations. Clower (1965/1969), too, assumed the Walrasian economic structure in which households sell factor services and buy goods and in which labour services are not differentiated from other factors of production. The clearest distinction found in Walrasian and neo-Walrasian theory is in Leijonhufvud (1968). Even there, the crux of the distinction between markets is relative speeds of price adjustment. Securities prices adjust to excess supplies and demands most quickly; then come goods prices and finally wage rates. These differences are assumed to follow from differences in the rates at which agents are able to acquire information in the financial, product and labour markets, respectively.

Keynes assumed that money-wage rates are relatively inflexible because workers are concerned primarily to defend their wage relativities. This assumption was clearly inductive, and he offered no theoretical justification for it. None the less, the assumption is analytically superior to the classical assumption that real wage rates tend in the long run to some unexplained socially determined subsistence level. The superiority of the Keynes assumption here stems from his demonstration that, at least in his analytical framework, flexible money-wage rates – which are the immediate subjects of the wage-bargaining process – have perverse effects on real-wage rates. Thus, real-wage rates are not determined by excess supplies and demands in the labour markets even over the periods of historical time sufficiently long to take in the economist's long run.

Keynes's argument turned on the proposition that reductions in money wages are unlikely to reduce real-wage rates because they are more likely to reduce than to increase planned production and therefore current employment of labour. The consequent increase in real-wage rates follows from Keynes's assumption of marginal cost pricing and diminishing marginal productivity of labour.

The two main reasons for Keynes's position on the effect of money-wage cuts were (1) that a decrease in money-wage rates, if expected to last for any length of time, diminishes actual and antici-pated demands for wage goods and (2) that any consequent fall in output prices increases the burden of debt on firms, thereby diminishing both the incentive to invest with borrowed funds and the available finance in excess of interest and principal payments on existing debts. Since these arguments imply that money-wage cuts are more likely to reduce than to increase employment, Keynes concluded that workers and their trade unions act wholly rationally in resisting such cuts (cf. Keynes, 1936, chapter 19).

Although Keynes's approach here was unexceptionable, there are two difficulties with his conclusions. One is that it rests crucially on the assumption that short-run production decisions are taken to equate the marginal costs of current production starts with prices expected to prevail one period of production hence. This assumption is neither descriptively accurate nor logically correct in markets characterized by long-run pricing. In those markets, the state of long-term expectation dominates the state of short-term expectation in the determination of prices.

The second problem is that the Keynes analysis, even if it were correct, is incomplete. For there is nothing in the Keynes theory to show how either the level of money-wage rates or changes in money-wage rates are determined. The latter particularly is important for any theory that explains inflationary processes. Keynes himself (1936, p. 265) simply referred to the 'system of free wage-bargaining'. Post-Keynesians who have considered the matter, such as Davidson (1972, 1974), Davidson and Kregel (1980), Eichner (1976, chapter 5) and Wood (1978), assume that wage bargaining takes place between individual firms or, occasionally, between employers' associations and the representatives of groups of workers in a trade, industry or firm.

Davidson lays particular stress on the duration of the wage contract, which, he suggests, is longer than the period of production of employers' products. If so – and this seems to reflect an American practice which is less evident in the United Kingdom – the duration of the wage contract is long enough to facilitate short-run planning on the basis of costs which are largely known in advance of decisions committing the firm to a particular volume of throughputs. Indeed,

Davidson and Kregel (1980, p. 144) go on to argue that 'it is [this] institution of forward labour contracting which provides a basis for the conventional belief in the stickiness of stability in prices over time'. Although it is not clear that wage bargains amount to forward contracts (in so far as wages but not volumes of employment are specified), much the same point is made by Eichner (1976, pp. 159–62), who argues that there are wage rounds in each of which the norm for wages or wage increases is established at the start in a 'bell-wether' industry. This is the 'key bargain', which sets the standard of fairness and equity accepted by most workers during the remainder of the wage round as they seek to maintain their wages relative to those of workers in the 'bellwether' industries.

There is, even apart from the question of 'forward labour contracting', a problem with this line of argument. It rests on the presumption that each group of workers knows its place in the league table of wage rates or wage incomes and, most importantly, accepts that place. When they do not, then models of the wage-bargaining process yield predictions about rates of wage inflation that are extremely sensitive to assumptions about, for example, the order in which groups within firms, or in which whole firms or industries, reach their wage bargains during the wage round (Wood, 1978, chapter 5). None the less, there is a general presumption that 'leap-frogging' will put upward pressure on money-wage rates whenever different groups of workers hold different views about what constitutes 'fair' wage relativities.

Distinct from these always-upward normative pressures on wages are what Wood calls 'anomic' pressures. Anomic pressures are based upon technological and competitive factors, whereas normative pressures are based on perceived social relationships in which incomes reflect status. The anomic pressures – for example, in conditions of high involuntary unemployment – can impose downward pressures upon wage settlements which, if extreme, will more than offset the upward normative pressures. Although he used different terminology, Phelps Brown (1977) argued a similar case and provided extensive evidence in support of this argument.

If wage relativities are an important determinant of the stance adopted by workers in the wage-bargaining process, then social (or normative) pressures can be shown analytically (Wood, 1978) to generate a tendency towards upward wage drift. Given the existence of wage drift, real (or anomic) pressures can either reinforce or counteract it. However, the initial assumption that wage relativities are important to workers is neither implied nor denied by anything in the theory developed in this book. We must therefore ask two questions: (1) Is the assumption of the importance of relativities in the wage-bargaining process compatible with the imbalance theory of the firm and markets? (2) Is the assumption fruitful in the sense that it generates disconfirmable hypotheses and policy prescriptions? Both of these questions will be answered in the affirmative. We turn now to the first question. The reason for the affirmative answer to the second question will become apparent in the macroeconomic analysis in chapters 8 and 9.

Imbalance theory and wage relativities

There are two aspects to the argument that relativities-determined wage demands by workers are compatible with imbalance theory. First, such a process is no less compatible with rational-maximizing behaviour by workers than are the processes assumed in equilibrium theories; second, and perhaps more important, relativities bargaining economizes on transactions costs in the labour markets in ways that are not possible in a Walrasian economic structure. The second aspect of the argument is that the assumptions that lie behind the wage-relativities analyses of, for example, Phelps Brown (1977) turn out to be demand-side analogues of supply-side propositions of the imbalance theory of the firm.

The cost to workers in formulating wage demands by taking the wages of a small number of well-defined bargaining groups as reference points is far less than the costs that would necessarily be associated with the sort of exchange activity assumed in equilibrium theories. In Walrasian models, the auctioneer is assumed to receive notification of the demands for and supplies of labour and then to bring these supplies and demands together until the lesser of the two is fully satisfied. Walrasians would have it that the auctioneer then raises the wage rate (presumably in relation to wage-good prices) if demand is the greater of the two and lowers the relative wage rate if supply is the greater. Neo-Walrasians would have it that household demands for firms' outputs are limited by the resulting wage income if supply exceeds demand and that firms' outputs are limited by the availability of labour services if demand exceeds supply. In either model, we again find that the auctioneer is processing all market information. If firms and households are rational, the cost of the auctioneer's activities to the participants in the market would necessarily be less than the addition to total transactions costs were he not to provide this service.

Compare the wage-relativities hypothesis with the assumption of the auctioneer. Each worker or group of workers will need to acquire and process a far smaller amount of information than does the auctioneer. This reduction in information requirements has two sources. One is that notions of fairness in relativities are assumed to be established by workers from a consideration of the wages paid to other workers in the same firm or the same trade or to workers in firms producing similar commodities or using similar technologies or, perhaps, to workers in firms located nearby. That is, the notion of a 'fair' relativity can be established by comparing as small a number of wage rates as can be accommodated by workers' computational capacities.

The second source of information economies is the wage round, which further limits the number of wage rates that each bargaining group of workers (or each worker) will wish to consider. If there is a well-defined wage round, any group of workers will know which of their reference wages have been established either in the recent past or since their own wage rate was last agreed. Furthermore, there is then no requirement to ascertain the outcome of wage bargaining processes being conducted simultaneously with one's own. If relativities are reasonably stable, and if other wage groups in similar positions have similar, recently agreed reference wages, then the wage relativities resulting even from simultaneously agreed bargains will not significantly change from one wage round to the next. Thus, the acquisition of a relatively small amount of information about recently concluded wage bargains will enable workers to stipulate their current wage demands as if they were able to determine from the auctioneer the other wages being agreed at the same time. In consequence, reliance by workers on information about wage relativities entails a minimum efficient scale in the acquisition of information that is far less that the scale of information that the auctioneer is assumed to acquire. Of course, this minimum efficient scale could also be a great deal larger than can be achieved by any individual worker. The achievement of this scale is one benefit of collective bargaining, although it was obviously by no means the main reason for the rise of the trade union movement.

Relativities bargaining by groups of workers yields a further economy in exchange. If each group bargains for standard wages, hours and other conditions of service, then each worker who is a member of that group cannot work just the length of time that, at the prevailing wage, will equate the marginal utility he derives from his real income with the marginal utility he derives from his leisure time. If such workers are rational utility maximizers, they will prefer to be part of such a bargaining group only if they, individually, incur smaller transactions costs and/or spend less time engaged in the transaction than would have been required in bargaining individually with employers. If the savings in time and transactions costs increases their utility, then they will rationally engage in group bargaining.

Firms, too, will patently realize transactions economies through bargaining with groups of workers instead of reaching agreements individually with each worker. These savings, for obvious reasons, increase with the number of workers employed by the firm.

The second aspect of the argument that the wage-relativities hypothesis and the imbalance theory of the firm are compatible is that certain propositions derived from imbalance theory constitute assumptions upon which the wage-relativities hypothesis is predicated.

Obviously, the notion that workers bargain for relative wages implies not only that they have in mind particular reference wages but also that they are bargaining over the wages attaching to a particular job. Since it can hardly be rational behaviour to bargain (or to pay intermediaries to bargain) over a wage rate that one will not be paid, it is clear that workers will be bargaining over the wages attaching to their own respective employments. The wage-relativities hypothesis as developed by Phelps Brown (1977) and Wood (1978) is based on the assumption that workers derive their prestige and social status from their employment and that this status is measured by their wages in relation to the wages of other bargaining groups. That is to say, Phelps Brown and Wood argue that the wage-relativities hypothesis conforms to what is known of social behaviour, whereas I have argued that the wage-relativities hypothesis conforms to behaviour that is efficient in exchange. These arguments are mutually reinforcing, and both imply that, in the bargaining process, workers are considering the wages and other conditions of employment attaching to their present jobs. It is this attachment of individual workers to existing employment that amounts analytically to a proposition about labour supply corresponding to a key proposition of imbalance theory about labour demand.

The relevant imbalance-theoretic proposition stems from the argument that periodically to assemble a whole new labour force would be irrational firm behaviour. One of the main arguments in support of the economic efficiency of focusing effects is that a labour force that is familiar with the technology of production or exchange employed in an expanded or even a different activity will start further along the learning curve associated with that activity than

would workers lacking that experience. It follows that the maintenance of the human resources of the firm with a small turnover in
personnel enables firms to plan investment and competitive strategies
that build on firm-specific knowledge, skills and experience of
known labour, supervisory and managerial resources, while at the
same time reaping the benefits of learning-by-doing in the short run.
In addition, the savings in information costs made possible by the
maintenance of a stable set of human resources are well known from
the theory of internal labour markets (Doeringer and Piore, 1971).
Evidently, the interest of firms in holding workers in their existing
employment is wholly compatible with the social and economic
interest of workers in bargaining over wages and conditions attaching
to those employments rather than searching for higher wages or
better conditions attaching to other, as yet unknown, employments.

The foregoing arguments imply that group bargaining over standard
conditions of employment, including wage relativities and real wages,
is wholly compatible with rational individual behaviour on both the
supply and the demand sides of the labour market. The inherent
rationality in such procedures and objectives stems from the savings
in information and transactions costs, which are simply not available
to either workers or firms in an economy with a Walrasian structure
or in an economy where individuals act as if the structure were
Walrasian.

Although real factors are important in determining the outcomes
of the wage bargaining process, the argument in this chapter does not
give such factors appropriate emphasis in comparison with social
(or normative) considerations. The reason for this is that the real
factors are macroeconomic in origin. As a result, they cannot be
considered in detail until our theoretical framework for macroeconomic analysis has been made clear. Once that has been done,
we shall find that our theory predicts pro-cyclical changes in real
wage rates over what, in section 1.4, was called the major macroeconomic cycle. The arguments in support of the existence of this
real-wage cycle will be set out in chapter 8.

6

The Macroeconomics of Output, Employment and Price Determination

6.0 INTRODUCTION

The purpose of this chapter is to derive an analytical framework for macroeconomic analysis from the microeconomic theory developed in the four preceding chapters. We shall find that, even taking full account of the institutional diversity of markets and complex technological relationships, the role of basic and non-basic commodities is precisely what we found in the simple model of chapter 1. Indeed, the theory of markets serves to make the basic/non-basic distinction not only natural but compelling.

As in chapter 1, we shall find that, whenever basic commodity producers respond to increased demands by selling their output to non-basic users, any upturns in economic activity will be weak and short-lived. When they respond by increasing their own rates of capacity growth, hence by demanding and using basic commodities rather than selling them to non-basic users, then upturns in economic activity are stronger and longer-lived. There is nothing surprising about this result once it is recognized that profit-maximizing, survival-motivated entrepreneurs cannot rationally maintain continuous markets in all second-hand capital equipment or the services thereof. The basic/non-basic distinction itself is a natural consequence of specialization in exchange which, we have found, is economically as advantageous as specialization in production.

In arguing for the importance of the macroeconomic analysis reported here, it is vital to be clear that it rests on no important unstated or implicit assumptions about microeconomic behaviour, relations or processes. It will therefore be appropriate to set out here the microeconomic propositions that were derived in the four preceding chapters from the assumption of rational, survival-motivated behaviour of firms' management teams and from explicit analyses and specifications of technology in both production and exchange.

1 Concepts of, or dependent upon, long-run equilibrium are inapposite because they require the adoption of special assumptions with no rationale in the assumption of individual rationality and because they lead to unnecessarily complex mathematical specifications of economic behaviour and processes.

2 Since the assumption of long-run profit or growth maximization violates the first proposition, some other assumption about long-run behaviour is required for any analysis of long-run processes. The assumption that has been found here to yield precise, simple and intuitively attractive results is that firms' managers are motivated primarily to secure the long-run survival of their firms. Nothing in particular has been assumed about the long-run motivation of households, although transactions cost minimization and a positive relationship between incomes and consumption expenditures has been assumed. These assumptions are compatible with standard choice theory.

3 The technology of exchange is no less important than the technology of production, and so both must be represented on an equal footing whenever technological specifications are required. The assumption of an arational auctioneer or other market-making agent is not required when exchange technologies are not differentiated analytically from production technologies.

4 Once the analysis of exchange is given an explicit foundation in technology and individual rationality, we find that continuous markets for all items of second-hand capital equipment cannot be assumed to exist.

5 Explicit analysis of the technologies of production and exchange, taken together, leads to the conclusion that, if exchange is allocatively efficient, some markets will be cleared continuously by flexible prices set, and changed, by profit-making intermediaries; but in other markets prices will be set with a view to longer-run considerations of finance and competition. In the latter class of markets, some commodities will be produced for stock while others will be produced only to order and customers will be queued so that the fixed capital equipment required for their production is continuously and fully utilized.

In this chapter we shall see what these propositions imply for a specification of the macroeconomic technology and how this technology can be used to determine prices, outputs, employment and capacity growth in the economy as a whole. These phenomena are, of course, associated particularly with the product markets. The financial markets will be considered in chapter 7, and the inter-actions between the product, financial and labour markets will be taken up in chapter 8. As in the microeconomic analysis, the macro-economic analysis is based as extensively and explicitly as possible on technological relationships. The advantage of these specifications over those that depend upon subjective relationships is that they render the theory more readily discomfirmable. Our microeconomic propositions imply our specification of the macroeconomic technology from which all our crucial propositions about dynamic macroeconomic processes are derived. If the technology is mis-specified, then no credence can be placed in our analysis of macro-economic processes, or therefore in the policy analysis predicated upon the identification of those processes.

In keeping with this approach, I begin in section 6.1 with the deduction of the macroeconomic technology of production and exchange from microeconomic propositions developed in earlier chapters. This technology is applied in section 6.2 to the dynamic analysis of capacity, output and employment growth and then in section 6.3 to macroeconomic price determination. We shall then see in sections 6.4 and 6.5 that the full macroeconomic framework for the analysis of industrial growth, employment and outputs is conveniently treated as a straightforward elaboration of the simple model of chapter 1. The real, but not the financial, effects of govern-ment expenditures are taken up in section 6.6 and the real effects of foreign trade are investigated in section 6.7.

6.1 THE MACROECONOMIC TECHNOLOGY OF PRODUCTION AND EXCHANGE

In Walrasian models, firms are represented by their production functions. In the present analysis it is more convenient to represent macroeconomic production possibilities by hypothetical processes which describe the range of input and output combinations available collectively to all firms. A hypothetical process represents an extreme set of inputs and outputs which it is technologically possible to produce in the whole economy; actual inputs and outputs can be represented by combinations of the hypothetical processes. Although some input and output combinations might be technologically feasible within the whole economy, it does not follow that they are actually feasible when capital equipment is not generally mobile in the short run. Some input and output combinations, though technologically feasible, would require firms to refrain from profitable uses of their capacities for production and exchange. For this reason the distribution of equipment among firms is likely to render it uneconomic to combine all inputs in all technologically possible combinations. The effect of any distribution of immobile capital equipment among firms is thus to limit the economically feasible combinations of extreme possibilities so that the extreme input combinations represented by some hypothetical processes cannot in fact be realized. In consequence, some output combinations will also be economically feasible.

The main advantage of this specification is that it reflects not only the short-run immobility of capital equipment, but also the embodiment of firms' technological opportunities in their capital equipment. Thus, the method of restricted combinations of hypothetical processes implicitly represents firms' production functions in the short run. By specifying the ways in which the restrictions on combinations of hypothetical processes can change over time, we can take into account not only changes in the quantities of capital equipment available to each firm but also the embodied technical changes adopted by firms.

I shall assume here that the hypothetical processes can be represented by vectors of fixed input and output coefficients so that actual inputs and outputs can be represented by linear combinations of these vectors. It is elementary that these assumptions reflect constant returns up to the point of full capacity utilization. Provided that inputs of materials and labour to actual processes and the percentages of capacities utilized are directly proportional to output volumes, the linearity assumption will not be in any way misleading. We shall see in the next section that technologically fixed inputs (i.e. input magnitudes that are required whatever the volume of outputs), and therefore technologically determined fixed costs, are readily incorporated here. This means that, although direct inputs to processes are linearly related to activity levels, average costs can decline up to the point of full capacity utilization. These fixed costs arise from the actual maintenance of plant and equipment and firms' organizations rather than from financial charges, which are in no sense technological. Fixed financial charges will be important in our macroeconomic analysis but they are not technologically determined, and the argument will be facilitated if technology and finance are not confused. In general, and apart from minor elaborations, the justification for assuming linear production relations is altogether standard.

The more innovative aspect of the specification of the macro-economic technology is the restrictions on combinations of hypo-thetical process activity levels. These restrictions and the ways in which they change over time are an elaboration of the basic ratios introduced in section 1.4. A basic stock ratio is the fraction of the stock of any basic commodity that is available for use in the pro-duction or exchange of current basic commodity outputs anywhere in the economy. A basic flow ratio is the fraction of the current output of a basic commodity that will be available in the next period for use in basic commodity production or exchange. The vector of maximum basic stock ratios gives us as complete a descrip-tion of the distribution of basic commodities as we shall require. Since, as will presently be seen, any vector of hypothetical process activity levels implies a vector of actual basic stock ratios, the combinations of activity levels are restricted by the maximum basic stock ratios.

For some purposes, it might be desirable to take into explicit account restrictions on macroeconomic activity levels arising from (say) the imbalances among individual firms' resources. In such cases, a further elaboration of the maximum basic stock ratios will be required so that the proportion of each basic (and possibly non-basic) commodity available to each firm is specified. Given the level of generality and abstraction at which the present argument is conducted, however, that additional elaboration is not warranted.

Joint production

Although the linearity assumption can be justified, the equally convenient assumption that each hypothetical process yields a single output cannot be sustained in light of the microeconomic argument in chapter 2.

Joint production is an important determinant of the direction of firm growth and investment because some focusing effects arise from the need to dispose of unwanted by-products which entail costly disposal. Any investment project that enables the firm to use or sell such by-products will improve the firm's cash flow and enhance its comparative advantage in the processes utilizing the by-products if it yields either a profit or a loss that is no greater than the cumulative disposal costs that would otherwise be incurred (cf. Moss, 1981, chapters 2 and 3).

In addition, Steedman (1983) has shown that joint production is, as a matter of fact, empirically widespread. Thus, even if the microeconomic foundation of our macroeconomic analysis did not require the joint-production assumption, that assumption would be required in the interests of generality of application of the theory reported here. In any case, by showing that the present theory yields relatively simple and comprehensible macroeconomic propositions on the basis of exceedingly complex microeconomic relationships, we shall have demonstrated that our macroeconomic theory is indeed robust.

Note that joint production is assumed here to be a strictly technological phenomenon which is independent of production costs. There might well be economies of scope (Teece, 1982) that make multiproduct firms more cost-efficient than single-product firms collectively producing the same commodities. Provided that the multi-product firm could, if it so chose, produce just any one of its outputs with the same personnel and capital equipment, then the production opportunities of the firm will be represented as linear combinations of hypothetical single-product processes. it is only when single-commodity production is technologically infeasible that the hypothetical processes must be specified to yield more than one output. In that case, the hypothetical processes will specify the extreme proportions in which the joint products can be produced.

Typically, there is some variability or substitutability in the proportions in which inputs are required and outputs can be produced. If the individual firm cannot change input or output proportions, different firms with capital equipment of perhaps different technological vintages will use inputs or will jointly produce outputs in different proportions. Provided that, for the economy as a whole, all input and output proportions can be varied, the macroeconomic technology can be described by the specification of a number of hypothetical processes that is equal to the number of commodities that are both produced and used (i.e. excluding primary inputs). Substitution is then captured in the usual way by varying linear combinations of hypothetical process activity levels.

Exchange and the basic/non-basic distinction

It will be convenient when considering the technology of exchange as well as production, to distinguish between products and commodities. A 'product' is defined as an output from a process of production and is described entirely by its physical characteristics. A 'commodity' is an output from a process of exchange and is described not only by its physical characteristics but also by the location in time and space that renders it suitable for exchange. Evidently, on these definitions all products that are sold in markets must first enter as inputs to one or more processes of exchange.

By defining commodities so that they are distinguished by their locations in time and space, and by including the technology of exchange in the specification of the macroeconomic technology, the basic/non-basic distinction is made a natural, theoretically sound and empirically accurate characteristic of that technology.

The theory of markets specifies the conditions in which intermediaries in general and retailers in particular will be active in resource-efficient markets. The retailers' operations are specified by processes of exchange, the outputs from which are transfers of products to households. By definition, such commodities do not themselves enter into further production: they are non-basic. Other exchange processes characterize allocatively efficient markets for transactions among firms. Some of these commodities will be used in further production and so might, but need not, be basic. Others will only be resold, perhaps several times, until they reach households, government agencies (not corporations) or cutomers abroad. Those products that are sold for use in non-basic activities are non-basic commodities even though the products could have been used in the production or exchange of basic commodities.

In other words, basic commodities can enter into the production and exchange of both basic and non-basic commodities. Indeed, some must do so if all basic commodities are to enter at least indirectly into the production and exchange of all commodities. It is convenient here to specify basic products that are sold via distinct processes of exchange to users who do not themselves produce basics as non-basic *commodities*. In so doing, these processes of exchange that yield sales only to households, government agencies and other non-producing agents can be identified as non-basic processes. Those processes of exchange that yield sales only to basic producers or to both basic and non-basic producers and traders are identified as basic processes.

Jointness and the technology of exchange

Although some production technologies are known to yield joint outputs, there is no reason to suppose that technology imposes jointness in exchange. Where there is joint exchange, it is a result of cost efficiency. But it is always possible to sell just one commodity on any one occasion. In the present context, this means that the technology of exchange can always be represented by hypothetical single-output processes.

The advantage of this specification is that it is always possible to identify hypothetical processes that yield only non-basic outputs. All retail activities can be represented by such non-basic processes provided that (say) a car sold by a retail trader to a household for personal use is treated as a non-basic but the same car sold by the manufacturer as part of a fleet for use by salesmen of machine tools is treated as a basic commodity. This is in keeping with the distinction made here between a commodity and a product. It follows that, by taking explicit account of exchange technology, it is always possible to identify basic and non-basic processes as well as commodities. To do so will afford us a very considerable expositional convenience.

In general, any production activities that do not entail technologically joint outputs can be represented by hypothetical processes that are either basic or non-basic, depending on whether the outputs are basic or non-basic. Similarly, any joint-production processes will be basic or non-basic if all of the outputs therefrom are basic or non-basic, respectively. The only complications arise when basic and non-basics are joint products, but these are easily taken into account. For the present, therefore, I shall assume that it does not happen. The modifications to the exposition that are required when it does happen will be considered at the end of section 6.5.

Input and output matrices

In the standard notation of the literature on joint production, there is an input matrix $\mathbf{A} = [a_{ij}]$ where a_{ij} is the input of the ith commodity to the jth process operated at the unit activity level, and there is an output matrix $\mathbf{B} = [b_{ij}]$ where b_{ij} is the output of the ith commodity from the jth process operated at the same unit activity level.

If there are distinct basic and non-basic processes, it is because all basic commodities are required directly or indirectly as inputs to all processes from which basic commodities emerge as outputs and no non-basic commodities are inputs to those processes. In addition, at least one basic commodity is a direct input to processes yielding only non-basic commodities. These remarks imply that the input matrix can be partitioned so that

$$\mathbf{A} \equiv \begin{bmatrix} \mathbf{A}_{11} & \mathbf{A}_{12} \\ \mathbf{0} & \mathbf{A}_{22} \end{bmatrix} \tag{6.1}$$

where A_{11} and A_{22} are square. That is, it is possible without loss of generality to order commodities and processes in such a way that the matrix is block-triangular. If there are distinct basic and non-basic processes, then all outputs from those processes that the non-basic commodities do not enter as inputs are basics and no outputs from the remaining processes are basic. The output matrix can therefore be partitioned so that, with the same ordering of commodities and processes as that adopted for the input matrix,

$$B \equiv \begin{bmatrix} B_{11} & 0 \\ 0 & B_{22} \end{bmatrix} \tag{6.2}$$

where B_{11} and B_{22} are square and of the same order as A_{11} and A_{22}, respectively. Since at least one basic commodity must be used in non-basic processes, A_{12} must be is semi-positive. It is assumed further that no ordering of commodities and processes will render sub-matrices A_{22} and B_{22} block-triangular. If A_{11} and B_{11} are block-triangular, then we would have several degrees of 'basic-ness' in the sense that one group of commodities would be required as direct or indirect inputs to the production and exchange of a second group but not vice versa, while the second group would stand in the same relationship to the non-basic commodities. If so, the exposition would be somewhat complicated but it would make no difference whatever to the principles enunciated here.

It is now a perfectly straightforward matter to show that the input–output matrix corresponding to this macroeconomic technology is decomposable and cannot be assumed to be non-negative. Let X_t be the vector of inputs during time period t; x_t is the vector of outputs, and q_t is the vector of activity levels. Then

$$X_t \equiv Aq_t \quad \text{and} \quad x_t \equiv Bq_t$$

so that

$$X_t \equiv AB^{-1}x_t$$

where AB^{-1} is evidently the input–output matrix. Taking the partitionings of the input and output matrices into account, the input–output matrix can be written as

$$AB^{-1} \equiv \begin{bmatrix} A_{11}B_{11}^{-1} & A_{12}B_{22}^{-1} \\ 0 & A_{22}B_{22}^{-1} \end{bmatrix}. \tag{6.3}$$

Clearly, a sufficient (but not necessary) condition for this input–output matrix to be non-negative is for the output matrix to be a non-negative, diagonal matrix since the diagonal elements of the inverse would be the reciprocals of the diagonal elements of the output matrix itself. If, however, the output matrix has any positive off-diagonal as well as diagonal elements – indicating joint outputs – then the inverse of the output matrix could, but need not, have negative elements. And so, in consequence, could the input–output matrix $\mathbf{AB}^{-1}$. The input–output matrix is clearly block-triangular, hence decomposable, because there are distinct sets of basic and non-basic processes.

Decomposable input–output matrices are not used in models comprising differential and/or difference equations because of the difficulty of deriving general results about time-paths of macro-economic processes (cf. Morishima, 1964). In the present analysis, however, nothing depends on the general solutions to systems of differential or difference equations because neither individual rationality nor any conceivable characteristics of technology imply behaviour that is compatible with exogeneous, unchanging lag structures of the kind required for dynamic input–output analysis.

The negativity of input–output coefficients has the same effect in the present theory as in previous theories. It implies that price and quantity signals in the short run could well be perverse. Steedman (1982), for example, has proved that fundamental propositions about prices such as the Stolper–Samuelson theorem and dual propositions about input substitution such as the Rybczynski theorem cannot be extended to technological systems in which there is any element of joint production because of the consequent possibility of negativity of some input–output coefficients. The relationships implied by these theorems might hold in particular cases of joint-production systems, but the conditions in which they will hold have not been determined. Certainly to assume that non-perverse price and quantity relationships hold would be decidedly *ad hoc* unless it were known in advance that there were no joint production at all.

The robustness of the present macroeconomic theory in comparison with previous theories is that it can accommodate Steedman's results. The source of this robustness is that its conclusions follow from the non-continuity (i.e. discontinuity or non-existence) of markets for second-hand capital equipment and from the basic/non-basic distinction, both of which are implied by allocative efficiency in exchange. They do not depend for their validity on the price regimes in different commodity markets or on the characteristics of any short-run price signals. The signals that will be generated in the upswing of the major macroeconomic cycle identified in chapter 1 will sustain that upswing until labour or financial constraints bring it to an end. If labour constraints end the major macroeconomic upswing, it will be because (by definition) full employment has been achieved. We shall determine the nature of the financial constraints and policy measures to avoid them in chapters 7–9.

6.2 CAPACITY, OUTPUT AND EMPLOYMENT GROWTH

Three types of accelerator process were defined in section 1.4. In the Type I accelerator process, increased demands for non-basic commodities (corn in the two-sector model) induce entrepreneurs producing and trading non-basics to increase their rates of capacity utilization without increasing their investments in capacity expansion. In the Type II accelerator process, entrepreneurs producing non-basic commodities respond to increased demands for their outputs by increasing their investments in capacity expansion while producers and traders of basic commodities face increased derived demands for their outputs but increase only their rates of capacity utilization. That is, in a Type II accelerator process basic commodity producers and traders do not respond to increased demands for basic commodities by investing in fixed capital equipment. In the Type III accelerator process, increased derived demands for basic commodities induce increased rates of capacity growth by producers and traders of basics.

We found in chapter 1 that, for the two-sector economy, only the Type III accelerator process leads to a self-sustaining major upswing in macroeconomic activity and growth. This property of the Type III accelerator process stems from the non-continuity (discontinuity or non-existence) of markets for second-hand capital equipment and the basic/non-basic distinction.

Given the basic/non-basic distinction, non-continuity of capital equipment markets implies that some individual items of basic capital equipment cannot be transferred in the short run between basic and non-basic production and exchange. This need not be true of all items of basic capital equipment, but it must be true of a substantial proportion of existing stocks of basic equipment which can enter directly as inputs to non-basic production. The representation of this immobility of second-hand items of basic commodities is by means of the basic ratios just as in the two-sector model in section 1.4.

Given the general immobility of capital equipment already in use, the driving force of the Type III accelerator processes is the trade-off between basic and non-basic capacity growth. In the two-sector model, increasing rates of basic capacity and output growth required rising basic stock ratios, which in turn required rising basic flow ratios. The basic stock ratio corresponding to any basic commodity is the proportion of the economy-wide stock of that commodity held in the basic sub-system. The basic flow ratio is the production of the output of the corresponding basic commodity retained or sold for use in further production and exchange of basic commodities. It is a crucial aspect of the Type III accelerator and the corresponding multiplier–accelerator interaction that rising basic stock ratios are associated with rising rates of basic capacity and output growth and short-run reductions in non-basic capacity and output growth. That this result survives the introduction of joint production into the analysis will be proved in the appendix to this chapter. It is possible (but unlikely) that the trade-off will not hold in some cases for short intervals of time. Such cases are easily taken into account in the present theory.

Before considering the three types of accelerator process, we require to specify the relationships between the distribution of stocks of capital equipment and materials and current outputs of basic and non-basic commodities.

Denote by X_{1t} the stocks of basic commodities held in the economy at time t and by X_{2t} the stocks of non-basic commodities. Similarly, let x_{1t} and x_{2t} be the gross outputs of basic and non-basic commodities, respectively, during time period t. $\tilde{X}_{1t}$ and $\tilde{X}_{2t}$ are the existing stocks of idle basic and non-basic commodities, respectively, held at the start of the period. It follows from the partitioning of the input matrix (6.1) that

$$X_{1t} \equiv A_{11}q_{1t} + A_{12}q_{2t} + \tilde{X}_{1t} \tag{6.4}$$

$$X_{2t} \equiv A_{22}q_{2t} + \tilde{X}_{2t}. \tag{6.5}$$

Non-negativity restrictions imply that non-basic activity levels are limited by the technology of basic production itself and by the availability of basic inputs to non-basic production. Formally,

$$A_{12}q_{2t} \leqslant X_1 - A_{11}q_{1t} \tag{6.6}$$

and

$$A_{22}q_{2t} \leqslant X_{2t}. \tag{6.7}$$

Since A_{11} and A_{12} are semi-positive, increasing any one basic activity level (i.e. any one element of q_{1t}) requires some reduction in the maximum possible activity levels of at least one non-basic process unless the non-basic processes are already constrained by supplies of non-basic inputs. The trade-off is symmetrical since an increase in non-basic activity levels reduces the supply of basics left available for basic commodity production and exchange.

The basic stock ratios are a device to enable us to take into account the short-run immobility of second-hand capital equipment. As such, they are strictly formal relationships which have no microeconomic meaning. They are in no sense decision variables. They are, however, reflections of the outcomes of decisions taken by producers and traders of basic commodities.

The vector of basic stock ratios during period t, Φ_t, is defined by

$$\hat{\Phi}_t X_{1t} \equiv A_{11} q_{1t}. \tag{6.8}$$

The circumflex over a vector symbol here and subsequently denotes a diagonal matrix with the elements of the vector on the principal diagonal. Since A_{11} is semi-positive, any increase in any hypothetical activity level entails an increase in one or more basic stock ratios, the elements of X_{1t} being fixed in the short run.

Substituting from identity (6.8) into condition (6.6),

$$A_{12} q_{2t} \leqslant (I - \hat{\Phi}_t) X_{1t}. \tag{6.9}$$

Since A_{12} is semi-positive, a necessary condition for q_{2t} to be semi-positive is that no basic ratio exceed unity while some are sub-unitary and that basic commodity stocks be positive. Furthermore, in the short run

$$A_{12}(\Delta q_{2t}) \leqslant - (\Delta \hat{\Phi}_t) X_{1t} \tag{6.10}$$

so that any increases in any basic ratios will require reductions in some activity levels of non-basic processes constrained by supplies of basic inputs.

If basic stock ratios were always positively related to net outputs of basic commodities in the short run – hence rates of growth of basic commodity stocks – the short-run trade-off between basic capacity growth rates and non-basic capacity and output growth rates would be established. In conditions of joint production, no such relationship is implied by the technology alone. The reason is entirely straightforward.

The vector of gross basic commodity outputs during period t is

$$x_{1t} \equiv B_{11}q_{1t}. \tag{6.11}$$

Since B_{11} is semi-positive, increasing any basic activity level will increase one or (if there is joint production) more gross outputs of basic commodities. In the absence of joint production, B_{11} will, without loss of generality, be a diagonal matrix. Its inverse will therefore also be a diagonal matrix and the principal diagonal elements will be the reciprocals of the corresponding elements of B_{11}. In conditions of joint production, however, at least one column of B_{11} will have at least two elements, so that we cannot presume that its inverse is semi-positive, though it might be.

Our hypothetical processes have been devised so that B_{11} will be non-singular. Therefore,

$$q_{1t} \equiv B_{11}^{-1}x_{1t}. \tag{6.12}$$

Since B_{11}^{-1} could have negative elements in conditions of joint production, it is possible (though by no means necessary) that increasing some gross outputs will entail reductions in some activity levels, although some activity levels must always increase. If some activity levels are reduced, then it is possible (though not necessary) that some inputs to basic production and exchange will be reduced. In the short run (with given stocks of capital equipment and materials), the reductions in aggregate inputs of any commodity to basic production and exchange is tantamount to a reduction in the corresponding basic stock ratio.

If the technology of basic commodity production is viable at all, then there must be some positive vectors of gross outputs implying semi-positive vectors of basic activity levels. Indeed, identity (6.11) asserts that there will be such vectors of activity levels. The implication of identity (6.12) is that there might also be some vectors of activity levels with negative elements corresponding to semi-positive gross output vectors. If there are such vectors of activity levels, then there will also be possible combinations of increases in outputs that reduce activity levels and, possibly, some inputs relative to outputs. The conditions in which this can happen are investigated in the appendix to this chapter and are found to require divergences from balanced growth that are impossible in some circumstances and unimportant in all circumstances. In the remainder of the main body of this chapter, I shall ignore perverse relationships between input changes and increases in outputs.

Although the hypothetical processes are a convenient analytical device, they are of no use in empirical studies. In order to specify the analysis in terms of observable variables, it is necessary to eliminate the activity levels of hypothetical processes from our identities. We are then left with input–output and output–input relationships.

Eliminating q_{1t} from identities (6.8) and (6.11), we have

$$\hat{\Phi}_t X_{1t} \equiv A_{11} B_{11}^{-1} x_{1t}. \tag{6.13}$$

Since the left side of this identity is the vector of inputs to basic processes and x_{1t} is the vector of gross outputs of basic commodities during time period t, $A_{11} B_{11}^{-1}$ is evidently the input–output matrix for basic commodities alone. It will be convenient henceforth to refer to the activities described by this matrix and its inverse as the basic sub-system. This sub-system is a technological concept the definition of which does not depend on either institutional arrangements or structures (though the technology will necessarily be compatible with, and perhaps implied by, these). The non-basic sub-system comprises the remaining input–output relationships even where the same firms produce both basic and non-basic commodities.

We require a specification of net outputs from the basic sub-system. This specification is conveniently derived from the vector of gross outputs implied by any composition and scale of inputs. From identity (6.13),

$$x_{1t} \equiv B_{11} A_{11}^{-1} \hat{\Phi}_t X_{1t}. \tag{6.14}$$

The determination of net outputs evidently requires some specification of physical depreciation. There is no problem about this specification in so far as direct material inputs to production and exchange processes are concerned: they are completely used up, although scrap could emerge as a joint output. The real problem arises when we consider fixed capital equipment. Plant and durable equipment clearly do not decay in the same way as radioactive isotopes. Nor are machines 'one year older' produced *for sale* jointly with other commodities, so that this ingenious device, developed in its modern form by Sraffa (1960, chapter 10), is not appropriate to an analysis in which the technology of exchange is represented on equal footing with the technology of production.

The most appropriate specification of the physical depreciation of fixed capital goods that I have been able to devise takes cognizance of the fact that, although fixed capital goods by definition survive utilization in production and exchange, they also typically require some maintenance. This maintenance requires inputs of materials and labour and perhaps other fixed capital equipment. Provided that these inputs are represented explicitly in the specification of the input coefficients of matrix $\mathbf{A}$, no further account need be taken of physical depreciation. This device is a physical analogue of Keynes's notion of user cost (1936, pp. 66–73). I therefore define the depreciation vector $\mathbf{d} \equiv (d_i)$ such that $d_i \equiv 1$ if the ith commodity is a direct material input to production or exchange and $d_i \equiv 0$ if the ith commodity is a fixed capital good. Whenever radioactive isotopes are used in processes of production and exchange (e.g. in electricity generation), there is no reason to preclude values of d_i between nought and unity.

With these comments in mind, we note that the vector of net outputs of basic commodities – which is here the change in the quantity of basic commodities available for use in production and exchange next period – is

$$\Delta \mathbf{X}_{1t} \equiv \mathbf{x}_{1t} - \hat{\mathbf{d}}(\hat{\mathbf{\Phi}}_t \mathbf{X}_{1t} + \mathbf{A}_{12}\mathbf{q}_{2t}) \tag{6.15}$$

where $\hat{\mathbf{d}}$ is the diagonal matrix of depreciation rates of basic commodities employed in production and exchange. Substituting for the gross output vector $\mathbf{x}_{1t}$ from identity (6.14), identity (6.15) can be written as

$$\mathbf{x}_{1t} \equiv \mathbf{K}\hat{\mathbf{\Phi}}_t \mathbf{X}_{1t} - \hat{\mathbf{d}}\mathbf{A}_{12}\mathbf{q}_{2t} \tag{6.16}$$

where $\mathbf{K} \equiv (\mathbf{B}_{11}\mathbf{A}_{11}^{-1} - \mathbf{d})$.

This identity is for net outputs of basic commodities in the whole economy, since the output vector is net of direct basic inputs to non-basic production and exchange. The vector of net outputs from the basic sub-system alone is

$$\mathbf{y}_{1t} \equiv \mathbf{K}\hat{\mathbf{\Phi}}_t \mathbf{X}_{1t}. \tag{6.17}$$

The basic sub-system is technologically viable if it can produce net outputs sufficient both for its own growth and in order to provide inputs to the non-basic sub-system. Formally, viability requires that there be some vectors of basic stock ratios for which all net outputs of basic commodities are positive. They need not actually be positive during every time-period, but it must be possible to produce positive quantities of all net basic outputs at the same time. It follows that the basic sub-system is technologically viable if there exists a set of positive vectors $\mathbf{\Phi}_t$ such that

$$\mathbf{K}\hat{\mathbf{\Phi}}_t \mathbf{X}_{1t} > 0 \tag{6.18}$$

If and only if this condition is satisfied, any semi-positive set of prices yields a value of gross outputs from the basic sub-system that is greater than the value of inputs to the basic sub-system; for, by a theorem of Gale (1960, p. 49), if and only if condition (6.17) is satisfied, there is no semi-positive price vector $\mathbf{p}'$ such that

$$\mathbf{p}'\mathbf{K}\hat{\Phi}_t\mathbf{X}_{1t} \leqq 0.$$

Thus, for any semi-positive vector of basic commodity prices, the value of net outputs from the basic sub-system is positive. Whether basic commodity production and exchange is actually profitable depends on the wage rate. All that viability implies is that, for the basic sub-system as a whole, value-added *can* be positive.

It should be noted here that condition (6.18) will not be satisfied only as a matter of chance. There are endogenous economic forces to ensure that it will be satisfied in the long run. For we know as a matter of history that growing shortages of raw materials, the sudden imposition of external supply constraints and/or sudden increases in demands for commodities give rise to searches for technical changes to overcome the supply deficiencies. Obvious examples of such episodes are the wood famine in Britain during the seventeenth and early eighteenth centuries, the capture by the Japanese of the main sources of supply of natural rubber in 1942 and the invention of the universal milling machine during the American Civil War. Moreover, each of these developments led to changes in a wide range of production and exchange processes. These and similar episodes were a major inspiration in the development of my analysis of focusing and inducement effects (Moss, 1981, especially chapter 3). The economic analysis of focusing and inducement effects implies that condition (6.18) will be satisfied in the long run if not in the short run (see chapter 8 on the timing of technical changes).

Suppose that there were no basic stock ratios satisfying condition (6.18). That is, the net output–input matrix of the basic sub-system does not permit the production and exchange of net outputs of all basic commodities simultaneously. Although this is a macroeconomic result, it implies that there are firms that cannot produce or exchange commodities for which there are demands during expansionary phases of the trade cycle when actual basic stock ratios are generally rising. Moreover, the demands for basic commodities are from firms requiring them either as direct or indirect inputs to production processes or in order to satisfy final demands from households and other agents who do not engage in production. Such recurrent and imperative excess demands will constitute inducement effects to economize on the requirements for these basic commodities. Rational individuals will seek technical changes which reduce or eliminate the demands for the commodities in short supply or which make possible substantial increases in the outputs of such commodities. In short, the imbalance theory of the firm implies that, whenever condition (6.18) cannot be satisfied, there will be micro-economic processes set in train to change the sub-system's net output–input matrix until that condition is satisfied.

Growth and the basic ratios

In the short run, with a given net output–input matrix **K** for the basic sub-system and a given vector of basic commodity stocks, the only means of changing net output levels from the basic sub-system is by changing the basic stock ratios. It is clear from identity (6.17) that equiproportional changes in the basic stock ratios yield the same proportional change in all net outputs from the basic sub-system. In conditions of joint production, however, some elements of **K** could be negative. It is therefore possible that increases in only some basic stock ratios could imply reductions in some net outputs from the basic sub-system and *mutatis mutandis* for reductions in some basic stock ratios.

Since fixed capital equipment is typically immobile in the short run, changes in the basic stock ratios can be effected only by changes in firms' rates of capacity utilization. It is therefore possible for relative values of the basic stock ratios to change dramatically in the short run if demand growth is declining and, in consequence, rates of capacity utilization in the basic sub-system are declining. Since, we have seen, some capital equipment is operated economically only at full capacity utilization, there can be dramatic changes in the relative rates of capacity utilization across establishments, and there-fore dramatic changes in the relative values of the basic stock ratios. These changes in capacity utilization rates are due to demand-induced reductions in the rates of growth of net outputs from the basic sub-system. But when there is increasing growth of demand for basic commodities, the rates of capacity utilization will rise and the net outputs from the basic sub-system – hence the basic stock ratios – will be constrained by the distribution of fixed, basic capital equip-ment among establishments. It follows that, during periods of growing basic commodity demands, the relative values of the basic stock ratios cannot change faster than the distribution of basic com-modity stocks among establishments. Since this distribution changes as a result of time-consuming investments in capacity expansion, the relative values of the basic stock ratios cannot change quickly during expansionary periods. For this reason, the growth of net outputs from the basic sub-system will be close enough to balance growth for there to be a positive relationship between the rates of growth of net outputs from the basic sub-system and the basic stock ratio. (The precise meaning of the phrase 'close enough to balanced growth' is established in the appendix to this chapter.)

This is an important result.

We found in the two-sector model in section 1.4 that the rate of growth of the machine stock in the whole economy was positively related to the actual basic stock ratio, while the rate of growth of the machine stock in the machine sector alone was positively related to the basic flow ratio. Furthermore, the maximum basic stock ratio – the proportion of machines held in the machine sector – would rise whenever the basic flow ratio exceeded the maximum basic stock ratio. As long as the pattern of growth of net outputs from the basic sub-system is close enough to balanced growth, the same results are obtained in the present more general specification of the macroeconomic technology.

The relationship between the growth of basic commodity stocks in the whole economy and the actual basic stock ratios is implicit in identity (6.16). Provided that the basic sub-system is viable and producing net outputs of all basic commodities, then increases in the basic stock ratios – the elements of Φ_t – yield increased net outputs from the basic sub-system while restricting or diminishing the use of basic materials in the non-basic sub-system. The positive term on the right side of identity (6.16) is increased while the negative term is, if anything, diminished. In the short run, with given stocks of basic commodities, increasing the basic stock ratios increases net outputs of basic commodities for the economy as a whole and, by definition, the rates of growth of basic commodity stocks in the whole economy.

It is convenient here to define the basic flow ratio corresponding to any basic commodity as the ratio of increases in basic commodity stocks available for use in the basic sub-system to *net* outputs of the commodity from the basic sub-system. Using this definition of the basic flow ratio, it follows that

$$\hat{\phi}_t \mathbf{y}_{1t} \equiv \Delta(\hat{\Phi}_t^* \mathbf{X}_{1t}) \tag{6.19}$$

where Φ_t^* is the vector of maximum basic stock ratios. That is, $\hat{\Phi}_t^* \mathbf{X}_{1t}$ is the vector of the total stocks of basic commodities held by firms that are active in the basic sub-system.

Expanding the right side of identity (6.19),

$$\phi_t \mathbf{y}_{1t} \equiv (\Delta\hat{\Phi}_t^*) \mathbf{X}_{1(t+1)} + \hat{\Phi}_t^*(\Delta \mathbf{X}_{1t}). \tag{6.20}$$

Substituting into this identity from identities (6.16) and (6.17) and rearranging, we have

$$\Delta\Phi_t^* \equiv \hat{X}_{1(t+1)}^{-1}[(\hat{\phi}_t - \hat{\Phi}_t^*)\,y_{1t} + \hat{\Phi}_t^*\hat{d}A_{12}q_{2t}] \qquad (6.21)$$

since

$$(\Delta\hat{\Phi}_t^*)\,X_{1(t+1)} \equiv \hat{X}_{1(t+1)}(\Delta\Phi_t^*).$$

It is clear from identity (6.19) (because it is implicit in the definition of the basic flow ratio) that an increase in any basic flow ratio amounts to a larger increase in the stocks of basic commodities that will be available for use in the basic sub-system in subsequent time-periods. Since the existing stocks are inherited from the past, the increase in the basic flow ratio is part and parcel of an increase in the rate of growth of basic commodity stocks in the basic sub-system.

Similarly, we see from identity (6.21) that for fixed capital equipment the maximum basic stock ratios rise if the current net output is positive and the basic flow ratio is above the maximum basic stock ratio. If the basic flow ratio is below the maximum basic stock ratio, the maximum basic stock ratio declines. In consequence, the maximum basic stock ratios corresponding to fixed capital equipment converge towards the basic flow ratios. This result follows from noting that the rows of $\hat{d}A_{12}$ corresponding to fixed capital equipment have only zero elements. For circulating or non-durable commodities (i.e. those that are used up in production), the maximum basic stock ratios rise when those materials are employed in the non-basic sub-system simply because the denominator of that ratio falls on that account. Thus, the maximum basic stock ratios of basic materials will be constant only when the basic flow ratio is somewhat below the maximum basic stock ratio. But, as for capital equipment, to increase any of the maximum basic stock ratios requires increases in the corresponding basic flow ratios. The speed of convergence of maximum basic stock ratios towards the corresponding basic flow ratio is positively related to the elements of y_{1t}, hence to the rates of capacity utilization in the basic sub-system.

These results confirm for the general case the results obtained in section 1.4. The rate of capacity growth over the whole economy is determined by the actual basic stock ratios. Therefore, the achievement of higher rates of macroeconomic capacity, output and employment growth requires increases in the basic stock ratios and eventually in the maximum basic stock ratios. To achieve these increases requires rising basic flow ratios (hence rising rates of basic capacity growth). In the short run, increasing basic flow ratios reduce the rates of growth of basic inputs available for non-basic production while increasing the rate of growth of basic production. In a fixed-coefficient model – which is technologically plausible on the definitions used here – the rate of employment growth in the basic sub-system must be increasing in these conditions while the rate of employment growth in the non-basic sub-system first declines and then converges towards the rate of basic sub-system employment growth as some balance is re-established in macroeconomic growth.

These results follow entirely from identities and the assumption that, even in conditions of joint production, increasing the rates of growth of net outputs from the basic sub-system requires reductions in the rates of growth of inputs to the non-basic sub-system. The conditions in which this assumption is justified and the consequences when it is not justified are taken up in the appendix.

The generalized accelerator processes

These relationships between the basic ratios and rates of capacity, output and employment growth are generalized versions of the relationships identified in the context of the two-sector model of section 1.4. It is therefore hardly surprising that the accelerator processes that these relationships were found to imply in the simpler case generalize to the macroeconomic technology specified here.

The Type I accelerator process entails no induced changes in rates of capacity growth anywhere in the economy. It follows that outputs of fixed capital equipment are unaffected by changes in household or other demands apart from those of domestic firms. Increased rates of capacity utilization will, however, be required to produce increased net outputs from the non-basic sub-system so that increased inputs of circulating capital goods (materials, semi-manufactures, etc.) to the non-basic sub-system will be necessary. Since some of these inputs will be basic commodities, the Type I accelerator will entail increased net outputs from the basic as well as the non-basic sub-system. This implication gives rise to the possibility that a Type I accelerator process will yield directly to a Type III accelerator process. This will happen when producers and traders in the basic sub-system respond to increased demands for circulating basic commodities by increasing their growth of investments in capacity expansion. Although such an outcome is possible, there are substantial theoretical grounds for rejecting it as unlikely. These grounds, specified in detail in section 6.5, turn on the finding that the state of long-term expectation in the basic sub-system will change only if the preponderance of entrepreneurs active in that sub-system *simultaneously* turn more optimistic or pessimistic about long-term demand trends. If only a few of these entrepreneurs change their expectations in the same direction, there will be no sustained changes in rates of capacity growth anywhere in the basic sub-system.

It is in the nature of a Type I accelerator process that the basic ratios attaching to circulating basic commodities decline. This is because the net outputs of these commodities from the basic sub-system are increased only to provide inputs to the non-basic sub-system. There will be declining growth rates of at least some basic production and exchange capacities because the corresponding basic stock ratios will be falling while the growth of non-basic outputs for non-productive uses increase until full capacity utilization is reached in the non-basic sub-system.

The Type II accelerator process is characterized by changed states of long-term expectation in the non-basic sub-system but not in the basic sub-system. If the process is expansionary, there will be increased *growth* of demands for both fixed and circulating (or durable and non-durable) basic commodities for use in the non-basic sub-system. The resulting market signals do not convince entrepreneurs in the basic sub-system that the increased demand growth will last long enough to warrant increased rates of capacity growth. In consequence, the basic flow ratios attaching generally to basic commodities employed directly in the non-basic sub-system will decline. (Other basic flow ratios can only take values of unity, so that rates of growth change only with rates of capacity utilization and with changing basic commodity distributions within the sub-system.) As the basic flow ratios decline, the maximum and, therefore, the actual basic stock ratios converge towards the now-lower and possibly falling basic flow ratios. It follows from our algebra that the rates of capacity, output and employment growth in the basic sub-system fall while non-basic capacity and output growth rates increase in the short run. In the long run, however, growth in the non-basic sub-system cannot be faster than the growth of the basic sub-system. Thus, after the initial increase in the growth of basic inputs to the non-basic sub-system, the rates of non-basic capacity, output and employment growth converge towards the lower or falling rates of growth in the basic sub-system. There is no substantial difference between this account of the Type II accelerator and that given for the two-sector model in section 1.4.

The Type III accelerator process, characterized by changed states of long-term expectation in the basic sub-system, is also a perfect parallel to the Type II process described in section 1.4. Once an expansionary Type II process is underway, the increased growth of demands for basic commodities could lead entrepreneurs in the basic sub-system to interpret the market signals to indicate a sustained increase in basic demand growth. They will then increase their rates of capacity growth so that basic flow ratios rise and, in the first instance, non-basic capacity and output growth rates fall owing to basic supply constraints. In the long run, however, the rates of basic capacity growth must stop rising and the non-basic sub-system growth rates can then converge towards the increased basic sub-system growth rates.

Although the characteristics of these three types of accelerator process rely heavily on entrepreneurial responses to market signals, they are insensitive to the form taken by those market signals that arise from allocatively efficient exchange. That is, the market signals generated by the various exchange technologies discussed in previous chapters all have the same effects during periods of expansion and during periods of contraction. This result makes the present theory very robust indeed in relation to alternative specifications of endogenous price and quantity changes.

The proof of this robustness requires the prior determination of the macroeconomic price relationships implied by our microeconomic theory. It is to that specification that we now turn.

6.3 MACROECONOMIC PRICE AND WAGE RELATIONSHIPS

The one general and clear macroeconomic relationship among prices and wages has already been identified in chapter 5. That is, any general increase in nominal wages and short-run prices will cause long-run prices to increase as well. If there is any joint production in the economy, then if only some wage rates and/or short-run prices rise, and the rise is not expected soon to be reversed, then some long-run prices will rise but others probably will not and yet others might actually fall. Also, if some or even all mark-ups are increased, then some long-run prices might rise, others might remain unchanged and others might fall. The results hold *mutatis mutandis* for reductions in short-run prices, wage rates and mark-ups.

These results make it implausible to treat prices as unambiguous market signals in any macroeconomic sense, although, as we have

seen repeatedly in previous chapters, prices do constitute unambiguous market signals in individual price-efficient markets. This
is not a problem in the present analysis, since real (as distinct from
financial) macroeconomic processes are insensitive to the price
regimes in individual markets. As we saw in chapter 1 (and is anyway
known), the absence of continuous markets in second-hand plant and
equipment implies that an economy comprising only price-efficient
markets can still be characterized by persistent Keynesian unemployment. Seemingly insuperable difficulties arise only for dynamic
analyses which depend upon non-perverse and unambiguous price
responses for the provision of market signals.

These points are made formally by elaborating the analysis of the
two preceding sections to include short-run prices, wage rates, mark-
ups and long-run prices. In light of the arguments of chapters 3 and
5, however, it cannot be assumed that every change in short-run
prices or in wage rates causes long-run prices to change immediately.
Nor can it be assumed that declining demands will not cause long-run
prices to fall. As was found in section 3.4, long-run prices will indeed
fall in the event of unusually severe and long-lasting depressions
in conditions of demand. This is one of the factors that makes it
possible for governments to reduce and possibly to reverse rates of
price inflation by means of deflationary demand management
measures. We also found that long-run prices will move in the same
direction as short-run prices only after the changes in short-run
prices turn out to be larger and/or more persistent than usual. Thus,
in this section, whenever wage rates and short-run prices are
specified, these are to be interpreted as 'normal' prices and wage
rates.

I argued in section 6.1 that, in general, exchange processes do not
yield technologically joint outputs. Even if they were to do so,
however, short-run-priced and long-run-priced outputs would never
emerge from the same exchange processes since the technologies of
exchange are different in each case. And, as I argued in section 5.4,
the allocatively efficient exchange technology in the labour markets
is unique. Moreover, the main categories of commodities that are
traded at short-run prices are mineral and agricultural produce,
which, clearly, are outputs from distinct processes and are not produced jointly with industrial commodities which constitute the main
class of commodities traded at long-run prices. I shall take these
remarks as my warrant for assuming that long-run-priced commodities are not produced jointly with short-run-priced commodities.
This implies block-diagonal output matrices for each sub-system. The
input matrix for each sub-system remains indecomposable.

Basic commodity prices

The output matrix for the basic sub-system can be partitioned so that

$$\mathbf{B}_{11} \equiv \begin{bmatrix} \mathbf{b}_{11} & 0 \\ 0 & \mathbf{b}_{22} \end{bmatrix} \tag{6.22}$$

where $\mathbf{b}_{11}$ is the matrix of outputs of short-run-priced basics and $\mathbf{b}_{22}$ is the matrix of outputs of long-run-priced basics. It will be convenient conformably to partition the basic sub-system input matrix so that

$$\mathbf{A}_{11} \equiv \begin{bmatrix} \mathbf{a}_{11} & \mathbf{a}_{12} \\ \mathbf{a}_{21} & \mathbf{a}_{22} \end{bmatrix}. \tag{6.23}$$

The basic sub-system labour-input matrix is $\mathbf{N}_1 = [n_{lj}]$ where n_{lj} is the input of the lth type of labour to the jth process operated at the unit activity level. This matrix is partitioned so that

$$\mathbf{N}_1 \equiv [\mathbf{n}_1 \ \ \mathbf{n}_2]. \tag{6.24}$$

The row vector of wage rates is $\mathbf{w}'$ and the row vector of basic commodity prices is $\mathbf{p}'$ where

$$\mathbf{p}' \equiv [\mathbf{p}_1' \ \ \mathbf{p}_2'] \tag{6.25}$$

with $\mathbf{p}_1'$ being the vector of short-run basic commodity prices and $\mathbf{p}_2'$ being the vector of long-run prices of basic commodities. Evidently, the block-diagonal sub-matrices in (6.22) and (6.23) are square and non-singular.

The gross profit from the jth process operated at the unit activity level is, when expressed as a proportion of direct costs,

$$r_j \equiv \frac{\sum_i p_i(b_{ij} - a_{ij}d_i) - \sum_l w_l n_{lj}}{\sum_i p_i a_{ij} d_i + \sum_l w_l n_{lj}} \tag{6.26}$$

where r_j is the rate of gross profits on actual costs, since the prices of fixed capital goods are multiplied by $d_i = 0$ as inputs although they enter into the determination of revenue from outputs. In matrix notation, with $\mathbf{r} = [r_j]$ being the vector of gross profit rates on actual costs and $\hat{\mathbf{r}}$ the corresponding diagonal matrix,

$$\mathbf{p}_1' \mathbf{b}_{11} \equiv (\mathbf{p}_1' \hat{\mathbf{d}}_1 \mathbf{a}_{11} + \mathbf{p}_2' \hat{\mathbf{d}}_2 \mathbf{a}_{21} + \mathbf{w}' \mathbf{n}_1)(\mathbf{I} + \hat{\mathbf{r}}) \tag{6.27}$$

where d_1 and d_2 are the vectors of depreciation rates of basic commodities traded at short-run prices and long-run prices, respectively. Identity (6.27) is the short-run price identity for the basic sub-system.

Since short-run prices are determined by intermediaries in light of current market conditions, the r_j must be residuals that are implied by the technology, the wage rates and the long-run prices. Even as residuals, the r_j cannot be interpreted as firms' profit rates since they attach to hypothetical macroeconomic processes rather than actual microeceonomic processes. None the less, if the r_j fall it is because the prices of outputs from firms producing short-run-priced commodities are falling relative to the prices of at least some of the inputs that those firms require, including inputs of labour. Thus, the profit rates on firms' input costs must be falling on average even if, in principle, the distribution of firms' profit rates could be so wide that some actually rise.

We now denote by m_j the mark-up on actual costs incurred in operating the jth process. The definition of the mark-up is the same as that of the profit rate except that the r_j are residuals while the m_j, being the outcomes of firms' financial and investment policy decisions, are given to the market.

Like the r_j, the m_j relate to hypothetical processes which need not be operated by any actual firm. The m_j therefore are macroeconomic manifestations of individual firms' pricing policies. Their analytical function here is to take account of the sluggishness of changes in long-run prices relative to the flexibility of short-run prices.

Denoting the diagonal matrix of these mark-ups on basic sub-system direct costs by $\hat{m}$, we have the long-run price identity for the basic sub-system:

$$p'_2 b_{22} \equiv (p'_1 \hat{d}_1 a_{12} + p'_2 \hat{d}_2 a_{22} + w' n_2)(I + \hat{m}). \qquad (6.28)$$

Any proportional increase in all wage rates and short-run prices yields the same proportional increase in all long-run prices. This is easily seen by rearrranging identity (6.28) and post-multiplying both sides by $(I + \hat{m})^{-1}$ so that

$$p'_2 M \equiv p'_1 a_{12} + w' n_2 \qquad (6.29)$$

where

$$M \equiv [b_{22}(I + \hat{m})^{-1} - \hat{d}_2 a_{22}].$$

We shall find in chapter 7 that prices are best denominated in some unit of account that is not identified with the price of any one commodity or group of commodities. In particular, there is no economic justification for normalizing prices on any basic commodities, so that long-run prices are seen in identity (6.29) to be homogeneous of degree one in wage rates and short-run prices denominated in some, for the moment, arbitrary unit of account. It follows that basic commodity price inflation will be general whenever wage rates and short-run basic commodity prices are rising in the same proportions.

If, however, relative wage rates and short-run prices change because some nominal wage rates and prices rise more than others or because only some rise at all, then some long-run prices will undoubtedly rise but others will, in some circumstances, fall. There is no mystery about this proposition. If b_{22} is not a semi-positive, diagonal matrix, then the sufficient conditions for M^{-1} to be semi-positive are not satisfied. This inverse matrix could have negative elements. Since, from identity (6.29),

$$\mathbf{p}_2' \equiv (\mathbf{p}_1' \hat{\mathbf{d}}_2 \mathbf{a}_{22} + \mathbf{w}' \mathbf{n}_2) \, \mathbf{M}^{-1}, \tag{6.30}$$

if M^{-1} has negative elements then it is possible that increases in some short-run prices and/or some wage rates will imply reduced long-run prices. The conditions in which this will happen are derived in the appendix. We shall also see in the appendix that any changes in any mark-ups could imply long-run price changes in either direction, though some must change in the same direction as the mark-ups. As a result, if some long-run prices should fall in response to an unexpectedly severe or persistent reduction in demands, some of the mark-ups on hypothetical processes might actually rise although some will necessarily fall.

Matters are much simpler when we turn to the determination of the residual profit rates on direct costs in the production and exchange of commodities traded in price-efficient markets. The definition of these profit rates – identity (6.26) – implies that any reductions in short-run prices relative either to wage rates or to long-run prices will reduce the values of the r_j; for long-run prices attach to inputs to, but not outputs from, the processes for the production and exchange of commodities traded in price-efficient markets. Thus, if short-run prices fall temporarily, then profits on the production and exchange of the corresponding commodities are squeezed. If short-run prices rise temporarily, then profit rates are increased. Once price-setting entrepreneurs see that changes in short-run prices have changed, there will be changes in relative long-run prices and therefore in residual profit rates. But when short-run prices and wages are generally rising, long-run prices will eventually begin rising at about the same rate so that residual profit rates will stabilize. Clearly, there will be a complicated lag structure here, since increased short-run prices take time to feed through into increased long-run prices. How much time depends on the size of stocks relative to rates of use and the speed with which users come to expect price increases to be sufficiently long-lasting to warrant increases in their own long-run prices. By their very nature, wage increases lead far more quickly to increases in long-run prices since they are the subject of negotiation and practice and because there are no stocks of labour services that can be purchased at current prices and stored against the day when wage rates might be increased. Long-term employment contracts lend an added certainty to wage increases, which will ensure that implied changes in long-run prices are affected as soon as the wage rates change.

Non-basic commodity prices

Apart from there being an additional category of inputs, the analysis of non-basic commodity prices is formally identical to the analysis of basic commodity prices. For exactly the same reasons as in the case of the basic sub-system, the non-basic sub-system output matrix is partitioned so that

$$\mathbf{B}_{22} \equiv \begin{bmatrix} \beta_{11} & 0 \\ 0 & \beta_{22} \end{bmatrix} \tag{6.31}$$

where β_{11} is the sub-matrix of outputs trading at short-run prices and β_{22} is the sub-matrix of non-basic outputs trading at long-run prices. The non-basic sub-system input matrices are partitioned conformably so that

$$\mathbf{A}_{12} \equiv [\mathbf{A}_{12}^s \ \mathbf{A}_{12}^L] \tag{6.32}$$

and

$$\mathbf{A}_{22} \equiv \begin{bmatrix} \alpha_{11} & \alpha_{12} \\ \alpha_{21} & \alpha_{22} \end{bmatrix}. \tag{6.33}$$

Denoting vectors for the non-basic sub-system by the Greek counterparts to the notation in Roman letters used for the basic sub-system, we have the short-run price identity for the non-basic sub-system:

$$\pi_1' \beta_{11} \equiv (\pi_1' \alpha_{11} + \pi_2' \alpha_{21} + \mathbf{p}' \mathbf{A}_{12}^s + \mathbf{w}' \boldsymbol{\nu}_1)(\mathbf{I} + \hat{\rho}) \tag{6.34}$$

and the long-run price identity for the non-basic sub-system is

$$\pi'_2\beta_{22} \equiv (\pi'_1\alpha_{12} + \pi'_2\alpha_{22} + p'A^L_{12} + w'\nu_2)(I + \hat{\mu}). \tag{6.35}$$

It is clear from identity (6.35) that basic commodity prices have the same effect on long-run non-basic commodity prices as do wage rates and short-run prices of non-basic inputs. In addition, it is clear from the non-basic short-run price identity (6.34) that basic commodity prices have the same effect on the residual profit rates – the elements of $\hat{\rho}$ – as do long-run, non-basic commodity prices and wage rates. Thus, any increases in basic commodity prices squeeze profit rates on the costs of direct inputs to processes for the production and exchange of short-run-priced non-basic commodities. In addition, they lead to changed long-run prices of the remaining non-basic commodities, although the directions of individual price changes cannot be ascertained in advance without full knowledge of the non-basic technology.

Inflation and relative prices in conditions of joint production

There are well defined limits, specified in the appendix, within which increases in some short-run prices and/or some wage rates imply that some or all long-run prices will rise and none will fall. Nothing in the present theory implies that wage-rate and short-run price rises will be within these limits, or, therefore, that such rises will not imply reductions in some long-run prices. In light of these results, the most transparent approach to the analysis of inflation in conditions of joint production is notionally to separate general rises in short-run prices and in wage rates into equiproportional rises equal to the rate of increase of the most slowly rising short-run price or wage rate, and then to take relative price and wage changes into account by further notional increases. The equiproportional rises imply that long-run prices rise in that same proportion. We can then notionally take into account those changes in relative short-run prices and wage rates that entail further rises in nominal short-run prices and wage rates within the above mentioned limits. This second stage implies further increases in some long-run prices and reductions in none. Finally, we allow for increases in short-run prices and wage rates outside the specified limits, implying that some long-run prices rise yet further while others decline. Once this process is completed it is possible that the total changes in some long-run prices will be negative, because the reduction in these prices at the third stage is larger in magnitude than the sum of the increases in these prices in the first two stages.

Within this framework, it is easy to consider how demand-pull and cost-push inflations can arise.

Demand-pull inflations will generally characterize Type III accelerator processes. As basic sub-system growth rates rise, and in the period after they have risen, there are necessarily excess demands for basic outputs. This is due to the prevalence of full capacity utilizations in the basic sub-system and the supply constraint on the non-basic sub-system. In consequence, short-run basic commodity prices will be rising. As a matter of fact, real wage rates rise fastest during strong macroeconomic upswings, for reasons that, as we shall see in chapter 8, are well explained by the present theory. Thus, we would expect both short-run prices and wage rates to be rising in the conditions of general excess demands attendant upon the Type III accelerator process, though not necessarily during the weaker and short-lived Type I and Type II accelerator processes. Although, as we have already found, general rises in wage rates and short-run prices do not imply that all long-run prices rise, it is certainly the case that the trend rate of long-run price inflation will be close to the trend rate of wage and short-run price inflation, though the variance of long-run price rises could entail some long-run price reductions.

Cost-push inflations in a closed economy start from rising nominal wage rates. In an open economy, rising import prices – arising perhaps from a falling domestic exchange rate – will have the same effect. Rising wage rates and import prices will unambiguously squeeze profit rates on direct costs in the production and exchange of short-run-priced commodities. In the face of falling profits, outputs of short-run-priced commodities will fall relative to outputs of long-run-priced commodities, which are not subject to the same profit squeeze, until the resulting supply deficiencies (or excess demands) cause short-run prices also to rise. Since both short-run prices and wage rates will then be rising, long-run prices will rise at a similar trend rate, although, again, reductions in some relative long-run prices could imply some price reductions.

We shall see in chapter 9 that demand-pull inflations are beneficial in that they help to sustain expansionary Type III accelerator processes. Cost-push inflations in a closed economy – if moderate – can ease the transition from major macroeconomic slumps to sustained major macroeconomic upturns, although in an open economy they are generally unhelpful.

It remains in this chapter to show that the importance of the direction of investment in determining employment, output and capacity growth in the whole economy is not affected by particular combinations of short- and long-run pricing regimes in the individual markets for commodities. Indeed, the results are not significantly different if all markets are price-efficient or none are. All we require is that individuals learn at limited rates and that continuous markets are not allocatively efficient for the exchange of all second-hand capital equipment. The satisfaction of the first of these conditions is required for the assumption of individual rationality to yield simple and general theories, while the satisfaction of the second condition is implied by the assumption of individual rationality.

6.4 THE MULTIPLIER

Both the employment multiplier and the investment multiplier analyses rest on the assumption that the net supplies of consumption commodities will accommodate the net demands. (As in chapter 1, these net supplies and demands exclude consumption by workers employed in the production and exchange of consumption commodities.) If there is no such accommodation, there is no multiplier process.

In distinguishing multiplier processes from accelerator processes and any spontaneous changes in employment or investment, it is necessary to identify what constitutes employment in the production and exchange of consumption commodities. Although this does not cause any difficulties in either one- or two-commodity models, the matter is by no means so obvious when a general multi-commodity macroeconomic technology is specified. The sort of issue that arises is to determine whether an increase in employment necessary to provide some indirect input to a final consumption commodity is to be treated as part of the accelerator process, because it is necessary for investment in inventories following an increase in incomes, or as part of the multiplier process, because it is a consequence of unintended inventory disinvestments. The change in employment is the same however we categorize it. What is involved here is only expositional convenience and clarity. I shall follow a procedure that is analogous to the elementary textbook accounts of the multiplier in a one-commodity model. Any expenditures on replacements for stocks used up as a result of increased net consumption demands will be treated as elements in the multiplier process. Any net investments in stocks are treated as elements in the accelerator process. All fixed capital formation is either spontaneous or a part of the accelerator process.

The basic/non-basic distinction makes it natural to define accelerator processes in relation to changes in the rates of growth rather than the levels of current expenditure (= income). This definition leaves for inclusion in the multiplier process all increases in employment required to maintain a realized increase in net consumption demands with a given stock of fixed capital equipment. Some of this employment will be in the basic sub-system and some will be in the non-basic sub-system. But none of it will result directly or indirectly from changes in rates of growth of fixed production or exchange capacities.

It follows that the multiplier is bound up with the state of short-term expectation while, with the definitions adopted here, the accelerator is bound up more closely with the state of long-term expectation. Net inventory investment is admittedly something of a borderline case in its relationship to short- and long-term expectations. In a given state of long-term expectation there can be only a Type I accelerator process, in which the effect of an increase in the growth of net consumption demands entails no increases in rates of capacity growth although there might be some increases in intended inventory growth. Any changes in macroeconomic activity will work mainly through the multiplier as a result of changes in short-term expectation. In these circumstances the magnitude and even the direction of multiplier effects are ambiguous.

Suppose, for example, that the government hires workers for some purpose that does not yield marketable outputs. (Any effects of government financing of the increased wage bill are ignored until chapter 8.) There will, in consequence, be some increase in the net demand for various consumption commodities. In a given state of long-term expectation, there will be different multiplier effects in different markets. In markets for consumption commodities sold from stock at long-run prices, there will be unanticipated inventory depletions. In markets where customers are required to queue for outputs, the queues will become longer. In price-efficient markets there will be some increases in sales volumes and some price increases. Provided that inventory depletions are made good, the multiplier effects will be just what the elementary textbooks suggest. Queue-lengthening will clearly have no multiplier effects and, in so far as consumers are prepared to wait for their orders to be filled, there will be a temporary increase in short-run savings relative to incomes. The result of price rises depends on the income and substitution effects. The income effects merely reduce the increase in net demands for consumption commodities and therefore the magnitude of the employment multiplier. The substitution effects mitigate the reduction in the magnitude of the multiplier in so far as expenditure is diverted to commodities sold at long-run prices from stock, but not in so far as expenditures are diverted to commodities for which customers are required to queue. Thus, the magnitude of the employment multiplier (and therefore the investment multiplier) depends on the composition of consumption demands even if marginal propensities to consume are constant.

6.5 MULTIPLIER–ACCELERATOR INTERACTION

The nature of multiplier–accelerator interaction in a general multi-commodity, joint-production technology in which basic and non-basic commodities can be identified is no different than that outlined in chapter 1. Since consumption commodities are non-basic outputs from exchange processes, any increases in the rates of capacity growth in the basic sub-system entail increased rates of basic sub-system employment growth and, therefore, increased growth of net consumption demands. In conditions of generally full capacity utilization, the upward employment multiplier effects generated by the rising rates of basic capacity growth cannot in fact be realized. There will be persistent excess demands for some consumption commodities combined with rising prices of others and increasing queue lengths for yet others. If basic sub-system capacity growth rates, and therefore employment growth rates, are falling, then net consumption demands must be falling as well. There will therefore be deflationary employment multiplier effects. Once basic sub-system growth rates cease changing, multiplier pressures will work to bring growth in the non-basic sub-system into line with basic sub-system growth. If all non-basic commodities were used only in consumption, then the trend non-basic sub-system growth rate would converge towards that of the basic sub-system. Other non-basic commodities will be considered in the sections following this.

The growth rates that can be attained in the basic sub-system we have seen to be limited by the maximum basic ratios, i.e. by the fraction of the total stock of each basic commodity available for use in the production and exchange of basic commodities. The immobility of basic commodity stocks is captured by the assumption that the maximum basic stock ratios can be changed only by changing the distributions and magnitude of current basic commodity outputs. Raising basic flow ratios, i.e. the fraction of current net outputs that becomes available for use as inputs to basic processes, raises the corresponding maximum basic stock ratios. If the basic flow ratios exceed the maximum basic stock ratios, then increasing the actual basic stock ratios – hence the rates of capacity utilization in the basic sub-system – will increase rates of basic capacity growth. If, however, basic flow ratios are below the maximum basic stock ratios, then increasing basic capacity utilization rates will diminish the maximum basic stock ratios and, therefore, the attainable rate of growth of the basic sub-system as a whole.

For any given composition of consumption commodity outputs, there will be one composition of basic commodity inputs to the non-basic sub-system and a different composition of basic commodity inputs to the basic sub-system. Thus, as basic capacity growth rates rise, the composition of basic commodity outputs will conform more closely to the composition of inputs required by the basic sub-system alone. As basic capacity growth rates decline, the composition of basic commodity outputs will conform more closely to the composition of inputs required by the non-basic sub-system. Provided that the extreme compositions of basic commodity demand can be met by linear combinations of the vectors describing the hypothetical processes, these changing compositions do not affect the analysis of multiplier–accelerator interaction; for the key element in that interaction is the growth of basic sub-system employment relative to non-basic sub-system employment.

The formal relationships among growth rates and basic ratios provide us with a framework within which to analyse dynamic macroeconomic processes. This framework is derived from the assumption of individual rationality and the explicit technological implications of that assumption. If the arguments that led to the present specification of the macroeconomic technology are correct, then the driving force of macroeconomic capacity, output and employment growth is the state of long-term expectation in the basic sub-system. I have no theory of the spontaneous determination of the state of long-term expectation that will prevail at any time; what I can do is to explain the dynamic limits to long-term optimism for the basic and non-basic sub-systems, respectively, as collective economic entities. There is nothing obscure or arcane about this explanation, although it does require there to be a collective state of long-term expectation in each sub-system. The justification for such collective expectational states is inherent in the description of the macroeconomic technology that has been developed in this chapter.

The state of long-term expectation in the basic sub-system

In the absence of technical change, there will be strong pressures to bring significantly deviant expectations among some entrepreneurs operating in the basic sub-system into line with the conventional expectations in that sub-system. Although these pressures might work on the supplies that will be available to the 'deviant' entrepreneurs, they will work mainly through the demands for their outputs.

Suppose, for example, that most entrepreneurs in the basic sub-system hold pessimistic long-term expectations. There is little, if any, growth of basic production and exchange capacities. If there are a few entrepreneurs operating in the basic sub-system who hold more optimistic long-term expectations, they will by definition be seeking to install new capacity at a faster rate than is the norm in the sub-system. In this circumstance, the demands for any direct inputs that they require, but do not themselves collectively produce, will be growing more quickly than the capacities necessary for their production. These demands could be met from increases in rates of basic capacity utilization by other entrepreneurs who sell from stock, but not by those who queue their customers. In the sort of depressed conditions hypothesized here, however, it is unlikely that production capacities will be fully utilized or that queues will be all that long. The supply constraints cannot then be binding until the 'deviant' growth rates have been maintained for some considerable time.

The real constraints on the optimistic entrepreneurs will be on the demand side. By hypothesis, demands for basic commodities for use in the basic sub-system are growing more slowly than the desired rates of capacity growth of the optimistic entrepreneurs. At least some of these optimistic entrepreneurs must sell their outputs, either to pessimistic entrepreneurs in the basic sub-system or to entrepreneurs in the non-basic sub-system. But the growth of employment in the basic sub-system as a whole is less than the optimistic entrepreneurs' desired rates of capacity growth. It follows that the growth of net consumption demands is also lower than the rates of capacity growth desired by the optimists. The multiplier effects therefore will not lead to sufficient growth in demands for basics by non-basic producers to enable the optimists fully to utilize their expanding capacities. Indeed, if they should increase their capacities at an abnormally high rate, their rates of capacity utilization will decline continuously.

There is nothing in this argument to suggest that some individual firms operating in the basic sub-system cannot grow faster than others. If it is not possible to sustain a relatively high rate of growth of the same outputs, then ambitious entrepreneurs will have an inducement to diversify into the production and/or exchange of other commodities, or to seek to take market share away from other firms or to take them over. The direction of such investment will depend on the focusing effects discussed in chapter 2 (cf. Moss, 1981, chapter 3).

Consider now the opposite case, in which optimism preponderates in the basic sub-system although the producers and traders of a small number of basic commodities remain pessimistic. In that case, as entrepreneurs in the basic sub-system increase their rates of capacity and employment growth, there will be upward multiplier effects in the non-basic sub-system. But, entrepreneurs in either the basic or the non-basic sub-systems or both will find themselves increasingly constrained by the slowly growing supplies of some basic commodities. This supply constraint constitutes a microeconomic inducement effect. That is, direct users of the commodities in limited supply will have a strong incentive to find alternative supplies or to integrate backwards in order to produce the requisite inputs themselves. There will also be some inducement effect on the producers and traders of the slowly growing basic commodity outputs to increase their capacities. They could hardly avoid being optimistic with regard to their short-term expectations; even at full capacity utilization, they will find the prices of their outputs rising or their stocks of finished commodities snapped up as soon as they reach the warehouses. In addition, the queues for those basic commodities that are produced only to order will continue to lengthen so that an increasing proportion of the capital costs of capacity expansion could be met out of the profits from existing orders. The markets for all these commodities will become increasingly attractive to potential entrants, and the firms producing and trading in these commodities will become increasingly attractive objects of take-over bids.

If this argument is right, then to conclude that the outputs and production and exchange capacities of a small number of basics could restrain the growth of the whole basic sub-system, one has to assume that all entrepreneurs who are either active or potentially active in the basic sub-system are for some reason unable or unwilling to diversify into clearly profitable lines of activity where they already have resources that will help to ensure the success of that diversification.

In summary, we have found that, under reasonable assumptions, there are price and quantity signals in the markets for basic commodities or, alternatively, profitable business strategies that would prevent a small number of entrepreneurs from either falling behind or running ahead of the capacity growth rates that predominate in the sub-system. This result is general. If, for example, the pattern of long-term expectations in the basic sub-system is such that there is a wide distribution of desired capacity growth rates between some relatively high rate and some relatively low rate, then the realized extreme growth rates will tend to converge towards some intermediate rate. The relatively low rates will be pulled up by the faster demand growth of the more optimistic entrepreneurs in the basic sub-system; the relatively high growth rates will be restrained by the slower growth of demands from the less optimistic entrepreneurs in the basic sub-system. It follows that, unless the whole range of desired capacity growth rates shifts upwards or downwards, the spread of actual and desired rates of basic capacity growth will tend to converge over time towards some common rate.

Although a given, linear technology has been assumed here for convenience, the foregoing argument is not substantially altered when this assumption is relaxed.

Clearly, stocks of innovatory fixed capital equipment will grow at very high rates simply because existing stocks are vanishingly small. If the new types of equipment are substitutes for previous technological vintages, then the outputs of the obsolescent vintages will presumably decline or cease altogether. Employment will shift from the production of the old to the production of the new vintages. If the innovation is a new circulating capital good, then the faster rate at which stocks turn over ensures that the growth rate of those stocks will rapidly converge to the rate of basic capacity growth in general. Obviously, different labour intensities and input compositions to innovatory processes will affect employment and other capacity growth rates during the period of diffusion. So, too, will economies of large-scale production and exchange – but only until minimum efficient scales are attained in the innovatory activities. None of these variations on the simple assumption alters the fundamental proposition that, over substantial intervals of time, capacity growth rates in the basic sub-system, and therefore in the non-basic sub-system, cannot diverge systematically and persistently.

Changing states of long-term expectation

One of the more important implications of the foregoing argument is that the expectations that determine macroeconomic growth paths are unlikely to be volatile. There are pressures on the most optimistic and pessimistic entrepreneurs operating in the basic sub-system to bring their long-term expectations regarding the profitability of individual production and exchange capacities into line with more moderate opinion. When all non-basic commodities are consumption commodities, the multiplier processes will keep long-term expectations in the non-basic sub-system broadly in line with expectations in the basic sub-system. If there is to be a substantial change in the rate of growth of employment and output in the whole economy, it will be the result of a wholesale change in the state of long-term expectation in the basic sub-system. Even if some individuals' expectations are volatile, turning points in any macroeconomic growth cycle require that their respective expectations – no matter how volatile – change in the same direction at the same time and then cease to be volatile. This is too much to be credible.

To put this point in a slightly different way, the effect of volatility in expectations held by individuals would be a large variance in the desired rates of growth of individual firms (rather than macro-economic capacities). Unless these expectations were determined either by the same or by different but highly correlated signals for all or most entrepreneurs, volatility would not affect the mean expectations. The technological factors considered above work to reduce the variance of expectations and therefore offset the effects of expectational volatility. If we are to determine the reasons for turning points of the major cycles in business activity, it is evidently necessary to identify the signals that the preponderance of entrepreneurs (at least in the basic sub-system) would take to indicate a change of future prospects in the same direction. No doubt there are cultural, social and psychological factors that are important in identifying both the signals and their effects. These matters are beyond the purview of this book. All that it is appropriate to seek here are technological characteristics of produc-tion and exchange relationships that would ensure that continuation of an existing state of long-term expectations would be incompatible with individual rationality. Following the approach taken when analysing the limits to speculation in chapter 5, we should look for factors that would ensure that unchanging expectations turn out to be wrong in some persistent and systematic way. Rationality would then imply that experience with such expectational errors will lead entrepreneurs to recognize the circumstances in which expectations must be changed before disaster actually strikes. We shall find that the assumption that entrepreneurs are concerned primarily with the survival of their firms leads to an analysis of the factors inducing expectational changes that is both simple and general.

The analysis of induced changes in the state of long-term expectations gives pride of place to financial relationships. These matters will occupy the whole of chapters 7 and 8. Before turning to them, we must investigate the technological relationships that are inherent in and limit the effects of changes in the state of long-term expectation. The key technological relationships in this regard determine how the distribution of basic commodities is likely to be changed as a consequence of changes in the state of long-term expectation.

Turning points and the technology of exchange

We have already seen that the multiplier–accelerator interactions implied by our microeconomic theory are insensitive to the mix of the allocatively efficient exchange technologies employed in transactions involving different commodities. It is equally important to demonstrate that analyses of the turning points of macroeconomic cycles are robust with respect to the technologies of exchange.

The limit to the rates at which basic sub-system capacities are growing at any time is imposed by the maximum basic stock ratios. As we saw in section 6.2, the maximum basic stock ratios corresponding to fixed capacities always converge towards the current basic flow ratios. The maximum basic stock ratio for any circulating capital good will converge towards some level that is directly related to the corresponding basic flow ratio but is not equal to it. In either case, the higher are the basic flow ratios, the higher will be the convergent values of the maximum basic stock ratios. Moreover, convergence to these values is always faster as the actual basic stock ratios (hence the rates of capacity utilization) are higher. It follows that changes in states of long-term expectation are reflected in changing basic flow ratios, distribution of current basic outputs between the two sub-systems – and the rates at which fixed capacities in the basic sub-system are being utilized and the rates at which stocks of material inputs to that sub-system are being used up.

The ways in which basic flow ratios change depend upon the procedures for allocating outputs among customers. Where customers queue for basic outputs and the processes are always operated, if at all, at full capacity utilization, then basic flow ratios rise when a higher proportion of users in the basic sub-system join the queue and reach the front. If they join the queue because of an improvement in the state of long-term expectation, then they are likely to join a more rapidly growing number of customers from the non-basic sub-system. In consequence, queue lengths increase and the lags between improvements in expectations and increases in some basic capacity growth rates get longer. When there is a deterioration in the state of long-term expectation, then the growth of customers from the basic sub-system joining the queues for these basic commodities declines. If the contractionary multiplier effects of the deterioration in long-term expectations proceed sufficiently quickly, then the growth of non-basic customers joining these queues will decline as well. Certainly the queues will shorten, but we cannot say whether the basic flow ratios fall in the first instance. Unless the growth of capacities for producing these basic commodities declines, however, queues will continue to shorten until they vanish and existing capacities will cease to be operated. While the state of long-term expectation remains depressed, any increases in demands for these basic outputs will be met by reducing the basic flow ratios. That is, the increased non-basic demands will join the relatively short queues and, because basic demands do not grow appreciably faster, will constitute a larger proportion of total demands. When these demands reach the front of the queue, the basic flow ratio will fall.

When commodities are sold from stock the lags are shorter than when commodities are produced only to order. A deterioration in the state of long-term expectation will be manifest by a reduction in the growth of demands from the basic sub-system, which precedes the multiplier-induced reduction in demands from the non-basic sub-system. The basic flow ratios fall initially on this account alone. As the contractionary multiplier process takes effect, the growth of demands from the non-basic sub-system will also decline, so that basic flow ratios could rise but only as rates of capacity utilization fall. It is clear from the argument of section 6.2 that declining rates of growth of basic commodity stocks held in the basic sub-system entail either declining basic flow ratios or declining basic stock ratios relative to their maxima, or both.

The basic flow ratios corresponding to commodities sold from stock will increase along with basic stock ratios when there is an improvement in the state of long-term expectation in the basic sub-system. In depressed macroeconomic conditions, the demands for such commodities initiated in the basic sub-system will be met by increasing the rates of capacity utilization. Once capacities come to be fully utilized, it is by no means clear that basic flow ratios will then continue to rise. There are two reasons for this. One is that we have identified no market signals that would lead basic commodity producers to give preference to the demands originating in the basic rather than the non-basic sub-system. The second is that the exigencies of goodwill competition will induce producers to give preference to the demands from their established customers without regard to the sub-system in which they are active; otherwise they could not expect to be given preference by their established customers when conditions of demand again deteriorate. It follows that one effect of goodwill competition is to restrict the rates of change of basic sub-system growth rates, and therefore the speed with which expansionary multiplier and accelerator effects can proceed.

Joint production of basic and non-basic commodities

The entire foregoing analysis would have to be substantially modified if it were to turn out that, in general, basic and non-basic commodities were produced jointly for wholly technological reasons. However, if we maintain the presumption that, in the main, basics and non-basics are not technologically joint outputs from the same processes, then the foregoing analysis requires only a slight modification to take the exceptional cases explicitly into account.

It will be convenient here to redefine the basic ratios to include in the numerators those basic commodities that are available as inputs to processes from which any basic commodities emerge as outputs even if non-basic commodities are produced jointly with basics in the same processes. As a result, rising basic ratios would imply growing outputs of those non-basic commodities that are produced jointly with basics; and falling basic ratios would imply that outputs of the same non-basics were falling relative to outputs of non-basics that are not produced jointly with basics.

During a period of improving states of long-term expectation, the growth of outputs of, say, consumption commodities produced jointly with basic commodities will diminish the net excess demands for consumption commodities in general. Even if the net supplies of other consumption commodities were growing more slowly than basic sub-system employment, and hence net consumption, demands, the supplies of consumption commodities produced jointly with basics would evidently be growing in line with basic sub-system employment and outputs. One would expect that short-run consumption goods prices would rise relative to the prices of this particular class of non-basics so that there would be some substitution. In consequence, demands for short-run-priced consumption commodities produced in the non-basic sub-system would not rise as much as they would if there were no joint production of basics with non-basics. For similar reasons, the excess demands for long-run-priced consumption commodities produced strictly in the non-basic sub-system would be diminished. In both cases, joint production of consumption and basic commodities evidently would reduce the magnitude of the multiplier effect – a reduction that would be more important as there were more consumption commodities produced jointly with basic commodities.

If, during a cyclical downswing, the growth rates of outputs of some basic commodities produced jointly with non-basics fall less than the growth rates of basic commodities produced in strictly basic processes, there will be some diminution in the profitability of the hybrid processes arising from the storage charges, wastage and disposal costs of the unwanted basic outputs. This would be a transitory phenomenon, however, since both basic and non-basic commodity demands generally grow in line with each other once the distribution of basic outputs between the two sub-systems has accommodated itself to the lower macroeconomic growth path. And if there were relatively short and mild recessions, which did not affect the state of long-term expectation, then the growing stocks of basics produced jointly with non-basics would be available for basic commodity production immediately the upturn came. In other words, the basic stock and flow ratios would rise so that the maximum basic stock ratios approached more quickly the values appropriate to the higher growth path. There would, in consequence, be a faster accelerator process.

A summary

In this section, we have found that the elaboration of the simple model of chapter 1 changes none of the essential relationships. The Type III accelerator process, characterized by increased basic sub-system growth, is the driving force leading to sustainable increases in the growth of the whole economy. In order to attain a higher growth path, basic flow and stock ratios must be increased. Market signals and profitable business strategies ensure that the state of long-term expectation in the basic sub-system, which determines the growth path of the whole economy, is well defined and stable. We have also shown that the directions of change of the basic flow and stock ratios when the state of long-term expectation changes in the basic sub-system is independent of the technology of exchange that is appropriate to particular markets. None the less, the rates at which the basic ratios change are sensitive to the exchange technologies.

In order to complete our analysis of dynamic processes within the real part of the economy, it remains to bring into consideration the two sectors that have so far been ignored: the public sector and the overseas sector. Although the financial aspects of government activity and international trade and capital movements cannot yet be taken into account, we can show the real effects of government purchases as well as of exports and imports.

6.6   REAL EFFECTS OF GOVERNMENT EXPENDITURE

If the aim of macroeconomic demand management policies is to bring about or to maintain a sustainable, full-employment growth path, then it is clear from the argument of section 6.5 that the success of such policies depends upon their effect on the state of long-term expectation in the basic sub-system. The state of long-term expectation determines the supply intentions of entrepreneurs who are active in the basic sub-system. Moreover, we have seen that, in a closed economy, supplies of basic commodities to basic commodity producers create their own (derived) demands via the multiplier and accelerator processes. It follows that to base macroeconomic policies on demand management alone is sensible only if there is an appropriate and reasonably stable relationship between the instruments of demand management on the one hand and the state of long-term expectation in the basic sub-system on the other hand.

In this section, we consider the relationships between government purchases of goods and services (excluding those of public sector companies) and the state of long-term expectation in the basic sub-system.

The effects of an increase in the government wage bill or an increase in transfer payments to households (e.g. pensions and other social security benefits) contribute to net demands for consumption commodities. The effects of exogenous increases in these net demands were considered at some length in section 6.5. Direct government purchases of commodities have slightly different effects, although there will be no systematically different multiplier effects on employment and outputs (hence incomes). The magnitude of the multiplier effects of government purchases of goods will depend on savings propensities with respect to the marginal profit and wage incomes and the distribution of income between profits and wages in the firms directly and indirectly supplying the government with the commodities in question. None the less, there will surely be multiplier effects.

In considering the accelerator effect of government purchases of commodities, it is useful to distinguish between its purchases of basic and of non-basic commodities. For example, the materials that governments acquire in order to maintain airports, roads and harbours are obviously basic since these elements of the economic infrastructure are essential to many classes of exchange – not least exchange in basic commodities. However, the buildings, paper, computers, pens and ink, etc., that are purchased for purposes of administration are non-basic, since they are not used directly in the production of any goods or services that are technologically required. The same is true of military goods. This is not to suggest that governments ought not to administer or defend the realm, any more than to classify consumption commodities as non-basics is to favour starvation by the naked in the open. But if the growth of public consumption, like that of private consumption, is so fast that it entails falling basic flow ratios, the consequence is a distribution of basic commodities that limits the ability of the economy to grow.

What is involved here is close but not identical to the choice between guns and butter or, even more pertinently, intertemporal substitution between current consumption and less current but more future consumption.

The choice between guns and butter can only be made once the availability of basic commodities for non-basic production and exchange is known. More of either guns or butter, but less of neither, in conditions of full capacity utilization entails lower basic flow ratios and so slower growth of employment, output and capacities in the long run. Faster growth entails higher rates of basic capacity utilization, hence higher basic flow ratios and so less butter or fewer guns or both. But this is not quite the Fisherian trade-off between present and future consumption, since no individual need choose among consumption magnitudes at different dates. It is none the less clear that, for the economy as a whole, there is such a trade-off, and that this trade-off is part and parcel of the trade-off between basic and non-basic production in conditions of full capacity utilization.

Of course, if capacities are not fully utilized in the basic sub-system, the economy as a whole can have more of both guns and butter, although the prospects for higher sustainable rates of macro-economic growth are not improved if the meeting of these non-basic demands further increases the proportion of holdings of basic commodities in the non-basic sub-system. Now, it is arguable that this last result is more likely when the government purchases goods than when it stimulates net consumption demands indirectly by increasing the government wage bill and transfer payments to households.

Increases in net consumption demands generate derived demands for basic commodities, but these derived demands are not especially likely to be given priority over the demands from the basic sub-system. Goodwill competition will work against priority being given to demands from either sub-system, even if sellers of basic commodities were interested in and could identify the sub-system for which their outputs were destined. But if the direct demands of government are backed by sufficient resources to outbid private firms, or if the government's financing methods raise interest rates so that users of basic commodities in the basic sub-system are unable or unwilling to invest in capacity expansion, then basic flow ratios and, possibly, rates of basic capacity utilization must fall. In other words, there will be a crowding-out effect in the short run which reduces the long-run growth of the whole economy.

This crowding-out occurs whenever increased growth of government expenditure leads to falling basic ratios. While crowding-out might be more likely when a government purchases goods directly, it can also happen when government-stimulated increases in net consumption demands do not induce Type III accelerator processes in which entrepreneurs in the basic sub-system increase their rates of capacity growth. In such cases, government expenditure will grow in a way that gives rise to some expansionary multiplier effects but, at the same time, to growth-depressing accelerator effects. Even if there is some short-run increase in the rate of growth of capacity in the non-basic sub-system, it cannot be sustained. If the growth of government expenditure is maintained while the basic flow ratios, and therefore the capacity for basic sub-system growth, is declining, then it follows as a matter of arithmetic that government expenditure must be growing as a proportion of total expenditure in the economy.

If these conclusions are correct on the assumption that the economy is closed, they have even more force for an open economy.

6.7   THE REAL EFFECTS OF FOREIGN TRADE

Exports of goods and non-financial services have the same effects on the supply side of the domestic economy as government purchases of commodities for non-basic uses. All exports are in effect non-basic since foreign trade always requires some specialized exchange processes and resources. To classify exports as non-basics simply reflects the point that basic commodities employed directly or indirectly in the production of commodities for export are not then available for the production and exchange of commodities for domestic use. These basic commodities are available for the production of new basic commodities on a smaller scale than if there were no exports.

This is by no means to suggest that exports are always undesirable. Clearly, national economies must export in order to import primary inputs that do not exist at home. It may be that in some cases fewer resources are required to produce commodities for export and then to use the resulting foreign exchange to import primary inputs that do exist at home, but are difficult to extract. In these circumstances foreign trade is simply technically and economically efficient: the home country has a comparative advantage in the production of certain manufactures, while the rest of the world has a comparative advantage in the extraction of certain raw materials.

However, not all foreign trade reflects comparative advantage, and it is possible that imports will prevent improvements in the domestic state of long-term expectation; for an important element in the expansionary multiplier–accelerator interaction discussed in section 6.5 is that excess net demands for basic commodities from producers of consumption commodities are a consequence of rising basic flow ratios in conditions of full capacity utilization. There are two ways in which imports unambiguously attenuate the strength of this interaction, as well as one ambiguous effect.

That imports reduce the magnitude of the multiplier effect is elementary. In a period of rising basic flow ratios, the net demand for consumption commodities is growing faster than net supply capacities, so either excess demands or rising prices (or both) will prevail in the various consumption markets. In either case, import penetration is likely to increase. We would therefore expect a weaker inducement for the producers and traders of consumption commodities to invest in capacity expansion.

Even if there were no such weakening of that inducement to invest, during periods of rising basic ratios and full capacity utilization, the growth of non-basic capacities must be falling while, import penetration apart, the demands for outputs of consumption goods and services are growing more rapidly. If growing consumption demands are not completely diverted to imports, rational entrepreneurs in the basic sub-system will look to foreign suppliers of fixed capital equipment and direct material inputs to their production and exchange processes when they are not able to acquire domestically produced capital goods and services.

Finally, we have seen that goodwill competition and the likely inability of producers to identify customers by sub-system (even if they had some inkling of the implications of the basic/non-basic distinction) limit the magnitudes of the basic flow ratios. If entrepreneurs in the basic sub-system wish to expand their production and exchange capacities faster than the competitively constrained basic flow ratios would allow, they will have to import some proportion of the required capital equipment and materials. The effects here are ambiguous. On the one hand, the faster growth of capacities in the basic sub-system makes possible a faster rate of employment growth and, therefore, a faster rate of growth of net consumption demands; that is, imports of capital goods for use in the basic sub-system will actually increase the magnitude of the multiplier effect. On the other hand, the accelerator effect is attenuated because queues for basic commodities produced only to order will be shorter while the prices of basic commodities traded on price-efficient markets will not need to be raised as sharply to cut off the excess domestic demands. If anything, therefore, the magnitude of the accelerator effect will be smaller while the magnitude of the multiplier effect will be greater. We cannot say *a priori* which, if either, will dominate.

Even if the net effect of importing inputs to the basic sub-system is expansionary, it cannot be maintained indefinitely. The faster rate of basic sub-system growth made possible by those imports increases the net demands for consumption commodities. There are four possible consequences of such growth in an open economy: there will be (1) persistent and growing excess consumption demands, or (2) continually falling real wages, or (3) increasing import penetration in the consumption commodity markets, or (4) increasing import penetration in the markets for non-basic capital goods. It is hard to imagine the social circumstances in which the first two possibilities can long prevail, since both continually depress standards of living. And increasing import penetration of the markets for both basic and non-basic commodities requires some alternative source of foreign exchange to finance the imports. Unless exports of financial services and other invisibles are growing or there is some sustainable growth of surplus on capital account, the imports will eventually be constrained by a lack of foreign reserves. This eventually could be avoided only if the contractionary accelerator effects of importing inputs to the basic sub-system dominate the multiplier effects, thereby depressing the state of long-term expectation and reducing the rate of macroeconomic capacity, output and employment growth.

The problems identified here do apply to economies that are undergoing an improvement in their respective states of long-term expectation. For an economy growing at a rate sufficient to maintain an existing state of tolerably full employment, the benefits of comparative advantage are quite likely to outweigh the disadvantages, if any, of a stable degree of import penetration. The problems arise when states of long-term expectation are depressed. Then, improvements in long-term expectations in the basic sub-system are necessary to bring about a sustained increase in growth and employment. But if the argument of section 6.4 is correct, the improvement in the state of long-term expectation in the basic sub-system can itself be sustained and reinforced only because the distribution of basic commodities in the economy is appropriate to the lower rate of macroeconomic growth. As that distribution shifts towards one that is appropriate to faster growth in the basic sub-system, a pattern of general excess demand or rising prices and unit profits emerges in all but the labour markets. If imports eliminate those excess demands and rising prices in either or both of the sub-systems, then improvements in the state of long-term expectation in the basic sub-system cannot be sustained.

If this argument is correct, then it would appear that the doctrine of comparative advantage and the principles of free trade are suitable for economies that are already growing as fast as technology and the size and growth rate of the domestic labour force will allow. Free trade will, however, be less appropriate for countries seeking to accelerate their macroeconomic rates of capacity, output and employment growth.

APPENDIX: QUANTITY AND PRICE RELATIONSHIPS
IN CONDITIONS OF JOINT PRODUCTION

Joint production gives rise to dynamic and comparative static results which, in the context of any mainstream theory, are perverse. However, these perversities will be seen to depend in no small measure on the assumptions that there are continuous markets for second-hand capital equipment as well as all other assets and commodities, and, in addition, that all markets are cleared by means of flexible prices. That is, in conditions of joint production, the assumption of the Walrasian economic structure and the efficient markets hypothesis lead to less general and less simple results than does the rational markets hypothesis and the economic structure that it implies.

It will be most transparent to develop the arguments concerning quantity (or input–output) relationships diagrammatically. The general case is not difficult to prove, although the economic meaning of those proofs are not obvious. Thus, I report the general method of these proofs in the analysis of price relationships. Because the distinction between long-run prices and short-run prices has no analogue in the quantity relationships, the price and quantity equations developed in section 6.2 and 6.3 are not duals. Thus, although the method used in proving general relationships among prices is readily applied to the quantity equations, the general proofs of the input–output relationships must be undertaken separately. I do not report the general proofs for the input–output relationships here.

Input–output relationships

Figure 6.1 is the standard activity analysis diagram relating inputs of two commodities to two production processes from which one or both commodities emerge as output. These processes constitute a basic sub-system since both outputs enter as inputs to both processes. Quantities of commodity 1 are measured along the horizontal x_1-axis while quantities of commodity 2 are measured along the vertical x_2-axis. Process 1 yields outputs only of commodity 1 although it requires inputs of both commodities. The gross output vector for process 1, Ob_1, is therefore coincident with the x_1-axis. The input vector for process 1 is Oa_1 along the ray OA_1 in quadrant III. Commodity 1 is a circulating capital good: it is some material that is used up in production. Commodity 2 is a fixed capital good such as a machine. Following the specification of depreciation in section 6.2, commodity 2 emerges unscathed from production processes while inputs of commodity 1 emerge only in so far as they are embodied in the saleable outputs from the process. Thus, the net output vector for process 1 is the gross output vector from which we subtract the horizontal magnitude equal to that of the x_1-coordinate of point a_1.

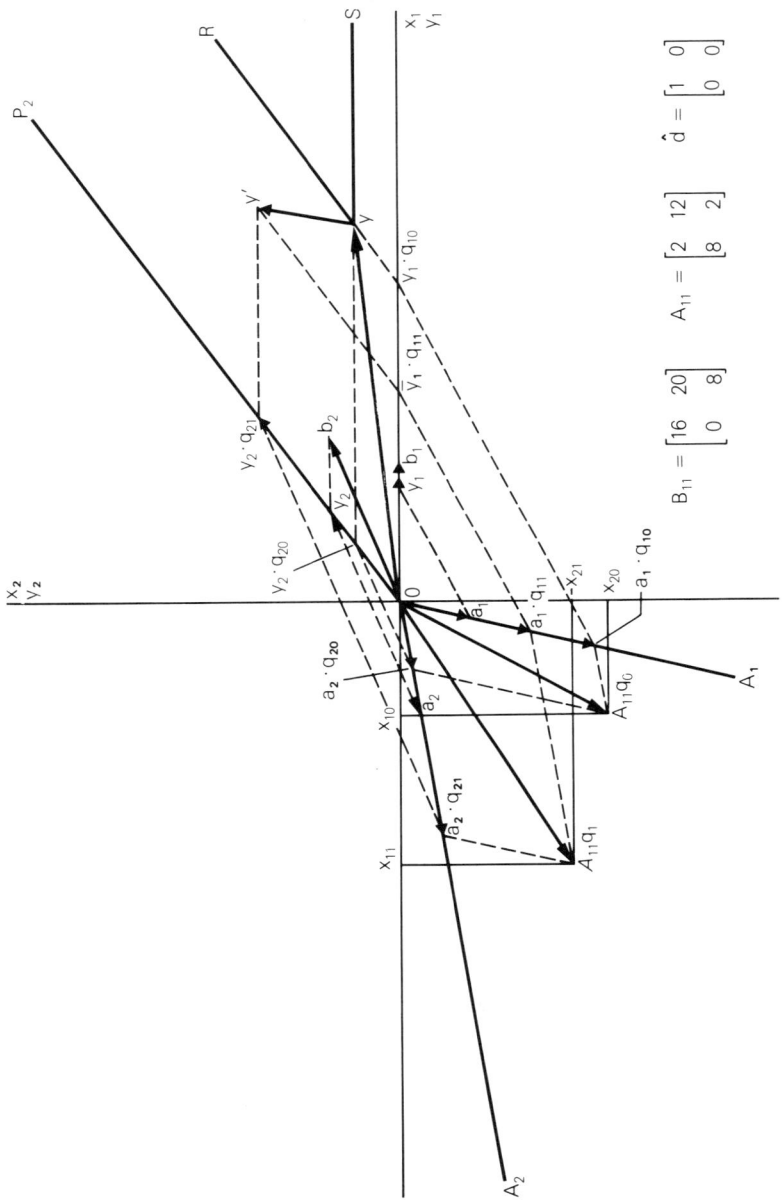

$$B_{11} = \begin{bmatrix} 16 & 20 \\ 0 & 8 \end{bmatrix} \qquad A_{11} = \begin{bmatrix} 2 & 12 \\ 8 & 2 \end{bmatrix} \qquad \hat{d} = \begin{bmatrix} 1 & 0 \\ 0 & 0 \end{bmatrix}$$

Figure 6.1   Input–output relationships in conditions of joint production

No subtraction is required in respect of inputs of commodity 2 since it is not in any sense used up. Thus, the net output vector for process 1 at the unit activity level is Oy_1 along the positive x_1-axis.

Process 2 is a joint-production process: net outputs include both commodities. The gross output vector for process 1 is Ob_2 in quadrant I. The input vector is Oa_2 along the ray OA_2 in quadrant III. Net outputs from process 2 at the unit activity level are found by subtracting inputs of commodity 1 but not commodity 2 from Ob_2. Thus, Oy_2 on ray OP_2 is the net output vector for process 2. The dashed line y_2b_2 has the same length as the x_1-coordinate of a_2.

Suppose that the net output from the basic sub-system during period 0 is given by the output vector Oy. To determine the activity levels of each process required to produce that net output, we need only employ the 'parallelogram of forces'. This shows that adding together the net output vectors $Oy_1 \cdot q_{10}$ and $Oy_2 \cdot q_{20}$ will yield Oy. q_{10} and q_{20} are the activity levels of the two processes during period 0.

To obtain the vector of total inputs required to produce the net outputs given by vector Oy we make use of the elementary properties of parallel lines. In a linear system, the ratio of the length of vector Oy_1 to $Oy_1 \cdot q_{10}$ will be the same as the ratio of the length of Oa_1 to $Oa_1 \cdot q_{10}$. To determine $Oa_1 \cdot q_{10}$ we require only to draw the dotted line y_1a_1 and then the parallel line from $Oy_1 \cdot q_{10}$ to the ray OA_1. The intersection must be $Oa_1 \cdot q_{10}$. Vector $Oa_2 \cdot q_{20}$ is determined in precisely the same way from the intersection of the dotted line from $y_2 \cdot q_{20}$, parallel to a_2y_2, and OA_2. From the 'parallelogram of forces', adding the input vectors for the two processes yields the vector of total inputs required for the production of net outputs given by Oy. That vector in quadrant III is $O(A_{11}q_0)$.

It is now an easy matter to show how increases in the net outputs of both commodities can imply reduced total inputs of one commodity, though inputs of at least one must be increased.

Suppose that the *incremental* net output between periods 0 and 1 is given by vector yy'. Since that vector is rising from left to right, there are increments to the net outputs of both commodities. To change net outputs in this way, the parallelogram of forces yielding the net output vector shows that the activity of process 1 must be reduced from q_{10} to q_{11} while the activity level of process 2 must be increased from q_{20} to q_{21}. With these particular processes, the reduction in inputs of commodity 2 to production process 1 is greater than the increase in inputs of that commodity to process 2. Thus, taking both processes together, inputs of commodity 2 have declined while inputs of commodity 1 have increased. This result depends on the absolute reduction in one activity level and the proportions in which the two commodities enter as inputs to each of the two processes. In Figure 6.1, the vector of inputs during period 1 is $O(A_{11}q_1)$, the x_2-coordinate of which is smaller in magnitude than the x_2-coordinate of $O(A_{11}q_0)$. In other words, the total inputs of commodity 2 are reduced.

Clearly, this result is never possible when the incremental output vector entails increases in both activity levels, since inputs of both commodities to each process must then be increased.

Because the line yR in quadrant I is parallel to the ray OP_2, any incremental output vector from y along yR implies no change in the activity level of process 1, as is immediately apparent from the parallelogram of forces corresponding to net output vector Oy. All increases in net outputs will be effected by increasing the activity level of process 2. The reason is that the proportions in which the net outputs of the two commodities are to be increased are the same as the proportions in which they emerge from process 2.

Similarly, because the horizontal line yS is parallel to net output vector for process 1, any incremental output vector from y along yS implies an increased activity level for process 1 but an unchanged activity level for process 2. The reason is that such incremental output vectors entail increases in the net output of commodity 1 alone and this is the only net output that emerges from process 1.

Evidently, the convex cone RyS is identical to P_2Ox_1 except that it emanates from point y in quadrant I rather than the origin. Any incremental net output vector from point y lying within RyS entails increases in both activity levels because the incremental output alone could have been produced by the two processes operated at positive activity levels. Output vectors above RyS entail reductions in the activity level of process 1 because the slope of such vectors is greater than the slope of OP_2. In consequence, those incremental net outputs alone could not have been produced because process 1 cannot be operated at negative activity levels. Incremental output vectors from y lying below yS entail reductions in the outputs of commodity 2, and therefore reductions in the process 2 activity level.

Since it is possible to reduce one activity level and increase the other without diminishing the total input of either commodity to both processes considered together, it follows that a necessary but not sufficient condition for there to be perverse relationships between inputs and outputs is that the incremental net output vector lie outside the convex cone P_2Ox_1, shifted to emanate from the current net output vector instead of the origin. With this result we can give a precise meaning to the assertion in section 6.2 that there will be no perverse input–output relationships provided that net output increments are sufficiently close to balanced growth of outputs.

In strictly balanced growth, the incremental net output vector is a linear expansion of Oy. Since Oy itself must be technologically feasible, the balanced-growth incremental net output vector must lie within RyS. The issue here is whether there are technological and/or economic reasons to expect divergences from balanced growth to be sufficiently small that incremental net output vectors typically lie within the general n-commodity analogue of RyS. There are just such reasons, and, although perverse input–output relationships are possible for short periods, they cannot be sustained over longer periods. In consequence, when perverse short-run results do occur, they have no serious effect on the results obtained in chapter 6.

The first, strictly short-run, limit on divergences from balanced growth is a result of the non-continuity of markets for second-hand capital equipment. In Figure 6.1 the incremental net output vector yy' implies a substantial reduction in inputs of commodity 2 – the fixed capital commodity – to process 1. Unless the same firms operate both processes within the same establishments, however, the capacity that is underutilized as a result of the reduction in the process 1 activity level will not be available for use in process 2. Thus, the increase in the activity level of process 2 in conditions of full capacity utilization is possible only if firms operating that process can acquire the necessary additional inputs of commodity 2 from purchases of current outputs. If it is necessary to queue for outputs of commodity 2, or if they are sold from stock but current outputs are insufficient to provide for the incremental capacity required to produce the additional outputs given by yy', then the activity level of process 2 must be smaller while there are no similar constraints on process 1. Thus, the incremental net output vector will turn out to be shorter. Certainly in conditions of a Type III accelerator process there is nothing to justify such an outcome; for if the change in output composition is part of an expansionary accelerator process, there will be excess demands for basic commodities for use in the non-basic sub-system. If commodity 1 enters directly as an input to the non-basic sub-system, there is no reason for firms operating process 1 to reduce their activity levels. It is far more plausible to suppose that the process 1 activity level will remain constant or rise more slowly than the process 2 activity level. In that case, the incremental net output vector cannot lie above Ry and the sufficient condition for non-perverse input–output relations is satisfied.

Suppose, for the sake of logical completeness, that the implausible happens. Even then, perverse input–output relations cannot persist indefinitely. To demonstrate this point, quadrant I of Figure 6.1 is reproduced as Figure 6.2. The slope of the ray OG in Figure 6.2 represents the proportions in which commodities 1 and 2 are required as inputs to the basic sub-system at the maximum feasible rate of balanced growth. If OG lies above OP_2, then maximum growth implies incremental output vectors along OP_2 itself. Process 1 will not be employed at all. The slope of the ray OH represents the proportions in which the two commodities enter directly as inputs to the non-basic sub-system. The faster the rate of capacity and output growth in the basic sub-system, the more closely will the composition of net outputs approximate to the slope of OG. The slower the rate of basic sub-system growth, the more closely will the composition of net outputs from the basic sub-system approximate to the slope of OH. Thus, in the course of an expansionary Type III accelerator process, the incremental net output vectors will point in the direction of OG. During a major macroeconomic downturn – a

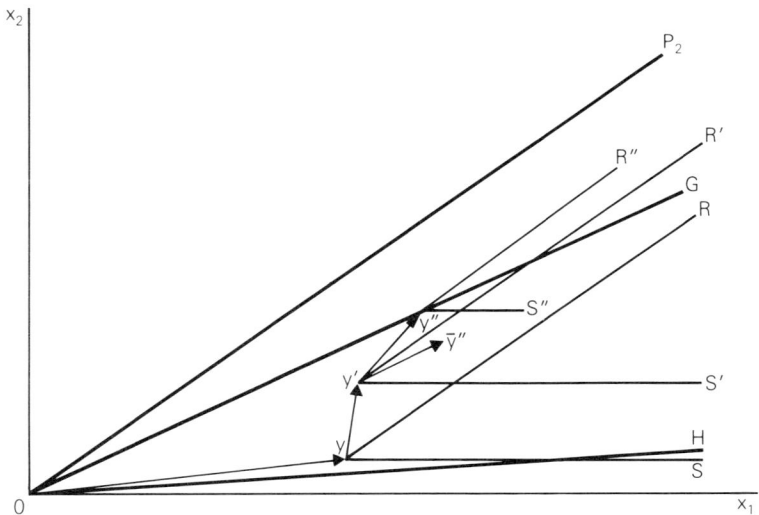

Figure 6.2   Time paths of net inputs and outputs in conditions of joint production

deflationary Type III accelerator process – the incremental net output vectors will point towards *OH*.

Consider an extreme, major macroeconomic upturn. Suppose that the incremental net output vector between period 0 and period 1 is yy' and then is $y'y''$ between periods 1 and 2. No non-basic outputs are produced after period 2 because the basic flow ratios are both unitary. We already know that inputs of community 2 decline between periods 0 and 1. Since $y'y''$ lies above the convex cone $R'y'S'$, the activity level of process 1 declines again between periods 1 and 2 so that, quite possibly, total inputs of commodity 2 decline again. But OG lies within $R''y''S''$ – the convex cone P_2Ox_1 shifted to emanate from y''. Thus, after period 2, further growth at the maximum feasible rate for the basic sub-system will entail increased activity levels for both processes. If, as is far more likely, growth rates stop short of the technological maximum (if only so that consumption commodities necessary for workers' survival can be produced), then the upward direction of the incremental net output vectors will become less pronounced as the rate of basic sub-system growth ceases to rise – or to rise as quickly. Incremental net output vectors will then be like $y'\bar{y}''$, which, since it lies within $R'y'S'$, implies that both activity levels are increasing. The sufficient condition for non-perverse input–output relations is therefore satisfied.

In general, the non-continuity of markets for second-hand capital equipment restricts the possible short-run divergences from balanced growth during an expansionary Type III accelerator process. Even if this restriction is not sufficient to preclude perverse input–output relationships, these perversities cannot last indefinitely since the composition of net outputs from the non-basic sub-system cannot change dramatically each period during a major expansion without reaching the maximum feasible rate of balanced basic sub-system growth. Since the rate of growth of the basic sub-system will be limited by workers' demands for non-basic consumption commodities, the technologically feasible rate of basic sub-system growth will never be reached. Even during periods of rising basic growth rates, however, there are market signals, identified in section 6.5, that induce convergence of the rates of capacity and output growth. It follows that, on economic grounds alone, perverse input–output relationships in conditions of joint production are not likely to be significant in the short run, and, even if they are, they cannot persist in the long run.

The problem raised by such perverse relationships is that they vitiate the trade-off between basic and non-basic sub-system growth rates in the short run. Their effect is, therefore, possibly to frustrate the transition from Type II to Type III accelerator processes. The excess demands from the non-basic sub-system for direct inputs of some basic commodities will be diminished, thereby to yield ambiguous market signals. If anything, this will make policy prescriptions to bring about major macroeconomic upturns even more necessary. The criteria for such policy prescriptions are derived in chapter 9.

Price relationships

The long-run price identity established in section 6.2 is reported here for convenience:

$$\mathbf{p}_2'\mathbf{M} \equiv \mathbf{p}_1'\mathbf{a}_{12} + \mathbf{w}'\mathbf{n}_2$$

where $\mathbf{M} \equiv \mathbf{b}_{22}(\mathbf{I} + \hat{\mathbf{m}})^{-1} - \hat{\mathbf{d}}_2\mathbf{a}_{22}$. It follows from the theorem of the separating hyperplane (Gale, 1960, pp. 44–5; cf. Filippini and Filippini, 1982) that the row vector of long-run prices $\mathbf{p}_2'$ is non-negative if and only if there is no column vector $\mathbf{y}$ such that

$$\mathbf{M}\mathbf{y} \geqq 0 \tag{6.36}$$

and

$$[\mathbf{p}_1'\hat{\mathbf{d}}_1\mathbf{a}_{12} + \mathbf{w}'\mathbf{n}_2]\,\mathbf{y} < 0. \tag{6.37}$$

In order to determine the economic meaning of this condition, let us suppose that inequalities (6.36) and (6.37) are satisfied. Inequality (6.37) implies that $\mathbf{y}$ must have some negative elements, since wage rates, short-run prices and technical coefficients are non-negative. But if $\mathbf{y}$ were semi-negative then there would exist a semi-positive vector or activity levels $\mathbf{q} \equiv -\mathbf{y}$ such that

$$\mathbf{M}\mathbf{q} < 0. \tag{6.38}$$

If this inequality has a solution for any semi-positive vector $\mathbf{q}$, then we know from the application of Gale's (1960, p. 49) theorem on pp. 178–9 that there is no non-negative vector of long-run prices such that

$$\mathbf{p}_2'\mathbf{M} > 0. \tag{6.39}$$

That is, not all processes could be profitable when all prices are non-negative. Since firms will not set negative long-run prices, they will not set mark-ups that collectively satisfy condition (6.38). That condition therefore specifies economically infeasible mark-ups.

It remains to consider vectors **y** with both positive and negative elements. If there is such a solution, then we can order processes so that

$$y = \begin{bmatrix} q^+ \\ -q^- \end{bmatrix}$$

where q^+ is semi-positive and q^- is positive.

Partitioning a_{22}, b_{22} and $\hat{m}$ conformably, we can write inequalities (6.36) and (6.37) so that, writing matrix **M** explicitly,

$$[b_{22}^+(I + \hat{m}^+)^{-1} - \hat{d}_2 a_{22}^+] q^+ \geqq [b_{22}^-(I + \hat{m}^-)^{-1} - \hat{d}_2 a_{22}^-] q^- \quad (6.40)$$

and

$$[p_1' \hat{d}_1 a_{12}^+ + w' n_2^+] q^+ < [p_1' \hat{d}_1 a_{12}^- + w' n_2^-] q^-. \quad (6.41)$$

These inequalities give us a set of restrictions on the mark-ups. To see this, note that neither q^+ nor q^- have negative elements and that the short-run prices and the wage rates are determined by means outside the control of individual firms – they result from conditions of supply and demand or from factors outside the purview of the present analysis. But these mark-ups are implied by firms' pricing policies. In practice, firms engaged in long-run pricing will not set negative prices, so that the prices they do set will not imply mark-ups that satisfy inequalities (6.36) and (6.37) simultaneously. Thus, if there exist vectors such as q^+ and q^- satisfying both of the above two inequalities, then the mark-ups given by m^+ are too low relative to the mark-ups given by $\hat{m}^-$. By raising diagonal elements of $\hat{m}^+$ and lowering those of $\hat{m}^-$, inequality (6.38) and therefore (6.40) can be reversed so that the vector of long-run prices is non-negative.

Given that long-run prices are, and remain, non-negative, we consider how they will change in response to increases in wage rates, short-run prices and mark-ups. We turn first to the effects of increases in wage rates and short-run prices. The result is analogous to our finding that increases in net outputs require increases and no decreases in activity levels, if any, only if they could have been produced alone with non-negative activity levels.

Let there be some row vector

$$(\Delta p_1') \hat{d}_1 a_{12} + (\Delta w') n_2 > 0. \quad (6.42)$$

This vector states that changes in short-run prices and wage rates (which need not all be positive) increase the labour and short-run-priced input costs to at least some processes for the production and exchange of long-run-priced commodities at any given vector of activity levels. None of these costs are reduced for any process.

For any given vector of mark-ups, it follows from the long-run price identity (6.29) that

$$(\Delta p_2') \, \mathbf{M} \equiv (\Delta p_1') \, d_1 a_{12} + (\Delta w') \, n_2 \geqq 0. \tag{6.43}$$

From the theorem of the separating hyperplane, either $\Delta p_2' \geqq 0$ or there is a column vector $\mathbf{y}$ satisfying condition (6.36) *and*

$$[(\Delta p_1') \, \hat{d}_1 a_{12} + (\Delta w') \, n_2] \, \mathbf{y} < 0. \tag{6.44}$$

If vector (6.42), i.e. the left side of condition (6.44), is a scalar multiple of a row vector satisfying condition (6.37), then condition (6.44) will also be satisfied: otherwise it will not. If long-run prices are positive at the prevailing levels of wage rates, short-run prices and mark-ups, then conditions (6.36) and (6.37) cannot be satisfied simultaneously. If and only if vector (6.42) is not a scalar multiple of any vector satisfying condition (6.37) when condition (6.34) is also satisfied, then the changes in wage rates and short-run prices generating vector (6.42) imply that some long-run prices will rise and none will decline. If the wage and price rises yield a vector (6.42) which is a scalar multiple of a vector satisfying condition (6.37) for some $\mathbf{y}$ that also satisfies condition (6.36), then those increases in wage rates and short-run prices imply some long-run price reductions as well as some increases.

While this result yields difficulties for orthodox derived demand theorems, it is of no consequence here and has already been taken into account in section 6.3. For the theory of markets implies that long-run prices are set not to clear markets but, instead, to cover all input costs and to provide a gross profit sufficient to meet firms' financial requirements over substantial periods of time. This pricing objective is wholly compatible with price reductions on some jointly produced commodities as long as the prices of other outputs from the same processes are increased when wage rates and short-run prices increase.

Much the same conclusion is reached when we turn to consider changes in mark-ups.

The mark-up is defined so that any increase entails increased gross profits at any activity level of the corresponding process. It does not imply that all prices of jointly produced commodities must increase whenever the mark-up is increased on the input costs to the joint-production process.

To see this, let Δm be a vector of mark-up increases; that is, Δm is non-negative. Then, from the long-run pricing identity (6.29),

$$\Delta p_2' \equiv p_2' b_{22} (\mathbf{I} + \hat{m})^{-1} \Delta \hat{m} [b_{22} - d_2 a_{22} (\mathbf{I} + \hat{m} + \Delta \hat{m})]^{-1}. \tag{6.45}$$

There is no reason to assume that the inverse matrix expression on the right side of identity (6.45) is semi-positive unless b_{22} is a semi-positive, diagonal matrix. This will be the case only if no long-run-priced commodities are produced jointly with other commodities. If this inverse has negative elements, then it is always possible to choose mark-up increases that imply reductions in at least one long-run price.

The purpose of an increase in any mark-up is to increase the internally generated finance available to firms. There is no reason to suppose that reductions in the prices of some joint outputs from a process are incompatible with this purpose as long as prices of other outputs from the same process are increased. All that is implied here is that it might not be possible for firms simultaneously to increase the prices of all joint outputs relative to the prices of all inputs. They can, none the less, simultaneously increase all mark-ups, provided that these increases do not imply that any long-run prices become negative.

7

Money, Finance and the Safe-asset Theory of Interest

7.0 INTRODUCTION

In order to complete the theory of macroeconomic processes, it remains to identify the determinants of the states of long-term expectation. Long-term expectations are concerned with events that are uncertain in the sense that they either cannot be well defined or, if well defined, cannot be given any probability of occurrence. It does not seem likely to be a fruitful enterprise to seek a theory of individuals' expectations. What is more fruitful is to follow the procedure of section 5.3 in determining the technological limits to price changes and other phenomena that are affected by expectations. These limits and the responses to them are then analysed on the assumption that individuals act rationally and, in particular, firms' managers act rationally to protect and enhance their respective firms' prospects for survival. We shall see in chapter 8 that these limits can be deduced from propositions developed in chapter 6 about employment, capacity growth and price determination and from the theory of money, finance and interest reported in this chapter. The novelty of this theory stems from its derivation from the theory of markets.

To develop a theory of money, finance and interest from the theory of markets is readily seen to be a natural undertaking. For money is commonly acknowledged to have no existence apart from its use or potential for use in exchange. Financial assets are always created by acts of exchange since the original sales of bonds, debentures, bills and the like are what establish the debt commitments of the issuers of these assets. Since interest arises only as a consequence of the existence of financial assets including, as we shall see, money, it is another phenomenon that depends upon acts of exchange in a sense in which produced commodities do not. It is conceivable, for example, that some agent could own land bearing whatever raw materials are required and could himself provide the necessary labour to produce some item without any act of exchange being involved. The existence of that commodity is then wholly independent of the technology of exchange. It follows that any complete analysis of money, finance and interest will entail an analysis of the exchange processes in which financial assets, including money, are created.

Before turning to the development of such an analysis, there is one issue that must be clarified in order to avoid subsequent misunderstandings. The issue turns on the definition of money.

We are told by the monetarist/new classical economists that money is a convenient *numeraire* because its main function is to serve as a unit of account. The temporary equilibrium theorists, following Clower (1967/1969), argue that the main function of money is to serve as a means of payment. Keynesians base their analysis of money and the role of monetary policy on the speculative motive and therefore on money's role as a store of value. None of these schools argue that money has only one function; it is just that each concentrates on one while effectively relegating the other two to the second rank of importance. The definition of money is not only a matter of exposition: it is a matter of substance. For money is neutral only if its role as a unit of account is predominant. That is an essential precondition for the validity of homogeneity postulate (i.e. the postulate that only relative prices determine the allocation of resources and composition of demand) in a Walrasian economic structure where all markets are price-efficient. The Clower analysis of the price inefficiency of markets is predicated upon the role of money as means of payment. Even when markets are simply assumed to be price-inefficient, the only justification for that assumption is that, by serving as means of payment, money prevents the supply of factor services from being interpreted by entrepreneurs as a subsequent demand for produced outputs. Finally, the Keynesian argument that the demand-for-money function is unstable (or volatile) rests on the speculative motive for holding money – a motive that depends upon money's role as a store of value (cf. Hicks, 1967, chapters 1–3).

These alternative emphases of the three aspects of the conventional definition of money are bound up with the alternative assumptions, discussed in chapter 4, about how markets work. In order to resolve the controversies to which these different emphases have given rise, I follow here the same procedure as in chapter 4 by determining the implications of individual rationality for those properties of money that can be said to be essential. In so doing, other implications of individual rationality that have been derived in previous chapters will be taken for granted.

7.1 ON THE DEFINITION OF MONEY

I shall argue in this section that only the most narrow definition of money as means of payment is at all satisfactory. Any definition that ascribes to money the role of unit of account is untenable on empirical grounds and is incompatible with the assumption of individual rationality and in particular with the rational markets hypothesis. To define money as a safe asset which is held to satisfy the Keynesian speculative motive is ambiguous, since different assets will be safe in different circumstances and, in any particular set of circumstances, the characteristics of a safe asset for one individual will not necessarily be the same as for another individual. The least unsatisfactory definition of money is that it serves as a medium of exchange or, equivalently, a means of payment. However, there are many means of payment, and, as we shall see, different means of payment will be used in different, allocatively efficient markets. Moreover, within any such market, different means of payment will rationally be used for different scales of transactions or in the context of different business relationships.

On balance, it seems most convenient to define money as means of payment that can be used in transactions without the necessity to engage in prior transactions. As long as we recognize that there are other (non-money) means of payment, this definition is unlikely to be confusing and it has the advantage of conforming to common usage. In order to justify this definition, we consider in turn the properties of units of account, means of payment and stores of value.

The unit of account

The purported role of money as a unit of account is bound up with its role as a medium of exchange. For example, Hawtrey's (1950) classic *Currency and Credit* starts by defining money as medium of exchange and store of value and then avers,

The practice which made the standard [i.e. money] commodity the common medium of exchange almost inevitably made it also the common measure of value. A market which priced each commodity separately in terms of every other would be impossibly complicated; the use of one standard commodity as money enables us to express all prices in terms of this one commodity.

Hawtrey's statement is representative of the mainstream view.

There are two objections to Hawtrey's statement and therefore to the conventional definition of money. One objection stems from the neoclassical theory of value and distribution (both partial and general equilibrium) and the other stems from the theory of markets.

Clearly, it is true that the adoption of a single unit of account in which to denominate all prices implies that each trader need perceive n prices of n commodities instead of $(n)(n-1)$ binary exchange relationships. But this saving in the complexity of observation does not mean that only n prices need be taken into account in determining optimal allocations of resources by firms and optimal compositions of commodity demands and factor supplies by households. For, according to the theory of value and distribution, firms and households take their allocative decisions by equating marginal rates of substitution with relative prices or, in imperfect competition, marginal input costs. Thus, if firms and households need to perceive n nominal prices, they will still have to calculate $(n)(n-1)$ binary exchange relationships in order to determine their optimal actions. It follows that any savings on the resources that must be devoted to perception are offset by the costs of the resources that must be devoted to calculation. As long as we maintain the assumption of individual rationality, we cannot argue that a common unit of account in which to denominate all prices reduces the complexity of the information required to reach production and exchange decisions.

If anything, a common unit of account actually increases the number of calculations that must be performed by individuals in the economy as a whole. For if the $(n)(n-1)$ binary exchange relationships were posted for all agents to see, then each would have to be calculated once; but if only nominal prices are posted, then all individuals will have to calculate all the binary exchange relationships that are of interest to them. It follows that, if we were to ignore the technology and costs of exchange, a common unit of account would actually increase the social resources that must be devoted to generating the information required for optimal decision-making.

As it turns out, however, a common unit of account does afford substantial savings in social transactions costs provided that it is not tied to any particular commodity or asset.

The price of a commodity, no matter how denominated, is but one of the measurable characteristics that are relevant to buyers and sellers. Consider, for example, the purchase of a bolt of cloth. The buyer will be concerned not only with the price of the cloth but also with its length, its width, the thickness or weight per unit of area, the composition of the cloth, its colour and pattern, etc. The cloth is likely to be sold in effect by the unit measure of area. Its price will have the dimensions both of unit of account and of unit of area measure. In deciding whether to buy the cloth and how much to buy, the purchaser will take into consideration the composition, the weight, and the colour and the pattern. In some cases, the desirability of the colour and pattern will be assessed by inspection. But the bulk purchaser – say a tailor – will purchase the cloth only by inspecting a sample on the understanding that all of the cloth is well standardized in respect to its colour and pattern.

The unit of account and the unit of area measure are specified in units of some mutually agreed and understood standard.

The tailor will not insist on applying his own measuring rod to the bolt of cloth before purchase provided that he has confidence that his conception of a unit of area is the same as that of the seller. The unit of area – say the 'metre' – is not in this case a concrete object but, instead, is an abstraction accepted by buyers and sellers alike. Such an abstraction is required whenever the costs of employing it are less than than the costs of employing a concrete measure such as a particular measuring rod. If the user of the cloth always purchased it in person from the producer in quantities that were sufficiently small, then he could take along his own measuring rod of any arbitrary length to determine how many square 'rods' of cloth were being purchased. Should the costs of purchasing the cloth be minimized when the area of measure is some common abstraction such as a metre, the rational buyer will specify his requirements in units of that measure. One such case is where the quantity purchased is such that the cost of the labour time and other resources required to apply a non-standard, arbitrary measure was greater than the expected cost of any shortages in the length.

Exactly the same principles apply with regard to the unit of account in which prices are denominated. In a complex economy in which bulk purchases are ordered, it is often convenient to specify the price in abstract units of account: so many pounds or dollars rather than so many pound notes or dollar bills or grams of gold or silver. Once the price is specified in such abstract units, any of a variety of particular means of payment can be used to effect the transaction. To be sure, a pound note will have the abstract value of £1 sterling just as a metre stick will have the length of one metre. But this is not to say that the length must always be measured by metre sticks or that pound notes must be used in payment. Cheques, trade credits, bills of various kinds and promissory notes will in various circumstances be employed as means of payment. That all of these means of payment will be *measured* in abstract units of account is by no means to say that they *are* units of account. Indeed, to identify means of payment with units of account is simply misleading.

The common adoption of a single abstract unit of account is more efficient than the adoption of a variety of different units of account. In relation to the activities of exchange – storage, transportation and communication – it is clear that abstract units of account do afford agents economies in communication. If individuals are rational, then the savings in the costs of communication from having prices denominated in units of account must exceed the social costs of computation from having prices expressed as a set of binary exchange relationships. The larger the number of units of account in common use, the smaller must be the savings on the costs of computation since the values of the various units of account relative to one another must be calculated before relative prices can be established. Evidently, the number of such calculations will be smaller as the number of units of account is smaller. And no such calculations are required when there is only one abstract unit of account. It follows that, if the computational costs are directly related to the number of calculations that must be performed, then computational costs are minimized when there is one, but only one, unit of account employed in denominating prices.

There is a significant advantage in recognizing that means of payment are not units of account but that the unit of account is one measure of means of payment. It enables us to analyse the role and effects of various means of payment without complicating the analysis of prices. As we shall now see, the same efficiency considerations that imply the optimality of a single unit of account also imply the optimality of a diversity of means of payment.

Means of payment

For any commodity or asset to be used as a means of payment by rational individuals, the giving and accepting of that commodity or asset in exchange must maximize the net benefits to both parties to the transaction. There is no reason, either in logic or in practice, to expect that any commodity or asset will be the optimal means of payment in all types of transactions.

Different means of payment entail different costs when employed in exchange. Otherwise there would be no reason to have more than one asset serving as means of payment. For transactions in any commodity, we can imagine one transactions cost curve for every means of payment where the total transactions cost in each case is a function of the physical volume of the transactions. Evidently, every point on the envelope of these transactions cost curves will correspond to a means of payment that minimizes total transactions costs for that scale of exchange of that commodity. Clearly, there is nothing in this that is in any way incompatible with elementary economic principles.

It is also an elementary tenet of the economics of money and banking that any means of payment must be compact, durable and well standardized. Compactness and durability are essential if storage and transportation costs are to be low. Storage costs must be low if means of payment are to be accepted by sellers for use in subsequent purchases. Transportation costs must be low if either the producers and users of goods are located at places that are widely distant, or if the number of buyers and sellers through intermediaries must be so large that they are inevitably widely dispersed. In general, means of payment will be compact and durable unless it is certain that they will not be used in transactions involving buyers and sellers widely separated in either time or space.

It follows from this discussion that any differences in the efficiencies of various means of payment in different transactions will be due to differences in standardization and the consequent differences in the appropriate technology of communication and, therefore, information costs.

An essential criterion for any seller in deciding whether to accept a means of payment is the likelihood that he will be able to use it either in further production or consumption or in exchange. Ignoring payment in kind, which is subject to the usual coincidence-of-wants inefficiencies of barter, we shall concentrate here on the likelihood that a means of payment will be useful in further transactions.

There are two broad classes of means of payment: those that have a widely recognized or legally enforced intrinsic value and those that are claims on (or debts of) their original issuers. Means of payment that have intrinsic value formerly included gold and presently include legal tender, which must by law be accepted in settlement of debts and in exchange for commodities. Unless the legal penalties for refusing to accept legal tender exceed the opportunity costs of accepting it, rational individuals will accord an intrinsic value to legal tender even when it carries no claim on any other asset or commodities. Those means of payments that have no intrinsic value and are therefore the debts of either the buyer in a transaction or some other agent will be accepted in general only if the seller is convinced of the financial probity and strength of the debtor or the guarantor of the debtor. This principle applies equally to bankers' drafts, individuals' cheques, trade credit or any other debt that is accepted in exchange for commodities or assets. In those cases where the original issuer of the means of payment is not known to the seller in a transaction, he may seek additional information from, for example, credit referral agencies, which function as intermediaries in the acquisition of information. These agencies achieve economies of scale in the acquisition and processing of information. In addition, they collect sufficient information to formulate statistically reliable multivariate frequency distributions relating repayment performances to other characteristics of debtors. Thus, if no information is available about a particular potential debtor, the decision to extend (say) trade credit can be based on characteristics statistically associated with good payment performance in the population as a whole.

Provided that both parties to a transaction are rational, they will use that means of payment which minimizes their joint transaction costs. If the use of one means of payment instead of some other lowers the total transactions costs of one party by more than it raises the total transactions costs of the other party to the transaction, the extra savings of the first party can be reflected in the price. If it is the buyer who gains the greater saving, he can offer to raise the price by an amount that does not exceed his saving and is greater than the seller's added costs from the use of that particular means of payment. Conversely, a seller could offer to lower the price by an amount that is less than his additional saving but more than the buyer's added costs.

It seems likely that, in the general case, both parties to a transaction will find that the same means of payment minimizes their respective transactions costs. In casual transactions involving small nominal values, means of payment of intrinsic value are likely to be employed because they entail no transactions costs. If, in such circumstances, the buyer were to offer a promise to pay at some future date in exchange for a commodity now, the seller would need to incur the information costs of ascertaining the buyer's financial probity and strength. Since this cost is independent of the value of the transaction, the recovery of the information cost by an increase in the price of the commodity would amount to charging interest at a rate that is far in excess of the prevailing interest rates. The buyer would do better to borrow means of payment of intrinsic value or the debt instruments of an agent of widely known financial strength and probity in order to effect such a transaction. When the value of the transaction is large or one of a long series of transactions of relatively small value, the information costs of extending credit to the buyer will be small in relation to the value of the transactions. In the case of individuals who engage in a large number of transactions of small values, the savings from making and receiving one larger payment periodically could well exceed the information costs and any interest income forgone by the seller.

It is clear from the foregoing discussion that the same principles that were used to deduce optimal exchange technologies and institutional arrangements in the theory of markets determine the optimal means of payment in transactions of varying frequencies and values. Even if the conclusions are by no means startling, to have derived them within the same analytical framework used to derive propositions about the macroeconomic technology of both production and exchange serves to show the generality and essential simplicity of the present analysis.

Stores of value

A store of value is presumably a durable asset that does not lose its value over time relative to other things. But unless relative prices never change, some durable assets are likely to be better stores of value with respect to some 'other things' and other assets will be better stores of value with respect to different 'other things'. Thus, we would expect that individuals who want stores of value will choose assets that are the best stores of value to them in light of their own future commitments and plans. Individuals who have commitments such as debts, which are denominated in the common unit of account, will hold as stores of value assets that they confidently believe will provide means of payment equal in value to the appropriate number of units of account at the time their commitments fall due. Individuals who rely on their wealth to provide for future consumption or other commodity purchases will hold their wealth in a form that they confidently believe will yield the appropriate purchasing power over the commodities they will want to buy at the time they want to buy them.

Provided that firms' managers are rational and survival-motivated, they will be averse to holding assets that they do not confidently believe will enable them to meet their debt commitments and purchase inputs to their production processes. In respect of their debt commitments, they are capital-uncertainty-averse. In respect of their future demands for inputs to production and exchange processes, they are income-uncertainty-averse. As we saw in section 5.3, the income-uncertainty aversion of financial institutions is manifest as a capital-uncertainty aversion. If, as is commonly assumed in economics, households are motivated to maintain well-defined consumption patterns over time, they will rationally be income-uncertainty-averse.

Unless the capital-uncertainty-averse and the income-uncertainty-averse are confident that their incomes will be sufficient for their known needs, they will rationally hedge their future commitments and purchases. In some circumstances they will be able to do so by buying and selling futures on the organized commodity exchanges. These are the circumstances that were analysed at length in section 5.3. As we know from that section, and from the theory of markets in general, organized exchanges are allocatively efficient only in respect of some commodities and assets. Thus, the motivation to hedge is more general than can be accommodated by organized commodity and financial exchanges. In order to generalize the analysis of hedging to include the hedging of commitments and commodity purchases that bear no close and direct relationships to assets traded on organized exchanges, we shall require a general analysis of what constitutes a 'safe asset' in different circumstances.

By developing a theory of safe assets as a generalization of the analysis of hedging, we necessarily identify rational behaviour in conditions of uncertainty. For a safe asset is one that provides a refuge from the capital or income uncertainty to which the commitments and preferences of individuals expose them and which entail the possibility that they will be unable to satisfy their (to them) most important objectives.

It is clear that such a theory differs from mainstream economics in so far as it relies on uncertainty. The circumstances that will be considered are those in which the sequence of short-run interest rates or asset prices from now into the indefinite future cannot be estimated even up to a subjective probability distribution. In consequence, it is not possible to define a utility function with arguments including either the first or the first two moments of such a probability distribution.

The safe-asset theory will also differ from Keynes's liquidity preference theory in that it relies crucially on the assumption of individual rationality. Because some of the analytical techniques adopted in the development of this theory are taken from Keynes, and, moreover, some of the conclusions are, if not identical, similar to Keynes's, it will perhaps avoid needless confusion and controversy if I explain why I believe liquidity preference theory to rely on arationality.

It is well known that both Hicks (1939, p. 164) and Robertson (1951, pp. 111–14) objected to liquidity preference theory because of its reliance on unexplained expectations. In Hicks's phrase, '[T]o say that the rate of interest on perfectly safe securities is determined by nothing else than uncertainty of future interest rates seems to leave interest hanging by its own bootstraps.' This is undoubtedly so. But Hicks's and others' way round this problem was to seek a theory of interest based on long-run equilibrium notions, therefore requiring long-run constrained maximization, and hence the absence of uncertainty. This procedure, we know from chapter 2, has its own problems. A better alternative (because it takes both uncertainty and rationality into account) will not ignore uncertainty of future interest rates but will deduce the effects of that uncertainty on rational individual behaviour.

That Keynes did not base his analysis of liquidity preference on individual rationality is clear from his defence of liquidity preference theory in the 1937 *Quarterly Journal of Economics* symposium. Keynes's (1937/1973, vol. 14, p. 116) main point there was that 'our desire to hold money as a store of wealth is a barometer of distrust of our own calculations and conventions concerning the future.' This desire is 'conventional or instinctive', and it operates 'at a deeper level of our motivation'. The interest rate is then 'the premium which we require to make us part with money' and its level is 'the measure of our disquietude'. Liquidity preference seems here a bit like primitive man's demand for caves and fire when he hears the call of the sabre-toothed tiger. But although the demand for the cave might be instinctive, the use of fire must have resulted from a process of learning and invention. Like fire, safe assets were invented relatively late in the history of man. It seems unlikely that the demand for any one asset such as money will have been installed in man's sub-conscious through any evolution of the species. Money is not, in this sense, like a cave. Indeed, when we analyse the demand for assets as hedges against uncertainty, we shall find that money is not the only safe asset; in fact, it is the optimal safe asset in only a limited class of circumstances.

Money defined

Whatever else money is, it is not a unit of account. To define money as anything other than a means of payment would be to deny it the one attribute that all analysts agree to be its main characteristic. But we need not and usefully will not define money to comprise all means of payment. If money is a safe asset at all, it is because it either has intrinsic value or is the debt of an agent of undoubted financial probity and strength. In such circumstances, and because as means of payment it must be denominated in the same units as all prices, money-as-safe-asset will be exchangeable directly for other commodities or assets which do not themselves serve as means of payment. This is the definition of money that will be employed here.

7.2   RATES OF RETURN

It is evidently of crucial importance here to be able to identify not only those assets that are safe with respect to an individual's commitments or planned purchases, but also which safe asset is optimally held by the individual. One possibility is always to purchase the asset or commodity that will be required and hold it until that requirement is realized. Suppose that asset j will be required at some future date. The question then is whether there is some other asset i that is preferable to j as a store of value with which to meet commitments to buy or sell asset j.

Keynes's (1936, chapter 17) definition of the rate of return provides an appropriate starting point for the determination of whether asset i or asset j is the better safe asset in these circumstances. Following Keynes, we define the net yield of an asset over the unit time interval as the increase in the quantity of an asset that holding it makes possible. This increase is represented as a proportion of the initial holding. The net yield is also the own-rate of return on the asset. For example, if a bond carries an annual interest payment that is made at the end of the year, the number of bonds that can be purchased with that interest payment when it is made divided by the number of bonds held during the year is the net yield or own-rate of return on the bond. If, alternatively, a wealth-holder should actually take possession of spot commodities, then the proportion of his holdings that would have to be sold in order to cover the storage and other carrying costs over the year will be the (negative) annual net yield of the commodity.

In general, denote the yield on the ith asset by y_i. If q_i^0 is the quantity of the ith asset held at the start of the period and q_i^1 is the quantity which that holding makes possible at the end of the period, then the net yield (or own-rate of return) on the ith asset is

$$y_i \equiv \frac{q_i^1 - q_i^0}{q_i^0}. \tag{7.1}$$

The rate of return on the ith asset when its value is denominated in units of the jth asset is the i-rate of j-return. It is defined analogously to the own-rate of return as the increase in the number of units of the jth commodity that could be acquired by holding the ith commodity expressed as a proportion of the number of units of the jth commodity that could be had in exchange for the initial holding of the ith commodity. Denoting the i-rate of j-return by ρ_{ij}, we have

$$\rho_{ij} \equiv \frac{p_{ij}^1 q_i^1 - p_{ij}^0 q_i^0}{p_{ij}^0 q_i^0} \tag{7.2}$$

where p_{ij}^t is the price of the ith asset denominated in units of the jth asset at time t. When all prices are denominated in the single, abstract unit of account, then p_{ij} is p_i/p_j, which is the number of units of the jth asset that must be sold at nominal price p_j in order to purchase a unit of the ith asset at nominal price p_i.

The proportional rate of capital gains of the ith asset denominated in units of the jth asset is

$$\gamma_{ij} \equiv \frac{p_{ij}^1 - p_{ij}^0}{p_{ij}^0} \equiv \frac{p_i^1/p_j^1}{p_i^0/p_j^0} - 1. \tag{7.3}$$

Substituting from identities (7.1) and (7.3) into (7.2), we have

$$\rho_{ij} \equiv y_i(1 + \gamma_{ij}) + \gamma_{ij}. \tag{7.4}$$

The question now is whether, in order to have a given quantity of asset j one period hence, a wealth-holder will hold asset j or asset i. Since the proportional increase in command over asset j as a result of holding asset i during that period is ρ_{ij} and the proportional increase in holdings of j is y_j, it is clear that asset i will be held if and only if

$$\rho_{ij} - y_j > 0. \tag{7.5}$$

Because rates of capital gains are generally recognized as rates of increase in nominal rather than relative prices, and because assets are normally bought and sold in exchange for means of payment dominated in the common unit of account, it is more efficient – requiring fewer resources devoted to calculation – to compare nominal rates of return rather than the i-rate of j-return and the own-rate of return on asset j. It is easily seen, however, that the nominal rate of return on asset i, ρ_{im}, is greater than the nominal rate of return on asset j, ρ_{jm}, if and only if condition (7.5) is satisfied. The difference on these nominal rates of return is

$$\rho_{im} - \rho_{jm} \equiv y_i(1 + \gamma_{im}) - y_j(1 + \gamma_{jm}) + (\gamma_{im} - \gamma_{jm}) \tag{7.6}$$

or

$$\rho_{im} - \rho_{jm} \equiv (1 + \gamma_{jm}) \; y_i \frac{1 + \gamma_{im}}{1 + \gamma_{jm}} + \frac{\gamma_{im} - \gamma_{jm}}{1 + \gamma_{jm}} - y_j \; . \tag{7.7}$$

We find from identity (7.3) that

$$\frac{1 + \gamma_{im}}{1 + \gamma_{jm}} \equiv 1 + \gamma_{ij} \quad \text{and} \quad \frac{\gamma_{im} - \gamma_{jm}}{1 + \gamma_{jm}} \equiv \gamma_{ij}.$$

Substituting these relationships into the right side of identity (7.7),

$$\rho_{im} - \rho_{jm} \equiv (1 + \gamma_{jm})[\, y_i(1 + \gamma_{ij}) + \gamma_{ij} - y_j] \tag{7.8}$$

or, equivalently,

$$\rho_{im} - \rho_{jm} \equiv (1 + \gamma_{jm})(\rho_{ij} - y_i), \tag{7.9}$$

the sign of which is the same as the sign of the left side of condition (7.5).

It follows from condition (7.8), and therefore from condition (7.5), that asset i will be preferred to asset j as a hedge for the meeting of commitments in asset j if and only if

$$y_i > \frac{y_j - \gamma_{ij}}{1 + \gamma_{ij}}. \tag{7.10}$$

7.3 CAPITAL UNCERTAINTY, INCOME UNCERTAINTY AND ASSET SAFETY

A safe asset is one that confers immunity from outcomes and events that would prevent an agent's primary objectives from being satisfied.

By holding a safe asset an individual knows that he will not be surprised either by an inability to follow plans and meet commitments or by a windfall gain of any kind, no matter what untoward or propitious events might occur. Once an individual holds a safe asset to hedge future commitments and plans, it makes no difference whether he has a well-defined subjective probability distribution or not. The outcome of his actions are circumscribed within narrow limits. If a capital-uncertainty-averse individual has debts denominated in the common unit of account, then a safe asset for him or her will be one that yields the value of those debts at the time they fall due. In these circumstances, the capital-uncertainty-averse will be concerned with the certainty of the nominal rates of return on assets held for hedging purposes. The income-uncertainty-averse will be concerned with the values of hedging assets in relation to the values of the commodities they will want to purchase. The rates of return on assets that will be of concern to the income-uncertainty-averse will therefore be asset rates of commodity return, where the commodities in question are those that the individual plans to buy or is committed to buying. We consider capital-uncertainty hedging and income-uncertainty hedging in turn. Since price expectations are of some importance here, these are considered at the end of this section.

Capital uncertainty

We begin with the normal position, in which firms' debt repayment and servicing commitments are denominated in the common, abstract unit of account. There are circumstances in which this position will not be acceptable to lenders, in which case those firms that borrow will have to incur debts denominated in other units. This point will be taken up below.

It is immediately clear that one safe asset for the capital-uncertainty-averse with debts denominated in the common unit of account is general means of payment, i.e. money. However, money is not necessarily the optimal safe asset for the capital-uncertainty-averse. It will not be the optimal safe asset if there is some other safe asset, say asset a, carrying a contractual, nominal rate of return that is higher than the nominal rate of return on money or, in Keynesian terminology, money's own-rate of return. Asset a will be held in preference to money as a hedge against uncertainty if the a-rate of nominal return is greater than the money-rate of nominal return. Since the rate of capital gains on money is identically zero, the nominal return is $\rho_{mm} \equiv y_m$. It is clear from condition (7.10) that asset a will be preferred over money as a safe asset only if

$$y_a > \frac{y_m - \gamma_{am}}{1 + \gamma_{am}}. \qquad (7.11)$$

The only sensible interpretation of y_m is as the rate of interest on money, taking into account both the interest actually paid on any money held as credits with banks or other agents and any charges against those credits for bookkeeping or the processing of payments. If the interest exceeds the charges, the effective rate of interest y_m is positive. If the charges exceed the interest, y_m is negative. The particular money asset that is relevant here is that which minimizes the transactions costs of the hedger against capital uncertainty. Although y_m can be negative it seems most implausible that y_a could be; for a non-money safe asset in this context is almost certain to be traded on an organized exchange. If it is a security, it will carry a positive interest payment and its price will be positive. Otherwise, lenders to the original issuers of the security would be paying for the privilege of making the loan. Since y_a is in all plausible cases positive, we see from condition (7.11) that a sufficient but not necessary condition for the nominal rate of return on asset a to exceed the own-rate of return on money is that money's own-rate of return be less than the rate of nominal capital gains on asset a.

Condition (7.11) implies that, given the current price of asset a and the interest payment due on asset a each period, asset a could be a better safe asset to hold than money, provided that the rate of capital gains on asset a exceeds the critical value implied by condition (7.11). In order to be a safe asset, the price of asset a at the date on which the hedger's commitment falls due must be known with certainty when the asset is purchased. That price can be known only if the safe asset itself matures at the same time as the hedger's commitment falls due.

It is evidently possible to hedge all future commitments by purchasing, say, gilt-edged stock maturing at or near each date at which a known commitment falls due. To do so, however, the proceeds from all new debts would have to be employed to buy assets maturing at the same times as the debts are due to be repaid and interest payments are due to be made. If any debts are incurred to finance either investments in capacity expansion or current production and exchange activities, these debts cannot be hedged. Nor can financial institutions hedge all of their debts if they are to lend to firms for investment. Just as industrial companies borrow in the hope of generating a positive cash flow from the use of non-financial assets, financial intermediaries need to hold assets that are less safe than the assets they create for their own creditors. Financial intermediaries take advantage of economies of massed reserves: in particular, the low probability that a high proportion of all short-term creditors will require repayment at the same time and the low probability that a high proportion of debtors will default. It follows that, for any investment to take place and for financial intermediaries to provide external finance for that investment, both the investing firms and the financial intermediaries must incur unhedged debt commitments. Moreover, to the extent that industrial and commercial firms finance their investments and financial institutions finance their lending internally, they will have to give up either the means of payment received as current revenue or the financial assets held as reserves in order to acquire real capital assets or claims to the value of (or future revenues from) those assets. Thus, internal finance by either industrial and commercial companies or financial institutions requires the firms in question either to reduce their current hedging positions or to reduce their capacity to hedge future commitments as they arise.

There are two possibilities here. Investing firms and their lenders could be flush with safe assets in excess of the debt commitments that might reasonably be hedged. Alternatively, they are becoming increasingly optimistic about the likelihood of generating the cash flows required to recover investment costs so that they are increasingly prepared to unhedge previously hedged commitments.

In order to have safe assets of a value in excess of the value of future hedged commitments, firms must place some limit on the interval of time over which they will hedge. It is hard to imagine that any firms will hedge commitments extending indefinitely into the future. Indeed, the analysis of speculation and hedging developed in section 5.3 indicates that a reluctance to hedge over the indefinite future is rational.

We saw in that section that there is a reasonably well-defined latitude within which speculative demands and supplies can dominate the determination of asset prices on the organized exchanges. If individuals learn from experience and history, they will come to recognize the limits to speculatively fuelled price increases and reductions. Although the latitude for speculative domination of bond and other financial asset prices is among the widest, there will be some experience of the duration of any cycles in these asset prices. There is no requirement here that these cycles be regular. But if a period of rising prices is always followed by a period of falling prices and vice versa, then there will be some maximum duration that has not in practice been exceeded in length. In these circumstances it will be reasonable to suppose that asset prices in general over the next, say, five or ten years will be favourable at some time to the hedging of commitments that will mature after that period. If so, it will be rational on the basis of past experience to hedge future commitments no more than that five or ten years ahead. Firms' holdings of financial assets that mature after that period are surplus to their hedging requirements. (That such cycles in financial asset prices are an endogenous property of macroeconomic processes will be demonstrated in chapter 8.)

Whether or not firms consider their longest-term commitments to be worthwhile to hedge, it is compatible with a general presumption that individuals have positive rates of time preference to assume that, whenever firms do unhedge commitments, they will choose those maturing furthest into the future. If the primary motivation of a firm's management team is to ensure the survival of the firm, then a positive rate of time preference implies that they will prefer a later rather than an earlier failure. In the event that there are inducement effects requiring some new investment, then firms will finance that investment internally by unhedging their most distant commitments. To the extent that the investments are financed externally, the investors will be undertaking new unhedged commitments.

In summary, the capital-uncertainty-averse will hedge their balance-sheet commitments by holding assets that are the debt instruments of firms or other agents whose financial probity and strength is understood to be no less than that of the agents whose debts are used as money. Those debt instruments will mature at the same time as the commitments they hedge. In general, a positive rate of time preference implies that internal finance for investment will entail the unhedging of commitments maturing furthest into the future. In any case, there is likely to be some limit to the future interval of time over which rational agents will hedge. This interval depends on the cycle of financial asset prices, which will be investigated in detail in chapter 8.

Income uncertainty

The income-uncertainty-averse are concerned to avoid situations in which they will be unable to purchase the commodities they require either for consumption (if households) or as inputs to production and exchange processes (if firms). There is no suggestion here that those who are income-uncertainty-averse cannot also be capital-uncertainty-averse. In some cases, capital-uncertainty aversion and income-uncertainty aversion are inseparable. In section 5.3, for example, we found this to be the case for financial intermediaries. More generally, agents hold some assets as hedges against capital uncertainty and others as hedges against income uncertainty. Sometimes these assets are identical, so that the values of the individual's safe asset holdings will be sufficient for both purposes.

Just as the relevant rate of return on assets held for capital hedging is the rate of money return (or nominal rate of return), the relevant rate of return to the income-uncertainty-averse is the rate of 'commodity' return, in which values are denominated in relation to the particular commodities the purchases of which are being hedged. The optimal safe asset for the income-uncertainty-averse will be the safe asset that has the highest rate of return relative to the individual's composition and time-pattern of planned commodity purchases.

The alternative to holding safe assets as income hedges is the holding of the commodities that will be required. Consider first the choice between money as an income hedge and the holding of a particular commodity c, which will be wanted for future use. Money will be preferred to commodity c if the money rate of c-return is greater than the c-rate of c-return (the own-rate of return on the commodity). Formally,

$$\rho_{mc} - \rho_{cc} = y_m(1 + \gamma_{mc}) + \gamma_{mc} - y_c > 0. \tag{7.12}$$

If this inequality is satisfied, then from the definition of the rate of capital gain

$$y_m > y_c(1 + \gamma_{cm}) + \gamma_{cm}. \tag{7.13}$$

That is, money will be held instead of the commodity itself only if the own-rate of return on money exceeds the c-rate of money return. This is the appropriate condition when money is valued in the same unit of account as the commodity price. In addition, it brings the real rate of interest on money into consideration since, in the absence of relative price changes, γ_{cm} is the rate of commodity price inflation.

It is immediately apparent from condition (7.13) that, although the real rate of interest on money is a determinant of the demand for money as a refuge from income uncertainty, a nil value of the real rate of interest on money has no special significance. For the net yield on commodity c (i.e. y_c) will always be negative if the commodity is held as a hedging asset but not actually used in production or exchange. Apart from the opportunity cost of the finance required for its purchase, any deterioration or storage cost (reckoned as a proportion of the price of the commodity) implies either that holdings of commodity c will decline over time or that the purchases and holdings of other commodities or assets will be reduced over time in order to meet the storage and interest costs. The real rate of interest on money holdings is, in the absence of relative price changes, $y_m - \gamma_{cm}$. If relative prices are changing, then $y_m - \gamma_{cm}$ is the rate of interest on money deflated by the price of commodity c alone. Money can rationally be held to hedge purchases or commodity c when

$$y_m - \gamma_{cm} > y_c(1 + \gamma_{cm}). \tag{7.14}$$

Since y_c is negative, the price-deflated rate of interest on money can be negative without diminishing this hedging demand for money. Clearly, the magnitude of the negative value of y_c will be greater as commodity c is less durable and less compact. Thus, for any given rate of price inflation, and ignoring changes in relative prices, money could be held to hedge the least durable and compact commodities but not necessarily the most durable and compact commodities.

It is obvious that rising nominal rates of interest on money raise the left side of condition (7.14) relative to the right side. If these rises proceed far enough, money will become a suitable (if not optimal) hedge for any future purchases of consumption commodities. The partial derivative of the left side of that condition respect to γ_{cm} is -1. The partial derivative of the right side with respect to γ_{cm} is y_c. Thus, provided that $y_c > -1$, rising rates of price inflation will raise the right side of condition (7.14) relative to the left side until the condition is no longer satisfied. This proviso must be met if anyone is ever to hold commodity c, since otherwise, $y_c \leqslant -1$ and the carrying cost of the commodity in terms of itself over the unit time-period will exceed the quantity held.

There is a condition equivalent to (7.14) for every consumption commodity. If the general rate of price inflation is rising, then one after another the conditions such as (7.14) corresponding to individual commodities will cease to be satisfied. In the absence of relative price changes, money will cease to be a possible hedge first for the most durable and compact commodities – those with the highest values of y_c. This conclusion will be mitigated to some extent by changing relative prices, although, as we saw in section 6.3, such changes are unlikely to be more important than the effects of general price inflation.

Non-safe money assets will provide the optimal income hedges if they carry higher rates of commodity return than either money or the commodities that will be required in the future. A non-money safe asset will be preferred to holdings of the required commodity if

$$\rho_{ac} - \rho_{cc} \equiv \frac{1}{1 + \gamma_{cm}} (\rho_{am} - \rho_{cm}) > 0 \qquad (7.15)$$

and the same safe asset will be preferred to money as an income hedge if

$$\rho_{ac} - \rho_{mc} \equiv \frac{1}{1 + \gamma_{cm}} (\rho_{am} - y_m) > 0. \qquad (7.16)$$

The magnitude of the difference between the two rates of return in each case is affected by the rate of commodity price increase, γ_{cm}.

Condition (7.14) determines which of these conditions will be relevant. If the rate of price increase is sufficiently small, condition (7.14) will be satisfied so that money will dominate commodities as an income hedge. Whether money or non-money safe assets will then be held as income hedges is determined by condition (7.16).

At rates of price increase that are high enough to violate condition (7.14), commodities will dominate money as income hedges and condition (7.15) will determine whether or not the non-money safe asset is the optimal income hedge.

The real rate of return on the non-money safe asset will be relevant only if commodities dominate money as income hedges; for condition (7.15) will be satisfied if and only if $\rho_{am} > \rho_{cm}$. From the definitions of these rates of return, we know that this condition amounts to

$$\rho_{am} - \gamma_{cm} > y_c(1 + \gamma_{cm}). \qquad (7.17)$$

Since a safe asset is, by definition, one that can be held to maturity to cover future commitments or discretionary purchases, the rate of return will be known and the net yield and rate of capital gains individually will be important except to the extent that they are taxed differently. The similarity of condition (7.17) with the analogous condition (7.14) for money *vis à vis* commodities as an income hedge is readily apparent. The same remarks that apply to the relative goodness of money and commodities as income hedges apply equally to the relative goodness of non-money safe assets and commodities for this purpose. Given the nominal rate of return on the non-money safe asset and the net yield of commodities, increasingly less compact and durable commodities will displace the appropriate non-money safe assets as income hedges as the rate of price inflation increases and, therefore, the real rate of return on non-money safe asset falls. As with money, the nil value of the real rate of return on non-money safe assets is of no special significance in this context.

Condition (7.16) will be satisfied if and only if the nominal rate of return on the non-money safe asset exceeds the own-rate of return on money. This is the same as the condition for the holding of non-money assets as capital hedges. In consequence, condition (7.17) will be satisfied whenever condition (7.11) is satisfied. Given that the rate of price inflation is not sufficiently high to displace money as an income hedge that is preferred to commodities, the actual level of the inflation rate is of no consequence. Thus, at low rates of inflation the same assets that are held as capital hedges will also be held as income hedges. As the rate of inflation increases, both money and non-money safe assets will increasingly be displaced by commodities as income hedges but not as capital hedges. As this displacement occurs, the real rate of return on safe assets becomes the relevant consideration to the income-uncertainty-averse, but, since the net yield on commodities is generally negative, this does not imply that the real rate of return on any asset need be positive in order for it to be preferred to commodities as an income hedge.

Expectations of inflation

Although the nominal rate of return on a safe asset, whether money or not, is known with certainty, the relevant inflation rate clearly cannot be known. The relevant rate of inflation is the expected future rate. This proposition, which is common to all schools of economists, obviously introduces an element of uncertainty into the concept of a real rate of return. For that reason, expectations of future inflation are important to the income-uncertainty-averse. For a different reason, the expected rate of inflation is also important in the hedging practices of the capital-uncertainty-averse.

As Irving Fisher (1933) pointed out, the rate of inflation (or deflation) determines the real burden of the debts that make firms averse to capital uncertainty. We have seen in the preceding discussion that inflation does not affect either the safety or the optimality of assets rationally employed in capital hedging. But a positive rate of price inflation will increase the nominal value of gross profits corresponding to any scale of activity. As long as a firm's share of aggregate gross revenue is not declining at a faster rate than the nominal revenue itself is increasing, gross profits must be growing relative to existing debts even if output levels are constant or declining. In consequence, the proportion of the firm's gross profits that is committed to debt repayments and, if the real rate of interest should fall, debt servicing will be declining.

This diminution in the real burden of debt can lead either to an increase in the demands for safe assets or to a reduction, depending upon the state of long-term expectation and consequent rate of investment growth. If the firms realizing diminishing real debt burdens use the increase in uncommitted incomes to hedge yet more future commitments, they will be unable to invest as rapidly but will be less subject to future reductions in both real and nominal incomes. If the state of long-term expectation is increasingly optimistic, then the increase in uncommitted revenue will be used for investments in capacity expansion. There is the further alternative that, in a depressed state of long-term expectation, the diminution of the real debt burden will lead to an increase in dividends and other profit distributions, or to the early repayment of debts. In general, in a pessimistic or unchanging state of long-term expectation, confident expectations of higher or continuously rising rates of price inflation will, if anything, induce the capital-uncertainty-averse to increase their demands for safe assets, thereby offsetting (and probably overriding) the declining demands of the income-uncertainty-averse. In an improving state of long-term expectation, confident anticipation of higher or rising inflation rates will be accompanied by a reduced demand for safe assets by the capital-uncertainty-averse, thereby reinforcing the declining demand from the income-uncertainty-averse.

It is evidently of some importance in this analysis to identify the determinants of individuals' expectations of future inflation rates.

Two sequences of events – one for demand-pull and the other for cost-push inflations – were identified in section 6.3. Demand-pull inflations begin with rising short-run prices which alter relative long-run prices and, probably but not necessarily, lead to some rises in wage rates as workers defend their real wages. (Short-run prices, it will be remembered, are those set to clear markets in the short run; long-run prices are set in light of longer-run financial considerations. Both can prevail in competitive markets.) Cost-push inflations begin with rising wage rates which, if supplies of raw materials and other short-run-priced commodities are to be maintained, lead to rising short-run prices as well. In consequence, long-run prices generally rise but, as shown in section 6.3, relative prices change less substantially than in the case of demand-pull inflation.

There is nothing in the present analysis to enable us to specify the time-lags involved in each of these inflationary sequences. In practice, rises in raw material prices are followed by rises in the Wholesale Price Index three to six months later and then, in another three to six months, by Retail Price Index rises. Widespread increases in wage rates lead more quickly and more uniformly to rises in both wholesale and retail prices. Since basic commodities are not sold at retail, these sequences are compatible with the analysis of chapter 6. It would clearly be rational for individual firms and households to interpret rising wages and rising short-run prices as signals that a more general inflation is on the way. Of course, these signals are for increased rates of inflation months, but not years, ahead. For this reason, it is quite possible to form expectations about future inflation rates over the short term but not over terms of a year or more.

Now, the key characteristic of any hedging transaction is that it eliminates uncertainty. During periods when inflation rates are perceived to be volatile, the income-uncertainty-averse will be unable confidently to hedge commodity purchases further into the future than that interval for which they have clear inflation signals. The capital-uncertainty-averse will be unable to predict with any confidence the real burden of debt beyond the same interval of time. Thus, the income-uncertainty-averse will have no clear guidelines as to which commodity purchases are optimally hedged, and the capital-uncertainty-averse will be unable to form confident expectations about the volume of internal finance that will be available for investment. These problems do not arise when firms and households believe inflationary conditions to be stable. It does not matter in principle whether it is the general price level or the rate of inflation (or rate of increase in the rate of inflation or any higher rate of change) that is stable. Provided that the ways in which nominal price levels change is thought to be known, then optimal hedging practices can be determined given the conditions of inflation.

This is not to suggest that inflation has no costs. Higher rates of inflation diminish the set of commodities that are optimally hedged by the holding of non-money safe assets and expand the set of commodities that will optimally be held for future use. Income-hedgers will therefore incur increased carrying costs while losing a real return on hedging assets if they respond rationally to rising expected inflation rates. However, there are no obvious costs in this regard to capital-hedgers since their aim will be to cover debts denominated in the same unit of account as the values of safe assets. There could, however, be some cost to firms as a result of inflation-induced constraints on the external finance that they can raise for their investment projects. This is a point of considerable importance which will be developed in chapter 9.

7.4   HEDGING, SPECULATION AND ENTERPRISE

The analysis of the hedging of future debt commitments by the capital-uncertainty-averse and the hedging of future consumption demands and purchasing commitments by the income-uncertainty-averse does not raise any questions or propositions that are fundamentally different from those raised in section 5.3. In particular, hedging is possible only if other individuals are prepared to assume the hedgers' uncertainty, and there will be such individuals only if they expect to be able to generate a positive cash flow by taking on that uncertainty.

Any increase in the net hedging of commitments maturing at any future date entails the purchase of assets that are safe with respect to that date, i.e. that mature at about that time. Evidently, the taking of such net hedging positions is possible only if those assets can be purchased either from individuals who hold existing assets or from individuals of known financial strength and probity who increase their commitments by offering new issues of the appropriate securities. Just as in the organized exchanges for commodities and futures contracts, individuals will be induced to take positions rendering them vulnerable to uncertainty only if they have some reason to anticipate a greater profit from such positions than from safer positions. In the organized exchanges for futures contracts, any net increase in long hedging (which entails purchases of commodity futures) requires the prices of futures contracts to rise enough to induce speculators to sell commodity futures in the expectation that, when those futures mature, the spot price will be substantially below the current futures price. For exactly the same reason, an increase in the net hedging of future debt, interest and dividend commitments or of future commodity purchases is possible only if the prices of safe assets are bid up until speculators or entrepreneurs become confident that the rates of return on other assets will be substantially greater than the rates of return on the assets demanded by hedgers.

Speculators' supplies of hedging assets

When speculators are induced to sell assets demanded by hedgers, they could do so in order to hold more money or to purchase assets maturing more quickly than those they sell or, alternatively, to buy assets that mature later or which, like equities, have no maturity dates.

Speculators will certainly not exchange assets demanded by hedgers for any shorter-term assets or money unless the rates of return on the shorter-term assets or money exceed the rate of return on the assets they already hold. It is perfectly obvious that a rate of return that is both higher and guaranteed over a long period of time is preferable to a rate of return that is lower and guaranteed over a shorter period of time. If it should be the case that there is an increase in the net hedging demands for assets maturing at some future date but not for assets maturing earlier, then the prices of the appropriate hedging assets will rise in the first instance relative to the shorter-term assets. The relative price increase on safe (hence fixed-interest) assets reduces the rate of return on those assets relative to securities that mature earlier. It is possible, but by no means necessary, that speculators will respond to this circumstance by selling their holdings of assets demanded by hedgers in order to buy the shorter-term assets. If they do, then the shorter-term asset prices are likely to be bid up until, eventually, the highest nominal rate of return on assets maturing before those demanded by hedgers is the own-rate of return on money. Thereafter, no one who holds the assets demanded by hedgers will sell them in order to buy any shorter-term asset. If they do not wish to hold longer-term assets or equities, they will increase their holdings of money as the securities in their portfolios mature.

Assuming that the proceeds from any sales of longer-term hedging assets are used to buy shorter-term assets with higher rates of return, the prices of the shorter term assets will rise until the differential rate of return is eliminated and the normal term-structure of interest rates is re-established. However, there is no reason to preclude the purchase of longer-term securities if the rate of return on those securities is expected to be greater than the rate of return on any of the shorter-term assets and greater than the own-rate of return on money. When the hedgers' demands lead speculators to go longer, then it is entirely possible that the shortest-term securities will offer higher rates of return than securities maturing later. That is, there will be a reversal of the normal term-structure of interest rates.

In general, there is some limit to the diversion of speculative holdings of assets demanded by hedgers to shorter-term assets and money. Once this limit is reached, any further shifts to the holding of money will take place only as money incomes are received and assets mature at their face values. If there is to be any further supply of the assets demanded by hedgers – ignoring, for the moment, newly created assets – then these supplies will have to be concomitants of a speculative portfolio shift to longer-term assets or equities.

The net supply of hedging assets in the organized exchanges is equivalently a net demand for futures contracts which just offsets hedgers' demands. That is, if hedgers collectively take a short position in futures, prices must move so that speculators are induced collectively to take a long position of the same value, and conversely. The issues involved here were discussed in detail in section 5.3. In the remainder of this section we consider only the inducements for speculators to exchange safe assets for fixed-interest securities and equities.

Suppose that the fixed-interest payment on a bond is D_b and that its current nominal price is p_b^0. The yield on the bond one period hence will be $D_b/[p_b^0(1 + \gamma_{bm})] \equiv y_b$. Similarly, the yield one period hence on the hedging asset is $D_a/[p_a^0(1 + \gamma_{am})] \equiv y_a$. Thus, if $\rho_{bm} > \rho_{am}$, identity (7.4), the general definition of a rate of return, implies that

$$\frac{D_b}{p_b^0} + \gamma_{bm} > \frac{D_a}{p_a^0} + \gamma_{am}. \tag{7.18}$$

The interval between the present and the redemption date of the safe asset a is taken as the unit time period. In that case, γ_{am} is simply the difference between the face value and current price of that asset as a proportion of the current price. The only value that is then not known and fixed in condition (7.18) is the rate of capital gain on the bond. A speculator will be induced to sell his holdings of asset a in order to purchase the bond only if the current price of asset a rises sufficiently that he believes that condition (7.18) will be satisfied for any likely rate of capital gain on the bond.

If it should happen that incumbent holders of the hedging asset (asset a) are unwilling to exchange their holdings for more speculative assets, then the price of the hedging asset will continue to rise until its nominal rate of return is no longer in excess of the own-rate of return on money. In that case, the inability to hedge by purchasing the requisite non-money safe assets will lead first to an increase in the demand for safe assets maturing sooner than the date at which the hedgers' commitments fall due and, ultimately, to an increase in the demand for money as the optimal safe asset.

The only complication that is introduced when we turn to consider the demand for equities as speculative assets is that their net yield is not known with certainty. But firms that will want to attract future equity finance will maintain as stable a dividend policy as they can, thereby reducing as far as they are able the uncertainty attaching to their equities in relation to the uncertainties attaching to the equities of other firms. Both the capital- and income-uncertainty-averse will prefer to hold assets that entail less rather than more uncertainty. Thus, these wealth-holders will not only be more likely to demand new equity issues when they appear; they will also maintain a stronger demand for existing equities so that prices are less likely to fall low enough to attract take-over raiders.

In summary, the supply of hedging assets will be forthcoming if the rates of return on those assets fall until speculative holders are prepared to trade them for equities or assets with different – generally more distant – maturity dates or, as we saw in section 5.3, futures contracts on the organized commodity exchanges. It is entirely possible that the rate of return on some hedging assets will fall to or below the level of the own-rate of return on money before speculative holdings are thrown on the market. In that case, there will be an increase in the holdings of money assets by hedgers as they cease to use the income they save and the principal repayments from their debtors to purchase non-money safe assets.

Entrepreneurs' supplies of hedging assets

Entrepreneurs become net suppliers of hedging assets either by increasing their issues of new, relatively short-term securities or by unhedging previously hedged commitments and purchases. New short-term securities will generally be issued only to provide finance for activities undertaken with existing production and exchange capacities. The threat to firm survival entailed in the short-term finance of long-term investments is well known to all students of finance. It happens only when available long-term finance is insufficient to satisfy demands in a confidently optimistic state of long-term expectation. However, the release of short-term assets previously held as hedges can result from improvements in either short- or long-term expectations. It is implausible to suppose that long-term expectations are improving in the face of deteriorating short-term expectations, even though an improvement in short-term expectations need not always lead to improved long-term expectations. When both expectational states are improving, there is no obvious irrationality in unhedging increasingly short-term commitments in order to provide the internal finance required for long-term investments as well as current production and exchange activities.

There is nothing in the present analysis to imply that falling rates of return on non-money safe assets will improve either the state of long-term expectation or the state of short-term expectation. If anything, declining rates of return arising from increased hedging demands imply that these states are deteriorating. It is possible that falling rates of return on short-term securities will reduce the cost of borrowing to such an extent that some firms find it economic to increase throughput rates that, at higher borrowing costs, were not thought likely to generate a positive cash flow. In such cases, the falling rate of return on non-money hedging assets could induce some firms to finance increased rates of production and exchange internally by selling assets previously used for hedging (thereby realizing unplanned capital gains on those assets) and externally by issuing new securities to firms and households seeking to increase their hedging positions. Thus, more profitable activities will be unhedged by some firms to enable firms engaged in prospectively less profitable activities and households to hedge their commitments and purchases.

Hedging and macroeconomic activity levels

The foregoing discussion has shown the importance of relative nominal rates of return in determining the composition of asset demands for purposes of hedging and, in the particular case of income-hedging, the importance of expected rates of commodity price inflation. It remains to consider the role of macroeconomic activity levels – or income – in the determination of hedging positions. We shall find that in some cases hedging demands are inversely related to current activity levels and in other cases they are directly related. Moreover, the transactions demand for money is itself but one object of hedgers' demands.

We begin with a consideration of the demand for hedging assets during a period of improving long-term expectations in the basic sub-system. To say that these expectations are improving or becoming more optimistic is precisely to say that entrepreneurs expect future demands to be buoyant enough to generate revenues that would cover not only direct costs of production and exchange but also the capital costs and any interest paid or forgone as a result of investments in capacity expansion. We saw in chapter 6 that improvements in the state of long-term expectation in the basic sub-system will increase the growth of demands for commodities throughout the whole economy. In particular, improving long-term expectations in the basic sub-system will generate excess demands in the non-basic sub-system, which – unless they are eliminated by imports – will lead rational entrepreneurs in that sub-system optimistically to revise their own long-term expectations. It is hardly rational for an entrepreneur to commit himself to the capital costs of capacity expansion if he is seriously worried that future revenues will be insufficient to enable him to meet his existing debt commitments. It follows that a general improvement in long-term expectations will entail the use of internal finance for capacity expansion and, if anything, increases in debt, interest and dividend commitments. Since, in addition, a general improvement in the state of long-term expectation follows from and depends upon an improvement in the state of long-term expectation in the basic sub-system, and an improvement in the state of long-term expectation in the basic sub-system generates an increase in macroeconomic capacity utilization and growth, it follows that hedging by firms and macroeconomic activity levels will *in these circumstances* be inversely related.

In a given and unchanging state of long-term expectation, any increase in demands for commodities will not be expected to presage a period in which revenues will cover more than direct costs of production and exchange and, possibly, the meeting of existing commitments. In such a circumstance, it will be wholly rational to use some part of current gross revenues to hedge commitments that have been undertaken during a period of greater long-term optimism. *A fortiori*, in conditions of deteriorating long-term expectations, any increases in gross profits that are not already committed will rationally be used by entrepreneurs to hedge future debt, interest and dividend commitments that are not already hedged. In short, any increases in gross profits corresponding to short-run increases in activity levels will be used for hedging, and, if the consequent hedging demands are sufficiently strong, it is possible that the rates of return on non-money safe assets will fall to the level of the own-rate of return on money. In that case – and only in that case – there will be a hedging demand for money that is positively related to the level of macroeconomic activity.

If nominal prices are generally stable, the relationship between the hedging demand for money and nominal income will be precisely what has just been found. If prices are rising, then at any level of macroeconomic activity, nominal revenues and gross profits will be rising relative to the nominal values of debts previously incurred. There will therefore be a larger absolute value of nominal income that can be used for hedging; so, if the state of long-term expectation is not improving, we would expect a stronger positive relationship between nominal incomes and the value of hedging demands. If anything, therefore, there will be a larger spill-over of hedging demands into money assets. During a demand-pull inflation, however, the demand for hedging assets is likely to be declining and a larger value of hedging assets already held will be required to finance any given capacity expansion. In such a circumstance there will be a larger nominal value of hedging assets sold, as price inflation is more pronounced. If any of these assets are money assets, the negative relationship between the hedging demand for money and nominal income will itself be more pronounced.

Transactions demands for money

Money is said to be held for transactions purposes in order to enable individuals to pay bills with money when the nominal value of those bills exceeds current money revenues. Since the transactions demand for money is generally assumed to be related to current real income levels, it follows that the bills in question arise from the purchases of inputs to production and exchange processes or for purposes of income-related consumption. In other words, transactions balances are a form of income hedge.

As we have seen, however, income hedges are by no means always held as money balances. Any safe asset maturing at the same time as the bills fall due will be a satisfactory income hedge. The optimal income hedge will be that safe asset that yields the largest positive difference between its nominal rate of return and the expected rate of increase in the price of the commodity to be purchased.

However, the transactions costs of hedging must, for completeness, be taken into account. Although these costs are unlikely to have any substantial effect on hedges maturing at all but the most immediate dates, they could eliminate the advantage of non-money safe assets over either money or the commodities required in a few days' or weeks' time. In that case – and provided that individuals believe that the bills falling due in the immediate future will exceed the value of money revenues over the same period – it will be rational to hold money instead of non-money safe assets. The money balances that are demanded for these purposes can be held from savings out of current money revenues or, if necessary, from the sale of hedging assets maturing furthest into the future or from the arrangement of short-term debts including overdraft facilities. By whatever means the money balances are acquired, the principles involved in the determination of their value are precisely the same as the principles that determine the composition and value of assets held to cover more distant commodity purchases.

If the nominal differences between receipts of money and required money disbursements for current purchases is positively related to activity levels, then, to the extent that money is the optimal income hedge, transactions demands for money will bear a positive relationship to real income levels.

7.5   THE SAFE-ASSET THEORY OF INTEREST

In this section, I set out a theory that explains why, during periods of declining investment and macroeconomic growth, rational individuals increasingly demand money as a hedging asset. The rationale behind this increasing demand is that rational, survival-motivated managers in the banking system will increase the own-rate of return on money as the rates of return on non-money safe assets fall. By adhering to the analytical method employed throughout this book, we shall see that rational behaviour by individuals who learn at limited rates yields the same broad conclusions as Keynes's liquidity preference theory of interest without being subject to the 'bootstraps' critique. Indeed, the theory presented here – the safe-asset theory of interest – avoids another important flaw in Keynes's theory without relying in any way on long-run equilibrium concepts.

Apart from the 'bootstraps' problem (i.e. Keynes's reliance on unexplained expectations to sustain the own-rate of return on money), liquidity preference theory is flawed because it confuses the own-rate of return on money with nominal rates of return on various non-money assets. For Keynes defined the liquidity premium on money as 'the amount (measured in terms of itself) which [people] are willing to pay for the potential convenience of security given by this power of disposal' of money (Keynes, 1936, p. 226).

This liquidity premium, which, net of carrying costs, is money's own-rate of return *in Keynes's theory*, is the nominal interest that wealth-holders are prepared to forgo in order to have 'this power of disposal'. The own-rate of return on money thus came to be identified with the nominal rate of return on a representative long-term asset such as consols.

To say, as Keynes did, that the own-rate of return on money is the lower limit on the nominal rates of returns on non-money assets because of money's liquidity is wholly compatible with the results obtained in section 7.4. But this does not imply that the own-rate of return on money is to be defined as the minimum nominal rate of return at which individuals will hold bonds or anything else. Any such definition renders the liquidity preference argument circular, but not just because of unexplained expectations. A more serious problem is that we end up saying that the liquidity premium is the difference between the nominal rate of return on a non-money financial asset and the proportional carrying cost of money, and in effect this difference determines itself. In consequence, the minimum rate of return on any non-money asset is simply the lowest value to which it falls. Keynes offered no independent means of determining this minimum. For reasons already discussed at length, the most satisfactory means will be identified by an analysis of what constitutes rational behaviour by those who have the incentive and market power to set the own-rate of return on money.

The determinants of the floor to the interest rate structure are suggested by the theory of markets. We must look to the demands for and supplies of money assets. Undoubtedly, there can be some speculative demands. The magnitude of these demands will be investigated in chapter 8. For the moment it is sufficient to note the implication from the argument of section 5.3 that the latitude for the speculative domination of bond and equity prices is as wide as for any asset. We have also identified the determinants of hedging (including transactions) demands for money. It remains only to consider entrepreneurs' demands for external investment finance. This, too, will be taken up in chapter 8. None the less, it is clear from the argument of chapter 6 that the demands for long-term investment finance will depend in substantial measure upon the state of long-term expectation in the basic sub-system. Without anticipating results that will be derived in chapter 8, it will be taken for granted here that these states do change as a result of endogenous factors, the timing of which is uncertain in advance. In short, there will certainly be some volatility in the demands for money. The more difficult questions turn on the supply of money; that is, we require to identify the means by which money is created and destroyed. The mechanisms that are involved here were widely recognized by earlier generations of economists (notably Hawtrey, 1950, chapter 10) and later economists working within the framework established by Gurley and Shaw (1960). Although I rely here on the same mechanics of money creation, my theoretical structure is very different from theirs.

The main point here is that the supply of money is not independent of the demand for money.

There are two kinds of money that can circulate in an economy: monies that are claims against the assets of agents that, for reasons that will soon be apparent, we shall call banks, and monies that are acknowledged to have some intrinsic value and are not redeemable claims against any agents. The first kind of money is bank money and the second we shall call 'intrinsic money'. (Intrinsic money is what Gurley and Shaw called 'outside money'. I do not use their term because its complement in their theory, 'inside money', includes means of payment not included here as bank money.) If we take for granted, for the moment, that there is intrinsic money circulating in the economy, we must still show that there are agents (i.e. banks) that profitably issue non-intrinsic money – in this case, bank money.

The first point to be made in this regard is that, in order to serve as money, an asset must have all of the characteristics that render it suitable for intermediated exchange. We found in section 7.1 that any money asset must be compact, durable and highly standardized. In addition, there can be intermediation in an asset only if there are economies of scale to be achieved in their exchange that cannot be achieved by agents on either side of the market. That there are such economies of scale to be had in borrowing and lending activities is such an elementary proposition that we can simply take it for granted here. And borrowing and lending is nothing other than the exchange of money assets for securities and other interest- or dividend-yielding assets.

Obviously, borrowing and lending via intermediaries does not itself require the creation of non-intrinsic money provided that the stock supply of intrinsic money meets all demands and is sufficient to make possible the achievement of economies of scale in financial intermediation with the existing technology of exchange. But if this condition is not met, then banks will have a clear incentive to create additional money unless it would necessarily be unprofitable to do so.

In fact, the demonstration that the creation of bank money will be profitable is a straightforward application of the analysis of intermediation within the framework of the theory of markets.

Banks can either buy large-denomination debt instruments from borrowers and 'break bulk' by selling their own small-denomination notes or other claims to the banks' lenders, or they can issue their own large-denomination debt instruments for sale on the organized financial exchanges and then re-lend their debts in smaller denominations. Like any other intermediaries, the banks will set a higher price on the assets they sell than they pay for the assets they buy. The difference covers the activities of exchange in which the banks achieve economies of scale that are not available to their own lenders and borrowers. The 'breaking of bulk' in either direction requires the banks to issue different debt instruments than they have accepted from their lenders. Some of these debt instruments can be fixed denominations – i.e. notes – and some are conveniently divisible claims against the banks – e.g. current account balances, deposit account balances and the like. Provided that the banks act in such a way that they are widely recognized to be honest and reliable in meeting any of their own debt commitments, and provided that they make known to any who care to enquire the nature of their assets, they can establish the reputation for financial probity and strength that is required for the successful issue of debts that pass as money.

It is also necessary, of course, that the lenders to and borrowers from banks should find that using the banks' services as intermediaries improves their cash flows. Individuals will lend to banks because the banks can achieve economies of scale in determining the likelihood that individual borrowers will be able to meet their commitments, and because the banks can achieve economies of massed reserves that are not available to those who lend either infrequently or on a small scale. In addition, the banks can achieve the economies of scale available to any warehouseman in the storage of customers' valuable holdings – in this case their holdings of money. Individuals will borrow from banks whenever the banks' information costs are sufficiently small in relation to the scale of their lending that they can profitably charge a lower rate of interest than other lenders or when the banks are able to lend larger amounts to a single borrower than non-bank lenders would want to lend. In the latter case, the borrowers save by negotiating loans with one bank rather than with each of a larger number of households or firms. It seems likely that, in normal practice, the scale economies available to banks is the more important of these reasons.

If there are financial intermediaries that themselves lend relatively large sums of money to each of several borrowers and then in effect issue a large number of notes each of relatively small nominal value, the information costs of the lenders to the intermediaries will be less if they can feel assured that the intermediaries are firms of substantial financial strength and probity. If this is the case, then individuals who borrow from the intermediaries will be able to accept in return for their own debt instruments the notes of the financial intermediary for use as means of payment. Unless these borrowers and lenders accept that the intermediaries are firms of substantial financial probity and strength, the costs of borrowing and lending will be very much greater, and therefore the scale of activities that can profitably be financed externally will be very much smaller. Borrowers and lenders alike are relying on the expertise and experience of these financial intermediaries in assessing the goodness of the loans they make. And the financial intermediaries in these markets will rationally be concerned to act in a way that maintains their reputations for probity.

In short, the assumption that firms' managers are survival-motivated and the propositions of the theory of markets imply that financial intermediaries that issue notes and other assets serving as money will have a profitable niche in the markets for loans. The assets issued by these intermediaries constitute bank money.

Although the foregoing argument explains the prevalence of bank money, it does not explain why anyone should want to hold intrinsic money. Clearly, banks would always hold intrinsic money to the extent that it is necessary to convince the public of the banks' financial strength and probity. We have already found such a banking posture to be rational. In addition, by creating money the banks incur unhedged commitments. Like any other capital-uncertainty-averse agents, banks will rationally undertake unhedged commitments only if they confidently expect that their holdings of acceptable means of payment to cancel those commitments will be sufficient as the commitments fall due. Of course, holders of bank money are unlikely to exercise their claims against the banks in order to exchange bank money for different bank money. Those claims will be exercised in order to acquire intrinsic money. And this, as every first-year student of money and banking knows, is the rationale for banks to limit the excess of bank money over the banks' holdings of intrinsic money and immediately realizable claims on intrinsic money held by other agents.

It follows that the reserve ratio maintained by banks is determined by the relationship between the minimum efficient scale of banking activities and the quantity of intrinsic money in existence as well as the record of claims by holders of bank money on banks' holdings of intrinsic money. Of course, banks will have an incentive to minimize the incidence of these claims. And this incentive, we shall see shortly, provides an explanation, based on the assumption of individual rationality, for the role of the own-rate of return on money as the effective floor to the whole structure of rates of return on financial assets.

Money supplies in relation to demands

If, for the present, we continue to ignore both banks' current expenditures and the existence of intrinsic money, the value of the total outstanding money supply will be equal to the value of banks' loans that have not yet been repaid. Although the points to be made here are entirely general, it will help to introduce them if we assume that all bank loans are repaid d periods after they are made. Denoting by $D(t)$ the net new loans made by banks at time t, the money supply at time T is

$$M(T) \equiv \Sigma_{T-d}^{T} D(t). \tag{7.19}$$

It is a characteristic of bank money created by lending that it ceases to exist when there is any net repayment of bank debts or any payments of interest to the banks. For this reason, the quantity of bank money in circulation when there is no intrinsic money must be sufficient to cover the servicing and repayment of bank loans falling due. In practice, the amount of bank money in circulation must be very much greater than these repayment and interest commitments to enable transactions to take place with money as means of payment. On the assumption made here, and the further assumption of a constant and uniform rate of interest i, the quantity of bank money must safisfy the condition

$$M(T) \geqslant i \, \Sigma_{T-d}^{T} D(t) + D(T-d). \tag{7.20}$$

Together with expression (7.19), this condition implies

$$D(T) \geqslant \frac{i}{1-i} D(T-d) - \Sigma_{T-d+1}^{T-1} D(t). \tag{7.21}$$

As long as bank lending is increasing, it is more than sufficient to provide the cash with which individuals can repay and service their debts to banks; for, unless the interest rate is close to unity, the right side of condition (7.21) will then be negative while new lending, the left side of condition (7.20), is positive. If, however, there should be an extended period during which the repayments of bank loans exceed new lending – so that the left side of condition (7.21) is negative – the value of the right side will be increased as time passes owing to the negative values of the $D(t)$.

The point here is both simple and general. If after any period of increasing bank lending there is a contraction, the quantity of bank money in circulation will decline relative to the commitments of the public to the banking system. If the expansion and then contraction are sharp enough, there is no doubt that debtors could be forced to default on their repayment and servicing of bank debts simply from a lack of cash. This result is only partly vitiated by the introduction of banks' expenditures and the existence of intrinsic money.

The supply of bank money is clearly increased *pro tanto* by banks' expenditures on wages, purchases of capital equipment and materials and distributions of dividends and net repayments of their own debts with interest. Although they will continue to meet their own debt commitments, it is hardly likely that a spate of defaults on bank loans will induce the banks to increase their current expenditures in order to provide the cash required by the defaulting debtors. If anything, the declining cash flows of the banks will induce them to reduce their current expenditures wherever possible in order to preserve their net assets and therefore their reputations for financial strength. If any amelioration of the cash shortage resulting from declining bank lending is to be looked for, it can be found only in an increase of the supply of intrinsic money.

There are two general sources of intrinsic money: flow-supplies of producible money assets such as gold, and the means of payment issued by the government for its own purchases. If the government prints money to buy goods and services from industrial and commercial firms, it will thereby increase the quantity of money that is available either for hedging and transactions purposes or for the repayment of bank debts and the payment of interest, or both. Of course, the banking crisis will be ameliorated only if the new issues of intrinsic money are used to purchase commodities or assets from the banks' debtors.

Suppose, however, that the money is issued to purchase second-hand financial assets from banks or other agents. If this money is hoarded by those agents because they are seeking safe assets and the nominal rates of return on non-money safe assets are no higher than money's own-rate of return, i.e. if the economy is in a liquidity trap, then the banking crisis will be in no way ameliorated. It is surely likely that banks will want to hold whatever intrinsic money comes their way during a banking crisis, particularly if that is the only way to assure depositors that bank money remains a safe asset. The only remaining means of ameliorating the banking crisis through open-market operations by the government or central bank is for the sellers of second-hand financial assets to use their increased holdings of intrinsic money received to buy new financial assets from the banks' debtors who are in distress or from those debtors' finance-constrained customers. Without anticipating results to be derived in chapter 8, we can only say that this is possible but less certain to be effective than expenditures by the government on goods and services.

In summary, a policy of Keynesian demand management in these circumstances is likely to be the most effective solution to a financial crisis that has its origins in a decline in bank lending.

Rational banking behaviour and money's own-rate of return

We have found that a decline in bank lending for any reason tends to create an excess demand for money. It will be argued in chapter 8 that such declines are certain to occur after periods of expansion in lending and increasing capacity growth. The timing of these declines is, however, uncertain. That uncertainty, together with the consequences of declining bank lending, render the supplies of bank money relative to the demands both unstable and unpredictable. Since money is also an asset that is well suited to intermediation, we have the conditions that were identified from the theory of markets for the 'price' of money to rise quickly to eliminate excess demands and to fall quickly to eliminate excess supplies. This conclusion is reinforced by the analysis of hedging in section 7.4.

In general, declines in bank lending are either a cause or a consequence of declining capacity growth rates, and therefore of deteriorating states of long-term expectation in the basic sub-system. In such circumstances we have seen that demands by hedgers for safe assets will become more urgent and will be constrained only by those cash flows from trading activities that are not already committed. It may be that the uncommitted cash flows are themselves declining in relation to commitments. Agents will then have to unhedge in order to provide the cash needed to pay bills currently falling due. In this circumstance they will rationally dispose of their longest-term hedging assets while continuing to hold on to their shortest-term assets, including both their existing money balances and the additions to those balances that become available as their non-money safe assets mature. Thus, hedging demands and, if possible, holdings of money will increase as bank lending and therefore the supply of bank money declines.

It is not difficult to show that the demands for money are likely to become less urgent and, indeed, to fall relative to the supply when bank lending is increasing; for increasing lending requires that banks have the confidence to lend and borrowers have the confidence to invest or to exchange safe assets for more speculative assets. Increased investment rates will be sustained only if the state of long-term expectation in the basic sub-system is improving so that, as argued in section 7.4, hedging demands for safe assets in general and money in particular are declining relative to incomes.

It follows from this discussion that expansions and contractions in bank lending, and therefore in the supplies of bank money, will be accompanied by opposite changes in demands for safe assets from hedgers as well as agents in debt to the banks. For reasons to be set out in chapter 8, speculative demands for safe assets will tend to change in the same direction as hedging demands. It remains only to demonstrate that, when bank lending is declining, the own-rate of return on money will rise relative to the nominal rates of the return on other financial assets and, in particular, on non-money safe assets.

Although it has been shown here that the market for money will be characterized by short-run pricing, it is not clear what can be meant by the price of money. An essential property of a generally acceptable means of payment is that it be denominated in the same units as commodity and asset prices – that is, in the common, abstract unit of account. The price of a non-money asset can rise or fall because those who buy and sell them are buying claims on payments of money. But the price cannot change relative to itself.

The usual argument in this regard is that, since the price of money cannot change relative to itself, it must change relative to the prices of other assets and commodities. That is, an excess supply of money causes the price of money to fall relative to the prices of goods, services and non-money assets, so that more money must be given in exchange for them. Thus, an excess supply of money results in price and wage inflation. Let us consider this argument briefly in relation to the theory of markets.

We have found that, for any asset to function as money, its physical characteristics must be those of any intermediated asset or commodity. Moreover, it is profitably introduced into circulation by intermediaries in means of payment at least some of whom will profitably create money assets. These results follow from the require-ments of efficient resource allocation in exchange. In the nature of financial intermediation, the intermediaries have the market power and the profit incentive to set prices that will equate supplies and demands. If we were to accept the usual argument that it is the commodity and non-money asset prices that rise and fall in response to excess supplies and demands for money, then banks would be the only intermediaries in the economy who have the power and incentive to set prices but wait passively for agents in other markets to change the prices of commodities and assets relative to the prices of those assets with which banks are most concerned. It is hard to see why, if banks were able to act in a manner that equated the supplies of and demands for money, they would refrain from doing so.

Note carefully that I am not suggesting that increasing the money supply never leads to price and wage inflation, or that contracting the money supply never leads to price and wage deflation (or reduced inflation). If the money supply is increased by means of expenditures that generate excess short-run demands for short-run-priced commodities, some price inflation is likely to result. If the money supply is reduced so sharply that the technologically feasible velocity of money is insufficient to enable existing commitments to be honoured or new commitments to be undertaken, then the consequent fall in demand will lead to falling short-run prices and probably to downward pressure on wages, and so to a general downward movement in the rate of inflation. This follows easily from the arguments of chapter 6. None the less, it offers no insight into the actions of rationally managed banks.

During a financial crisis resulting from reductions in bank lending, perhaps accompanied by government sales of non-money assets that are not then matched by expenditures, banks will be compelled to act to maintain the attractiveness of holding bank money; otherwise individuals who already hold bank money will claim the intrinsic money to which bank money entitles them, and in addition bank money will become unacceptable in payment of debts for use in transactions. In the latter case bank lending will be reduced yet further, and so bank profits will be further squeezed unless lending rates can be raised relative to the rates banks offer to their depositors and other creditors.

Since there is no price of money that banks could raise in order to attract 'sellers' of money assets, they will need to make the money assets created by them more attractive by offering a higher return to the holders of those assets. As hedgers and speculators are seeking non-money safe assets, thereby inducing intermediaries in those assets to raise their prices, banks will rationally offer higher own-rates of return on bank money in order to induce hedgers and speculators to hold their wealth as time deposits or current account balances with banks. The own-rate of return on money will not usually need to rise very far to satisfy the needs of the bankers, since the growing demand for safe assets in general will be raising the prices of non-money safe assets, thereby lowering the nominal rates of return that agents could realize on additional purchases or continued holdings of those assets.

In general, during a period of excess money demands the own-rate of return on money will rise relative to the nominal rates of return on non-money financial assets. The reason for money's uniqueness in this regard is that, unlike banks, intermediaries in non-money assets have no rational incentive to maintain any particular price level or therefore nominal rates of return on the assets in which they trade. What is of concern to them is only the spread between the prices at which they buy and sell assets and the volume of turnover. Banks, however, can continue in business only if claims upon them continue to be acceptable as money. To make these claims acceptable the banks manipulate the one relevant variable that they control: the own-rate of return on bank money. Since a decline in lending for any reason leads to a decline in banks' cash flows, which, if compounded by a drain of banks' reserves of intrinsic money, would cast their reputations for financial probity and strength in doubt, rational, survival-motivated bankers will act to prevent existing holders of bank money from exchanging that money for intrinsic money. To do so, they must make the holding of bank money more attractive relative to both intrinsic money and other safe assets, and this they can do only by offering a higher rate of return.

7.6   THE ADVANTAGES OF SAFE-ASSET THEORY OVER OTHER THEORIES OF INTEREST

The theory of interest rates reported in this chapter is preferable to the theory of liquidity preference because it relies on the assumption of individual rationality to explain the importance of the money rate of interest as a stabilizing force that prevents cumulative downward movements in the structure of interest rates. Consequently, this theory is not open to the 'bootstraps' charge of Hicks. This safe-asset theory is also preferable to Hick's alternative and to the portfolio selection theories that rely on subjective specifications of at least the first two moments of probability distributions of future rates of return. For, unlike those theories, the safe-asset theory takes for granted limited learning rates, and so does not lead to the logical conundrums discussed in chapter 2.

There is, moreover, a general attraction of combining the assumption of well specified rational behaviour with the assumption of limited learning rates and the consequent uncertainty (rather than risk) of future outcomes. Together, these assumptions make it possible to predict the nature, if not always the magnitude, of both microeconomic and macroeconomic processes without having to find implausible specifications of expectations-forming mechanisms. Nor is it necessary to conclude that everything depends on expectations that are, in their nature, unpredictable. This advance over previous theories relies crucially on the application of the assumption of individual rationality to processes of exchange as well as production. In consequence, a single analytical approach based on a small number of basic assumptions provides a general analysis in which the issues raised by money and speculation do not figure as either special cases or anomalies requiring us to make *ad hoc* auxiliary assumptions.

8

Macroeconomic Cycles

8.0   INTRODUCTION

Both the analysis of multiplier–accelerator interaction in chapter 6 and the analysis in chapter 7 of the demands for and supplies of hedging assets depend crucially on individuals' expectations. Although this is by no means the first theory in which expectational factors have been found to be important, it is, as far as I know, the first theory in which it is possible to analyse endogenous changes in expectations in conditions of uncertainty (as distinct from risk). The analysis reported in this chapter admittedly does not provide a theoretical foundation for predictions of the timing or the magnitudes of the effects of expectational changes. Indeed, I shall argue here that no such theory is possible. None the less, the present theory enables us to identify the reasons for inevitable, endogenous changes in the state of long-term expectation in the basic sub-system. As was demonstrated in section 6.5, such expectational changes necessarily generate turning points of major macroeconomic cycles. Our theory should therefore improve econometric analyses of the turning points. By identifying the sources of these turning points, we are also in a position to derive the criteria for efficient macroeconomic policies that will delay and ameliorate the downturns and accelerate the up-turns of the major cycles, thereby keeping the economy closer to its full-employment growth path in the long run.

8.1   EXPECTATIONS AND UNCERTAINTY IN TRADE CYCLE ANALYSIS

The reliance of the present theory on expectational states harks back to the trade cycle analyses that were common before the advent of large-scale macroeconometric modelling. The same issues (though not the same conclusions) are resurrected by the Lucas (1976/1981) critique of macroeconomic policy evaluations undertaken with these models.

The view that prevailed from the time of Marshall, and was accepted by Keynes, has been described clearly and succinctly by Kregel (1976, pp. 213–14, n.1):

> The traditional explanation of unemployment linked the mistaken expectations of entrepreneurs (too optimistic in the boom and too pessimistic in the slump) to fluctuations in output and employment . . . . Lavington [(1922), for example] gives the view that 'these cyclical changes in business activity are probably the most important single cause of unemployment' (p. 16) and that these cyclical changes 'in the current activity of business depend on the estimates made by business men of future market conditions, and that these estimates in their turn are affected materially by the general state of confidence in the business outlook' (p. 29) while 'the principal influence lies in the tendency of confidence to rise or fall cumulatively'. In his Preface Lavington indicates this to be a summary of views held by Marshall, Pigou, Robertson, W. C. Mitchell and Aftalion.

Kregel went on to point out that Keynes's objective was to establish a theory that determined positions of short-run equilibrium given the prevailing state of long-term expectation and, subsequently, to determine what would happen when the state of long-term expectation changed. Although Keynes had no theory of the determination of the state of long-term expectation itself, he did take for granted the position described by Lavington. Moreover, as I pointed out in section 1.3, Keynes believed that the direction of investment would always be appropriate to the maintenance of full employment in the long run provided that, in the prevailing state of long-term expectation, current demands were sufficient fully to employ the existing labour force.

We found in chapter 6 that, contrary to Keynes's presumption (for which he adduced no reason), the direction of investment is important whenever the macroeconomic technology entails the basic/non-basic distinction. This distinction is inherent in any macroeconomic technology that can be described by an input–output matrix exhibiting any degree of block triangularity when sufficiently disaggregated. In these cases, the state of long-term expectation in the basic sub-system determines the growth path of output and employment for the whole economy in the long run, and in the short run it determines the magnitude of government real expenditure required to bring about full employment. In addition, the state of long-term expectation in the basic sub-system cannot be volatile, and rates of basic capacity growth will converge over time to a central limit.

In summary, Keynes's advance over pre-Keynesian trade cycle theories was the invention of a theory of short-run equilibria consistent with any given state of long-term expectation. I claim for the present theory that, in its macroeconomic aspects, it identifies the long-term expectations that determine the growth path of the whole economy, and, by virtue of its microeconomic foundations, the macroeconomic theory implies that the key, long-term expectations are not violently unstable.

As stated in the opening paragraph, the purpose of this chapter is to extend the analysis of long-term expectations so that it provides a theory of the turning points of the major macroeconomic cycles. In other words, we seek to identify the factors that lead to changes in the state of long-term expectation in the basic sub-system since it is that expectational state that determines the growth trend of capacity, output and employment in the whole economy. Before turning to the identification of the sources of the turning points, it is important to be clear why I am not offering a deterministic or stochastic model of behaviour over the whole of the cycle.

We have already seen that the Type III accelerator process, by virtue of its interaction with the employment multiplier process, is self-reinforcing and therefore cumulative. Expansionary Type III accelerator processes, unlike the Type I and Type II processes, will be brought to an end only by systematic and persistent inducements for entrepreneurs in the basic sub-system to reduce their rates of investment in capacity expansion. A contractionary Type III accelerator process will be ended only by an equally persistent and systematic inducement to increase rates of basic capacity growth. There is nothing in the multiplier–accelerator interaction to create these inducements. Thus, we need to identify the endogenous sources of the turning point in order to complete our account of the economic forces that underlie the major macroeconomic cycle in all of its phases. A stochastic or deterministic model would be possible only if, in addition, we could identify general forces that impose upper and lower bounds on both the magnitude and the timing of investment and financial decisions by entrepreneurs thoughout the economy.

The issues involved in the development of a trade cycle model are clearly seen in relation to the Lucas critique. Because Lucas was arguing from the presumption that the economy is characterized by long-run equilibrium and a Walrasian structure, it is clear that we cannot accept his critique in full. None the less, the critique has a more general substance, which was for a time taken seriously by those who use macroeconometric models to simulate the effects of alternative policy regimes.

The thrust of the Lucas critique is that, if policy measures are announced or in any way perceived by rational individuals, their reactions to some economic events and phenomena will generally be different than if they had not known about the policy change. In Lucas's own words (1977/1981, p. 220),

[T]he ability of a [macroeconometric] model to imitate actual behaviour in the way tested by the Adelmans (1959) has almost nothing to do with its ability to make *conditional* forecasts, answer questions of the form: how *would* behaviour have differed had certain policies been specified in different ways? This ability requires the *invariance* of the structure of the model under policy variations of the type being studied. Invariance of the parameters in an economic model is not, of course, a property which can be assured in advance, but it seems reasonable to hope that neither tastes nor technology vary systematically with variations in countercyclical policies.

Lucas's hope that technology will not change systematically as a result of macroeconomic policies is not well founded. Certainly, if technical changes are embodied in new capital equipment, then any macroeconomic policy that successfully increases rates of investment in capacity expansion will systematically increase rates of technical change. This point is important to the policy analysis reported in chapter 9. It also implies a more general critique of the Lucas critique itself.

In addition to systematic changes in the rate of technical change, there are likely to be many other sources of bias in econometric modelling of this sort. There is no evidence that the structural changes suggested by Lucas predominate over these other sources. Nor is there any way of knowing whether all of these sources of bias do or do not cancel one another out. As a result, the Lucas critique is not necessarily anything more than the identification of one unexplained factor in the determination of macroeconomic outcomes. Since statistical models explain only some part of the variances of the dependent variables, the Lucas critique is nothing more than the identification of one source of part of the unexplained variances.

Of course, the point of the Lucas critique was that macroeconometric models ought to include the structural implications of the rational expectations hypothesis. This point cannot be accepted here because of the reliance of the rational expectations hypothesis on the assumption that individuals learn at unlimited rates. To take account of the Lucas critique but not the rational expectations hypothesis is, in principle, possible. But we should need to know in advance the information set that individuals could perceive, process and act upon. There is no reason to suppose that this information set includes the values of all of the variables that rational agents would like to know if information were scarce in relation to their capacities to use it.

My theory of markets is, in effect, a theory of the information that will be available in the economy as a whole and to individuals who trade in each of the various markets. It also shows how markets evolve so that a manageable flow of information is received by individuals. It is conceivable that, given an appropriately limited structure and quantity of information, individuals would be able to devise decision rules that could be specified by behavioural relations and reaction functions in a stochastic – if not a deterministic – model. Though conceivable, the Lucas critique, when stripped of the implicit assumption of unlimited learning rates, leads to the conclusion that such an outcome is not in practice possible. For, as Lucas goes on from the above quotation to say (1977/1981, pp. 220–1),

[A]gents' *decision rules will* in general change with changes in the environment. An equilibrium [i.e. Walrasian general equilibrium] model is, by definition, constructed so as to predict how agents ... will choose to respond to a new situation. Any disequilibrium model [which, in Lucas's lexicon means any model that is not a Walrasian general equilibrium model], constructed simply by codifying the decision rules which agents have found it useful to use over some previous sample period, without explaining *why* these rules were used, will be of no use in predicting the consequences of nontrivial policy changes.

In chapters 2–5, we investigated the decision rules that rational agents will use in various markets. In chapter 6 we considered the effects of these decision rules in various circumstances and how individuals' decision rules would change in response to certain endogenous and exogenous macroeconomic developments. We found that very different decision rules are compatible with rational individual behaviour, although neither the rules nor the ways in which they are changed are described by any long-run equilibrium theory – including Walrasian theory. None the less, if we can show that the decision rules used by rational individuals do change with the economic environment, then the general point of the Lucas critique – though not the implication that all models should encompass the rational expectations hypothesis – is correct. The remaining issue is the possibility of predicting the timing and the sharpness of changes in individuals' decision rules. If we stick to the assumption that individuals learn at limited rates, then we must conclude that these characteristics of decision-rule changes cannot be predicted.

The essential point here is that accelerator–multiplier interaction determines the timing and the sharpness of macroeconomic cyclical upswings and downswings, and that this interaction involves all markets for basic commodities as well as some or all markets for non-basic commodities. An important characteristic of market forms and procedures in this regard is that they enable individuals to take decisions on the basis of limited information with no direct knowledge of events that, individually or cumulatively, will affect the outcomes of their own decisions. Since they have no direct knowledge of these phenomena, the individuals themselves cannot predict the optimal timing of changes in their own decision rules since they cannot predict when the broad characteristics of the economic structure (or environment) will make such changes optimal.

In short, the complexity of multiplier–accelerator effects on individual markets renders it impossible for individuals who learn at limited rates to predict the timing of their own optimal decision-rule changes. Thus, even the assumption of rational behaviour does not yield determinate time-paths of any individuals' decision rules. If rationality does not determine the timing of specific behavioural reactions, then no theory resting on the assumption that individuals are rational can predict that timing.

It is, however, of the utmost importance to note that this argument does not imply the impossibility of identifying endogenous economic forces that will and must eventually lead to certain kinds of decision-rule changes. We shall see in this chapter that the changing financial structure of the economy during a major macroeconomic upswing will eventually bankrupt firms in the basic subsystem unless they first reduce their rates of capacity growth. That is, the prospect of firm survival becomes increasingly less certain as the upswing proceeds. Moreover, the sharper the upswing and the longer it lasts, the greater is the reliance of each firm on the continued growth of other firms' investments in capacity expansion. It is impossible for each firm to predict changes in the decision rules and, hence, the investment propensities of firms they do not know. At the same time, those firms that are not among the first to contract or abandon their expansionary activities, even though market signals have not changed, will be less well placed to survive the ensuing depression in economic activity than firms that are quickest to consolidate and contract their investment activities.

A similar result pertains with respect to speculative holdings of financial assets.

There is an equivalent result as the downswing and trough of the macroeconomic cycle progress. Firms and, in the financial markets, speculators become increasingly less dependent on other individuals' actions and decision rules the longer the economy is in the major cyclical trough. Moreover, the potential loss if the wrong decisions are taken declines continuously.

The effect of these findings, which will be derived in the remainder of this chapter, is that the financial structure of the economy changes over the cycle. These changes are endogenous. They raise the potential costs of optimistically maintained decision rules relative to the potential benefits as the major macroeconomic upswing progresses; they reduce the potential costs relative to the benefits as the major macroeconomic downswing progresses and the slump persists. In economies where individuals learn at limited rates, they will recognize the thrust of these structural changes but will be unable to assign even subjective probability distributions to the timing of the events that precipitate the costs. It is this that makes it impossible for rational agents to determine the optimal moment at which to change their decision rules and, therefore, for observers to predict when they will do so.

The results derived in this chapter, though they bear some resemblance to the Lucas critique, are much stronger. The Lucas critique identifies one possible source of unexplained variances of the dependent variables in macroeconometric models, with no argument about the importance of that source relative to any other, so far unidentified, sources of unexplained variances. The argument developed here will identify endogenous changes in the economic environment that are persistent, systematic and cumulative. Unless decision rules change, survival-motivated managers will see their firms fail and will know in advance that the threat to firm survival is increasing. If they do not change their decision rules in the appropriate way, their firms must fail as the upswing progresses or be squeezed out of their markets or taken over as the slump progresses. Even if there are long periods during which the changing structure does not induce changes in decision rules, eventually the appropriate decision-rule changes will be made or the firms that do not change their decision rules will cease to exist. If this argument is correct, then macroeconometric models that perform satisfactorily with an invariant structure during the major cyclical upswings and down-swings are likely to yield biased predictions at the cyclical turning points. In general, they will miss or underestimate the sharpness of the upturns and the downturns.

Finally, it is important to emphasize that the cumulative changes in the macroeconomic structure are endogenous and not, as Lucas assumed from his Walrasian perspective, restricted to exogenous changes. As a result, econometric predictions of the turning points ought to be improved by taking into account the endogenous cyclical changes identified in this chapter.

8.2 THE DOCTRINE OF INCREASING UNCERTAINTY
I: CAPACITY GROWTH CYCLES

The microeconomic foundation of the theory of the turning points rests on the identification of a phenomenon that is common to both the product and the financial markets. We shall find in both classes of markets that, during periods of expanding scales of activity, individuals are exposed to increasing financial losses relative to potential gains, and as any expansionary phase proceeds the realization of losses or gains by any individual depends increasingly on the strategies (or decision rules) adopted by other individuals. Conversely, during periods of diminishing scales of activity potential losses decline relative to potential gains, and the outcomes of each individual's decisions in these markets become increasingly less sensitive to the strategy choices of other individuals. The proposition that such relationships characterize all but the labour markets I shall call the 'doctrine of increasing uncertainty'.

A special case of the doctrine of increasing uncertainty is Kalecki's (1937) principle of increasing risk. Although, as we shall see presently, the Kalecki principle is defective in detail, the thrust of his argument accords well with the theory reported here.

Kalecki argued that the cost of capital to the firm includes a risk premium which increases with the ratio of the firm's debts to its liquidity. The risk identified by Kalecki was said by him to be due to the 'illiquidity' of capital equipment. Although Kalecki identified the ratio of debts to liquidity with the financial leverage of the firm, this identification is neither essential nor, since the net assets of a firm are not necessarily held as liquid assets, correct. What is essential to the Kalecki principle is that a larger rate of expenditure on investment requires a reduction in the liquid assets of the firm in relation to its debt commitments, thereby rendering the survival of the firm less certain in the event of a downturn in demands for its outputs. The greater the value of debt and interest payments relative to the value of a firm's liquid assets, the greater the risk of firm failure. To compensate for this risk, lenders will require a risk premium over and above the prevailing rate of interest. The larger the rate of investment, the greater the risk and so the greater will be the required risk premium. The rationally managed, competitive firm, according to the Kalecki principle, will invest until the marginal efficiency of investment is equal to the prevailing rate of interest plus the marginal risk premium – this being the marginal cost of capital to the firm. Since the marginal risk premium increases with the magnitude of investment, the rate of investment by the firm will be limited even when the marginal efficiency of investment is constant because of constant returns to scale. Clearly, provided there is some minimum efficient scale of production and exchange for the commodities sold by a given firm, the rising risk premium will limit investment by the firm in conditions of increasing as well as constant returns to scale.

Kalecki also recognized a role for the macroeconomic conditions of demand – what he called 'the economic situation'. Since an increase in aggregate investment increases aggregate profits *pro tanto*, as well as increasing income and employment via the multiplier process, Kalecki presumed that increasingly buoyant macroeconomic conditions would increase profits without affecting the marginal risk premium corresponding to each debt–equity ratio, thereby increasing the rationally chosen rate of investment. This presumption is unwarranted since, as we shall see, increasing investment rates or, more precisely, increasing investment growth and capacity growth will diminish investing firms' holdings of safe (including liquid) assets even though their profits grow more quickly.

While Kalecki's presumed connection between macroeconomic activity levels and the risk or uncertainty faced by individual firms cannot, if the argument of this book is correct, be sustained, the microeconomic principle is clearly correct. Provided that we take into account all holdings of safe assets rather than those that are strictly liquid, the safe-asset theory enunciated in chapter 7 provides a sound theoretical foundation for the Kalecki principle. As we saw in that chapter, any investment in capital goods requires the under-taking of new unhedged debt commitmens or the unhedging of previously hedged commitments. The increase in unhedged commit-ments exposes the investing firm to increased capital uncertainty. It is possible that the revenue from using the newly acquired capital goods will enable the investing firm to acquire additional safe assets to hedge the debts incurred to finance the investment externally or to replace the safe assets sold to finance the investment internally. But if there is either a substantial gestation period for the invest-ment, during which costs are incurred, or if there is a substantial pay-back period (whether or not the length of this period is an investment-choice criterion), then there will be some substantial interval of time during which the value of hedging assets held by the firm falls relative to its capital commitments and the value of its ongoing purchasing requirements.

It is a matter of simple algebra that the age distribution of capital equipment entails ever higher proportions of younger relative to older equipment as the rate of investment and therefore capacity growth is higher. Thus, taking all firms together, the faster the macroeconomic rate of capacity growth, the greater will be the ratio of gestating and new capacity to total capacity. In consequence, the value of unhedged commitments to total revenues in conditions of full capacity utilization must increase for the economy as a whole as rates of growth increase unless both the gestation and pay-back periods of new production and exchange capacities are negligible. In the absence of continuous markets for second-hand capital equip-ment, the real assets acquired by investing firms cannot themselves be safe assets. Since continuous markets for these assets will not be widespread in economies comprising rational individuals, we can take it as a theoretically justified norm that more rapid rates of capacity growth entail a smaller value of safe asset holdings relative to current revenues and profits as well as a larger value of unhedged com-mitments. Although there may be some firms that do not increase their rates of capacity growth, those that do must suffer increased exposure to both income and capital uncertainty as macroeconomic growth rates increase.

The major cyclical upswing

The crucial case here is the major upswing in which basic ratios are increasing as rates of capacity growth in the basic sub-system rise. The rates of capacity growth of firms operating in the basic sub-system will therefore be increasing at least as fast as those of firms operating in the non-basic sub-system. Once full capacity utilization rates are reached in the basic sub-system, further increases in rates of basic capacity growth will entail reductions in non-basic capacity growth. In consequence, the exposure to capital and income uncertainty of firms operating in the basic sub-system will be increasing as the basic ratios rise while the exposure to uncertainty of firms that operate mainly or entirely in the non-basic sub-system will be increasing more slowly and, once basic capacities come to be fully utilized, are very likely to diminish. The diminution of exposure to uncertainty in the non-basic sub-system is due to the excess demands for their outputs consequent upon increased employment growth in the basic sub-system and the forced curtailment of their purchases of new capital equipment. Provided that the utilization of their existing capacities is profitable, the curtailment of their investment growth will imply a reduction in the proportion of gestating and new capacities relative to outputs and, therefore, an increase in profits relative to new or newly unhedged commitments and purchasing requirements.

Evidently, so long as the basic ratios are rising, firms' exposure to capital and income uncertainty engendered by activity in the basic sub-system continues to grow, while the exposure to the same uncertainty engendered by activity in the non-basic sub-system declines. These points will be taken up and extended formally in the macroeconomic analysis in sections 8.4–8.6. It is already clear however that, prima facie, basic activities will become increasingly vulnerable to any macroeconomic financial constraints that should arise as the major cyclical upswing proceeds. Non-basic activities will, at the same time, be getting less vulnerable. Such financial constraints could be the result of either declining gross profits owing to falling demands or declining supplies of external finance.

The trough and upturn of the major cycle

Although the major cyclical upswing entails increasing exposure of firms in the basic sub-system to capital and income uncertainty, minor cyclical upswings reduce that exposure.

The minor upswings result from Type I or Type II accelerator processes. In other words, either there are no increases in investment in capacity expansion anywhere in the economy (Type I), or there are increases in investments only in non-basic capacity expansion.

In the event of an increase in demands for non-basic commodities, which induces only a Type I accelerator process, there will be some improvement in the current cash flows of firms in both sub-systems. Rationally managed firms will not increase their production and exchange rates unless increased rates of capacity utilization generate revenues in excess of the direct costs of production and exchange, including any interest charges in respect of working capital. If there is a Type II accelerator process, increased utilization of basic capacities will improve cash flows in the basic sub-system since there will be no consequent increases in investments in basic capacity expansion. Gross profits will be used either to increase hedging of capital commitments and purchases of direct inputs to production and exchange or to repay debts or enhance share values by maintaining or increasing dividend yields. At the same time, presuming that gestation and pay-back periods of capacity investments are non-negligible, firms will be increasing their exposure to capital and income uncertainty in the non-basic sub-system as they unhedge commitments and purchases to finance their investments internally or take on new unhedged commitments in order to finance the investments externally.

Clearly, a Type II accelerator process will yield a greater improvement in the security of firms active in the basic sub-system than will a Type I accelerator process. If there is a Type I process, the derived demands for basic commodities will be restricted to direct and indirect inputs of circulating basic commodities to non-basic production and exchange. But a Type II accelerator process entails demands for fixed basic and non-basic capital equipment (and therefore derived demands for circulating basic inputs to their production) as well as the demands for basic commodities that result from a Type I accelerator process.

It follows that every minor upturn during a major cyclical trough cumulatively insulates firms in the basic sub-system from capital and income uncertainty. When these minor upturns are characterized by Type II accelerator processes, the improvement in the financial positions of firms in respect of their activities in the basic sub-system is more substantial than the improvements resulting from Type I accelerator processes. In addition, the exposure of firms to capital and income uncertainty in the non-basic sub-system will be increased as a result of Type II accelerator processes unless the duration of the minor upswing exceeds the sum of the gestation and payback periods of their investments in non-basic capacity expansion.

This argument does not imply that all firms operating in the basic sub-system will be able to increase their holdings of safe assets and/or diminish their unhedged commitments. If demands for basic commodities decline absolutely during the downturn following the minor boom, then the queues for commodities produced only to order will shorten, perhaps to the vanishing point, and the fixed capacities for the production of commodities sold from stock will eventually be under-utilized. The fixed costs associated with these capacities – particularly those capacities required for the production of commodities to order – will constitute a drain on the safe assets of the firms that own them unless they incur additional unhedged commitments by borrowing in an attempt to tide themselves over until the next boom.

If the slump is sufficiently deep and long-lasting, those firms that suffer the worst drains on their holdings of safe assets relative to their commitments will inevitably face dissolution, or at least will close down their operations in the basic sub-system before brankruptcy is forced upon them. Once the remaining operational basic capacities are reduced to the point that they are more or less fully utilized during even the deepest slumps, each successive minor upswing will increase the holdings of safe assets of the firms that use those capacities.

Evidently, surviving firms' operations in the basic sub-system must eventually enable them to reduce their collective exposure to capital and income uncertainty. Provided that minor booms do occur from time to time, the threat to those firms' survival from unsuccessful investments in capacity growth will continue to diminish. The diminished threat is not itself sufficient to bring about a major upturn with increasing rates of basic capacity growth. None the less, uncertainty becomes increasingly less of an impediment to investment by firms in the basic sub-system with rational survival-motivated managers.

The argument of this section shows that the exposure to capital and income uncertainty of firms in the basic sub-system changes systematically over the major macroeconomic cycle. If these systematic changes influence the state of long-term expectation in the basic sub-system, and therefore the decision rules that determine the magnitudes of investments in basic capacity expansion, then the implications drawn from our generalization of the Lucas critique would have theoretical confirmation. However, there is nothing in the argument so far to compel us to accept this conclusion. The complete and, I believe, compelling argument requires the complementary analysis of speculation in the financial markets undertaken in the following section and the macroeconomic argument set out thereafter.

8.3   THE DOCTRINE OF INCREASING UNCERTAINTY
II: SPECULATIVE CYCLES

The doctrine of increasing uncertainty applies to the financial markets as well as to the markets for capital commodities; for as we have seen, the latitude for speculative domination of financial asset prices is as wide as for any asset. Indeed, there is no obvious physical limitation on holdings of debt and equity instruments as there is on cereals and even precious metals. None the less, prices on the organized financial exchanges do not rise without limit or (generally) fall to zero. There are alternating periods of bear markets with falling long-run securities prices and bull markets with rising prices. In the absence of technological limitations on the abilities of speculators to drive prices up or down, we must identify rational behavioural limitations in conditions of uncertainty. If we are successful in this endeavour, we shall have broadened the theoretical basis of the analysis of uncertainty reported in section 5.3 and thereby completed the foundations of the safe-asset theory of interest introduced in chapter 7. In that chapter it was shown why net hedging demands for safe assets could raise the prices of those assets to the point where speculative holders would be prepared to sell them while net supplies resulting from the unhedging of previously hedged commitments and purchases would reduce prices until speculators were prepared to take up those supplies.

Finally, there is the question of external and equity finance for investments. We have established that external, e.g. bond and bank, finance of investment projects entails increases in unhedged capital commitments. We have not established the limits to these commitments, which are imposed by the willingness of lenders to accept this increased exposure to capital uncertainty, albeit at one remove; for the failure of a debtor reduces the value of lender's wealth and income-generating assets without reducing their own capital and income commitments. The capital uncertainty of debtors is, therefore, also the capital uncertainty of lenders.

The relationship between speculative demands for equities and long-term, fixed-interest securities on the one hand and, on the other hand, speculators' demands for shorter-term securities has already been analysed in chapter 7. We shall therefore be concerned in this section only with their demands for the more speculative assets. The implications for the supply of and demand for hedgers' safe assets are then determined by appeal to the results of section 7.4.

Increasing uncertainty and the rates of return on fixed-interest securities

The nominal rate of return on a long-term, fixed-interest security was found in section 7.4 to be

$$\rho_{bm} \equiv \frac{D_b}{p_b^0} + \gamma_{bm} \tag{8.1}$$

where ρ_{bm} is the nominal rate of return on a bond, D_b is the fixed interest payment per period, p_b^0 is the issue price and γ_{bm} is the nominal rate of capital gains.

We are concerned here, however, with the effects and time-paths of securities prices over time. In order to take these into account, we note that at any time t the price of (say) the bond is

$$p_b^0 \Pi_0^{t-1} [1 + \gamma_{bm}(T)]$$

so that the nominal rate of return on the bond at time t is

$$\rho_{bm}(t) \equiv \frac{D_b}{p_b^0 \Pi_0^{t-1} [1 + \gamma_{bm}(T)]} + \gamma_{bm}(t). \tag{8.2}$$

The only element on the right side of this identity that is not simply inherited information is the current period's rate of capital gains $\gamma_{bm}(t)$. Since the rate of capital gains depends on changes in the demands for the bond relative to the stock supply, the value of the rate of capital gains can be predicted only as accurately as the changes in demands over the period ahead plus any flow-supply of new securities. Those who buy and sell securities for purposes of hedging will not be concerned with the immediate rate of capital gains. They will decide whether or not to hold these securities on the basis of their value in relation to commitments at the time those commitments fall due. If hedgers decide to dispose of such assets, it will be in order to purchase real assets yielding future incomes rather than capital gains. Whether it is thought worthwhile to dispose of any particular asset will depend on the date of its maturity and its current price rather than on future rates of capital gains. It is, therefore, only speculators seeking to maximize the nominal returns on their portfolios who will buy and sell securities in light of their expectations of the rates of capital gains in the immediate future.

The magnitude of the effect of capital gains on the nominal rate of return depends upon the history of capital gains on a security. Every period during which the rate of capital gains is positive increases the denominator of the net yield term on the right side of identity (8.2); every period during which the rate of capital gains is negative reduces that denominator. It follows that, as long as the price continues to rise, the net yield on the fixed-interest security declines and the nominal rate of return increasingly approximates to the rate of capital gains alone. As a result, the longer the duration of a bull market in fixed-interest securities, the greater is the reliance of securities-holders on the demands by all other traders in the determination of the rate of return on their holdings.

Conversely, as the sequence of periods during which capital gains are negative gets longer, the net yield term on the right side of identity (8.2) continues to increase so that the nominal rate of return is dominated increasingly by the net yield – hence the fixed interest payment – and less by the rate of capital gains. Consequently, as the rate of capital gains continues to fall, the rising net yield becomes dominant and causes the nominal rate of return to rise. Moreover, the rate of return cannot then decline until there has been a period of substantial bullishness in the market.

In order to make this last point, we note that the first difference of identity (8.2) is

$$\Delta \rho_{bm}(t) \equiv \Delta \gamma_{bm}(t) - \frac{D_b}{p_b^0} \cdot \frac{\gamma_{bm}(t)}{\Pi_0^t[1 + \gamma_{bm}(T)]} \tag{8.3}$$

so that the nominal rate of return on the fixed-interest security is rising if and only if

$$\Delta \gamma_{bm}(t) > \frac{D_b}{p_b^0} \frac{\gamma_{bm}(t)}{\Pi_0^t[1 + \gamma_{bm}(T)]}. \tag{8.4}$$

The minimum value of $\Delta \gamma_{bm}(t)$ is obviously $-[1 + \gamma_{bm}(t)]$. Otherwise, the price of the security would turn negative. Whilstever $\gamma_{bm}(t)$ is negative, the right side of condition (8.4) is negative and declining, period by period. The left side of condition (8.4) thus has a minimum that is rising as long as $\gamma_{bm}(t)$ remains negative while the right side is falling without limit. It follows that, eventually, condition (8.4) must come to be satisfied; that is, a prolonged bear market leads to the position identified above in which the nominal rate of return is rising as long as the rate of capital gains remains negative.

The effect of a rise in the rate of capital gains is to render the left side of condition (8.4) positive while, so long as the level of the rate of capital gains remains negative, the right side of condition (8.4) is negative. This amounts to an easing of the sharpness of the bear market – the security price continues to fall but does so more slowly. The consequence is a faster rise in the nominal rate of return. Once the rate of capital gains turns positive, i.e. a bull market gets underway, there can still be no immediate, sustained decline in the nominal rate of return. There must first be a substantial rise in the value of $\Pi[1 + \gamma_{bm}(T)]$ in the denominator on the right side of condition (8.4). This will come about only with a sequence of positive values of $\gamma_{bm}(t)$.

These results are parallel to those of section 8.2.

As speculators drive up the prices of fixed-interest securities, they become increasingly exposed to capital uncertainty, and as a result increasingly vulnerable to the effects of a pessimistic turn in other speculators' expectations. As entrepreneurs in the basic sub-system continue to invest in capacity expansion, they suffer the same increase in exposure to uncertainty and vulnerability to others' pessimistic turns. In addition, as speculative pessimism drives securities prices down, both the exposure to capital uncertainty and the vulnerability to market outcomes decline. This is analogous to the effects of growing financial strength in the basic sub-system as a major slump continues. Although the mechanisms in each case are different, the general pattern and effects are the same. The doctrine of increasing uncertainty applies to the markets for fixed-interest securities no less than it applies to the markets for fixed basic capital equipment.

Equities and the doctrine of increasing uncertainty

The obvious difference between fixed-interest securities and equities as speculative assets is that the net yield on the one is known with certainty (apart from the chance that the issuer of the security will fail) while the net yield on the equity is neither certain or riskless. There is no reason to expect this difference to affect the application of the doctrine of increasing uncertainty to a bull market in equities. The longer the rate of capital gains remains positive, the smaller will be the net yield on equity shares unless the dividend payment each period is growing at a rate no less than the rate of capital gains. If it is, then the potential loss from holding these equities longer than other speculators is diminished by the maintenance or rise of the dividend yield. Conversely, if the dividend payment should be reduced, the net yield on shares falls that much faster and the doctrine of increasing uncertainty applies with greater force. Evidently, what is involved here is a difference in the magnitude and perhaps the timing of cost increases as between the markets for fixed-interest securities and equity shares when prices are rising.

In a bear market for equities, the time-path of the rate of return will be broadly the same as the nominal rates of return on fixed-interest securities in the same market conditions as long as publicly quoted companies sustain their dividend payments. This they will have two incentives to do. Both follow from the proposition that sustained dividend payments in a bear market, for the reasons seen in relation to fixed-interest securities, eventually generate a phase of rising nominal rates of return. In consequence, these shares become increasingly more attractive to speculators than the shares of firms that do not maintain their dividend payments. The relative prices of the shares with sustained dividends will therefore rise. One effect of these relative price increases is to deter take-over raiders (cf. Marris, 1964; Kahn, 1972a). This will obviously be an important incentive to survival-motivated management teams. The second effect is to make any future equity finance cheaper for any given dilution of existing share-holdings. The ability to raise relatively cheap equity finance will be useful during a Type II accelerator process for firms in the non-basic sub-system and during a Type III accelerator process for firms active in the basic sub-system.

The firms that are unable to generate gross profits during a major macroeconomic slump will clearly be unable to sustain their dividend payments. If these firms hold real assets that are valuable to other firms – because the productive resources of the firms are complementary – then the weak firms will become increasingly desirable take-over targets as their share prices fall; otherwise they will simply struggle on until the next major upturn if they can survive that long.

For both the weak and the strong firms, the constraint on dividend payments is their hedging practices. (Dividends paid obviously cannot be used to hedge future capital commitments or purchases of inputs.) The determinants of these practices have already been discussed at length.

In summary, rational managers of surviving (and survivable) firms will maintain dividend payments implicitly to ensure that the rates of return on their outstanding shares exhibit the same broad time-patterns that we found to be followed by rates of return on fixed-interest assets. This finding renders the doctrine of increasing uncertainty applicable to the markets for equity shares as well, and in the same way, as it applies to the markets for bonds.

8.4 THE DOCTRINE OF INCREASING UNCERTAINTY
III: IMPLICATIONS FOR THE THEORY OF THE TURNING POINTS

The doctrine of increasing uncertainty, in its applications to both the capacity growth and speculative cycles, implies that the potential costs of pursuing an optimistic strategy increase over the cyclical upswings and diminish through the downswings and troughs.

As the upswings of each cycle proceed, moreover, the disparity between the costs that will be realized by those who first switch to a safe strategy and by those who switch later increases over time. It is therefore rational for individuals to take ever more notice of signals that might indicate an impending downturn. Signals that are rationally ignored in the trough are rationally acted upon with alacrity in the boom. Consequently, the parameters of the reaction functions describing rational individuals' responses to market signals will change systematically over the relevant cycle.

Among firms in the basic sub-system, the safe strategy is to refrain from investments in capacity expansion. A switch to such a strategy, if at all widespread, will induce a major cyclical downturn. The firms that continue to invest in basic capacity expansion longest will suffer the largest magnitudes of negative cash flows in relation to assets. Among speculators, the safe strategy is a portfolio shift in favour of safe assets. Widespread portfolio shifts of this nature will induce the onset of a bear market. The largest capital losses in relation to asset values will then be realized by those speculators who hold on longest to non-safe assets. Clearly, it is rational for entrepreneurs and specu-lators to switch to safe strategies ever more readily as the upswings in the capacity growth and speculative cycles, respectively, proceed. This behaviour implies increasing downside instability in the product and financial markets during the upswings.

For symmetrical reasons, upside instability increases during the major downswing and trough in the product markets and as long as bearishness predominates in the financial markets. In each case, the potential costs of a non-safe strategy decline. At the same time, the realization of these costs is continually less sensitive to the strategy choices of other agents. If there are widespread switches from safe to non-safe strategies, those who switch first will gain the most.

The instabilities identified here are crucial to the theory of the turning points reported below. Their relationship to the generaliza-tion of the Lucas critique, developed in section 8.1, will be obvious.

8.5 ACCOUNTING CATEGORIES FOR A THEORY OF THE TURNING POINTS

In the remainder of this chapter, we bring together the two applications of the doctrine of increasing uncertainty. In so doing, we provide a general theory of the turning points of the major cycles in macroeconomic activity. The accounting framework within which the turning points theory is reported is that of flow-of-funds accounting.

Flow-of-funds accounting is uniquely well suited to the present analysis because it relates changing financial asset and liability positions of whole sectors of the economy to current sales and purchases of both real and financial assets. In particular, as Roe (1973) has pointed out, these relationships underlie the financial instabilities created when investment and capacity growth are buoyant. The specification of these instabilities and their sources is rightly identified by Roe with the work of Minsky (e.g. 1975, 1982, although Minsky – I believe wrongly – claims only to have elaborated Keynes's *General Theory*).

Minsky, along with Davidson (1972), emphasized the role of financial intermediaries in controlling the flow of funds to non-financial firms to enable them to undertake real investment. Although a number of concerns that occupied Minsky and Davidson are of no interest here – particularly the prices of second-hand capital equipment – the main difference between their analyses and mine is that they followed Keynes in giving no regard to the direction of investment. Minsky (1975, p. 148), for example, quotes with approval Keynes's (1936, p. 379) remark that he saw 'no reason to suppose that the existing system seriously misemploys the factors of production which are in use.... It is in determining the volume, not the direction, of actual employment that the existing system has broken down.' Unless I have made a fundamental algebraic error in chapter 6, Keynes was wrong. There is nothing to prevent a macroeconomic direction of investment that persistently and systematically reduces the economy's capacity for employment and output growth. This proposition is virtually self-evident once we distinguish between basic and non-basic commodities and recognize the importance of the technology of exchange.

Although the distinction between basics and non-basics is crucial to the macroeconomic theory reported here, so too is the distinction between industrial and commercial activities on the one hand and financial activities on the other. For we have seen in sections 8.2 and 8.3 that the doctrine of increasing uncertainty applies in different ways to the holding of real assets and the holding of financial assets. Since this doctrine is crucial to our theory of turning points, it must be maintained side by side with the basic/non-basic distinction. The analysis of financial instability based upon the doctrine of increasing uncertainty is compatible, in the main, with the Minsky–Davidson arguments. By introducing the basic/non-basic distinction into that line of analysis, we are able to ascertain the forces that determine macroeconomic growth cycles.

One of the advantages of the flow-of-funds framework for this development is that it enables us to define sectors according to the requirements of our analysis and, at the same time, to make distinctions among assets and liabilities that are as fine or as broad as are found to be useful. In the remainder of this section we establish first the sectoral categories implied by the analysis from chapter 6 onwards, then the categories of financial assets that must be represented. In section 8.6 we set out an algebraic statement of the accounting identities implied by these two disaggregations.

The sectoral categories

The sectors that must be established here for our flow-of-funds analysis will entail, at the minimum, the basic/non-basic distinction and the distinction between firms engaged in the acquisition of real assets for use in production and exchange and firms engaged in the acquisition and sale of financial assets. In addition, we must take households into account in order to determine the flows of funds resulting from consumption purchases, and in order to analyse public policies we shall need to take cognizance of the government sector. The introduction of the rest-of-the-world sector is then a straightforward matter which can be undertaken subsequently.

First, we consider the relationship between the basic/non-basic distinction and the distinction between financial and non-financial companies.

The basic/non-basic distinction is strictly technological. It is derived from the technologically rather than institutionally determined patterns of inputs to the production and exchange of goods and services. Money and finance are not technologically required as inputs to any processes. Even money is not a technologically required input to processes of exchange. This follows from the demonstration in section 7.1 that money – as distinct from means of payment in general – is required in exchange only when transactions take place between economic agents who are not well known to (and trusted by) each other. In consequence, a take-over or merger that has no effect on the macroeconomic technology will typically eliminate the use of money in the production and exchange of some commodities or assets. More generally, the need for external finance is not technological since the purpose of that finance is to provide the money needed to purchase the equipment, materials and labour required to effect investment projects. The quantity of money required for this purpose will, we have seen, be determined by the institutional rather than the technological structure of the economy.

Since money and finance are not technologically required, either directly or indirectly, in the production and exchange of all commodities, the services of financial intermediaries that give rise to finance and bank money are non-basic; that is, banks and other financial institutions operate in the non-basic sub-system.

There is nothing in this argument to suggest that production and exchange are possible in practice without finance and money. Indeed, we saw in section 8.2 that a dearth of finance (or the fear thereof), and in section 7.5 that a consequent dearth of money, will bring an end to growth in the scale of production and exchange activities. But this does not imply that money or finance are basic any more than the constraining effects of a dearth of labour make labour services basic. Both labour and finance, albeit in decidedly different ways, are essential to the carrying on of production and exchange activities although neither is basic in any technological sense.

In our sectoral disaggregation, therefore, we shall distinguish between non-basic production and exchange activities and non-basic financial activities. All basic activities constitute a sub-sector within the non-financial companies sector for purposes of flow-of-funds accounting.

It will be convenient in the present analysis to combine households and financial institutions as two sub-sectors within a single flow-of-funds accounting sector. We have already analysed at some length the role of consumption demands in relation to the basic/non-basic distinction and therefore the economy's capacity for growth. In relation to flows of funds, however, we are concerned with the disposition of households' savings as well as the financial effects of their consumption. In practice, and for reasons elucidated in section 7.5, households' savings are held either as bank money or as non-money financial assets which arise from lending to firms via the agency of financial intermediaries. Since these intermediaries are the main conduit between the external finance of investment and household and financial intermediaries' saving, and since, moreover, the doctrine of increasing uncertainty applies to households and financial intermediaries in the same way, the analytical simplicity afforded by treating these two groups of agents as parts of a single accounting sector outweighs any advantages from a complete dis-aggregation into two sectors. Within the financial institutions and household sector, however, it will be important to recognize the effects of intra-sectoral flows of funds on consumption.

In establishing these two sectors, we have an analytical frame-work that is virtually identical to that used by Keynes in his *Treatise on Money* (1930/1971). The quantity of money held by non-financial companies is what Keynes called the industrial circulation of money, and the quantity of money held by financial institutions and households is what Keynes called the financial circulation of money. The flows between these circulations on capital account are controlled virtually entirely by financial intermediaries – a point that will be taken up in some detail in presenting our algebraic specifica-tion of the flow-of-funds accounts.

It remains here to consider the government sector. This sector is treated separately because, as we found in section 7.5, it makes a considerable difference to the financial constraints on investment in real assets whether the government undertakes open-market operations in what we can now call the financial circulation or contributes directly (through its current expenditures) or indirectly (through its employees' and beneficiaries' consumption) to the industrial circulation. However, if there are public corporations engaged in basic activities or in non-basic activities yielding outputs that are subject to exchange in the same way as the outputs of private firms, then these corporations are naturally included in the non-financial companies sector. While this categorization is at variance with UK national accounting practice, it conforms to the present analytical requirements.

Categories of financial assets

Three categories of financial assets were discussed in chapter 7: money, non-money safe assets and non-safe assets including non-money means of payment. Of these, only money and non-money means of payment can be clearly distinguished from the others in a general and unambiguous fashion.

A safe asset to one individual will not necessarily be a safe asset to another individual. An asset is 'safe' only in relation to capital commitments and ongoing purchasing requirements. Admittedly, some short-dated, non-money assets such as Treasury bills will always be safe assets with respect to purchasing requirements near the dates of the assets' maturities. Also, equities are never safe with respect either to capital commitments or purchasing requirements, since neither their future capital values nor the dividend payments attaching to them can be known with complete confidence. None the less, a bond that is suitable to hedge one individual's future capital commitments (because all previously maturing commitments are hedged by matching securities) will not be suitable as hedges for another individual's commitments, either because they all mature earlier than the bond or because previously maturing commitments have not yet been hedged.

The impossibility of determining a generally and unambiguously applicable division between safe and non-safe assets does not in any sense vitiate the importance of that distinction. What is involved here is analogous to the specification of commodity demand curves. Their general characteristics can be determined from the standard properties of individual preference sets even though the individuals' demand functions cannot in general be established. In chapter 7 we found that rational behaviour implies that a widespread shift from speculative to safe strategies in the markets for financial assets will reduce the demands for longer-term fixed-interest securities and for equities. It is not necessary to assume that all individuals switch strategies in this way, and it is not implied that all firms will be unable to float new issues of securities. But if we take all non-financial companies together, this general switch in portfolio strategies implies that borrowing that augments the industrial circulation of money will be constrained on the supply side.

It will make no difference to our turning point theory whether it is the supply of bond finance or equity finance or both that is diminished. We do need to know that the sum of the two will be diminished by such a strategy shift by wealth-holders in the personal and financial institutions sectors of the economy. That the demands for holdings of both fixed-interest securities and equities must be increasingly unstable in the downward direction as long as wealth-holders remain bullish is sufficient to generate the main characteristics of the macroeconomic downturn. Similarly, it is sufficient for the turning point theory to have demonstrated that upside instability increases so long as wealth-holders remain bearish. Since both of these propositions were demonstrated in the previous section, it will not be necessary to distinguish between fixed-interest securities and equities in the general analysis of the turning points.

We have a general category of non-safe assets that cannot be distinguished clearly from the category of safe assets. Safe assets are those that are the debts of firms noted for their financial probity and strength or the debts of government agencies and which, in the main, mature within a few years.

The analysis of safe asset demands in chapter 7 provides our warrant for specifying macroeconomic accounting categories that do not distinguish between non-safe assets and non-money safe assets. In that chapter we found that continuing demands for more safe assets will eventually force the rates of return on those assets downward until, in self-defence, banks put a floor under the whole structure of rates of return by raising the own-rate of return on money. This is the essence of the safe-asset theory of interest. It follows that, during periods of deteriorating expectations held by entrepreneurs and speculators, demands for both non-safe assets and non-money safe assets must eventually decline. There will be a general portfolio shift towards money. It is altogether possible that, before rates of return come to be held up by the own-rate of return on money, the upside instability following a widespread deterioration in expectations will result in a general improvement in expectations, and therefore in increasing flow-demands for production and exchange capacities by non-financial companies, as well as in increased bullishness in the financial markets. Since our purpose here is not to determine the timing of such an upturn but only to establish that it must eventually occur, we need show only that the conditions creating increasing upside instability will occur at some extreme. Such extreme conditions occur when the demand for safe assets amounts to a demand for money. It will therefore be sufficient for our purposes to distinguish only between money and non-money assets, whether or not those non-money assets are safe.

In considering the downturn, we need only show that there will be an increasing shortage of both internal and external finance in the basic sub-system. Whether a shortage of external finance results from an excessive stock supply of safe or non-safe assets is not germane to the demonstration that there will be downside instability arising from an increasing dearth of such finance.

It follows that, whether we are concerned with the upturn or the downturn, we need only distinguish between money and non-money assets.

It remains here to consider the distinction between money and non-money means of payment. Because our purpose is to demonstrate the forces that render turning points inevitable, it is not necessary to analyse the supplies of and demands for non-money means of payment at all in the present analysis.

We saw in section 7.1 that households and financial institutions rationally require that any payments due to them from non-financial companies be made in money, in order to minimize information costs associated with subsequent transactions. Thus, a dearth of money in the industrial circulation will restrict the abilities of non-financial companies to meet their wage bills and to repay and service debts. This alone is sufficient to bring about a downturn as downside instability increases through a strong boom. Conversely, an increase in the industrial circulation of money during a slump will enable non-financial companies to meet wage and debt commitments without facing catastrophic liquidity crises in the earliest stages of the upturn.

In short, if we consider the financial flows between the two Keynesian circulations of money, they conform to and enhance the doctrine of increasing uncertainty as it applies to non-financial companies alone, and they provide the crucial link between the applications of that doctrine to non-financial companies and to households and financial institutions.

8.6   THE ACCOUNTING IDENTITIES

The flow-of-funds accounts report net acquisitions of financial assets by the various sectors. In establishing our own accounting identities, we have three sectors and two classes of financial assets. The money in the non-financial companies sector is the industrial circulation of money; the money held by financial institutions and households is the financial circulation of money; money held by the government is irrelevant to our purposes. The flow-of-funds accounts summarize the changes in the two circulations and the activities that bring about those changes as well as changes in the sectoral holdings of non-money financial assets. We are also concerned with the ways in which activities in the two sub-sectors of each sector change the distribution and quantity of money. We consider first the industrial circulation and then the financial circulation.

The industrial circulation

The change in the industrial circulation of money during any interval of time is simply the sum of all receipts of bank and intrinsic money by non-financial companies from the other sectors of the economy, *minus* the sum of all money payments to the other sectors. The receipts include payments by households for consumption commodities (denoted by C), payments by financial institutions for the commodities they require as inputs to their intermediation and other activities (denoted by I_f), payments for commodities purchased by the government in excess of all taxes on non-financial companies (G_c) and the net proceeds of any sales of financial securities to individuals in the other sectors (ΔF_c). ΔF_c is the negative of net acquisitions of financial assets by non-financial companies. If ΔF_c is negative, then non-financial companies are increasing their financial asset holdings or reducing their liabilities by repaying debts of a larger value than their new debts to the other sectors, and/or they are increasing their holdings of non-money assets for hedging purposes.

Payments to other sectors not included in the calculation of net receipts are the wage bill of non-financial companies (W_c) and profits distributed to households and financial institutions, $(1 - s_c) P_c$, where P_c is the sector's gross profits and s_c is the fraction of gross profits retained as additions to reserves.

Denoting the change in non-financial companies' holdings of intrinsic and bank money by ΔL_c, the change in the industrial circulation is

$$\Delta L_c \equiv C + I_f + G_c + \Delta F_c - [W_c + (1 - s_c) P_c]. \tag{8.5}$$

We know from national income accounting conventions that, for any sector, profits and wages together are equal to the value of purchases of commodities produced in the sector net of indirect taxes and subsidies, plus net 'exports' to the other sectors of the economy. Since all taxes and subsidies are already taken into account in the value of G_c, we can specify the total value of transactions among non-financial companies by I_c, which is current investment expenditures in the sector. It follows that

$$W_c + P_c \equiv I_c + C + I_f + G_c. \tag{8.6}$$

Substituting from this identity into identity (8.5),

$$\Delta L_c \equiv \Delta F_c + s_c P_c - I_c. \tag{8.7}$$

That is, the increase in the industrial circulation of money during any arbitrary interval of time is the excess of net new debt and additions to reserves out of trading income (less any increases in holdings of non-money hedging assets) over gross investment by non-financial companies.

Identities (8.5) and (8.7) are clearly different ways of expressing the same thing. Identity (8.5) expresses an increase in the industrial circulation as the outcome of actions taken wholly outside the non-financial companies sector, while identity (8.7) expresses the increase in the industrial circulation as the outcome of actions taken within the non-financial companies sector. Since these actions entail sales and purchases of commodities and assets, it cannot be surprising that we get the same results whether we consider the sales or the purchases (or the effects thereof). An increase in household consumption, for example, increases the sum of non-financial companies' wage bills and gross profits. In identity (8.5) the increase in consumption minus any wages and profit distributions resulting from that increase is clearly seen to be a net acquisition of financial assets, which, to the extent that it is held in the form of money, is an increase in the industrial circulation. In identity (8.7) that same acquisition of financial assets is represented simply as a retention of current gross profits. In general, each identity focuses our attention on different decisions and flows although the outcomes and transactions involved are the same.

Basics, non-basics and the industrial circulation of money

With this accounting framework, it is a perfectly straightforward matter to separate the basic from the non-basic processes employed by non-financial companies. In so doing, we see that firms engaged in basic activities will clearly bear the brunt of the increasing uncertainty during a major upswing.

The argument has three independent elements: the application of the doctrine of increasing uncertainty to the capacity-growth cycle; the relationship between current rates of capacity growth and the age-profile of existing and gestating capital equipment; and the inverse relationship between cash flows from trading and the basic flow ratios. The first of these elements was argued in detail in sections 8.2 and 8.4; the second is an elementary algebraic point which need not be restated here; the third element is easily demonstrated. It is to that demonstration that we now turn.

The sources of financial assets in the basic sub-system from trading alone are sales to the non-basic sub-system and other non-basic users of basic commodities such as the government. The uses of finance are entirely to pay wages and, in an open economy, to purchase imports. We continue to assume for the present, however, that the economy is closed. Using the notation of chapter 6, the nominal value of current basic commodity outputs sold to non-basic users and traders is

$$\mathbf{p}'(\mathbf{I} - \hat{\phi}_t)\,\mathbf{B}_{11}\mathbf{q}_{1t}$$

where ϕ_t is the vector of basic flow ratios, $\hat{\phi}_t$ is the corresponding diagonal matrix, $\mathbf{B}_{11}$ is the basic sub-system output matrix, $\mathbf{q}_{1t}$ is the vector of basic activity levels during period t and $\mathbf{p}'$ is the row vector of basic commodity prices. The uses of finance in production and exchange by the basic sub-system as a whole are in the payment of wages to workers in the basic sub-system. The basic sub-system wage bill, again in the notation of chapter 6, is

$$\mathbf{w}'\mathbf{N}_1\mathbf{q}_{1t}$$

where $\mathbf{w}'$ is the row vector of wage rates earned by the various categories of workers and $\mathbf{N}_1$ is the matrix of the various categories of labour inputs to the basic processes of production and exchange.

The net acquisition of financial assets from current production and exchange activities in the basic sub-system is evidently

$$[\mathbf{p}'(\mathbf{I} - \hat{\phi}_t)\,\mathbf{B}_{11} - \mathbf{w}'\mathbf{N}]\,\mathbf{q}_{1t} \tag{8.8}$$

or, in scalar notation,

$$\sum_j \left[\sum_i p_i (1 - \phi_{it})\, b_{ij} - w n_j \right] q_{jt}. \tag{8.9}$$

It is perfectly clear that increases in the ith basic flow ratio reduce the basic sub-system's acquisition of financial assets without reducing the use of financial assets for the payment of wages. Moreover, as the basic flow ratios tend towards unity, the net acquisition of funds becomes negative and tends in magnitude to the value of the basic sub-system wage bill.

We must be clear, however, that the diminution in the net acquisition of financial assets from the trading activities of the basic sub-system does not imply any lack of profitability of those activities. For we have in effect eliminated the gross profits of individual firms from sales within the basic sub-system by consolidating the income accounts of those firms in respect of their basic production and exchange activities. The increasing growth of transactions within the basic sub-system will generate increasing profits. However, the assets received will be the debts – generally the trade debts – of other firms operating in that sub-system, or they will have been acquired by increases in external finance or the use of financial reserves. Since there will be a limit to the volume and duration of trade debt that firms extend to one another, eventually the reserves of firms operating in the basic sub-system must decline and their borrowings and issues of equity shares must grow relative to current revenues.

In short, even if the industrial circulation of money as a whole were to be growing and non-financial firms were to be adding to their net financial asset positions, activities of non-financial firms in the basic sub-system would still be a drain on holdings of financial assets in general, and, since money must be paid to workers and creditors, the distribution of the industrial circulation of money will shift away from firms active mainly or entirely in the basic sub-system in favour of those with activities concentrated in the non-basic sub-system.

The financial circulation

The change in the financial circulation of money during any accounting period comprises the receipts of money by households and financial institutions from non-financial companies and the government *minus* payments by households to their other sectors and payments by financial institutions to those other sectors in excess of any bank money that is created during the period. That is, when a bank loan to a non-financial company takes the form of the creation of a deposit with the bank, the industrial circulation of money is increased but the financial circulation is not diminished. Similarly, when a bank creates a deposit as a loan to a household in order to purchase a security from another household or a financial institution, the financial circulation of money is increased. In general, therefore, the financial circulation of money is diminished only to the extent that payments by financial institutions and households to the other sectors of the economy exceed the creation of bank money. Thus, the financial circulation of money could increase as a result of the creation of bank credit used for speculation and consumption by households even though non-financial companies and the government are net borrowers from households and financial institutions.

Households' and financial institutions' receipts from non-financial companies have already been identified as distributed profits

$(1-s_c)P_c$, reductions in the net indebtedness of non-financial companies to financial institutions and households together with increased holdings of non-money hedging assets, denoted by ΔF_c, and the non-financial companies' wage bill W_c. Payments to non-financial companies by financial institutions are for materials and capital equipment employed as inputs to the provision of financial services (I_f) and payments by households are for consumption purchases (C). The value of purchases of financial assets by the government from financial institutions and households is denoted by G_f, and the government wage bill and transfer payments to households is denoted by W_g. Both G_f and W_g are net of all direct and indirect taxes. The creation of bank money during the period is denoted by ΔM_b.

With this notation, the change in the financial circulation of money during any time-period is

$$\Delta L_f \equiv (1-s_c)\,P_c + W_c + W_g + G_f - I_f - C - \Delta F_c + \Delta M_b. \quad (8.10)$$

Upon substitution from the social accounting identity (8.6) we have

$$\Delta L_f \equiv (I_c - s_c P_c - \Delta F_c) + (W_g + G_c + G_f) + \Delta M_b. \quad (8.11)$$

The terms in the first set of parentheses on the right side of this identity are the negative of the change in the industrial circulation. The terms in the second set of parentheses are the value of all expenditures on goods, services and assets by the government sector; it is therefore the flow-supply of government (or intrinsic) money and will be denoted by ΔM_g. Identity (8.12) can therefore be written as

$$L_f \equiv \Delta M_g + \Delta M_b - \Delta L_c. \quad (8.12)$$

In other words, the increase in the two circulations of money is equal to the net flow-supply of bank and intrinsic money. This result shows the coherence of our accounting framework.

The macroeconomic financial relationships identified by means of the accounting framework developed above will be used here in two ways.

In the remainder of this chapter they will be used to identify endogenous forces that induce the turning points of the major macroeconomic cycle. The analysis of increasing asymmetrical instabilities in sections 8.2–8.4 implies only that the upswings and downswings will be cumulative in their early stages once the downturns and upturns, respectively, have been brought about by other economic forces. In chapter 9 the accounting framework, together with the identification of the endogenous sources of the turning points, will be used to derive the criteria for (and an example of) effective and allocatively efficient macroeconomic policies to delay and ameliorate the severity of the major downturns and to accelerate and sharpen the major upturns.

8.7   THE MAJOR CYCLICAL TURNING POINTS

In this section we shall identify the reasons why both an upturn and a downturn are inevitable over the course of the major cycle. This analysis is necessary because we have so far identified only the conditions that favour these turning points, rather than the events that bring them about. The events that bring about the major upturn are identified by returning to the analysis of focusing and inducement effects on firms. These two effects were summarized briefly in chapter 2 on the basis of my previous detailed analysis of these phenomena (Moss, 1981, chapter 3). The downturn is brought about by the macroeconomic inducement effects defined in section 2.3. We consider first the major upturn and then the major downturn.

The upturn

Any analysis of the upturn that conforms to the general analytical approach taken in this book will be predicated upon the assumption of rational individual behaviour, the survival motivation of firms' managers and a technological, rather than introspective, subjective basis for action. There are three classes of upturn-generating events, which have been extensively analysed in the trade cycle literature and which meet these criteria of analytical conformity. These are (1) replacement investments, (2) technical changes requiring increases in the rate of investment to embody innovations in new capital equipment and (3) exogenous increases in demand such as government expenditures or tax reductions, leading to increased household consumption or increased export demands. Government policies and other sources of exogenous increases in demands will be considered in detail in chapter 9. We consider here, therefore, only the first two classes of events that are said to generate upturns in macroeconomic activity.

Undoubtedly, some patterns of replacement investment could provide the stimulus to a major upturn as upside instability increases in the markets for capital equipment and long-term financial assets. However, there is no reason to expect stock replacements, though they will certainly generate a Type I accelerator process, to induce a major upturn. Stock replacement orders and purchases are short-lived phenomena that, in practice, are well understood by entrepreneurs. Moreover, stock-holdings will be limited by existing storage capacities and, as we saw in chapter 7, will not be substantially and permanently increased relative to the rates of use that are possible with existing capacities unless inflation rates are thought to be rising to exceptionally high levels. It is elementary that investments in capacity expansion are wholly uneconomic unless the demand flows increase for periods of time longer than the gestation and payback periods of the new fixed capital equipment.

Fixed capacity replacements could not provide the requisite expansionary market signals unless either they were bunched – and this was not realized by capital goods producers – or there were a lengthy trend of rising rates of investment in fixed-capacity replacements which led to the full utilization of capacities in the basic subsystem. There is no technological reason to expect any bunching of this kind of replacement investment, nor have I been able to identify any reasons for bunching based on the assumption of rational, survival-motivated, entrepreneurial behaviour. The financial relationships identified in sections 8.2 and 8.6, however, indicate that growing rates of replacement investment are compatible with our behavioural assumptions.

The argument here is perfectly straightforward. Firms that are able to survive in the trough of the major cycle will, we have seen, generally be able to improve their financial positions over time. This is the source of upside instability. In consequence, they will be increasingly well placed to invest in replacements for their deteriorating or outmoded capital equipment. If there should be any disruption to production and exchange as a result of the investment – perhaps while old machinery is removed and new machinery put in its place – the costs of such disruption will be less during periods of slack demand than during periods of growing demand. Customers will generally require the firm's outputs less urgently, so less goodwill is lost during the slump than during the boom.

The upturn arising from the replacements of fixed capacities could simply peter out once existing capacities in the capital goods industries (whether basic or non-basic) are fully utilized. 'Bottlenecks in production' will then be blamed for the weakness and brevity of the boom. In other words, there will be a minor boom induced by a Type I accelerator process. If, however, firms in the non-basic sub-system respond to the full utilization of their capital equipment by increasing their own rates of capacity expansion, there will be a stronger Type II accelerator process and expansionary multiplier–accelerator interaction. In the now usual way the Type II accelerator could give way to a Type III accelerator process, though it need not. And if there should be a Type II or Type III accelerator response, we cannot say *a priori* how strong it will be.

Stronger results will follow from our consideration of technical change.

During a deep and prolonged depression, there are no inducement effects leading firms in general to expand their production and exchange capacities. Indeed, that is the essence of the slump. If there are any inducement effects, these will lead firms to merge or to acquire other firms in order to protect markets or to diversify away from the production and exchange of commodities in slack demand. In the nature of the major trough, firms will not in general be constrained either by their existing production and exchange capacities or by their organizational structures. Focusing effects, however, are internal to the firm, and so can continue to be a force even during periods of slack demands for inputs and outputs; the personnel of individual firms will face routine problems requiring routine solutions using their accumulated and collective skills and experience. Those firms with management teams that are sufficiently ambitious to seek growth even during a major cyclical trough need not confine their activities to acquisitions of, or mergers with, other firms. They will rationally seek ways of increasing their shares of markets in which demands are weak. In these circumstances, cost-reducing process and product innovations will be at a premium, and, whenever focusing effects lead to the definition of the appropriate technical changes, ambitious management teams will rationally encourage their development.

When these focusing effects lead to successful innovatory strategies, the innovating firms will be able either to undercut the prices of their competitors or to offer new capital equipment to their customers that will reduce their customers' costs. The innovating firms will invest in new capacities in order to increase their market shares or to create new markets. In either case, firms in the industries to which the innovation applies will have a clear incentive to bunch replacement investments and/or to invest in capacity expansion. Since, moreover, technical changes in one line of production or exchange are often applicable in other areas of activity (cf. Rosenberg, 1976; Moss, 1981, chapter 3), the capital goods producers will, at least in some cases, have a product innovation on their hands that provides them with new, originally unforeseen marketing opportunities; their existing marketing channels, together with the innovatory product, will constitute a focusing effect on the capital goods producers to adopt a strategy entailing the marketing of the technical change to firms in industries other than the one for which it was first developed.

In general, focusing effects within rationally managed firms during a major slump will sometimes lead to technical changes that can generate upturns in the demands for capital equipment. If the innovatory capital equipment is specialized to non-basic uses, the technical change will have the same effect as any non-basic demands for basic commodities. The basic commodity producers and traders could simply meet the new demands, thereby generating a minor upturn, or they could respond by increasing their own rates of capacity growth and so generate a major upturn. But if the technical change affects the basic sub-system directly, its introduction will entail the use of basic outputs in the production of basic commodities; basic flow ratios will rise, and the Type III accelerator process will generate a major upturn. The process of innovation and imitation in the basic sub-system must generate a major upturn; innovation and imitation in the non-basic sub-system *might* generate a major upturn but, equally, the resulting upturn might be minor.

The identification of these sources of the major upturn gives some indication of the periodicity of the cycles. The innovatory cycle conforms to the Mensch cycle, which appears to run roughly in tandem with the 50-year Kondratieff cycle. It must be said, however, that the evidence for these cycles has not convinced all observers. These innovatory cycles, if they exist and if the foregoing argument is correct, act as something of a long-stop: they will generate the major upturn when the replacement cycles are not sufficiently strong to do so.

In the end, of course, the periodicity of these cycles is an empirical matter which cannot be settled without a time-series of input–output tables sufficiently disaggregated to exhibit block triangularity and, equivalently, to differentiate between basic and non-basic activities.

The downturn

It is clear from the argument of sections 8.2 and 8.4 that the upward phase of a major cycle could be brought about by the failure of entrepreneurial nerve in the basic sub-system as firms active in that sub-system switch from expansionary to safe strategies. The longer the upward phase lasts, the greater is the incentive for entrepreneurs in general, but not least in the basic sub-system, to cease investing in capacity expansion in order to build up financial reserves against any major downturn in demand growth. It is equally clear from the argument of sections 8.3 and 8.4, together with the accounting identities of section 8.6, that the downturn could be brought about by a wholly rational and increasing reluctance on the part of financial institutions and households to lend to firms that are active in the basic sub-system; for an increasing proportion of the assets of these firms will be in the form of trade credits, and their cash flows from trading will be negative and increasing in magnitude. The interdependence of these firms, not only for demands but also to preserve their balance-sheet values, exposes substantial lenders to considerable capital uncertainty.

Although it is plausible that a rational failure of entrepreneurial or *rentier* nerve, or both, will bring an end to the upward phase of a major cycle, they are not inevitable. In consequence, they will not make the downturns themselves inevitable. That inevitability has a more strictly technological source.

Higher basic ratios in a given macroeconomic technology entail the employment of a larger proportion of the labour force in the basic sub-system and, obviously, a smaller proportion in the non-basic sub-system. In consequence, the domestic production and exchange of non-basic commodities – including consumption commodities – per head of the employed population must be lower as the basic stock ratios are higher. Indeed, that is the key element in the expansionary multiplier–accelerator interaction that brings about a major rather than a minor boom.

In a closed economy either real wage rates must fall if prices are flexible, or there must be shortages of consumption commodities or increasing propensities to save out of wages. There is no evidence for the last possibility and, certainly, it is not implied by the orthodox theory of choice. Whether real wage rates fall or there are persistent shortages of consumption commodities, the quantity of goods and services that workers can consume for each additional hour of work must decline as basic stock (and therefore flow) ratios rise. In the limit, basic ratios are unitary and there is no production and exchange of consumption or any other non-basic commodities. Orthodox choice theory implies that the supply of labour will decline towards nil as the quantity of consumption commodities that can be bought with the wage rate declines. Even if there is a substantial surplus of unemployed workers, the supply of labour services will increasingly constrain the utilization of production and exchange capacities as the rates of capacity growth increase. In such circumstances the full-employment ceiling will be declining as the rates of basic capacity growth are rising. At full employment, the rate of basic capacity growth will necessarily decline to the rate of growth of the labour supply. In conditions of declining real wages, of course, orthodox choice theory implies the possibility that the rate of growth of the labour supply could be negative even if the rate of population growth is positive.

The implications for the continuation of the major cyclical upswing are not altered if workers defend their standards of living. Indeed, the analysis of market power in section 3.2, together with the flow-of-funds relationships identified in section 8.6, imply the existence of a wage cycle in phase with the major macroeconomic cycle.

This wage cycle results from the deteriorating hedging positions and cash flows of firms that concentrate their activities in the basic sub-system. Operations in the basic sub-system render firms ever more vulnerable to interruptions in their cash flows as the major upswing progresses. At the same time, the demand for labour is growing. What is involved here is a straightforward issue of market power. The costs of industrial disruption are increasing for firms that have been investing in capacity growth and, by virtue of operating in the basic sub-system, find their profits increasingly accounted for by trade credit and/or their debt commitments growing in relation to revenues. The costs faced by workers as a result of industrial disruption are, if anything, diminishing, since, even if they force their employers into bankruptcy, other jobs are becoming available with other firms. Since the costs of extended industrial disruption are becoming increasingly intolerable to employers in the basic sub-system but not to workers, the analysis of market power reported in section 3.2 implies an unambiguous power shift in the labour markets towards workers and away from firms in the basic sub-system. As real wages rise in the basic sub-system in consequence of this power shift, the financial squeeze on firms engaged in basic activities becomes tighter and the downward instability of the basic sub-system becomes more pronounced.

During the major slump, market power shifts towards firms in both sub-systems and away from workers. Weaker firms will be unable to survive substantial increases in wage rates relative to their output prices, and if they should fail workers' prospects for alternative employments are less favourable than in the upswing and are (perhaps) deteriorating. Stronger firms, however, are able to improve their financial positions with each successive minor boom and so are increasingly well placed to withstand industrial disruption. Thus, both weak and strong firms increase their market power *vis-à-vis* workers during the slump. This downward pressure on real wage rates adds to the factors that improve the hedging positions of surviving firms and so increases upside instability as the major slump continues.

If workers defend their wage relativities, and we saw in section 5.4 that this presumption is compatible with the present theory, then the real wage cycle in the basic sub-system will extend to the non-basic sub-system as well. As a result, there will be added demand pressures on the producers and traders of consumption commodities, though the growth of available internal finance will be reduced. However, provided that the speculative cycle moves up more or less in phase with the major macroeconomic cycle, there will be an easing of the constraints on external finance for investments in capacity expansion and the increased inducement to invest will dominate in the non-basic sub-system. Thus, once entrepreneurs pause to consolidate their investments in the basic sub-system, the demands for basic inputs to non-basic production and exchange will prevent excess supplies of basic commodities from becoming in any way general. The Type III accelerator process will give way to a Type II process. It is quite possible that the Type II process will then give way to the Type III process again once firms in the basic sub-system have repaired their finances; that is, there could well be a sequence of minor downturns during a major upswing and boom.

The major upturns and downturns compared

The common element in the foregoing analysis of the upturns and downturns of the major macroeconomic cycles is the doctrine of increasing uncertainty. This doctrine entails the demonstration that both internal and external finance of investment by non-financial companies will become an ever more imperative constraint as the major cyclical upswings proceed and will be increasingly abundant as the major cyclical slump continues. This result leads to the conclusion that booms are marked by increasing downside instability and slumps by increasing upside stability.

Although we have found that the general analysis of uncertainty and instability applies to both the upturns and the downturns of the major cycles, the events that bring them about are different in character. Specifically, the upturns are due to microeconomic phenomena – the focusing and inducement effects on individual firms described in chapter 2, which I have previously analysed theoretically and historically in detail (Moss, 1981). While they are not inevitable, the inventions and innovations arising from the focusing effects and the technological imitation necessitated by the inducement effects are the products of rational behaviour by survival-motivated management teams. There is nothing *ad hoc* or lacking in clear microeconomic foundations in our analysis of the upturn. The downturns, however, are due to macroeconomic phenomena – ultimately to macroeconomic inducement effects arising ineluctably from the nature of the macroeconomic technology. But the key characteristics of this technology were deduced from our microeconomic analysis of allocative efficiency in exchange – an analysis predicated more consistently and generally on rational microeconomic behaviour than any previous theory or analysis of exchange. Thus, albeit at one remove, the analysis of the downturn has a clear microeconomic foundation which is in no sense dependent on *ad hoc* assumptions.

9

Policy Analysis

The theory put forward in this book implies that the direction of macroeconomic investment, including government spending, is a policy issue of the first order of importance. It is a policy issue in its own right because rational entrepreneurs cannot establish the markets or other institutions that provide signals to entrepreneurs in the basic sub-system leading them to invest in enough capacity expansion to generate full-employment growth. An increase in current demands could in principle lead to either declining or increasing basic capacity growth. In the first case the result will be a minor, self-terminating macroeconomic upswing, while in the latter case the result will be a major, self-sustaining macroeconomic upswing which will be ended only by financial or labour constraints.

For this reason, Keynesian demand management is not sufficient to maintain full employment in the long run. The effect of demand management is to maintain high rates of capacity *utilization* in the short run but not high rates of capacity *growth* in the long run. If capacity growth rates are lower than the rate of growth of the labour force, then Keynesian policies will not only fail to eliminate growing structural unemployment; they might actually aggravate it.

Of course, it is hardly to be expected that capacity growth rates will rise when existing capacities are under-utilized. It follows that Keynesian demand management can be used to fulfil a necessary condition – full capacity utilization – for capacity growth. None the less, demand management may have to be supplemented by policies that affect supplies either by the establishment of appropriate institutions or by direct government intervention in the basic sub-system. In those cases where rational entrepreneurs cannot profitably establish the appropriate institutions, then these must be established by government. In this chapter, the sort of institutional arrangement that I have in mind is a NEDO with teeth: a forum for government, business managers and trade unions that can offer incentives to each sector in order to generate agreed macroeconomic outcomes. Essentially, the policy measures discussed below are either indicative planning measures or they depend for their success on other non-market forms of supply-side coordination. Because the theory from which these policy implications are drawn depends on the assumption of decentralized decision-making by rational individuals, I do not consider any form of central planning that would take investment decisions out of the hands of independent firms' managers.

The theory developed above implies the rejection of the institutional arrangements and economic behaviour that would make a natural unemployment rate meaningful. We have found that, in general, the Walrasian structure in which the natural rate of unemployment can be defined requires irrational individual behaviour. It is, therefore, open to us to adopt full employment as our primary policy objective. The growing body of evidence linking stress-related illness to unemployment is, to my mind, sufficient reason to do so.

Formally, I shall define full employment as that macroeconomic condition in which output growth is constrained by the growth of the labour force.

Although I shall consider when anti-inflation policies are required in order to achieve and maintain full employment, I will not take the control of inflation *per se* to be a primary policy objective. Nothing in my theory implies that the control of inflation ought to take precedence over the maintenance of full employment.

9.1 DEMAND MANAGEMENT OVER THE MAJOR CYCLE

Even if expansionary demand management policies in the trough of the macroeconomic cycle are not sufficient to bring about a major upturn, they do facilitate upturns induced by other forces. Each minor upturn that is induced by demand management policies increases the financial strength of non-financial companies, thereby reducing the severity of the consequences of falsely optimistic programmes of investment in capacity expansion. In addition, the minor booms are likely to prolong the operations of some financially marginal firms so that their existing capacities will be available once the major upturn gets underway. And, even during the trough of the major cycle, expansionary demand management increases current employment, although the growth of the maximum possible employment of labour may be static or declining.

If expansionary demand management does not increase rates of basic capacity growth, then the employment-generating effects of government policy will eventually be offset by the deflationary effects of unchanging or even declining rates of employment growth in the basic sub-system. To counter these effects, the government will need to undertake a further round of expansionary demand management. The result is similar to what some monetarists have claimed: maintenance of full employment will require repeated rounds of expansionary demand management, with the result that the government share of gross domestic expenditure will continually increase while the share of the basic sub-system continually declines.

If policies are to be devised that generate rising rates of basic capacity growth, it is important that these policies not be frustrated by inappropriate forms of demand management. On obvious efficiency grounds, we should require that the particular increases in capacity utilization brought about or encouraged by demand management do not deny resources to the basic sub-system. Formally, demand management policies at the major upturn or during the major upswing of the macroeconomic cycle must not result in reduced or falling basic flow ratios. The expansionary demand management policy itself – independently of its direction – will ensure that actual basic stock ratios rise towards their short-run maxima.

The practical force of this caveat is that neither the government nor its direct or indirect suppliers must be in a position to outbid basic commodity producers and traders in their demands for basic commodities. Since individual households do not typically have market power *vis à vis* firms producing and trading basic commodities, it does not seem likely that government action to increase household incomes will diminish basic ratios. It is quite possible, however, that the building of munitions factories and hospitals could divert basic commodities from the basic sub-system. This is not to say that weapons and hospitals should not be built; but if the purpose of these and other items of government expenditure is to achieve and sustain full employment, then final demands by the government must be restricted to that magnitude which takes up any excess basic and non-basic production and exchange capacities and which does not displace any demands emanating from the basic sub-system.

The determination of the direction of government expenditure in these circumstances is clearly a matter of some complexity. The building of roads that facilitate the transportation of basic inputs and outputs evidently raises basic ratios and so, on the criteria suggested here, will be appropriate elements in a policy of demand management. Since, however, the government does not sell the services of the road, and since, if the road should fail to generate a profit, the government will not cease to survive, there is nothing in the present theory to suggest that government expenditures on roads and other items of the economic infrastructure will not run ahead of, or fall behind, the trend rate of basic sub-system growth. If government expenditures on basic public goods such as roads persistently run ahead of the basic sub-system growth trend, the production and exchange capacities of the basic sub-system will be distorted. There will be under-utilized infrastructure and constrained supplies of basic commodities in other activities over an unnecessarily long interval of time. Capacity, output and employment growth in general will be held back.

Evidently, the optimal growth of government expenditures on social overhead capital – the economic infrastructure – will depend on the growth of the whole basic sub-system. This growth rate in turn depends on the state of long-term expectation in that sub-system. Since these are issues that affect the supply side of the economy, they are best considered in detail when we turn to such issues in the following section. The general point here should none the less be clear. Demand management will be most effective if the growth of direct government purchases of goods and services is restrained relative to the growth of direct government employment, transfer payments to households and expenditures to rectify deficiencies in the economic infrastructure.

Managing full employment

If financial conditions do not bring an end to the major macro-economic upswing, then the trend rate of capacity growth in the economy as a whole must decline to the natural rate of growth once full employment is reached. The objective of demand management at this point in the major cycle will be to maintain full capacity utilization in both sub-systems so that the downturn does not give way to a headlong slump. The optimal composition of government demands once full employment is reached will depend upon a measure of the relative labour intensities of the two sub-systems and, within the non-basic sub-system, of the labour intensities of processes yielding outputs for government and private consumption.

The conventional measure of labour intensity is the capital–labour ratio. It has been well established for two decades and more that there is no technologically meaningful definition of real capital in an economic system producing more than one commodity (Harcourt, 1972). Moreover, a major portion of Sraffa's seminal *Production of Commodities* (1960) was devoted to the demonstration that, except in relation to a particular *numeraire* for each technology, the same result applies to the basic sub-system (as it is called here) alone. It applies to the non-basic sub-system no matter what *numeraire* is employed. The capital–labour ratio therefore cannot be of use in the present theoretical context.

The effect that economists seek to capture with the concept of relative labour intensities is the change in demand for labour as the activity levels of any one group of processes increases relative to the activity levels of other groups of processes. It will suffice for our present needs, therefore, to say that the basic sub-system is more labour-intensive than the non-basic sub-system if, in conditions of generally full capacity utilization – apart from under-utilizations arising from resource imbalances within firms – increased basic flow ratios initially raise the growth of demands for labour. The non-basic sub-system is the more labour-intensive if the impact effect of an increase in basic flow ratios is to reduce the rate of growth of labour demand. In the long run, of course, the rate of growth of labour in the whole economy will converge towards the trend rate of basic capacity growth.

Once full employment is achieved, so that the rate of basic capacity growth with full capacity utilization is forced down towards the natural growth rate, the supply of labour will be growing more slowly than the demand if the non-basic sub-system is labour-intensive relative to the basic sub-system. In consequence, the labour constraint will prevent full capacity utilization in the whole economy.

There are several possible results of the labour constraint. One is that firms that are unable to attract enough labour to utilize all of their existing capital equipment will simply scrap or 'mothball' their least efficient establishments. There is clearly a limit to this process, since capital equipment will have to be taken out of use continually as long as basic flow ratios do not fall and the natural rate of growth does not increase. In the end, the production and exchange capacities in use will tend to vanish. In the presence of the labour constraint, producers and traders are more likely to reduce their rates of capacity growth. If consumption commodity producers and traders reduce their capacity growth rates, the excess demands for basic commodities will be diminished while the excess demands for consumption commodities will be increased. The market signals should lead firms in the consumption industries to maintain their investments in capacity expansion. Reduced rates of capacity growth in the basic sub-system lead to both reduced growth of net consumption demands and reduced excess demands for basic commodities. Thus, either basic stock ratios or basic flow ratios or both must decline, as must the growth of demands for consumption commodities. All of the market signals in these circumstances will be contractionary. Unless the state of long-term expectation in the basic sub-system should change smoothly to one characterized by that degree of optimism which is just appropriate to the natural rate of growth, it could become too pessimistic, so that the full-employment constraint gives way to a major macroeconomic downswing. It cannot, for reasons we have just seen, remain too optimistic.

The role of government policy and activity in these circumstances must be to smooth the transition to full-employment growth, thereby to ensure that the macroeconomic downturn does not give way to a major downswing. One element of this policy will be to restrain the downward trend in basic flow ratios to those that are compatible with a rate of growth and composition of output that is appropriate to the natural rate of growth and market demands for consumption commodities. Since the reduction in basic ratios stems from declining capacity utilization, it is natural to employ demand management policies that maintain full capacity utilizations as the basic flow ratios fall. The reductions in basic flow ratios must be managed by other means, since fall they must.

Since the falling rates of capacity utilization are themselves due to the full-employment constraint, the objective of demand management must be to increase the supply of labour available for employment in the production of both basic and non-basic commodities. To achieve this objective, the government need only reduce the rate of growth of government employment so that it is less than the rate of growth of private labour demand. How much less depends on the relative labour intensities of the two sub-systems. If there is little difference between them, employment by the government will continue to grow but at a reduced rate. If there is a sufficiently large difference between the labour intensities of the two sub-systems, government employment will have to decline. In the latter case,

simply that basic sub-system employment is growing faster than non-basic sub-system employment. If technical change in the basic sub-system reduces the relative labour intensity of that sub-system, employment growth in the basic sub-system corresponding to any given time-path of capacity growth rates will be reduced. This is just what we would expect to happen if technical change increases the average real productivity of labour; for when basic capacities are growing faster than non-basic capacities, new technologies are being embodied in basic processes more quickly than in non-basic processes.

This brings us to the first of the two additional advantages of basic innovations. Because the rate of growth of actual employment in the basic sub-system corresponding to any rate of basic capacity growth is reduced by technical change, consumption commodity output per worker in the whole economy does not fall as much during the major macroeconomic upswing. Real wage rates can thus be higher or excess net consumption demands can be lower, or both. It follows that the major upswing corresponding to any level or pattern of consumption per worker in the whole economy can be sharper and faster. If the upturn is not first brought to an end by financial constraints, the scale of basic commodity outputs that can be reached before workers resist further reductions in consumption per head will be larger.

The second advantage of basic technical change concerns demand management at the downturn. If technical change reduces the relative labour intensity of the basic sub-system, there will be a larger transitory increase in the growth of demand for labour as the basic flow ratios fall with capacities fully utilized. So much follows from the argument of the preceding section. As a result, the government will have to contract its activities to a greater degree than if the basic technical changes had not been introduced. It turns out, therefore, that an industrial policy at the major cyclical trough that successfully induces the expansion of labour-saving, innovatory, basic processes leads at the major cyclical peak to a larger reduction in government activity on the demand side if capacities are not to be under-utilized for lack of labour to operate them.

Although this second 'advantage' will be seen as such immediately by those who believe that less government activity is always preferable, no such ideological view is taken here. It does seem possible, however, that demand management will be more effective in the downswing and major trough if it starts from a smaller base. The quantity of resources required to effect full capacity utilization by means of demand management will be smaller if an upturn in government spending follows a decline rather than amounting to just another in an unbroken sequence of increases in government spending.

Although there are clear advantages to industrial policies that succeed in increasing the rate of growth of innovatory production and exchange capacities in the basic sub-system, there is no reason to believe that the number and importance of such processes will be sufficient to raise the rate of capacity growth in the basic sub-system as a whole. We can show, on the basis of the argument of section 6.5, that there is some minimum number and magnitude of basic production and exchange capacities that must be made to grow at a higher rate if the growth of the sub-system is to be raised. The same argument implies that there is no reason to influence the growth rates of all basic capacities directly by industrial policy.

We found in section 6.5 that basic capacity growth rates converge over time. If the firms collectively operating some basic capacities are expanding them more slowly than the average rate of basic capacity growth, the users of their outputs in the basic sub-system will be constrained by the supply of inputs to their production and exchange processes. The suppliers of these inputs will face inducement effects to expand their production and exchange capacities. The users of these inputs will face inducement effects indicating vertical integration to assure the supplies they require. Potential new entrants will find that the production of the basic commodities in short supply holds the promise of a profitable business venture. It follows that industrial policies need not be addressed directly to increases in the lowest rates of basic capacity growth. As long as full capacity utilization is maintained in the major cyclical trough and upswing by means of demand management, there will be appropriate market signals and profitable business strategies to bring the lagging growth rates into line with the rising trend rate of capacity growth in the basic sub-system as a whole.

At the other extreme, the highest basic capacity growth rates are under downward pressure as a result of demand constraints in both the basic and the non-basic sub-systems. If these capacity growth rates are sustained or increased, the only result will be a faster growth of stocks of unsaleable commodities and under-utilized capacities. What is required here is to justify the optimism of the entrepreneurs investing at the highest rates by means of industrial policies that raise some of the lower (but not the lowest) rates of basic capacity growth. Any such industrial policy must eliminate the downward pressure on the highest capacity growth rates.

The importation of basic commodities will optimally be restricted to those that do not reduce domestic rates of capacity utilization or the rates of growth of basic sub-system capacities. At the same time, importers of these basic commodities will require access to the foreign exchange necessary to purchase the imports. Ignoring the capital account of the balance of payments until section 9.4, it is clear from these remarks that exports of non-basic commodities will be required in order to avoid deficits on current account, which eventually exhaust domestic reserves of foreign exchange and thereby bring an end to importation. The production and exchange of non-basic commodities for export will evidently require employment of workers who will add to the demands for – but not the supplies of – consumption commodities. This result is in keeping with our previous (by no means novel) finding that, in a closed economy, a sharper major upswing of the macroeconomic cycle requires a larger reduction in consumption per worker in the whole economy. There is, however, a cushion available in the open economy that is not available in the closed economy.

We saw in section 6.7 that exports have the same effects as demand management in raising rates of capacity utilization but (possibly) depressing long-run capacity, output and employment growth. That is, in terms of long-run employment and growth policies, exports and expansionary demand management are substitutes – just as Keynesians have shown to be true with respect to short-run employment and capacity utilization. In order to minimize reductions in domestic living standards, the government will reduce its own employment growth or, if necessary, shed some labour. This policy will reduce net demands for consumption commodities and so must not proceed so far that there are excess net consumption supplies.

The problem is then to generate non-basic exports of sufficient value to pay for imports of basic commodities, and at the same time to generate faster growth in the basic sub-system. What is required here is complementarity of industrial and exchange rate policies.

An undervalued domestic currency, by rendering the prices of domestic exports competitive in foreign markets while making import prices uncompetitive in domestic markets, will depress the growth of the basic sub-system. Exporters and their domestic suppliers will be able to outbid domestic users of both basic and non-basic commodities. Industrial policy will therefore be required to ensure that basic sub-system growth rates rise while imports for direct use in the basic sub-system are subsidized by the government. Clearly, the growth of imports to the basic sub-system will be limited by the ability of the economy to produce non-basic commodities for export. Increasing basic sub-system growth, we have shown, implies declining growth in the non-basic sub-system. Unless living standards can fall without limit, there will be some decline in the growth of the non-basic export volume. In general, therefore, we could expect such policies to make possible some increases in the basic sub-system growth during the major upswing, although such increases are not unlimited and must be bought at the expense of domestic consumption per worker.

Of course, it is not possible for all countries to pursue these policies simultaneously. If one country's currency is under-valued, then by definition other countries' currencies are over-valued. And, unless different countries' economies are characterized by very different technologies, one country's imports of basic commodities will be other countries' exports of basic commodities. Similarly, one country's exports of non-basics will be others' imports of non-basics. It follows that any one country can pursue these growth policies only at the expense of growth in other countries.

The alternatives to the policies outlined above are either the imposition of import and export controls – thereby to lose the benefits of comparative advantage – or expansionary industrial policies and complementary demand management by all countries, with each maintaining a rough balance between imports and exports of basic and, separately, non-basic commodities. In this way, comparative advantage can be realized with foreign exchange rates which maintain a rough current account balance.

In this discussion I have ignored both the capital account of the balance of payments and differing inflation rates among trading countries. These matters will be taken up in the two following sections.

9.4 INTEREST RATES, PUBLIC FINANCE AND MONETARY POLICIES

It can hardly be efficient for governments to adopt contradictory economic policies. Thus, when we consider government activities in the financial markets, it is important to identify strategies that complement the policies, described in sections 9.1–9.3, that work primarily through the markets for goods and non-financial services. Since different demand management and industrial policies are appropriate to different phases of the major macroeconomic cycle, it is to be expected that, at different phases of the cycle, different measures to affect interest rates, the money supply and public finance will also be appropriate.

In this section I shall consider interest rates first, then government borrowing and taxation and finally management of the money supply. We shall see just how and why optimal policy configurations change over the cycle. These results are then extended to the open economy.

Interest rates

The conventional Keynesian propositions that low interest rates are wanted at the cyclical trough and high interest rates are wanted once full employment is reached are amply justified here. Although the result is conventional, it is important to understand how it arises from the present macroeconomic theory, which differs from Keynesian theory by taking into account the endogenous determination of the state of long-term expectation.

The advantage of low interest rates at the major cyclical trough is that they entail low interest payments by non-financial companies on their *existing* debts. In consequence, they are able to build up their financial resources more quickly than is possible in the face of higher interest payments. If low interest rates also extend the margin of profitable investment projects in a given state of long-term expectation, that Keynesian outcome is an additional advantage. In the present context, however, the main purpose of a low-interest-rate policy is to bring forward the macroeconomic conditions in which unsuccessful investments by a significant proportion of non-financial companies will not end their respective existences.

During the major cyclical upswing, low interest rates and payments provide for higher cash flows to non-financial companies than do higher interest rates and payments, thereby, delaying financially induced major downturns. If a financially induced downturn is delayed long enough, full employment can be reached. At that point, the government will want to constrain the growth of the industrial circulation of money and to raise interest rates as part of its management of the transition to long-run, full-employment growth.

The advantage of rising interest rates as full employment is reached is that they put more downward financial pressure on investment in basic capacity expansion than on investment in non-basic capacity expansion. This proposition follows from the demonstration in chapter 8 that, as the major upswing progresses, the growth of the industrial circulation of money declines and the distribution of the industrial circulation shifts in favour of the non-basic sub-system. Thus, the money required for the payment of wages and distribution of profits (including interest payments) by firms operating mainly in the basic sub-system must come increasingly from increases in their debts.

To be sure, it is perfectly possible for some firms to operate both basic and non-basic processes. In such cases they could finance their basic activities out of the money revenues from their non-basic activities. If firms typically operate equally in both sub-systems, then rising interest rates cannot be relied upon to reduce basic capacity growth rates relative to non-basic capacity growth rates. There is no reason, however, to believe that the focusing effects will *generally* lead to such concatenations of activities within firms.

Firms that operate mainly or entirely in the basic sub-system will require higher debt–revenue ratios during the major upswing than firms operating mainly or entirely in the non-basic sub-system. As a result, a rise in interest rates will claim a larger marginal proportion of the revenues of firms oriented towards the basic sub-system than will be the case for firms oriented towards the non-basic sub-system. Thus, firms relying on basic activities for their gross profits will find that the growth of their internal finance is reduced in greater proportion than the growth of internal finance of firms relying mainly on non-basic activities. It follows that a rise in interest rates late in the major macroeconomic upswing will put relatively more downward financial pressure on investments in basic capacity expansion than on investments in non-basic capacity expansion. Since the objective of macroeconomic policy as full employment is reached is precisely to reduce basic relative to non-basic capacity growth in order to facilitate the transition to balanced, full-employment growth, allowing interest rates to rise will evidently be an effective policy measure.

Note that the objective of the rise in interest rates is *not* to reduce all investment but, rather, to reduce the growth of basic relative to non-basic investments by reducing the after-interest profits of firms to a greater degree as their activities are concentrated more heavily in the basic sub-system. This objective is met by increases in short-run interest rates as well as by increases in long-run interest rates. Indeed, to the extent that long-run interest rates are fixed, rises in short-run interest rates will be the more effective.

Public finance

The interest rates on long-term loans and financial assets have the most important effect on the magnitude of overall capacity expansion in all phases of the cycle. Although the government can have some effect on these interest rates through its open market operations, it must always face the possibility that speculative activity in the organized financial exchanges will frustrate its interest rate policies. This follows from our finding that the latitude for speculative domination of securities prices is very wide. I am not suggesting that the government should never borrow from the public by selling its own securities, or that it should never make net repayments of its debts by repurchasing its own securities. It is none the less important that the government finance its policy measures by means that directly affect the industrial circulation. Two such means of public finance are considered here: 'printing' money (typically by government borrowings from its own central bank) and taxation.

The 'printing' of money to finance expansionary demand management and industrial policies adds to the industrial circulation in the first instance, although some of this increase will end up in the financial circulation as wages are paid to households and dividends and interest are paid to households and financial institutions. Borrowing from the public to finance expansionary demand management and industrial policies transfers money from the financial to the industrial circulation, although, for the same reasons as in the 'money-printing' case, some of the initial increase in the industrial circulation will return to the financial circulation.

The theory of markets and the safe-asset theory of interest together provide an explanation based on rational behaviour (rather than speculative expectations alone) for the proposition that flow-supplies of government securities increase interest rates. That is because the physical and contractual characteristics of securities have been evolved to ensure that the corresponding markets meet the conditions for price efficiency. Rational intermediaries in the organized financial exchanges will have both the market power and the incentive to reduce prices of government securities when the supplies exceed the demands (section 5.3). Hedgers' demands will then increase because the price reduction makes government securities more attractive as safe assets while money becomes relatively less attractive (section 7.3).

It is possible, of course, that speculators will take government demand management and industrial policy measures in the trough to presage a general macroeconomic upturn. In consequence, they will increase their demands for long-term securities to such an extent that interest rates remain at or near the minimum that the banking system can rationally allow (section 7.5). This outcome is more likely the longer and more severely have bearish trends prevailed in the financial markets (section 8.3). If this outcome should be realized, then government borrowing will not, in the event, raise interest rates. But our theory predicts only that the speculative turning point will become increasingly likely; it does not predict the timing of the turning point. Without a theory of the timing of the turning point, it would be rash to rely on a bullish turn following upon expansionary demand management and industrial policies. The safer form of public finance in these circumstances is government borrowing from its own central bank or some other form of 'printing' money.

This is by no means to suggest that the government can rely on falling or static but low interest rates when it 'prints' money. Bear financial markets can prevail even in the face of expansionary government policies, so that interest rates rise in the trough of the major macroeconomic cycle. In such circumstances the government will certainly not want to add to the upward pressure by borrowing from the public. Even if it 'prints' money with which to buy its own securities in the financial markets, the latitude for speculative dominance of securities prices is wide enough to make a continued rising trend in long-term interest rates possible. In these circumstances, taxation measures will be useful.

It is an elementary proposition of mainstream Keynesianism that tax rates ought, if anything, to be reduced in the trough of the macroeconomic cycle as part of the expansionary demand management package. The same proposition applies equally to expansionary industrial policies. If reduced tax rates increase the magnitude of multiplier effects and therefore private expenditure on goods and non-financial services, the industrial circulation and non-financial companies' profits will be increased. Such increases in the industrial circulation complement the thrust of expansionary monetary policies. The increase in profits will accrue mainly to the producers and traders of consumption commodities, and so will enhance the effects of demand management rather than industrial policies. But the main policy objective in the major cyclical trough is to increase rates of basic capacity growth relative to non-basic (including consumption) capacity growth. It will therefore be desirable to change tax rates in such a way that the bulk of the increase in the industrial circulation accrues to the basic sub-system.

Although the argument is easily extended to take indirect taxes into account, the principles of the policy analysis can be fully elaborated in relation to direct taxes alone. Consider, in particular, the effects of taxes on companies' profits and on personal incomes.

A reduction in the companies' profit tax rate obviously improves the cash flows of companies in proportion to their accounting profits. Growth of investment in basic capacity expansion will necessarily increase profits accruing to firms in respect of their activities in the basic sub-system. At the same time, increasing net consumption demands increase the profits accruing to firms in respect of their activities in the non-basic sub-system. As far as I can tell, there is nothing in the present theory that enables us to predict the *general* effect of the major macroeconomic upturn on the distribution of profits from activities in the two sub-systems. Thus, we cannot say what will be the effect of a reduction in profit tax rates on the relative tax payments from the two sub-systems. We do know, however, that the current cash flows of the basic sub-system will be under downward pressure, while the cash flows of the non-basic sub-system will be increasing (section 8.5). It follows that, if profits (hence profit tax payments at any given tax rate) are growing at least as fast in the basic sub-system as in the non-basic sub-system, the cash flows after taxes in the basic sub-system will be reduced in greater proportion than in the non-basic sub-system. Since cash flows and profits arising from the non-basic activities will be growing during the major macroeconomic upswing, the loss of cash flow would be felt more keenly in the basic sub-system even if its profits were growing more slowly than those arising from non-basic activities.

Evidently, companies' profit tax rates ought to be reduced if taxation policy is to increase the cash flows arising from basic activities relative to the cash flows arising from non-basic activities. In this way, current trading will shift the distribution of the industrial circulation in favour of the basic sub-system and so reinforce expansionary industrial policy.

Reductions in personal income taxes stimulate consumption expenditures by households. Since, for reasons given in section 7.1, payments for consumption goods are generally in money rather than non-money means of payment, reductions in personal income tax rates will increase the industrial circulation of money. Some part of this increase in the industrial circulation will return to the financial circulation as wage payments and profit distributions (including interest payments). The increase in the industrial circulation accrues entirely to firms operating in the non-basic sub-system (producing and selling consumption commodities) in the first instance. It is passed on to the basic sub-system only to the extent that the resulting increase in outputs requires direct inputs of basic commodities. And, of course, some of that increase in the cash flows from basic activities will be paid out again as wages and profit distributions. As a result, the increase in the industrial circulation accruing to the basic sub-system will be only a part of that initially accruing to the non-basic sub-system. Reductions in personal income tax rates will therefore shift the distribution of the industrial circulation in favour of the non-basic sub-system.

We must conclude that, in general, the structure of tax rates is rationally reduced in the trough of the major macroeconomic cycle in order to increase the industrial circulation. In order to increase the share of the increased industrial circulation that will be available for investments in basic capacity expansion, the companies profit tax rate will be reduced relative to the personal income tax rate.

The financial management of the transition to long-run, full-employment growth is the converse of the management of the major macroeconomic upturn. The government will rationally increase its flow-supply of securities in order to put what upward pressure it can on interest rates, and it will increase the structure of direct tax rates. In order to shift the distribution of the industrial circulation in favour of the non-basic sub-system, companies' profit tax rates will be increased relative to personal income tax rates.

Managing the money supply

The policy conclusions reached so far entail a passive approach to monetary management. I have presumed that the government's contribution to the money supply will be whatever is necessary to achieve the appropriate distribution and rate of growth of the industrial circulation over the major macroeconomic cycle. However, influential schools of macroeconomic thought have convinced governments that their contribution to monetary growth has a dominating role in the determination of price and wage inflation rates. It is therefore important to determine whether a passive or actively constrained monetary policy is preferable.

If the means of public finance proposed above are adopted, then the growth of the money supply will be anti-cyclical. The combination of 'printing' money and reducing tax rates in the trough of the cycle while restricting the flow-supply of government securities will obviously increase the stock-supply of government money. The opposite policies to assist in managing the transition to sustained full-employment growth will reduce the rate of monetary growth.

Prices and wages move pro-cyclically. The reasons, however, are real rather than monetary. Price increases result from rising nominal wage rates and short-run prices. That wage rates tend to move pro-cyclically was shown in chapter 8 to be a consequence of the doctrine of increasing uncertainty. Short-run prices increase during the upswing as demands grow at increasing rates. Long-run prices, of course, increase as rises in wage rates and short-run prices turn out to be permanent or, at least, unusually persistent.

If we take into consideration the stock-supply of bank money, then the aggregate stock of money will move pro-cyclically simply because the cycle is defined by real growth of investment, output and employment. To the extent that these phenomena are financed externally by the banking system, then for reasons that have been well understood – if not universally agreed – since Gurley and Shaw (1960) developed their analysis of inside and outside money, the supply of bank money must grow at faster and slower rates as investment, output and employment grow at faster and slower rates. If the present theory is correctly derived from the assumption that individuals behave rationally, then cyclical movements in real magnitudes generate similar cycles in wage and price movements and in the stock-supply of government and bank money. If the quantity of bank money is much greater than the quantity of government (or any intrinsic) money, then the total money supply *must* change pro-cyclically.

Although it is clear from the foregoing argument that monetary growth does not necessarily cause inflation, it *can* give rise to either a cost-push or a demand-pull inflation.

The passive monetary policy described above can certainly make possible a wage-induced (hence, cost-push) inflation; for increasing the money supply to whatever extent is necessary to finance investments in capacity expansion effectively removes all limits to nominal wage bargains. Firms can accede to any wage bargain and then borrow whatever is necessary to meet the resulting wage bill in confidence that the ensuing price inflation will reduce the resulting burden of debt.

We know that high rates of inflation impose costs on rational individuals. The increased hedging costs resulting from hyperinflations were described in section 7.3. In addition, we know from the argument of 7.1 that means of payment that hold their value in relation to commodities are essential for allocatively efficient exchange. For these reasons, a passive monetary regime must be supplemented by a policy of imposed or negotiated wage restraint. The alternative is a restrictive monetary policy that frustrates expansionary industrial policies. We shall see in section 9.5, however, that a real-wages policy (or wages and prices policy) is an important concomitant of industrial and demand management policies even in the absence of inflation. To use the requisite policy machinery to control any tendencies towards cost-push inflation is, in that context, a small and entirely natural step.

Monetarists and new classical macroeconomists, relying on the Walrasian homogeneity postulate, have convinced governments that increasing the money supply faster than the rate of labour productivity growth always generates a demand-pull inflation. It is therefore important to determine in the present theoretical framework the conditions in which such inflations result.

Suppose that the government increases the rate of monetary growth by 'printing' money which it then introduces into circulation by increasing its own nominal wage bill or by purchasing goods and services from non-financial companies. The effect will certainly be to raise short-run prices as government purchases lead to direct and derived demands for non-basic and basic commodities and as government employees contribute to increased net consumption demands. We saw in section 7.3 that rates of commodity price inflation can rise so fast that rational individuals increasingly hold the commodities they will require in the future as hedges against income uncertainty. This phenomenon, though it is characteristic only of hyperinflation, will increase current commodity demands and therefore put further pressure on short-run prices.

Suppose instead that the money 'printed' by the government is deposited with the banking system, thereby increasing the nominal value of the loans that banks are willing to make. If the loans are to speculators in financial assets, then nominal prices will rise in the financial markets and interest rates will fall – other things being equal. Loans to households for consumption expenditures will increase net consumption demands without increasing basic subsystem growth, and so will eventually lead to excess consumption demands, rising non-basic prices and, therefore, rising nominal wage rates as workers seek to defend their real-wage rates. The easy availability of finance will enable firms to meet these wage demands, and, if workers in the basic sub-system defend their wage relativities, basic commodity prices must also begin to rise.

It must be stressed, however, that an expansionary monetary regime such as this has no connection with the passive monetary regime suggested previously. That regime was the concomitant of demand management and industrial policies intended to generate growth in the basic sub-system appropriate to the attainment and sustenance of full-employment growth. The wanton increase in the government money supply discussed here, however, does not increase basic capacity growth rates. It is for this reason that demand-pull inflations with low growth rates ensue. Provided that the flow-supply of government money is the outcome of public finance measures that complement demand management and industrial policies, pro-cyclical changes in inflation rates will be a normal adjunct to real cyclical factors.

It remains here to consider whether restrictive monetary policies amount to efficient anti-inflation policies.

Certainly, restrictive monetary regimes can reduce inflation rates. Suppose, for example, that the government reduces its net sales of its own securities and, possibly, places restrictions on domestic bank credit. Firms that have incurred debts to finance investments in capacity expansion will face liquidity shortages even if they remain profitable (section 7.5). Moreover, the shortage of money, non-money safe assets and new loans will induce rationally managed financial institutions and non-financial companies to develop new kinds of financial assets to get round the government restrictions. This is a paradigmatic inducement effect of the sort discussed in chapter 2. In this circumstance, managerial resources are diverted from the encouragement and coordination of investments in technical change and generally in capacity expansion – investments that are essential to the generation of major cyclical upturns and upswings. This is in addition to the attendant barriers to the accumulation of financial resources required for major upturns.

The effect of restrictive monetary regimes is to extend and deepen the major cyclical trough. Short-run prices will be under downward pressure from diminishing demands. Wages will be under downward pressure as market power shifts increasingly towards surviving firms. If this process is so severe that prices actually fall, the real burden of firms' debts is increased so that there will be further downward pressure on surviving firms' rates of capacity growth. Firms that would be at the financial margin of survival in a less restrictive monetary regime will go out of business.

In general, then, a passive monetary regime, which reflects the public finance measures appropriate to efficient demand management and industrial policies, will generate a useful degree of inflation that diminishes the burden of company debt during the major cyclical upswing and so complements the set of active macroeconomic policies. If the monetary regime, though expansionary, is not simply the result of demand management and industrial policy measures, then it will be inflationary whether or not full employment prevails. A sufficiently restrictive monetary regime will reduce inflation rates – but only at the cost of endemic low growth, capacity under-utilization, high unemployment and, therefore, needlessly low standards of living.

The open economy

That the effects of domestic policies on the capital account of the balance of payments restrict the government's freedom of action is hardly a surprising proposition. Once the basic/non-basic distinction and its implications are recognized, it is possible to identify the nature of those restrictions more clearly and more soundly on a coherent theoretical basis, and thereby to formulate policies to generate full-employment growth within those restrictions. One result of this analysis is a simple and testable theoretical explanation of Britain's economic problems in this century.

The main restriction of concern here is on exchange rate and interest rate policies. In section 9.3 I suggested that exchange rates should, in the absence of coordinated international economic policies, be under-valued in order to encourage exports and discourage imports. Provided that this policy is combined with an expansionary industrial policy, including subsidization of essential imports to the basic sub-system, balance on the current account of the balance of payments would be consistent with a policy-induced major macroeconomic upswing. Nothing further would need to be said only if it could be assumed that the domestic exchange rate that preserves a current account surplus never generated capital account deficits. That condition is clearly not met. The capital account surplus is determined by other countries' interest rates, and so is outside of the control of the domestic authorities. It is elementary that large and persistent capital account deficits will eventually exhaust the holdings of foreign exchange required to pay for imports to the basic sub-system.

Although foreign countries' exchange rate policies restrict domestic freedom of action, they do not make necessary tariffs and quantitative import controls which effectively close the economy. We have found in this section that domestic interest rate and tax rate policies are substitutes when used to complement industrial policies and demand management. Thus, interest rates can be maintained at a level that attracts foreign currency in sufficient quantities to cover any current account deficits resulting from imports to the basic sub-system. If the foreign exchange rate is then over-valued in relation to current account balance, taxation policy will be required to minimize the importation of non-basic commodities while improving the cash flows of firms that are active in the basic subsystem. Increasing personal income tax rates reduces consumption demands and will presumably reduce demands for imported consumption commodities; reducing tax rates on company profits improves the cash flows of all firms. Thus, in an open economy, where the sustainable exchange rate is incompatible with a current account *and* balance of payments surplus, recovery from a major cyclical trough will require higher interest rates than in a closed economy and a tax rate structure in which personal income tax rates are yet higher relative to company profit tax rates. The greater the capital account deficit required to maintain current account surplus, the higher will be the required structure of domestic interest rates, the higher will be the required personal income tax rates, and the lower will be the required rates of tax on company profits.

It must be remembered that these conclusions are valid only if the government is pursuing expansionary demand management and industrial policies as described in sections 9.1 and 9.2.

The British experience

It will be instructive to develop the foregoing argument as an explanation of the failure of successive British governments' policies to secure long-run, full-employment growth. What is involved here is the de-industrialization of Britain.

The British economy has been characterized since the Second World War by a declining share of manufacturing output and an increasing share of services – particularly financial services – in gross domestic product. This trend is well documented and ascribed to different sources by different commentators (cf. Bacon and Eltis,

1976; Singh, 1977/1983; Blackaby, 1978; Pollard, 1982). The shift away from manufacturing in favour of services is what is meant by de-industrialization. If manufacturing is growing more slowly relative to other sectors of the economy, then the basic sub-system must be growing more slowly as well. This trend is well explained in the present theory by the use of public policy measures to protect the position of the City of London in the international financial markets.

The provision of financial intermediation and exchange services in international markets takes place, from the point of view of the domestic economy, within the non-basic sub-system. In this, it is like any other processes for export exchange. Where it differs from other non-basic activities, however, is that high domestic interest rates and exchange rates of the domestic currency increase its contribution to both current and capital account balance of payment surpluses; for high domestic interest rates and strong exchange rates render the domestic currency suitable for use as means of payment in international transactions. In addition, if the domestic currency is in net demand on the foreign exchanges, foreign currency reserves are thereby in good supply domestically and so are available for use in both financial and real transactions in which the foreign currencies are the means of payment. Domestic firms will then be well placed to provide intermediating services in these transactions.

Domestic firms' intermediation in international real and financial transactions will, of course, generate revenues in foreign currencies and so add to the surplus on current account. In other words, there will be a favourable balance of trade in invisibles. To sustain the balance of payments surpluses necessary to carry on these activities, British governments have maintained high interest rates and high tax rates along with bouts of deflationary demand management in order to hold down imports. In practice, personal income taxes are high, and only some 20 per cent of companies pay mainstream corporation tax. The difficulties arise because the deflationary demand management policies create capacity under-utilization in the non-basic sub-system – apart from that sub-system's financial intermediation capacities – and therefore slow growth of derived demands for basic commodities. Net consumption demands therefore arise increasingly from workers in the non-basic sub-system who are not employed in the production and exchange of consumption commodities. As financial and public sector employment and productive capacities grow relative to manufacturing employment and capacities, the basic stock and flow ratios are necessarily declining. The capacity for growth of the whole economy is therefore declining, and must be declining ever more rapidly if the financial and public sectors alone are growing at constant or, worse, increasing rates.

These developments give rise to two problems whenever the balance of payments is sufficiently in surplus to enable the government to undertake some expansionary demand management. One is that slow growth in the basic sub-system implies that the proportion of the labour force that could be employed in the basic sub-system is small in the sense that the basic sub-system wage bill at full capacity utilization will generate net consumption demands that are small in relation to total supplies. It follows that the expansionary multiplier–accelerator interaction identified in section 6.5 must be far weaker than in an economy where, historically, basic sub-system growth has been significantly higher. Even if the state of long-term expectation in the basic sub-system were to improve, the benefits in terms of derived demands from the non-basic sub-system – in particular, producers and traders of consumption commodities – will be relatively small and the corresponding expansionary signals relatively weak until basic sub-system growth has been rising for some time. What is required here is to increase the proportion of net consumption demands arising in the basic sub-system.

The second problem is that, unless interest rates fall and the domestic currency declines on the foreign exchanges, import penetration will increase as government expenditures on non-basics increase net consumption demands. If the basic sub-system growth rate does not rise, then the growth of net consumption demands from the non-basic sub-system must eventually exceed the net supply capacities of the consumption industries. If the basic sub-system growth rates do rise, then the growth of net consumption supply capacities must decline until the basic sub-system growth stops rising. Either way, there must be a period of increasing import penetration of markets for non-basics. If the effect on the balance of payments induces the government to raise interest rates and deflate the economy by means of contractionary demand management, the expansionary market signals to the basic sub-system will be superseded by contractionary signals. And this supposes that a sequence of such contractions will not prevent improvements in the state of long-term expectation in the first place.

If this argument is right, then de-industrialization in Britain or anywhere else will be part and parcel of a declining trend in the growth of the basic relative to the non-basic sub-system. If it is desired to follow policies that protect the international financial sector of the domestic economy, then that objective must be tempered by a prior commitment to the growth of the basic sub-system. In an open economy, it might well be necessary to maintain the value of the domestic currency on the foreign exchanges by a regime of high interest rates. But we have found that such interest rates are more appropriate to full-employment growth than to the trough of the major macroeconomic cycle. If full employment is the primary objective of government policy, then that objective will be better served if foreign exchange reserves are allowed to decline and the interests of firms engaged in international finance and trade are sacrificed for a time to the requirements of basic capacity growth. After all, we found in section 6.7 that an economy that is able to provide for its own consumption and investment will be better able to enjoy the benefits of comparative advantage without chronically unfavourable balances of trade, and will therefore be better able to export financial services.

9.5   WAGES AND PRICES POLICIES

If the policies described in sections 9.2–9.7 are successful in bringing about major macroeconomic upturns and sustained full-employment growth, the speed with which this result can be brought about will depend on the shape of the wage cycle. Indeed, it is possible that a sharp upswing of the wage cycle will prevent the attainment of full employment in the first place.

The wage cycle, we found in section 8.7, is roughly in phase with the major macroeconomic cycle of capacity, output and employment growth. Wage rates rise during the macroeconomic upswing as labour market power shifts in favour of workers and decline during the macroeconomic downswing as labour market power shifts back in favour of employers. This wage cycle can bring about the major downturn as wage rates rise relative to prices – particularly in the basic sub-system – and so lead to the premature exhaustion of firms' financial resources. Moreover, the increasing basic capacity growth rates, which drive the major upswing, require falling rates of non-basic output growth, including the growth of consumption commodity outputs. Even if basic capacity growth rates are more or less constant, the higher the level of those growth rates, the lower is non-basic output per worker in the whole economy. It follows that a sharper major macroeconomic upswing and a faster approach to full employment from the major cyclical trough requires less consumption per employed worker until full employment is reached.

Presuming that consumption is positively related to real disposable incomes, a faster realization of full employment necessarily requires lower real wage rates after the deduction of taxes. I have already argued that the mix of personal income tax rates and company profit tax rates can be chosen to restrain consumption while at the same time increasing the growth of cash flows to the basic sub-system. However, the labour market analysis in section 5.4 and the analysis of the wage cycle in section 8.7 imply that there will be some limit to the effectiveness of these taxation measures. As the major upswing proceeds, workers could well succeed in raising their nominal wage rates in order to increase their real wage rates net of taxes. Since they will be best placed to achieve rising nominal wage rates in the basic sub-system, it follows from the analysis of section 6.3 that nominal prices will, as a result, be rising throughout the economy. There will, in short, be a cost-push inflation. If income tax rates rise during this period, workers will have an added incentive simply to accelerate their wage demands and so generate rising rates of cost-push to accelerate their wage demands and so generate rising rates of cost-push price inflation.

Either workers will succeed in raising their real wage rates, and will possibly disrupt firms' cash flows by strikes and similar actions, or there will be some form of real-wage restraint. In the first case, firms in the basic sub-system in particular will lack the internal finance required to sustain investments in capacity expansion, while in the second case the major upswing will be able to proceed more quickly and over a period of time long enough for full employment to be realized. The social and political conditions in which workers will exercise sufficient self-restraint in their wage demands is a matter that is outside our purview. If the policy objective of the government is to secure full-employment growth over the long run, then the government will need to adopt measures that influence both wages and prices, since it is the relationship between the two that constrains rising basic capacity growth. Furthermore, if the labour markets are to be free from direct government control, it is apparent that the increases in nominal wage rates relative to price increases must be agreed by workers and firms' managers or their representatives. In reaching such agreements, the role of government will be the same as in its industrial policies: it will be providing information that is not available to individuals from market signals. For the essential problem here is that there are no profitable opportunities for individual firms to acquire the necessary market power to enforce real-wage constraint or to signal effectively that short-run real-wage restraint will yield long-run benefits to the working population as a whole.

The issues involved here evidently turn on the social rate of time-preference and workers' collective desire for full employment. More consumption can be had now at the expense of slower employment growth in the long run. If a faster approach to full employment is wanted *by workers currently in employment*, then they will have to agree to smaller real-wage-rate increases or even falling real wage rates once production and exchange capacities are fully utilized. Clearly, a faster approach to full employment from a state of chronic unemployment will require a degree of altruism on the part of employed workers. Equally clearly, agreement on real-wage increases must cover both wage and price increases in a single package.

Unless workers are appraised of the long-run consequences of their current wage bargains, however, there are no signals for their altruism (if they have any) to act upon. It is therefore a plausible (though not analytically demonstrable) proposition that the fastest tolerable approach to full employment will be achieved through negotiations among entrepreneurs', workers' and the government's representatives concerning prices, wages and rates of basic capacity growth. Such an institutional arrangement will also be useful in managing the transition from the major upswing to long-run full employment. The demand management, industrial and public finance policies of the government at the upturn and during the transition to full employment would usefully be determined within this institutional structure, since their effectiveness depends upon real-wage movements.

References

Alchian, A. A. and Demsetz, H. (1972), 'Production, Information Costs and Economic Organization', *American Economic Review*, pp. 777-95.

Andrews, P. W. S. (1949), *Manufacturing Business* (London: Macmillan).

Andrews, P. W. S. (1964), *On Competition in Economic Theory* (London: Macmillan).

Arrow, K. J. (1959), 'Towards a Theory of Price Adjustment', in A. Abramovitz (ed.), *The Allocation of Economic Resources* (Stanford: University of California Press).

Arrow, K. J. and Hahn, F. (1971), *General Competitive Analysis* (Edinburgh: Oliver and Boyd).

Bacon, R. and Eltis, W. (1976), *Britain's Economic Problem: Too Few Producers* (London: Macmillan).

Barro, R. J. and Grossman, H. I. (1976), *Money, Employment and Inflation* (Cambridge: University Press).

Blackaby, F. (1978), *Deindustrialisation* (London: Heinemann).

Buiter, W. (1980), 'The Macroeconomics of Dr Pangloss', *Economic Journal*, pp. 34-50.

Caves, R. E. (1980), 'Industrial Organization, Corporate Strategy and Structure', *Journal of Economic Literature*, pp. 64-92.

Chandler, A. D., Jr (1962), *Strategy and Structure* (Cambridge, Mass. and London: MIT Press).

Chandler, A. D., Jr (1977), *The Visible Hand* (Cambridge, Mass.: Harvard University Press).

Clark, J. B. (1893), *The Distribution of Wealth* (New York: Macmillan).

Clower, R. W. (1965/1969), 'The Keynesian Counter-revolution: A Theoretical Appraisal', in F. Hahn and F. Brechling (eds), *The Theory of Interest* (London: Macmillan); reprinted in Clower (1969).

Clower, R. W. (1967/1969), 'A Reconsideration of the Microfoundations of Monetary Theory', *Western Economic Journal*, pp. 1-19; reprinted in Clower (1969).

Clower, R. W. (1969), *Monetary Theory* (Harmondsworth: Penguin).

Coase, R. H. (1937), 'The Nature of the Firm', *Economica*, pp. 386-405.

Davidson, P. (1972), *Money and the Real World* (London and Basingstoke: Macmillan).

Davidson, P. (1974), 'Disequilibrium Market Adjustment: Marshall Revisited', *Economic Inquiry*, pp. 146-58.

Davidson, P. and Kregel, J. A. (1980), 'Keynes's Paradigm: A Theoretical Framework for Monetary Analysis' in E. J. Nell (ed.), *Growth, Profits and Property* (Cambridge: University Press).

Doeringer, P. and Piore, M. (1971), *Internal Labour Markets and Manpower Analysis* (Boston: D. C. Heath).

Eichner, A. S. (1973), 'A Theory of the Determination of the Mark-up Under Oligopoly', *Economic Journal*, pp. 1184-1200.

Eichner, A. S. (1976), *The Magacorp and Oligopoly* (Cambridge: University Press).

Filippini, C. and Filippini, L. (1982), 'Two Theorems on Joint Production', *Economic Journal*, pp. 386-90.

Fisher, F. M. (1976), 'The Stability of General Equilibrium: Results and Problems', in Artis, M. J. and Nobay, A. R. (eds), *Essays in Economic Analysis* (Cambridge: University Press).

Fisher, I. (1933), 'The Debt Deflation Theory of Great Depressions', *Econometrica*, pp. 337-57.

Friedman, M. (1969), 'The Role of Monetary Policy', in *The Optimum Quantity of Money and Other Essays* (London and Basingstoke: Macmillan), pp. 95-110.

Gale, D. (1960), *The Theory of Linear Economic Models* (New York: McGraw-Hill).

Goodwin, R. M. (1951), 'The Non-linear Accelerator and the Persistence of Business Cycles', *Econometrica*, pp. 1-17.

Goss, B. A. and Yamey, B. S. (1978), *The Economics of Futures Trading* (2nd ed.) (London and Basingstoke: Macmillan).

Gurley, J. G. and Shaw, E. S. (1960), *Money in a Theory of Finance* (Washington: Brookings Institution).

Hahn, F. (1973), *On the Notion of Equilibrium in Economics* (Cambridge: University Press).

Hahn, F. (1977), 'Keynesian Economics and General Equilibrium: Reflections on Some Current Debates', in Harcourt (1977).

Hahn, F. (1980), 'Monetarism and Economic Theory', *Economica*, pp. 1-17.

Harcourt, G. C. (1972), *Some Cambridge Controversies in the Theory of Capital* (Cambridge: University Press).

Harcourt, G. C. (ed.) (1977), *The Microeconomic Foundations of Macroeconomics* (London and Basingstoke: Macmillan).

Harrod, R. F. (1939), 'An Essay in Dynamic Theory', *Economic Journal*, pp. 14-33.

Hawtrey, R. (1950), *Currency and Credit* (4th ed.) (London: Longmans, Green and Co.).

Hicks, J. R. (1939), *Value and Capital* (Oxford: University Press).

Hicks, J. R. (1950), *A Theory of the Trade Cycle* (Oxford: University Press).

Hicks, J. R. (1965), *Capital and Growth* (Oxford: Clarendon Press).

Hicks, J. R. (1967), *Critical Essays in Monetary Theory* (Oxford: University Press).

Jefferys, J. B. (1946), 'The Denomination and Character of Shares, 1855–85', *Economic History Review*, pp. 45–55.

Kahn, R. F. (1972a), 'Notes on the Rate of Interest and the Growth of Firms', in *Selected Essays on Employment and Growth* (Cambridge: University Press), pp. 208–32.

Kahn, R. F. (1972b), 'Notes on Liquidity Preference', in *Selected Essays on Employment and Growth* (Cambridge: University Press), pp. 72–96.

Kaldor, N. (1934), 'The Equilibrium of the Firm', *Economic Journal*, pp. 60–76.

Kalecki, M. (1937), 'The Principle of Increasing Risk', *Economica*, pp. 440–7.

Keynes, J. M. (1930/1971), *A Treatise on Money* (London: Macmillan); reprinted as vols 5 and 6 of *The Collected Work and Correspondence of John Maynard Keynes* (London and Basingstoke: Macmillan).

Keynes, J. M. (1936), *The General Theory of Employment, Interest and Money* (London: Macmillan).

Keynes, J. M. (1937/1973), 'The General Theory of Employment', *Quarterly Journal of Economics*; reprinted in *The Collected Work and Correspondence of John Maynard Keynes* (London and Basingstoke: Macmillan), vol. 14, pp. 109–23.

Kregel, J. A. (1976), 'Economic Methodology in the Face of Uncertainty', *Economic Journal*, pp. 209–25.

Langrish, J. et al. (1972), *Wealth from Knowledge* (London and Basingstoke: Macmillan).

Leijonhufvud, A. (1968), *On Keynesian Economics and the Economics of Keynes* (New York: Oxford University Press).

Lucas, R. E. (1975/1981), 'An Equilibrium Model of the Business Cycle', in *Journal of Political Economy*, pp. 1113–44; reprinted in Lucas (1981), pp. 179–214.

Lucas, R. E. (1976/1981), 'Econometric Policy Evaluation: A Critique', in K. Brunner and A. H. Meltzer (eds), *The Phillips Curve and Labour Markets*, Supplement to the *Journal of Monetary Economics*, pp. 19–46; reprinted in Lucas (1981), pp. 104–30.

Lucas, R. E. (1977/81), 'Understanding Business Cycles', in K. Brunner and A. H. Metzer (eds), *Stabilization of the Domestic and International Economy* (Amsterdam: North-Holland), pp. 7–29; reprinted in Lucas (1981), pp. 215–39.

Lucas, R. E. (1981), *Studies in Business Cycle Theory* (Oxford: Basil Blackwell).

Lucas, R. E. and Prescott, E. (1974/1981), 'Equilibrium Search and Unemployment', *Journal of Economic Theory*, pp. 188–209; reprinted in Lucas (1981), pp. 156–78.

Malinvaud, E. (1977), *The Theory of Unemployment Reconsidered* (Oxford: Basil Blackwell).

Malinvaud, E. (1980), *Profitability and Unemployment* (Cambridge: University Press).

Manara, C. F. (1980), 'Sraffa's Model for the Joint Production of Commodities by Means of Commodities', in Pasinetti (1980), pp. 1-15.

Marris, R. (1964), *The Economic Theory of 'Managerial' Capitalism* (London: Macmillan).

Minsky, H. (1975), *John Maynard Keynes* (London and Basingstoke: Macmillan).

Minsky, H. (1982), *Inflation, Recession and Economic Policy* (Brighton: Wheatsheaf).

Morishima, M. (1964), *Equilibrium, Stability and Growth* (Oxford: University Press).

Moss, S. J. (1981), *An Economic Theory of Business Strategy* (Oxford: Martin Robertson).

Muellbauer, J. and Portes, R. (1978), 'Macroeconomic Models with Quantity Rationing', *Economic Journal*, pp. 788-821.

Muth, J. (1961), 'Rational Expectations and the Theory of Price Movements', *Econometrica*, pp. 315-35.

Newbery, D. M. G. and Stiglitz, J. (1979), 'The Theory of Commodity Price Stabilization Rules: Welfare Impacts and Supply Responses', *Economic Journal*, pp. 799-817.

Newbery, D. M. G. and Stiglitz, J. (1981), *The Theory of Commodity Price Stabilization* (Oxford: University Press).

Newbery, D. M. G. and Stiglitz, J. (1982), 'The Choice of Techniques and the Optimality of Mavhet Equilibrium with Rational Expectations', *Journal of Political Economy*, pp. 223-46.

Okun, A. M. (1981), *Prices and Quantities* (Oxford: Basil Blackwell).

Pasinetti, L. L. (1980), *Essays on the Theory of Joint Production* (London and Basingstoke: Macmillan).

Penrose, Edith (1959), *The Theory of the Growth of the Firm* (Oxford: Basil Blackwell).

Phelps, E. S. (1969), 'Money Wage Dynamics and Labor Market Equilibrium', in Phelps et al., *The New Microeconomics in Employment and Inflation Theory* (New York: W. W. Norton).

Phelps Brown, H. (1977), *The Inequality of Pay* (Oxford: University Press).

Pollard, S. (1982), *The Wasting of the British Economy* (London: Croom Helm).

Radner, R. (1966), 'Competitive Equilibrium Under Uncertainty', *Econometrica*, pp. 31-59.

Robertson, D. H. (1951), 'Some Notes on the Theory of Interest', in *Utility and All That* (London: Allen & Unwin), pp. 111-14.

Robinson, J. (1960), *Exercises in Economic Analysis* (London and Basingstoke: Macmillan).

Roe, A. R. (1973), 'The Case for Flow and Funds and National Balance Sheet Accounts', *Economic Journal*, pp. 388-420.

Rosenberg, N. (1976), *Perspectives on Technology* (Cambridge: University Press).

Shannon, H. A. (1931), 'The Coming of General Limited Liability', *Economic History*, pp. 18-32.

Singh, A. (1977/1983), 'UK Industry and the World Economy: A deindustrialization?', *Cambridge Journal of Economics*, pp. 113-36; reprinted in C. H. Feinstein (ed.), *The Managed Economy* (Oxford: University Press).

Sraffa, P. (1960), *Production of Commodities by Means of Commodities* (Cambridge: University Press).

Steedman, I. (1980), 'Basics, Non-Basics and Joint Production', in Pasinetti (1980), pp. 44-50.

Steedman, I. (1982), 'Joint Production and the Wage-Rent Frontier', *Economic Journal*, pp. 377-85.

Steedman, I. (1983), 'The Empirical Importance of Joint Production', University of Manchester, Department of Economics, Discussion paper 31.

Teece, D. (1980), 'Economies of Scope and the Scale of the Enterprise', *Journal of Economic Behaviour and Organization*, pp. 223-47.

Tobin, J. (1980), *Asset Accumulation and Economic Activity* (Oxford: Basil Blackwell).

Watson, J. D. (1970), *The Double Helix* (Harmondsworth: Penguin).

Weintraub, E. R. (1979), *Microfoundations* (Cambridge: University Press).

Williamson, O. E. (1975), *Markets and Hierarchies* (New York: Free Press).

Williamson, O. E. (1981), 'The Modern Corporation: Origins, Evolution, Attributes', *Journal of Economic Literature*, pp. 1537-68.

Wood, A. (1975), *A Theory of Profits* (Cambridge: University Press).

Wood, A. (1978), *A Theory of Pay* (Cambridge: University Press).

Wright, B. D. and Williams, J. C. (1982), 'The Economic Role of Commodity Storage', *Economic Journal*, pp. 596-614.

Index

Index